Corporate Social Responsibility and Law in Africa

This book examines the conception of corporate social responsibility (CSR) in Africa, expanding its frontiers beyond corporate reporting, voluntary corporate charity and community development projects.

Taking a corporate law perspective on CSR, the author combines theory and practice to explain how CSR interacts with sustainable development and sets an agenda for effective operationalization in Africa. The book not only devises an enforcement mechanism towards embedding effective CSR and sustainable development in Africa but also addresses CSR greenwash on the continent. The author critically examines CSR practices, legal and regulatory techniques in Nigeria and South Africa in the context of international regulatory dialogues and shows how corporate socially responsible behaviour can be effectively embedded within business communities in Africa.

Increasing our understanding of the theoretical, legal and regulatory frameworks supporting corporate responsibility, this book will be of interest to scholars, policy makers and practitioners in the fields of Africa law, corporate law, corporate social responsibility and African business.

Nojeem A. Amodu is Post-Doctoral Research Fellow at the Centre for Comparative Law in Africa (CCLA), Department of Commercial Law of the University of Cape Town (UCT), South Africa. He also holds an appointment as Research Associate in the School of Oriental and African Studies (SOAS) School of Law, University of London, United Kingdom.

Routledge Contemporary Africa Series

Introduction to Rwandan Law
Jean-Marie Kamatali

State Fragility and Resilience in Sub-Saharan Africa
Indicators and Interventions
John Idriss Lahai and Isaac Koomson

Press Silence in Postcolonial Zimbabwe
News whiteouts, Journalism and Power
Zvenyika E. Mugari

Urban Planning in Rapidly Growing Cities
Developing Addis Ababa
Mintesnot G. Woldeamanuel

Regional Development Poles and the Transformation of African Economies
Benaiah Yongo-Bure

Nature, Environment and Activism in Nigerian Literature
Sule E. Egya

Corporate Social Responsibility and Law in Africa
Theories, Issues and Practices
Nojeem A. Amodu

Greening Industrialization in Sub-Saharan Africa
Ralph Luken and Edward Clarence-Smith

For more information about this series, please visit: www.routledge.com/ Routledge-Contemporary-Africa/book-series/RCAFR

Corporate Social Responsibility and Law in Africa

Theories, Issues and Practices

Nojeem A. Amodu

LONDON AND NEW YORK

First published 2020 by Routledge

2 Park Square, Milton Park, Abingdon, Oxon OX14 4RN
605 Third Avenue, New York, NY 10017

Routledge is an imprint of the Taylor & Francis Group, an informa business

First issued in paperback 2021

Copyright © 2020 Nojeem A. Amodu

The right of Nojeem A. Amodu to be identified as author of this work
has been asserted by him in accordance with sections 77 and 78 of the
Copyright, Designs and Patents Act 1988.

All rights reserved. No part of this book may be reprinted or
reproduced or utilised in any form or by any electronic, mechanical,
or other means, now known or hereafter invented, including
photocopying and recording, or in any information storage or
retrieval system, without permission in writing from the publishers.

Notice:
Product or corporate names may be trademarks or registered trademarks,
and are used only for identification and explanation without intent to
infringe.

Publisher's Note

The publisher has gone to great lengths to ensure the quality of this reprint
but points out that some imperfections in the original copies may be apparent.

British Library Cataloguing-in-Publication Data
A catalogue record for this book is available from the British Library

Library of Congress Cataloging-in-Publication Data
A catalog record for this book has been requested

ISBN: 978-0-367-43631-5 (hbk)
ISBN: 978-1-03-217310-8 (pbk)
DOI: 10.4324/9781003009825

Typeset in Bembo
by Apex CoVantage, LLC

To Debola

Contents

Acknowledgments	viii
Abbreviations	ix
List of figures	xii
Foreword	xiii

PART I
Background, theories and global outlook — 1

1	Introduction	3
2	Theoretical underpinnings of CSR practices	38
3	CSR implementation and international regulatory framework	85

PART II
CSR conceptual and regulatory framework in Africa — 127

4	CSR in Nigeria	129
5	CSR in South Africa	157

PART III
CSR and regionalism in Africa — 173

6	Roadmap to embedding CSR in Africa	175
7	Model CSR framework for Africa – the Responsible Stakeholder Model	196

Bibliography	215
Appendix: tables of cases and statutes	227
Index	232

Acknowledgments

But for Professor Ada Ordor, the idea to publish this book in its present scope may never have been conceived. I also thank her as Director, Centre for Comparative Law in Africa, University of Cape Town, South Africa (CCLA) and acknowledge the post-doctoral research funding at CCLA under the TY Danjuma Fund for Law and Policy Development in Africa.

I thank Professor Joseph Abugu and Dr Adewale Olawoyin, *SAN* for their painstaking reviews of my PhD research upon which this book is based.

I am indebted to Professor Emilia Onyema, and the School of Oriental and African Studies (SOAS) School of law, University of London for the appointment as Research Associate and access to materials required to complete this book. The warm reception and support of Professor Mashood Baderin, Professor Imran Oluwole Smith, Dr Olivia Lwabukuna and Mrs Henrietta Onyema facilitated the right frame of mind to complete the book.

This book benefited from the mentorship of Professor Janet Dine; her insights at different crucial moments remain priceless.

I am also grateful to Professor CK Agomo, Professor PK Fogam, Professor IO Bolodeoku, Professor AO Sanni, Professor AO Oyewunmi and Professor Yemi Oke for their respective invaluable guidance at different times.

Finally – but in no way the least – for the gift of life, health and sustenance, I express my immense gratitude to the Almighty Allah and my parents, Afusat and Fatai Owolabi Amodu.

Nojeem A. Amodu
London, November, 2019.

Abbreviations

3TG	Tin, tantalum, tungsten, and gold
AEC	African Economic Community
AfCFTA	African Continental Free Trade Area
All	ER All England Law Reports
ALBA	Bolivarian Alternative for the Americas
APPER	Africa's Priority Program for Economic Recovery
ASEAN	Association of South-East Asian Nations
ATCA	Alien Torts Claims Act
BBBEE	Broad-Based Black Economic Empowerment
BEIS	Department for Business, Energy and Industrial Strategy
BIT	Bilateral Investment Treaty
BWI	Bretton Woods Institution
CAN	Andean Community
CAMA	Companies and Allied Matters Act
CEN-SAD	Community of Sahel – Saharan States
CBI	Confederation of British Industry
CDA	Community Development Agreement
COMESA	Common Market for Eastern and Southern Africa
COP	Communication on Progress (under the UN Global Compact)
CSR	Corporate Social Responsibility
CSI	Corporate Social Investment
EAC	East African Community
ECCAS	Economic Community of Central African States
ECA	United Nations Economic Commission for Africa
ECOWAS	Economic Community of West African States
EFTA	European Free Trade Association
EITI	Extractive Industries Transparency Initiative
ESG	Environmental Social and Corporate Governance
ESV	Enlightened Shareholder Value
EU	European Union
FDI	Foreign Direct Investment
HL	House of Lords
HRC	Human Rights Council

x *Abbreviations*

ICC	International Chambers of Commerce
ICSID	International Centre for the Settlement of Investment Disputes
IGAD2	Intergovernmental Authority on Development
ILO	International Labour Organization
IMF	International Monetary Fund
ISA	Investments and Securities Act
LFN	Laws of the Federation of Nigeria
LPA	Lagos Plan of Action and the Final Act of Lagos
MCO	Mining Cadastre Office
MDA	Management's Discussion and Analysis of Financial Condition and Results of Operations
MECD	Mines Environmental Compliance Department
MID	Mines Inspectorate Department
MMSD	Ministry of Mines and Steel Development
MNC	Multinational Corporation
MNE	Multinational Enterprise
MREMC	Mineral Resources and Environmental Management Committee
NAICOM	National Insurance Commission
NAFTA	North America Free Trade Agreement
NAP	National Action Plan
NCC	Nigerian Communication Commission
NCP	National Contact Point
NDA	Niger Delta Avengers
NEITI	Nigerian Extractive Industries Transparency Initiative
NEPAD	New Partnership for Africa's Development
NGO	Non-Governmental Organisation
NHRI	National Human Rights Institutions
NNPC	Nigerian National Petroleum Corporation
NMMA	Nigerian Minerals and Mining Act
NSWG	National Stakeholders Working Group
OECD	Organisation for Economic Cooperation and Development
OEEC	Organisation for European Economic Co-operation
PENCOM	National Pension Commission
PIB	Petroleum Industry Bill
PRT	Promoting Revenue Transparency
REC	Regional Economic Communities
RSM	Responsible Stakeholder Model
SACA	South African Companies Act No. 71 of 2008
SADC	Southern African Development Community
SEC	Securities and Exchange Commission
SGSR	UN Secretary-General's Special Representative
SIA	Sustainability Impact Assessment
SIP	Specific Instance Procedure
TBL	Triple Bottom Line
TFTA	Tri-Partite Free Trade Agreement

TNC	Transnational Corporation
UDHR	Universal Declaration of Human Rights
UK	United Kingdom
UKHL	United Kingdom House of Lords
UMA	Arab Maghreb Union
UN	United Nations
UNCTAD	UN Conference on Trade and Development
UNCTC	UN Commission on Transnational Corporations
UNECA	United Nations Economic Commission for Africa
UNGC	UN Global Compact
UNGPs	UN Guiding Principles on Business and Human Rights
USA	United States of America
WBCSD	World Business Council for Sustainable Development
WCED	World Commission on Environment and Development
WTO	World Trade Organization

Figures

1.1	Carroll's initial pyramidal structure of CSR categories	15
1.2	Robust and comprehensive CSR practices occupying the core of corporate operations	18
2.1	Illustration of RSM formulation	72
7.1	Illustrating RSM formulation and regulatory features	204

Foreword

This book is a fine work of scholarship. It is erudite, challenging and interesting. As a cross-disciplinary subject, corporate social responsibility (CSR) has attracted the attention of many scholars offering varying perspectives. From Friedman's controversial statement that "there is one and only one social responsibility of business – to use its resources and engage in activities designed to increase its profits so long as it stays within the rules of the game, which is to say, engages in open and free competition without deception or fraud" many scholars take a softer definition, which includes moral or ethical undertones.

From a Pan-African corporate law perspective, Dr Amodu uses his unique exposure as both an experienced legal attorney in multinational businesses in Africa and a corporate law scholar to conceptually clarify CSR as a comprehensive regulatory construct beyond philanthropy, corporate charity or large companies undertaking community development projects. The author argues that most scholars tend to agree about the core values of CSR in addressing human rights violations, environmental degradation, social exclusion and other imbalances between individuals, states and powerful companies.

He analyses the socio-legal subject matter as a corporate governance topic, which broadens the fiduciary duties of corporate executives to consider, manage and balance the social, economic and environmental impacts of corporate decisions in a wider social context. Beyond the assemblage of protective rules for enhancing shareholder value, the book underscores the pursuit of a corporate law objective to promote aggregate welfare, social efficiency, transparency and accountability to corporate stakeholders such as employees, host communities, consumers, creditors, the government and the environment among others. CSR implementation is discussed within the context of Africa's business communities as warranting the prescription of legal obligations to check the otherwise narrow pursuit of profit and the raw exercise of corporate powers.

The book makes a bold and original contribution to the corporate objective discourse by its proposal of an alternative corporate law theory known as the responsible stakeholder model (RSM) embodied in the two notions of: a default legal duty to balance competing stakeholder interests and a presumption of verifiable corporate irresponsibility whenever alleged by qualified stakeholders. Unlike many stakeholder-oriented models lacking practicable paradigm

xiv *Foreword*

with which corporate executives may effectively manage and balance competing interests in the best interest of the company, the author concludes the book in Chapter 7 with a pioneer prescription of a workable set of model CSR-oriented provisions for adoption within the corporate law systems of Nigeria and South Africa. The recommended framework provides a practical guide for directors to balance legitimate but competing stakeholder interests in the long term interest of the company.

For an improved conceptualization and implementation of CSR in Africa, the book demonstrates that there is nothing antithetical between CSR and its core value of sustainable development and trade liberalization. It depicts how CSR is accommodated within the World Trade Organization rules and agreements, and, for the purpose of drawing important lessons for African regional integration arrangement, it shows how CSR is implemented within the context of the European Union operations.

Overall, in light of the dearth of standard materials on CSR in Africa from corporate law regulatory viewpoint and devoid of the prevailing moralistic approach to the subject, Dr Amodu's book is unique and timely. Policy makers, industry practitioners, business executives, legal consultants, academics and postgraduate students of company law and corporate governance across the continent of Africa and beyond will not only find the book very interesting in terms of its contributions but also an indispensable companion.

Janet Dine
Professor of International Economic Development Law
Queen Mary University of London
November 2019

Part I

Background, theories and global outlook

1 Introduction

1 Background

Corporate social responsibility (CSR) is a corporate governance and business management model used as a catalyst for economic prosperity for businesses and sustainable growth in the society. Although CSR may be shrouded in mystery coupled with a number of issues and debates, many scholars in the field, however, agree that situating CSR within a proper conceptual and implementation framework offers great prospects for achieving sustainable development for both business communities and the society.

Despite varying definitions, debates and approaches on the CSR subject as shall be later demonstrated in this chapter, the subject has nonetheless received general recognition in many jurisdictions around the globe. Many businesses are now desirous of been tagged as good corporate citizen, socially responsible, environmentally conscious, enlightened business and economically sustainable. CSR has become very popular around the world including in Africa. While it is commonly known as 'corporate social responsibility' (CSR) in Nigeria and 'corporate citizenship' in South Africa, it is called 'corporate responsibility' (CR) in the United Kingdom and 'corporate citizenship' (CC) in the United States of America, 'maatschapelijk verantwoord ondernemen' (MVO) in The Netherlands, 'responsabilite social des enterprises' (RSE) in France, 'responsabilidad social empresarial' (RSE) in Spain, 'responsabilita socialedelle impresse' (RSI) in Italy, 'unternehmerische gesellschaftsverantwortung' (UG) in Germany, amongst other nomenclatures in other countries.

Notwithstanding the different CSR nomenclatures across different jurisdictions as highlighted earlier, this chapter highlights the emergence of the CSR subject in corporate governance discourse of both the United States of America and the United Kingdom. It also shows differences in CSR conceptions and definitions together with their respective associated problems and underscores the interconnectedness between CSR and corporate governance. Following its CSR conceptual analyses and clarifications and summaries of all subsequent chapters in the book, the chapter concludes by setting an agenda for investigating the philosophical underpinnings of corporate actions and CSR with a view to situating effective CSR practices within an acceptable theoretical, regulatory and enforcement framework within African business communities.

4   *Background, theories and global outlook*

1.1 Emergence of CSR

Although capitalism provided efficient means of optimal distribution of resources, it also engendered market failures together with economic recession, and accordingly public trust in businesses continues to dwindle. The fundamental assumptions of the free market shareholder primacy theory continues to gather queries about the efficacy of the most developed 'invisible hand' of the free market in sustainably distributing resources in the society. Therefore, a few ideological and policy questions have become inevitable in the manner in which the world's largest economies are run. There are questions, for instance, surrounding the role of state institutions and governments in economies; such questions pertain to identifying whose responsibility it must be to provide public goods and social services in the society. The present economic structure has been incapable to counterbalance the recurrent negative ethical, social and environmental developments in terms of poverty reduction, decreasing unemployment and inequality. This has reinforced arguments for systemic economic reforms and better corporate governance mechanisms. These systemic reforms have taken different shapes including agitations for social inclusion and the gradual shift from using the traditional (transaction-oriented) economic parameters of gross domestic product (GDP) to gauge the health of any economy to more some progressive and people-oriented parameters such as the gross national happiness (GNH)[1] amongst others.

Corporate social responsibility emerged as one of the systemic reform responses to the previously mentioned economic imbalances, corporate irresponsibility and sustainability challenges attributable to capitalism. CSR enjoins corporations not just to 'do well' economically in the course of their operations but also to do good; corporate success is nowadays measured in terms of the success of all relevant stakeholders of companies, not just the success of the business owners. However, in view of the manner in which CSR was introduced into corporate governance discourse, coupled with issues, debates and policy questions inherent in the CSR concept itself, the relevant ultimate question is: (at least as CSR is presently conceived in many jurisdictions around the world including in Africa) is CSR really capable of addressing the fundamental queries and inadequacies of corporate capitalism and of the dominant shareholder primacy model[2] in the business community? To put it differently, to what extent can the responsibilities and obligations of businesses and companies be broadened in reaction to societal pressure for effective CSR practices and sustainable development?

1.1.1 Historical perspectives from the United States of America

Many writers and commentators have traced CSR to different origins. Historical accounts of early developments of corporate responsibility include the following:

(i) In ancient Mesopotamia around 1700 BC, King Hammurabi was reported to have introduced a code in which builders, inn keepers and farmers were put to death if their negligence caused the deaths of others or major inconvenience to citizens;

(ii) In ancient Rome, senators reportedly grumbled about the failure of business to contribute sufficient taxes to fund their military campaigns;

(iii) In 1622, disgruntled shareholders in the Dutch East India Company were said to have also issued pamphlets complaining about management secrecy and self-enrichment;[3]

(iv) CSR history also finds a place in the philanthropic work of wealthy business owners such as John D. Rockefeller, Andrew Carnegie and Henry Ford who gave away millions of dollars for social uses and causes. Rockefeller and Carnegie believed that they were stewards of a social contract between business and society and as such were required by way of philanthropy and good management to hold society's resources in trust in order to increase total social welfare;[4]

(v) CSR origins also has a place in the United States' 19th-century boycotts of foodstuff produced with slave labour.[5]

However, the history of the modern conception of CSR as discussed in this book dates back to the corporate governance debates, largely captured in the published works of Professors Adolf Berle and Merrick Dodd in the Harvard Law Review[6] and calls for reforms in the early 1930s.[7] Many scholars have concluded that the majority of issues and problems which characterized discussions in corporate governance and CSR among academics are traceable to Adolf Berle and Gardiner Means' postulations on the theory of separation of ownership from control in their 1932 work, *The Modern Corporation and Private Property*.[8] For instance, Douglas Branson contended that the ideas of the Columbia Professors Berle and Means:

> have proven more durable still. The separation of ownership from control, problems it poses, whether indeed it poses any problems at all, and proposals to 'reform' corporate governance by filling the void the separation of ownership from control creates, continue to monopolize corporate governance theorists' discussion to the present day.[9]

Corporate governance reform in its earliest form centred around finding an effective check on the raw exercise of corporate power, and these checks began in respect of the social and environmental concern about businesses. Consequently, the advent of government intervention in terms of prescriptive legislations to check corporate powers appears widely accepted as characterizing the beginning of the CSR movement. Therefore, when in the United States of America, a large number of large corporations consolidated to the detriment of the public in 1890, there was government intervention by way of

6 *Background, theories and global outlook*

regulation of utilities together with the anti-trust movements. Also in 1914, the government passed further anti-trust laws in order to prevent the formation of monopolies. Further strict government regulations were made even in the 1960s up to 1970s to curb raw exercise of corporate powers. It is important to note that one of the early writers espousing on this check on corporate powers was the Harvard economist, John Kenneth Galbraith, who theorized on the incidence of government's exercise of a 'countervailing power', which should serve as a check on the raw exercise of corporate powers by way of farm legislations, labour and minimum wages legislation et cetera.[10] While there were other notable early contributions on the CSR subject by writers such as Keith Davis, William C. Frederick and Joseph W. McGuire amongst others,[11] it was not until 1954 that the expression 'corporate social responsibility' was first introduced into corporate America by Howard R. Bowen in his book, *Social Responsibilities of the Business.*[12] Howard Bowen defined CSR as:

> the obligation of businessmen to pursue those policies, to make those decisions, or to follow those lines of action which are desirable in terms of the objectives and values of our society.[13]

Bowen also contended that corporate executives must perform the ethical duty and ensure that the broader social impacts of their decisions are considered and that all corporations failing to give due regard to the social impacts of their activities ought not to be seen as legitimate. However, in spite of the important contribution of Howard Bowen, the crucial moment in the emergence of modern CSR movement did not come until the 1970s from the wave of legal academics who suggested methods of governmental intrusion in response to the problems posed by the separation of ownership from control. The thesis of the movement was that, in order to solve the ills of society thought in large part to be the product of corporate behaviour (in turn thought to be the result of the separation of ownership from control), some sort of government intervention must remain essential to make large corporations and their managers alike accountable, if not to the owners of such corporations, then to the society as a whole. Essentially, justifications for CSR activism were based on the fact that large corporations were no longer merely aggregations of private property. It was further argued that corporations had become so large – and their behaviour affected so many in the society – that the law should regard them as public, or quasi-public, institutions and regulate them as such. Lawrence Mitchell summarized the influence of these corporations on the society as follows:

> No institution other than the state so dominates our public discourse and our private lives. . . . Corporations make most everything we consume. Their advertising and products fill almost every waking moment of our lives. They give us jobs, and sometimes a sense of identity. They define communities and enhance both our popular and serious culture. They

Introduction 7

present the investment opportunities that send our children to college, and provide for our old age. They fund our research.

. . . They pollute our environments. They impoverish our spirits with the never-ending messages of the virtues of consumerism. They provide a living, but often not a meaning. And sometimes they destroy us; our retirement expectations are unfunded, our investment hopes are dashed, our communities are left impoverished. The very power that corporations have over our lives means that, intentionally or not, they profoundly affect our lives.[14]

At the core of this argument was the need to impress on senior executives and directors of these large corporations the notion that, as a matter of general corporate law, those managers had responsibility for the welfare of workers, to make products safe, to be good citizens in the communities in which their corporations operated, to protect and promote clean air and clean water, and so on. In a nutshell, CSR agitations centralized on compliance with occupational health, safety, clean water, clean air and other labour and environmentally friendly legislations.

It is also important to note that while efforts at reforming corporate governance and checking corporate powers in the early 1970s and its preceding years had taken the shape of increased government intervention, things took a different dimension in the late 1970s and early 1980s. The CSR construct as a countervailing power was not received with open arms by many academics, corporate managers and executives. Perhaps the response of certain corporate managers to CSR advocates is best captured in Calvin Coolidge's retort that 'the business of business is business'. Furthermore, as a result of the stagnation in the mid-1970s, legal academics who delved into economics began to question the potency and efficacy of national governments and their prescriptive legislations to bring about sustainable development and act as a sufficient check on corporate capitalism together with the enormous corporate powers of giant corporations. The World Bank and the International Monetary Fund (IMF), which were founded to ensure that national governments could manage temporary balance of payment problems, eventually saw government interference in such businesses and economic planning as an ineffective and inappropriate way to stimulate economic growth.

It is interesting to note that the historic use of CSR as an effective countervailing power received criticism mostly from apologists of the influential assertions of the Nobel Prize-winning economist from the University of Chicago, Milton Friedman. To Friedman:

there is one and only one social responsibility of business – to use its resources and engage in activities designed to increase its profits.[15]

As a corollary of Adam Smith's 'invisible hand of market forces', Friedman further argued that the markets were so accurate in their allocation of capital

8 Background, theories and global outlook

and pricing of inputs that a corporation that had funds to spend on CSR activities must be reaping monopoly profits, at the expense of consumers and many others in the society.[16] Friedman had also noted that any discussion of CSR is utter hogwash that CSR could thoroughly undermine the very foundations of our society and that it is a fundamentally subversive doctrine.

Upon the perceived failure of government countervailing power and intervention, the 'invisible hand of the market'[17] therefore gained traction as a substitute countervailing power on the raw exercise of corporate power. Branson[18] explained the occurrence as follows:

> The questions early generations had asked still existed. What prevented managers from lying down on the job, playing golf three times a week and neglecting their management duties? What prevented managers from "ripping off" the owners, by misuse or embezzlement of corporate funds or property or by other forms of purposeful venality? The answer law and economics gave was not 'more regulation' or 'public interest directors,' or 'intervention by the federal government,' but 'market forces.'

The prevailing market forces intervention in corporate governance climaxed into the contractarian[19] movement (comprising economist cum legal academics) in the 1980s, which suggested that corporate legislation should not only be minimalist but should have no mandatory content at all. It was further argued that the role of corporate legislations should stop at providing an 'off the rack' standard form contract whereby parties to an incorporated venture would negotiate, absent transaction costs et cetera. To the contractarian, even the basic conception of fiduciary duties of directors and corporate managers can be varied or eliminated by way of contract, e.g., through a majority vote of the shareholders. In essence, the corporation is taken in terms of the private contractual arrangements of its statutory constituents (shareholders, directors and officers), governed largely by market forces.[20] Finally, from corporate America's perspective and in reaction to the market forces theory and contractarian movement of the 1980s, what is closest to the modern day conception of the CSR construct became more prevalent in the USA in the late 1990s. The CSR movement has now evolved to accommodate the government interventionist models of stakeholder theory and the communitarian model of the corporation. Basically, the stakeholder theory enumerates a number of stakeholders – including a company's work force, consumers, suppliers, the society, the environment where it operates and the investors in such a corporation – as key actors in the corporation and whose stakes in the company must be equally safeguarded. The communitarians emphasized the sociological and moral phenomenon of the corporation as a community, in contrast to the individualistic, self-reliant group of purely economic actors who are the only significant players in a corporation. This new CSR movement also comprised academics who advocated a legal responsibility of corporations to workers and their families.

Introduction 9

1.1.2 Historical perspectives from the United Kingdom

Just as the first book on something on 'company law' was first published in the United States of America in 1932 as opposed to latter publication in the United Kingdom in 1836,[21] the phrase 'corporate governance' appeared first in American journals before it was imported into the United Kingdom (UK). Corporate social responsibility (CSR) as a corporate governance construct was virtually non-existent in the UK before 1970. As a matter of fact, it was not until 1973 that the most influential business community pressure group in the UK – the Confederation of British Industry (CBI) – accorded some recognition and made a statement on the CSR subject.[22] The emergence of CSR in the UK also followed a similar pattern as in the USA, having arisen as a form of corporate governance countervailing power to checking the raw exercise of corporate powers. The UK witnessed a sudden insolvency of major large companies which had, until then, issued financial statements showing they were in a healthy economic and financial state. This led to the setting up of various committees to defuse public pressures for corporate governance reforms. The reform reports on corporate governance by the various committees culminated into the bulk of the provisions of the Combined Codes of Best Practices, which is now known as United Kingdom Corporate Governance Code. Consequently, the present UK Corporate Governance Code could be traced in history to the Cadbury Committee Report,[23] which was published in 1992. The Cadbury report was followed by the Greenbury Report of 1995;[24] both of which were combined in the Sir Ronald Hampel-chaired Committee Report of 1998.[25] And then came the Turnbull Report[26] of 1999 to address the scope and extent of Internal Control in corporate governance. There was also the Derek Higgs Review of the code in 2003.[27] Subsequent to these published corporate governance reports, the UK Financial Reporting Council (FRC) has been undertaking regular review of the code. The latest version of the code is the July 2018 version,[28] which is applicable to accounting periods beginning on or after 1 January 2019. Enforcement method adopted for earlier versions of the code was through the listing rules of the Financial Services Authority, which required all listed companies registered in the UK to comply with the provisions or give good reasons why they had not in their annual report to the Authority. As the Competent Authority for audit in the UK, the FRC now monitors and takes action to promote the quality of corporate reporting in accordance with the provisions of the code. Starting from 1 January 2019, the code is applicable to all companies with premium listing, whether incorporated in the UK or elsewhere. The traditional 'comply or explain' enforcement approach of the UK Corporate Governance Code has been retained in the new code, which approach has become the trademark of corporate governance approach in the UK.

Although the acronym CSR did not feature specifically in the UK Corporate Governance Code, the code has, however, always featured elements of modern CSR conception. For instance, CSR elements appear in the 1998

10 *Background, theories and global outlook*

Sir Ronald Hampel Committee Report stating that 'good corporate governance ensures that constituencies (that is stakeholders) with a relevant interest in the company's business are fully taken into account'.[29] Further, directors are enjoined to set the company's values and standards and ensure that its obligations to its shareholders and 'others' are understood and met.[30] A reasonable and necessary inference from this is a deliberate introduction of government interventionist obligations on businesses to consider the interests of 'others', which would mean obligations to certain stakeholder group of creditors, suppliers, contractors, employees and so on, apart from the shareholders.

In rounding off discussions on historical perspectives, CSR is clearly evolving.[31] It has evolved from mere charity or philanthropy into more contemporary advocacy for sustainable development. In modern times, CSR is construed in terms of a business management model, which requires the consideration of the interests of a certain stakeholder group in the day to day activities of business associations and organizations. The concept of CSR has broadened the roles of companies, especially large multinational corporations; it has increased the responsibilities of corporate managers and has raised the bar on the expectations of the society from corporate owners. From the foregoing, it is no longer business as usual; it is no longer commercially wise to simply declare huge profit margins in annual reports without justifying how such bottom lines were legitimately reached without contravening accepted core values of the society. Otherwise, such businesses run the likely reputational risks of losing their so-called social license to operate[32] and its attendant effects.

Suffice to conclude on the note that the evolution of CSR is ongoing and is more likely to continue in corporate governance reforms and corporate law discourse to address key economic and corporate governance issues as they arise. The relevance of the CSR construct in the 21st century is perhaps best summarized by Bryan Horrigan thus:

> CSR is a major feature of the 21st century business environment. For better or worse, it affects the work of corporate insiders (e.g. corporate shareholders, boards, managers, and employees), corporate advisers (e.g. company secretaries, in-house counsel and external legal and business financiers), and all of the communities in which the corporations operate (e.g. local business sites, transnational consumer markets and global supply chains). Everyone in the world therefore belongs in one CSR camp or another, whether you support CSR, tolerate it or condemn it.[33]

1.2 CSR conception, definitional attempts and debates

Conceptualizing CSR is not a simple task in corporate governance discourse. This difficulty is not unconnected to the interdisciplinary and multidisciplinary nature of this socio-legal subject; CSR is relevant and therefore discussed in many disciplines ranging from accountancy, geography, economics, sociology, law, and many management studies; this multi-disciplinary nature sometimes rears its face even within a particular discipline. For instance, in the law discipline, varying scholars in different aspects of the law (industrial law, environmental law, corporate law, human rights law and so on) write differently and each sometimes with varying conception of the CSR subject.

1.2.1 The Berle/Dodd debate

CSR is perhaps inseparable from the popular debate in the academic circle of the early 1930s. Notably at the centre of the debate are the arguments of Professors Adolf Berle and Merrick E. Dodd. The crux of the debate is that while Berle argued in 1931 that 'all powers granted to a corporation or to the management of a corporation . . . are necessarily at all times exercisable only for the rateable benefit of all shareholders',[34] Dodd argued against Berle's 'single-minded devotion to stockholder profit'[35] in his celebrated 1932 article. Dodd maintained that

> the view that business corporations exist for the sole purpose of making profits for their shareholders is apt to give way to a theoretically defensible and law-informing view of the business corporation as an economic institution which has a social service as well as a profit-making function.[36]

Although Berle succumbed to Dodd's pro-CSR arguments at some point in the mid-1960s, there are relevant corporate law implications from the arguments proceeding from the debate, which are still the basis of fierce arguments and counter-arguments among scholars. For instance, the submissions of Milton Friedman as shown at 1.1.1 earlier and as underpinned by the shareholder primacy model (discussed in detail in Chapter 2) appear still largely premised on Berle's arguments. Unlike Friedman, however, some others rather align with Dodd's position seeing a company as a social institution fundamentally underpinned by a public purpose. This approach is concerned with not just the shareholders but also the non-shareholding stakeholders. In the stakeholder model, corporations do not have an obligation to maximize societal wealth, but they do have a duty to be good corporate citizens.[37] Dodd's stakeholder perspective is still relevant to date and underpins recent arguments and theories attempting to explain the nature of firm, corporate actions and CSR practices.[38] The dichotomy of views in terms of stakeholder model versus shareholder primacy model and their coloration on the CSR discourse constitutes a rich field for independent and separate research outside the scope of the present chapter. These views are accordingly discussed in detail in Chapter 2.

The relevance of the previously highlighted debate together with its modern day argumentative colorations to CSR literature is not far-fetched. One implication has been that a scholar's conception, views and arguments around CSR are almost automatically polarized and dependent on the side of the debate from which such views originate. For instance, the adoption of a CSR that is intrinsically based on voluntariness as initially advocated at the level of the

12 *Background, theories and global outlook*

European Union and the Organization for Economic Cooperation and Development appears to align with Professor Berle's perspective and is *friedmanesque* in nature. This will likely also skew such thoughts on consequential issues such as CSR regulation and enforcement towards adoption of self-regulatory regime by the business community, whereas views aligning with Professor Dodd's position will likely influence a writer's thoughts for a CSR conception beyond voluntary actions of companies and possibly also call for some form of external regulation of corporate behaviours. More thoughts about this point are discussed in Chapters 2 and 3 to follow.

1.2.2 Definitional approaches and associated problems

There is a definitional problem in CSR discourse; CSR is very popular and everybody is talking about it, yet so far nobody has been able to give a generally acceptable definition. In fact, some scholars are rather of the view that a generally accepted definition of the CSR concept is simply impossible.[39] Since CSR is multidisciplinary, it has caught the attention of many scholars and experts in different disciplines and, each of these scholars usually offers his or her biased perspective on the subject. As will be demonstrated later in respect to business management scholars, legal scholars have similarly struggled to offer a generally acceptable definition of CSR. David Engel defined CSR as:

> The obligations and inclinations, if any, of corporations organized for profit, voluntarily to pursue social ends that conflict with the presumptive shareholder desire to maximize profit.[40]

Evident from Engel's attempt is that CSR was originally conceived as anything done by companies outside their core operational objects; this would therefore ordinarily involve voluntary corporate charity and philanthropy. Little wonder many companies primarily understand CSR initiatives in this light in terms of absolutely discretionary provision of public goods and social services by companies and giving back to the society a portion of the company's profits. This sort of definition and CSR conception has drawn criticisms from many commentators and scholars as an approach serving no one any particular good – from the most conservative business person to the most ambitious ideals-driven civil society or the most market-oriented government official. For instance, a voluntary CSR will most likely not serve a traditional capitalist businessman any particular good since such a voluntary idea of giving back can only constitute sheer detraction from his core business of profit maximization.[41] Similarly, the very ambitious ideals-driven civil society may also not derive so much utility from a centrally voluntary CSR concept, as such approach is likely to jeopardize an efficient compliance framework under which businesses should be held accountable. In other words, if demonstrating effective CSR is very important as recognized in the business community, where it is voluntary, what then happens in cases of non-compliance or demonstrated sheer irresponsibility? A voluntary CSR will definitely fall short in providing answers to such questions; the same argument may also be advanced in the case of government officials whose traditional objective of ensuring an efficient legal framework may also be jeopardized if a central theme of voluntariness is adopted on the CSR discourse. This approach to CSR and its consequences in CSR regulation and enforcement discourse are discussed in detail in Chapters 2 and 3.

Marydee Ojala had defined CSR as:

> the obligation of both business and society to take proper legal, moral-ethical and philanthropic actions that will protect and improve the welfare of both society and business as a whole, all of which must be accomplished within the economic structures and capabilities of parties involved.[42]

As commendable as the previous definition may be, it can be criticized for its seeming emphasis on CSR as some moral philanthropic burden on corporations to discharge in response to societal pressures. A more appropriate definition of CSR, especially within its conception in the modern business world, appears cited by Bryan Horrigan as the:

> Obligations (social or legal) which concern the major actual and possible social impact of the activities of the corporation in question, whether or not these activities are intended or do in fact promote the profitability of the particular corporation.[43]

The previous more recent definitions rather reflect the gradual shift from the usual primary focus on wealth maximization philosophy of companies and business enterprises and show that CSR in recent times now transcends the ideology of simply giving back to the society out of the excess or surplus of the business. In modern times, therefore, CSR has broadened responsibilities beyond the traditional obligations of businesses to focus on wealth maximization for business owners first, then giving back to the society on a second note if there are surpluses. It has extended the responsibilities of businesses towards obligations for environmental protection, ethical business practices and social inclusion in their operations amongst others. It is now desirable to speak of intrinsically responsible companies and businesses; a business that is not primarily focused on wealth maximization for its owners 'at all costs' but considers the legal, social and ethical repercussions of its operations on its employees, local communities where it operates, the society, the government and the environment in general; a business that is not solely after the race to the bottom line of profit but rather the more inclusive triple bottom line; a balanced business with the right blend of the interests of its shareholders and stakeholders altogether.

In the business management field, CSR appears mostly conceived as the responsibility of businesses to the wider societal good, not only beyond but also in addition to the economic performance of the business. A number of CSR models have evolved since its introduction in corporate governance discourse.

14   *Background, theories and global outlook*

However, Professor Archie Carroll's model, in his *A Three-Dimensional Conceptual Model of Corporate Performances*, appears most useful and interesting.[44] He opined:

> The social responsibility of business encompasses the economic, legal, ethical, and discretionary expectations that society has of organizations at a given point in time.[45]

From the previous work, Carroll identified four CSR components:

(i)   Economic Responsibilities;
(ii) Legal Responsibilities;
(iii) Ethical Responsibilities; and
(iv) Discretionary/Philanthropic Responsibilities.

The economic responsibilities of a corporation or business entail its responsibility to make profits for its investors. The legal category of responsibilities represents the responsibilities of the business to operate within the framework of legal requirement. Carroll explained that, just as society had sanctioned the economic system by permitting business to assure the productive role, as a partial fulfilment of the social contract, it has also laid down the ground rules – the laws and regulations – under which business is expected to operate. He clarified that the ethical responsibilities of a corporation entail 'the responsibility to do what is right, just, and fair'. These ethical responsibilities are meant to include society's expectations of business over and above (any) legal requirements. In other words, the corporation must endeavour to surpass legal duties and obligations in its relation to the members of the society. Finally, the discretionary responsibility, which appears to be the most controversial of the categories among scholars, represents society's expectation that a business should assume social roles above and beyond its economic, legal and ethical responsibilities. These discretionary duties, which naturally mean that a business not engaging in them is not necessarily breaching any other legal or ethical duties, include contributions to various kinds of social, educational, recreational or cultural purposes.

Carroll's categorizations of CSR are not mutually exclusive of one another but ordered in their fundamental role in the evolution of their importance. In Carroll's pyramidal structure, economic responsibilities are at the bottom, topped by legal responsibilities, then ethical responsibilities and ultimately topped by discretionary responsibilities.

This categorization and conception of CSR by Carroll was later criticized as outdated by Andrew Zur and Jody Evans[46] who rather discussed CSR in terms of *business orientations* and identified heterogeneous capabilities including: (i) Environmental Capability entailing environment-friendly business culture and practice; (ii) Work place capability representing good health and safety for employees; (iii) Market place capability entailing long-term relationship with

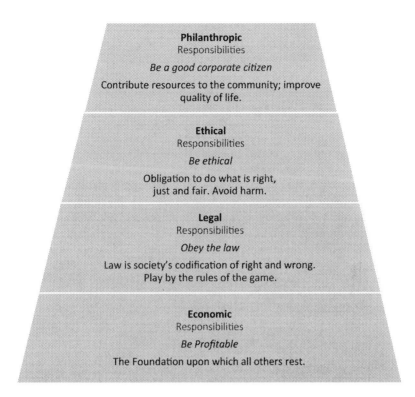

Figure 1.1 Carroll's initial pyramidal structure of CSR categories[47]

suppliers, customers and business partners and (iv) Societal capability, which involves short-term investment into the local community for future generations. Zur and Evans posited that:

> the traditional four obligations of CSR represent outdated thinking and do not lend themselves to conceptualisation of CSR as a business orientation . . . we conclude that a broader, but more specific classification is needed in order to examine CSR orientation in a manner that better reflects the current business retail climate.[48]

Zur and Evans' counter-proposals on the four heterogeneous CSR dimensions are not only commendable but also relevant towards improved understanding and operationalization of the CSR subject; however, their criticism of Carroll's categories as being archaic appears, after all, unfounded. This author is of the view that the authors appear not to have averted their minds to the fact that Carroll had maintained that there were in existence certain 'issue' elements to which his categories or elements of CSR are tied.

16 Background, theories and global outlook

In any event, Carroll later modified his CSR model. In the later analysis, a Venn diagram with three CSR elements or domains was proposed in place of the earlier four-domain pyramidal structure.[49] Schwarz and Carroll proposed the three categories of economic, legal and ethical responsibilities. Carroll's earlier discretionary or philanthropic category was abandoned as an independent category and rather subsumed within the ethical and the economic responsibilities. Amongst other reasons, the three-domain approach was adopted by the authors because, in their view, the philanthropic category was unnecessary, inaccurate and a misnomer as a CSR element. The contention underpinning the change of mind appears to be that CSR is a responsibility and an obligation, and it is inaccurate and a misnomer to simultaneously describe it in terms of discretionary and voluntary activities. It is also argued that it is difficult to really distinguish between ethical responsibilities and philanthropic responsibilities, and many philanthropic or discretionary activities are actually based on economic interests. This correction turned out to be crucial to his earlier postulations and has been greeted with more acceptability.

The author aligns with the CSR conception of Carroll to a large extent, especially as initially categorized into the four elements. While the philanthropic category as an independent element has been rejected by a number of scholars as being considered inaccurate and a misnomer – since an activity cannot be an obligation or responsibility and at the same time described in terms of discretion or voluntariness[50] – unlike Carroll and others who abandoned the fourth philanthropy domain, this author begs to differ and has accordingly retained it as an independent element for a few reasons as discussed in the following.

First, the terms 'discretion' and 'obligation'/'responsibility' are not necessarily mutually exclusive in all connotations. There are instances in law (especially for administrative and judicial decisions) where there might be an obligation to exercise discretion or which obligation entails the exercise of discretion. Further, discretionary activities constitute an integral part of any business operations. There will always be elements of discretion in the manner in which business managers carry out operations and CSR policies of the business. There is also discretion in the manner in which obligations and responsibilities, whether legal, ethical or economic responsibilities, are carried out. In most cases, the framework under which an obligation is exercised usually warrants the exercise of discretion. For instance, it is a regulatory obligation on employers to pay salaries and wages to a certain group of employees as agreed with them. However, the same regulatory framework usually admits of discretion as to the manner in which such obligation or responsibility is to be exercised, for instance which exact time of the week or month or how such salaries are to be paid. It is therefore not so much of a misnomer having discretion or voluntary activities in respect to such obligations.

Second, the level of CSR integration in businesses and manner of practice in some jurisdictions, especially amongst the less-industrialized economies of Africa and Asia, are still suggestive that philanthropy, charity and discretionary activities constitute an integral part of CSR conception.[51] For instance in

India, by virtue of Section 135 of the 2013 Indian Companies Act, CSR is still largely perceived in terms of voluntary philanthropic community development projects, as the activities that may be included by companies in their Corporate Social Responsibility Policies Activities relate to: (i) eradicating extreme hunger and poverty; (ii) promotion of education; (iii) promoting gender equality and empowering women; (iv) reducing child mortality and improving maternal health; (v) combating human immunodeficiency virus, acquired immune deficiency syndrome, malaria and other diseases; (vi) ensuring environmental sustainability; (vii) employment-enhancing vocational skills; (viii) social business projects; (ix) contribution to the Prime Minister's National Relief Fund or any other fund set up by the Central Government or the State Governments for socio-economic development and relief and funds for the welfare of the Scheduled Castes, the Scheduled Tribes, other backward classes, minorities and women and (x) such other matters as may be prescribed.[52]

Besides, despite the seeming policy innovations in some jurisdictions as shall be discussed in Chapters 4 and 5 respectively, many business actors across Africa including but not limited to Cameroun,[53] Nigeria,[54] South Africa,[55] Zambia,[56] Uganda[57] and Kenya,[58] still restrictively conceive of CSR in terms of corporate charity, philanthropy, donations and just giving back to the society out of excess profits.[59]

For the previous reasons, this author confirms that the CSR elements may be represented in a Venn diagram as opposed to a pyramid. The author also differs in the representation of the relationship existing among the four CSR elements. As a result of the inseparable and interwoven nature of the four elements, efficient CSR practice is (or should be) at the core of any business operations involving the right balance and integration of the entire four CSR elements. In other words, CSR should simply underlie the obligations of businesses (whether legal, ethical, economic or philanthropic). Consequently, therefore, this book rather situates CSR at the centre and as the foundational core from which economic, legal, ethical and philanthropic obligations of any company emanate as shown in Figure 1.2.

1.2.3 Institutional attempts to define CSR

The World Business Council for Sustainable Development (WBCSD) is a merger of the Business Council for Sustainable Development and the World Industry Council for the Environment in January 1995. It is a CEO-led organization of forward-thinking companies that galvanizes the global business community to create a sustainable future for business, society and the environment. The WBCSD defines CSR as:

> The continuing commitment by business to behave ethically and contribute to economic development while improving the quality of life of the workforce and their families as well as of the local community and society at large.[60]

Figure 1.2 Robust and comprehensive CSR practices occupying the core of corporate operations

To the WBSCD, CSR defines what a company has to do in order for it to win and enjoy the confidence of the community as it generates economic wealth and responds to the dynamics of environmental improvement. The Organisation for Economic Cooperation and Development (OECD) in its Guidelines for Multinational Enterprises[61] defined CSR as 'voluntary principles and standards for responsible business conduct consistent with applicable laws'. The International Chamber of Commerce (ICC) proposes the following definition of corporate responsibility from a business perspective as the voluntary commitment by business to manage its activities in a responsible way. According to a Green Paper issued by the European Commission in 2001,[62] CSR is 'a concept whereby companies integrate social and environmental concerns in their business operations and in their interaction with their stakeholders *on a voluntary basis*' and clarifying further that 'being socially responsible means not only fulfilling legal expectations, but also going beyond compliance and investing "more" into human capital, the environment and the relations with stakeholders'.[63]

It is apt to reiterate the earlier mentioned attention to the recurring theme of voluntariness pervading the previously cited CSR definitions. The significance of this point is most appreciated on the question of enforcement mechanisms of CSR. This question of whether or not CSR obligations ought to be enforced mandatorily or left to self-regulation remains a major CSR debate. Such a voluntary approach already discernible from a definition puts too much emphasis and rather shows bias for a particular regulatory and enforcement regime. Essentially, this approach has also been criticized because usually in the end it turns out that effective CSR practice in many cases is mostly embedded upon adopting the right balance and combination of different regulatory techniques, be it voluntary or mandatory amongst others.

Arising from the previous, little wonder therefore that attitudes appear to change towards CSR definitions. While the ICC jettisoned the word *voluntary* from its CSR definition, the European Union also in its 2011 communication deviated from its earlier narrow voluntary approach. A new definition depicting a modern understanding of the CSR subject was given as 'the responsibility of enterprises for the impact on society'.[64]

Having reviewed the foregoing varying definitional attempts and approaches, this author submits that the CSR is a 'neutral' concept, and there is nothing inherently voluntary or mandatory about it. It is a business model that actors, players and parties concerned may choose to adopt on a voluntary basis and accordingly base on a soft law self-regulatory regime for efficacy or on a hard law (legal prescription) and probably based on mandatory regime for efficacy. For instance, Section 135 of the 2013 Indian Companies Act mandates certain CSR obligations on a specific class of companies within the Indian business community. Therefore, varying circumstances and challenges faced in any society and the societal attitude about CSR values will ultimately inform whether or not the CSR business model is better adopted on a voluntary basis or otherwise.

CSR should therefore be defined as a corporate governance and business management model that broadens the responsibility of companies in an attempt to align the interests of business managers and the interest of not only the shareholders but also that of a stakeholder group within the environment of such companies. The environment referred to includes the company's physical environment (its surrounding land, air, water and the like), its human environment (such as its shareholders and employees), its social environment (its relations with and reputation in the society or local community where it operates), its economic environment (entailing the interests of investors to create and distribute resources and wealth) and its political environment (the substantive government and agencies regulating its operations). Therefore, such stakeholders within a company's environment include the company's employees, contractors, suppliers, creditors, customers or the community where the company operates, the government, the media and so on. The danger of everybody or anything claiming to be part of the stakeholder group of a business is appreciated here. This would mean that each business would have to reasonably qualify and delimit its stakeholder group within an acceptable business framework. A qualification of relevant and legitimate stakeholders for businesses, for instance, has been proposed in Chapter 2. A robust adoption of CSR as a

20 *Background, theories and global outlook*

corporate governance and management model will ensure business enterprises reasonably balance out the following interests and pressures:

(i)   The need to create wealth for business owners;
(ii) The need to comply with laws, rules and regulations as set by constituted authorities governing operational activities;
(iii) The need to demonstrate fairness, responsiveness and high ethical standards in its operations;
(iv) The need to show responsibility in response to societal pressures and needs to the best of its ability whether or not such responsibility will create wealth for the business or not.

This CSR conception would mean that while not necessarily taking over the role of government, the business community can no longer see the provision of public goods and social services as fundamentally secondary to its primary focus of wealth maximization for its owners. It would also mean that no company will be able to claim effective intrinsic CSR practice without demonstrating efficient balancing and aligning of certain necessary interests as highlighted previously. The world economy is simply too important to be anchored on a self-regulating business community and hinged on the neoliberal assumption of an efficient or perfect free market. It is too significant for us to continue to adopt the view that public goods and social services should be the exclusive responsibility of the government or that CSR model should only entail voluntary corporate responses to societal pressures.

1.3 Nature and reception of CSR within the business community

Despite the debates surrounding the CSR conception, a few of which were highlighted in Section 1.2, by its nature, certain basic values appear generally agreed upon as integral to CSR.[65] These core values include, amongst others:

(i)   Human rights protection;
(ii)   Employee rights;
(iii) Environmental protection;
(iv)   Community development;
(v)   Information disclosure;
(vi)   Stakeholder engagement and management;
(vii) Combating bribery;
(viii) Consumer protection;
(ix)   Sustainable development.

Such a broad value system is probably responsible for its adoption across different disciplines and fields and is probably also responsible for difficulties surrounding a generally acceptable definition. Notwithstanding its wide interdisciplinary reach and benefits to companies in manifold ways as they are largely able to avoid unnecessary costs associated with irresponsible corporate behaviour, the introduction of CSR discourse in businesses has been nonetheless attended by a few problems. A few academics, corporate managers and business owners continue to view CSR as just a source of undue public pressure, a detraction from serious business and a deviation from the primary economic object of doing business, which is primarily profit maximization for shareholders.[66] Such a view was expressed in *The Economist* that:

> The most fundamental criticism of CSR is what executives spend on it is other people's – i.e., shareholders' – money. They may mean well, and it may give them satisfaction to write a cheque for hurricane victims or disadvantaged youth, but that is not what they are hired to do. Their job is to make money for shareholders. It is irresponsible for them to sacrifice profits in the (sometime vain) pursuit of goodness.[67]

Further, while CSR appears very popular, it has perhaps become a victim of its own popularity. Every business claims to be involved in CSR, whether genuinely or otherwise;[68] while many companies may actually be conducting their businesses responsibly and communicating the same effectively to stakeholders, others rather merely tick boxes in corporate reporting and constitute free riders, paying lip-service to CSR and involved only in CSR greenwashing.[69] Corporate *greenwashing* is faux CSR; it means making fake, insincere, dubious, inflated or misleading environmental claims. The term was first used by an American environmentalist Jay Westerveld in 1986 in response to a hotel's efforts to encourage guests to re-use towels in order to help the environment by saving water and energy. Westerveld had suspected that the true motivation was profit maximization for the hotel. Greenwashing appears to have also dovetailed into regulatory and enforcement debates. There are concerns regarding CSR conception as mere tokenism or voluntary corporate charity subject to the whims and caprices of the companies involved, a conception that seems to have been popularized at the EU. It has thus been difficult to embed effective and intrinsic CSR values within the business community as a result of (what this book will argue) desperate clinging to voluntary and self-regulatory CSR techniques at the intergovernmental level. This difficulty significantly hinders an effective and efficient CSR implementation framework at the global level that should legally bind companies.

CSR has also been greeted with the argument that it has no real value as it cannot be legally enforced. Without a regulatory or implementation approach, CSR appears not to have sufficient impact on solving the problems it is expected to solve. Put differently, Saleem Sheikh noted that CSR may be criticized for the notion that companies have a direct responsibility for solutions to many problems that plague society and that they have the ability to unilaterally solve them.[70]

22 *Background, theories and global outlook*

In Africa, there also appears to be some CSR antipathies as an irrelevant and distracting Western concept targeted at further impoverishing the continent. This argument comes to life in trade liberalization and regional integration discourse across countries of Africa. Many developing states, especially in Africa, would argue for instance that CSR principles and standards only constitute unnecessary trade barriers to free flow of goods and services from Africa to the rest of the developed world market. It could therefore be seen as a concept that forestalls the delivery of the promises of globalization to Africa. Further explanations and discussions around this issue are detailed in Chapters 6 and 7 of this book.

However, more ethically conscious and enlightened corporate executives now place increasing significance on CSR. CSR is now seen as a creative opportunity to fundamentally strengthen businesses while contributing to society at the same time. Corporate organizations and corporate managers appear more receptive towards CSR values seeing that they stand to profit in manifold ways by spending on CSR projects and avoid otherwise unnecessary costs attending irresponsible corporate behaviour. Richard Smerdon has succinctly summarized modern attitude to CSR in the following words:

> the debate has moved on from the position five or so years ago when, as a generalization, companies and their investors were ambivalent as to whether investment in social and environmental projects was justified in terms of shareholder value, to a position where there is a much greater understanding by a significant proportion (but not by any means all) of investors and companies of the necessity for a business model which puts sustainability as a high priority, followed closely by ethical practices and a significant social contribution: all are seen as simply good business.[71]

The modern economic realities as a result of global financial crisis appear to have whittled down arguments that CSR only constitutes a deflection from serious business. To this end, Bryan Horrigan quoted the former Australian's Minister for Superannuation and Corporate Law (Senator Nick Sherry) as saying:

> the world financial crisis is not just a corporate issue; the economy is not a private product but a critical piece of the social infrastructure. . . . While some commentators have speculated that the financial crisis will put a stop to CSR programs – I believe this not to be the case. Such views are driven by a misunderstanding of what CSR is all about. If anything the current crisis should accelerate its adoption. Companies may need to refocus their efforts, and concentrate on the shared values between them and the wider community in which they operate. I believe the current circumstances highlight the realities of CSR as an important means of companies to manage non-financial risk and maximise their long term value.[72] ·

Therefore, CSR has not only become the rhetoric of every business enterprise (whether genuinely or just paying lip service), especially those engaged in natural resource development, but it also occupies a pre-eminent position in board room discourse. Effective and efficient CSR strategy and initiatives have now been directly linked to growth in businesses and mitigation of social risks that may have profound effects on the bankability of an enterprise and the rate of returns on its projects. In addition, in research conducted at the Canadian Centre for Social Performance and Ethics at the University of Toronto, it has been found that, over the long term, companies that rate highest on ethics and CSR usually turn out to be most profitable.[73]

Further, in the EU, a lot of progress has been recorded on CSR implementation among companies. More EU enterprises have signed the United Nations Global Compact (arguably the world's foremost CSR implementation framework[74]); many more (beyond Europe) are also signing trade and investment agreements incorporating CSR clauses. This is further discussed in Chapters 3 and 6.

It is important to clarify that although CSR is usually discussed in relation to the activities of large companies or multinational enterprises and corporations because of their enormous powers and influence, this is not, however, saying that CSR only applies to them. Intrinsic, effective and efficient CSR is a corporate governance and business management model applicable to all corporate forms: companies and corporations, small or big, domestic or transnational, private or public.

Finally, it is useful to clarify that while some scholars may draw distinctions in the use of the terms 'corporate accountability' or 'corporate responsibility' or 'corporate social and environmental responsibility' or 'corporate sustainability' or even 'corporate social responsibility and accountability', this book does not see any real value in such exercise (as shown in Chapter 5) and therefore uses the terms interchangeably to all represent the responsibility of companies (used interchangeably with 'businesses') to consider, manage and balance the social, economic and environmental impacts of corporate decisions and operations.

1.4 Interconnectedness of corporate governance and CSR

Corporate governance is about the administration of a company, the relationship between the board of directors and management. Colin Tricker, who originally coined the term 'corporate governance' in 1984, made the important distinction between 'management' and 'direction'. Management is about running business, and governance is about seeing that it is run properly and confirming the old distinction between doing things right and doing the right thing. Corporate governance is also ultimately about accountability. To Monks and Minow, corporate governance is the 'relationship among various participants in determining the direction and performance of corporations'.[75] It is about power and influence: in what manner is the power in a business

24 *Background, theories and global outlook*

distributed, who plays a role in conveying this power and how is this power used? A comprehensive definition is given by the Organization for Economic Cooperation and Development (OECD). The OECD originated in 1948 as the Organisation for European Economic Co-operation (OEEC) for the reconstruction of Europe after World War II. Its mission is to help its member countries to achieve sustainable economic growth and development and to raise the standard of living in member countries while maintaining financial stability in order to contribute to the development of the world economy. The OECD described corporate governance as follows:

> Corporate governance is one key element in improving economic efficiency and growth as well as enhancing investor confidence. Corporate governance involves a set of relationships between a company's management, its board, its shareholders, and other stakeholders. Corporate governance also provides the structure through which the objectives of the company are set, and the means of attaining those objectives and monitoring performance are determined.[76]

It is mostly accepted now that discussions on the proper governance of businesses are probably as important as the proper governance of countries. The reforms in corporate governance discourse are mostly premised on the concept of separation of ownership from control and the agency cost problem. Spearheading[77] this reform was the work of Adolf A. Berle and Gardiner C. Means, *The Modern Corporation and Private Property* first published in 1932, and the subsequent history of corporate governance and its reform have since focused on solutions to problems posed by the phenomenon of separation of ownership from control in companies. Douglas Branson summarized thus:

> with public offering of shares on a widespread basis, many industrial and mercantile corporations were widely held. Because of modern communications and other mechanisms such as stock exchanges, the holders of shares in these corporations were dispersed, perhaps from Maine to California, and their holdings were atomized into 100, 500 or perhaps 1000 share lots. Thus, the shareholders who owned the corporations which, in turn, owned vast amounts of property, no longer controlled the property. Those corporations' assets represented a new form of property in that the persons who owned it no longer controlled it. There had come to exist a 'separation of ownership from control'.[78]

Closely related to the theory of separation of ownership from control is the problem of agency costs in corporate governance discourse. This problem appears to be premised on an age-long assumption that corporate managers, being human beings that they are, will find it difficult to prudently manage corporate funds the way they would manage their personal funds, and efforts by corporate owners to check the excesses of these corporate managers will further add to the agency costs. To Ige Bolodeoku, the problem of agency cost is a characteristic feature of the concept of separation of ownership from control.[79] As a concept, it describes the issue of how the shareholders (as corporate owners or principals) can provide the agents (the corporate managers) with incentives to induce behaviour beneficial to the shareholders. In similar words, the agency cost analysis studies the costs of providing such incentives and the costs resulting from the extent to which agents will still deviate from the interest of the principal even in the presence of such incentives. Under this agency cost discourse, the crux of comments and articles attempt to align the interests of both the principals and the agents in business ventures such that despite the myriad agency problems, principals may still have proper welfare and sufficient motivation to remain in business in terms of returns on investment. Agency cost is the sum of the monitoring expenditures by the principal, the bonding expenditures by the agent and the residual loss. In other words, the agency problem is rooted in the opportunity cost of ensuring that corporate powers in the hands of corporate managers are properly utilized in the best interest of the owners of the companies. These costs, that is, the costs attributed to monitoring, bonding and aligning the interests of both the corporate owners and managers alike, sometimes eventually serve as disincentives to corporate owners; the bottom line, for instance, which would have been available to the corporate owners, would have been reduced significantly. Bolodeoku had also noted that the dynamics between agency costs and separation of ownership from control is such that it is the degree of separation of ownership from control that will determine the acuteness of the associable agency problems and the measures that should be taken to solve the problems. It is observed that subsequent postulations and modern writings in corporate governance are almost all still addressed to solving the agency problem. This is usually by means of redefinition and expansion of duties of directors and managerial structures and broadening the responsibilities of companies and corporate owners to accommodate more recent values such as CSR core values of human rights protection, dignity of labour, environmental protection, sustainable development and many more.

From the previous discussions, it is evident that while CSR and corporate governance are two distinct concepts, they share some common agenda. By way of explanation, since it is not humanly possible for legislators to envisage or anticipate every mischief scenario in the corporate law and practice discipline, it is also virtually impossible to strictly provide for every possible corporate law and practice issue. This in turn also means that there will exist certain lacunae to be filled by case law and agreed standards, norms, rules, regulations, traditions, customs, conventions or codes that have not passed through legislative processes. The principles of both CSR and corporate governance as presently usually expressed in codes are thus largely applicable to fill in these gaps. CSR and corporate governance also share the common objective of giving effects to legislated provisions especially in the absence of case law. Tineke Lambooy in her *Corporate Social Responsibility: Legal and Semi-legal Frameworks Supporting*

26   *Background, theories and global outlook*

CSR Developments 2000–2010 and Case Studies[80] reflects on the previous point in respect to Dutch Law in the following words:

> CSR and corporate governance apply mainly to the conduct of companies, their executives and financiers. Statutory provisions on corporate conduct leave considerable margins of discretion commonly filled in by case law through reasonableness tests. CSR and corporate governance contribute towards filling in these margins by introducing new standards for the conduct of businesses and their executives. These new standards have largely developed from initiatives taken by the business sector itself. They could be regarded as standards of behaviour or codes of conduct.

In spite of the shared features, CSR and corporate governance are not exactly one and the same; they are distinct concepts with different (though related) values and issues. The development of CSR is aimed at adjusting corporate behaviour for the purpose of: preventing depletion of the Earth's natural resources, preventing unsustainable and irresponsible corporate actions aimed solely at profit maximization, promoting human rights protection and promoting a fair and social corporate policy for all employees in all countries where the company carries out business operations amongst others. On the other hand, the development of corporate governance codes, for instance, is targeted at restoring the balance between corporate bodies with an aim to boosting shareholder confidence in company directors and the capital market.

Interestingly, it had been argued that corporate governance only constitutes a subject of CSR and that CSR encompasses corporate governance.[81] Walsh and Lowry had contended that:

> corporate governance is an increasingly important aspect of CSR. And, as they continue to develop, corporate governance principles will continue to provide the more solid foundations on which broader CSR principles – and business ethics – can be further enhanced.[82]

The previous assertion may not hold much water in modern times; it appears now settled that CSR rather constitutes an integral part of corporate governance and one of the modern trends in corporate governance discourse. The words of Bob Tricker lent credence to this modern conception when he explained that:

> The original corporate governance codes, dating from the early 1990s, were voluntary. At the time they were derided by some company chairmen as being no more than expensive, box ticking exercises. But since then three significant changes have taken place. Firstly, corporate governance compliance has increasingly become mandatory, enshrined in regulation or in some cases law. Complaints now tend to be about the cost of compliance not about the need of corporate governance codes. Secondly,

risk analysis and risk management have become an integral part of the corporate governance process. Thirdly and most recently, corporate social responsibility and sustainability have been added to the corporate governance portfolio.[83]

Summing up on this heading, it is instructive to simply note that CSR in terms of responsible business practices constitutes an integral part of sound corporate governance practices. Therefore, CSR may be simply seen, especially from historical perspectives, as one of the modern constructs or devices used in addressing the age-long agency problems in corporate governance discourse; that is to say, with CSR, companies are being reconceptualized as social institutions with proposals over the years to broaden the duties of directors and ensuring that corporate managers do not only enhance shareholder value but also balance the interests of a larger group now popularly referred to as stakeholders.

1.5 Methodology and scope

As CSR is both multidisciplinary and interdisciplinary, it is capable of several definitions and also appears differently to experts and scholars across different disciplines and fields. For the avoidance of unchecked generalization, while there are relevant allusions to business management, human rights, environment, labour law and international law principles in this book, such allusions are only necessitated for an overarching discussion of the socio-legal subject; the book has not made any postulations or advanced analysis in such fields. Rather, it places emphasis on corporate law and governance. It explores CSR based on corporate law principles with a view to synthesizing ideas and principles related to embedding effective CSR in Africa.

While it is usually convenient to justify CSR practices normatively using purely moral persuasions, the analyses in this book are undertaken with the consciousness of excluding such moral considerations (from, for instance, seeking theoretical justifications for CSR within corporate law). This is deliberately done to dissociate the findings and recommendations from the idea of morality otherwise.

Although necessary references are made to other states in Africa as required in the course of discussions, the book has specifically examined CSR in the two jurisdictions of Nigeria and South Africa as case studies. These two countries are the biggest economies in Africa, and Nigeria represents the largest market for business activities in the whole of Africa. The author has proceeded on the assumption that considerations of policy innovations and legislative advancements in these two jurisdictions in Africa will not only provide sufficient CSR insights about these countries but also reflect CSR theories, issues and practices in other countries in Africa.

Structurally, the book has three parts of seven chapters. The first part provides foundational conceptual clarifications, definitions, theoretical underpinnings and CSR implementation mechanisms around the world. The second

28 *Background, theories and global outlook*

part reviews CSR definitions, theoretical underpinnings, practices and legal and implementation framework in the two selected case study countries of Nigeria and South Africa. Part III appraises the role of CSR in the African regional integration discourse. Each part covers a general theme, while specific topics are discussed in the chapters. The last chapter strings all major points in previous chapters together and proposes a CSR theoretical, legal and implementation framework for adoption in corporate Africa. A synopsis of the chapters together with their respective headings is set out in the following.

Chapter 1: Introduction

This chapter introduces the subject matter to the audience and provides relevant background information. It discusses the emergence of CSR from corporate governance discourse, providing materials on its history, popular debates, definitions and conceptual analysis, among other foundational matters. It underscores the neutrality of the CSR concept, clarifying that there is nothing intrinsically voluntary or mandatory or inherently 'Western' about it (other than historical perspectives) and that it transcends corporate charity and philanthropy. The chapter closes with summaries of chapters in the book together with the scope, methodology and perspective from which the book was written.

Chapter 2: Theoretical Underpinnings of CSR Practices

This chapter contributes to the open-ended corporate purpose discourse. It undertakes an investigation of the theoretical underpinnings of companies and their CSR practices. The chapter provides insights into the fundamental assumptions underpinning different schools of thought in relation to CSR implementation within corporate law systems. It highlights the shortcomings of analyzed ideological models in providing an acceptable corporate objective or offering a workable normative foundation towards embedding effective CSR practices in Africa and beyond.

Chapter 3: CSR Implementation and International Regulatory Framework

Towards demonstrating how CSR is being implemented around the globe, the chapter shows the various CSR regulatory methods adopted at intergovernmental and international law levels. It examines a few international regulatory initiatives in the CSR domain including: the United Nations Global Compact (UNGC), the Organisation for Economic Cooperation and Development Guidelines for Multinational Enterprises (OECD Guidelines) and the Guiding Principles on Business and Human Rights: Implementing the United Nations' 'Protect, Respect and Remedy' Framework (UNGPs). Largely from the prism of corporate law and practice, the chapter analyses the tale of struggling international initiatives to implement

CSR or combat corporate social and environmental irresponsibility. It also discusses policy responses to corporate irresponsibility at the regional level of the European Union and in a few foreign jurisdictions including the United Kingdom, the United States of America and India. It pinpoints specific challenges of conflicting national interests, fear of over-regulation, the doctrine of sovereign equality of states and sometimes just the lack of sincerity of purpose coupled with an unwarranted desperate clinging to voluntarism and self-regulation. Despite the seeming inadequacies of the international regulatory initiatives on CSR implementation, several policy innovations and regulatory advancements were nonetheless identified and discussed for possible transplantation in Africa.

Chapter 4: CSR in Nigeria

This chapter localizes the initial global outlook of the subject matter to Africa, taking corporate Nigeria as the first case study. It introduces the reader to CSR conceptualization, practice, issues, debates and regulation in corporate Nigeria. It provides information about its history in Nigeria and gives instances of specific CSR conception and practices by different companies, small or big in the country. Despite some promising provisions in the secondary legal instruments demonstrating CSR conception as a robust and comprehensive corporate governance construct, the chapter underscores the popular confinement of the subject to corporate philanthropy and, at best, undertaking community development projects. The chapter also interrogates aborted, extant and proposed CSR implementation legislations in Nigeria. The chapter exposes factors militating effective CSR implementation including (i) the popular confinement of CSR in Nigeria to corporate charity; (ii) the faulty legal transplantation involved in attempts to implement a few foreign policies and principles and (iii) the incoherence and policy misalignment in the primary and secondary legal instruments on CSR implementation. Drawing on lessons from discussions in the preceding Chapter 3, this chapter argues for reforms in CSR conceptualization, implementation and practices in Nigeria.

Chapter 5: CSR in South Africa

This chapter discusses CSR in the Republic of South Africa as the second case study. It introduces CSR as conceptualized, practiced, and regulated in corporate South Africa. While a number of CSR implementation legislations were identified, the chapter interrogates two regulatory instruments on CSR implementation in South Africa that are directly within corporate law and governance context. Relevant comparative analysis and allusions were also made to the first case study, Nigeria. The chapter underscores a few factors militating against effective CSR implementation in the country namely: (i) the 'disguised' underlying ideological corporate model of shareholder primacy within the South African primary corporate

30 *Background, theories and global outlook*

legislation; (ii) the lack of clarity in the operational terms of the 'social and ethics committee' introduced by the 2008 Companies Act; (iii) the largely soft law regulatory and voluntary CSR implementation approach adopted within the South African business community, which appears to foster corporate greenwashing and mindless compliance with code requirements, among other factors. Leveraging relevant lessons from discussions in Chapter 3, this chapter also highlights a few recommendations to engender effective CSR implementation in corporate South Africa.

Chapter 6: Roadmap to Embedding CSR in Africa

Leveraging findings in Chapters 4 and 5, this chapter sets a roadmap for a continent-wide CSR implementation as a comprehensive corporate governance and business management model. It underscores the significance of CSR to the sustainable development discourse in Africa. With a view to reversing CSR antipathies in Africa, especially in relation to the notion that CSR counteracts Africa's trade liberalization agenda or constitutes an unnecessary trade barrier, the chapter confirms the compatibility of CSR on the one hand with the World Trade Organization rules and trade liberalization objectives of African countries on the other hand. The chapter traces the origins of the African regional integration scheme and highlights legal instruments underpinning the Pan-African integration discourse leading to contemporary discussions about the African Continental Free Trade Area (AfCFTA). The chapter juxtaposes the AfCFTA agreement for its CSR implementation against implementation within regional integration discourse in the global North, especially within the European Union as discussed in Chapter 3. It underscores that the lack of attention to CSR implementation within the AfCFTA agreement diminishes the seriousness of the African integration scheme towards achieving the sustainable development goals (SDGs) in Africa. Towards attaining the SDGs, the chapter closes by setting the tone for effective mainstreaming of CSR core values into African regionalism.

Chapter 7: Model CSR Policy Framework for Africa – the Responsible Stakeholder Model

This chapter strings together earlier discussions and recommendations in other chapters into a model CSR implementation framework useful across Africa and within the intergovernmental and regional integration discourse of Africa. Leveraging the synthesized responsible stakeholder model (RSM) in Chapter 2, the chapter reiterates the earlier dismissal of the fundamental assumptions of the two dominant corporate law models and, in their place, argues for an alternative CSR implementation strategy in Africa. In a pioneer manner, it provides a set of model CSR provisions for incorporation/integration within the corporate law systems of the two case study jurisdictions (corporate Nigeria and South Africa) and beyond. Further, the chapter builds on arguments in Chapter 6 and indicates specific benefits for mainstreaming CSR within the African integration scheme. It also proposes the adoption of a CSR implementation protocol to the African Continental Free Trade Area (AfCFTA) agreement together with regular releases of directives for legal transposition within domestic corporate law systems across African countries. This provides a shared CSR policy framework in Africa and harmonizes the overall sustainable development agenda across the continent towards the attainment of the sustainable development goals.

1.6 Chapter summary

In summary, CSR is both interdisciplinary and multi-disciplinary. It is capable of several definitions, and the multiplicity is reflected even within the academic community where scholars and experts of international law, environmental law, labour law, human rights law, immigration law and business or corporate law amongst others adopt different definitions and viewpoints on issues as they relate to CSR. This chapter (and indeed the book) examined CSR and conceptually clarified the subject from a corporate law perspective.

In this chapter, the book noted that the definitional stance of scholars on CSR appears to often polarize such scholar's viewpoints on issues as they relate to CSR and its implementation. For instance, on the issue of CSR regulation and enforcement mechanisms, it was shown that an adoption of a CSR construct largely on a voluntary basis has almost automatically pre-conditioned the adoption of soft law self-regulatory mechanisms and in turn resulted in a CSR implementation framework largely underpinned by non-binding corporate governance codes and guidelines. Adopting such a rather restrictive approach has only contributed to the current global challenge of corporate greenwashing whereby companies only pay lip service to a robust and effective CSR practice. Consequently, the author submitted that CSR should be conceptualized as a neutral subject (neither voluntary nor mandatory) to which either soft or hard law or a combination of both may be applicable to implement. CSR is simply what it is; it is a comprehensive corporate governance and business management model through which the economic, legal, ethical, and discretionary responsibilities of a company may be balanced for the sustainable development of both the business community and society. There is nothing intrinsically voluntary or mandatory about it.

Also in this chapter, it was observed that, notwithstanding the disparate views on CSR issues, it is still widely accepted across many jurisdictions that CSR offers the prospects for solutions to several sustainability questions and constitutes a potent tool to mitigating the adverse impacts of cold corporate capitalism, the raw exercise of corporate powers, and shareholder primacy-oriented corporate objective of companies. CSR continues to find acceptance in the hearts of many corporate executives as it appears to be settled that companies cannot be given unrestrained freedom, even in a free market economy, to simply

32 *Background, theories and global outlook*

focus on enhancing shareholder value. Put differently, further to the contributions of CSR in corporate governance discourse, it is no longer acceptable to strictly privatize or propertize corporate powers for the sole interest and benefits of the so-called corporate owners. Finally, following the appreciation of the meaning and significance of effective CSR conception amongst others, the ultimate target is to provide a clearly-defined CSR conceptual, regulatory, and implementation framework in Africa. But first, in order to avoid delineating the ambits of a CSR framework, which may be considered antithetical to investment or the commercial focus of businesses in Africa, it is imperative to investigate the theoretical underpinnings of corporate practices and CSR towards understanding the nature and purpose for which companies anywhere in the world operate and within what ideological background a robust and comprehensive CSR model can be undertaken in corporate Africa. This forms the focus of discussions in Chapter 2.

Notes

1 Karma Ura, Sabina Alkire, Tshoki Zangmo and Karma Wangdi, *An Extensive Analysis of GNH Index* (Bhutan: Centre for Bhutan Studies 2012) 4, 5 *et seq.*
2 Detailed discussions on the shareholder primacy model are contained in Chapter 2.
3 Nuntana Udomkit, 'CSR Analysis: A Reflection from Businesses and the Public in Thailand' (2013) 3 *Journal of Management and Sustainability* 155.
4 John Meehan, Karon Meehan and Adam K. Richards, 'Corporate Social Responsibility: The 3C-SR Model' (2006) 33 *International Journal of Social Economics* 386.
5 Michael Blowfield and Jedrzej George Frynas, 'Setting New Agendas: Critical Perspective on Corporate Social Responsibility in the Developing World' (2005) 81 (3) *International Affairs* 499–513, 500.
6 Adolf Berle, 'Corporate Powers as Powers in Trust' (1931) 44 *Harvard Law Review* 1049; E. Merrick Dodd, 'For Whom Are Corporate Managers Trustees?' (1931) *Harvard Law Review* 1049; Adolf Berle, 'For Whom Are Corporate Managers Trustees?' (1932) *Harvard Law Review* 1365.
7 Uwafiokun Idemudia, 'Corporate Social Responsibility and Development in Africa: Issues and Possibilities' (2014) 8/7 *Geography Compass* 421; Douglas Branson, 'Corporate Governance "Reform" and the New Corporate Social Responsibility' (2001) 62 *University of Pittsburgh Law Review* 605, 606.
8 Adolf Berle and Gardiner Means, *The Modern Corporation and Private Property* (New York: The Macmillan Company 1932).
9 Branson (n 7) 608; see also generally, Paddy Ireland, 'Making Sense of Contemporary Capitalism using Company Law' (2018) 33 *Australian Journal of Corporate Law* 379–401.
10 John Kenneth Galbraith, *American Capitalism: The Concept of Countervailing Power* (Boston: Houghton Mifflin 1952), 135–141.
11 Archie B. Carroll, 'Corporate Social Responsibility: Evolution of a Definitional Construct' (1999) 3 (38) *Business & Society* 268, 269–273 citing Keith Davis, 'Can Business Afford to Ignore Social Responsibilities?' (1960) *California Management Review* 2; Keith Davis, 'Understanding the Social Responsibility Puzzle: What Does the Businessman Owe to Society?' (1967) *Business Horizons* 10; William Frederick, 'The Growing Concern over Business Responsibility' (1960) *California Management Review* 2; and, Joseph McGuire, *Business and Society* (New York: McGraw-Hill 1963).
12 Howard Bowen, *Social Responsibilities of the Businessman* (New York: Harper and Row 1953).
13 Ibid. 6.

Introduction   33

14 Lawrence E. Mitchell, *Progressive Corporate Law*, Lawrence E. Mitchell ed. (Boulder, Colorado: Westview Press 1995) xiii.
15 Milton Friedman, 'The Social Responsibility of Business' in Kurt R. Leube (ed.), *The Essence of Friedman* (Stanford: The Hoover Institution Press 1987) 36–38.
16 Milton Friedman, 'The Social Responsibility of Business Is to Increase Its Profits' *New York Times* (13 September 1970) Section 6.
17 This is an adjunct of the Open Economies Movement of the Chicago school. They advocated that market forces governed human behaviour more effectively than laws or lawsuits ever could. The term 'invisible hand' was first used by Adam Smith to describe the guiding force that leads to the efficacy of the free market. In 1776, Smith stated that the guiding force is the propensity of human nature to pursue self-interest. '*It is not the benevolence of the butcher, the brewer, or the baker, that we expect our dinner, but from their regard to their own interest*'. Adam Smith, 'An Inquiry into the Nature and Causes of the Wealth of Nations' Vol. 1, in Robert L. Heilbroner (ed.), *The Essential Adam Smith* (New York: W. W. Norton Company 1987) 169.
18 Branson (n 7) 619.
19 For detailed discussions on contractarianism, see Chapter 2.
20 The contractarian argument has no regard for the function corporate legislation ought to and actually plays in the society. However, as shall be further shown in Chapter 2, it is not everything that could be or should be contractually varied or eliminated in reality.
21 In the USA was first published Joseph Angell and Samuel Ames, *Treatise on the Law of Private Corporations Aggregate* (1st edn, Hilliard, Gray, Little & Wilkins 1832), then later in the UK came Charles Wordsworth, *The Law Relating to Railway, Bank, Insurance, Mining and Other Joint Stock Companies* (1st edn, Henry Butterworth 1836).
22 *The Responsibilities of the British Public Company* (CBI 1973) cited in LCB Gower, *Gower's Principle of Modern Company Law* (4th edn, London: Stevens & Sons 1979) 62, 63.
23 The Committee on the Financial Aspects of Corporate Governance, *Report with Code of Best Practice* [Cadbury Report] (London: Gee Publishing Ltd 1992).
24 Greenbury Committee, *Directors' Remuneration: Report of a Study Group Chaired by Sir Richard Greenbury* (London: Gee Publishing Ltd 1995).
25 Hampel Committee, *Final Report of the Committee on Corporate Governance* (London: Gee Publishing Ltd 1998).
26 The Turnbull Report was first published in 1999 and set out best practice on internal control for UK listed companies. In October 2005 the Financial Reporting Council (FRC) issued an updated version of the guidance with the title 'Internal Control: Guidance for Directors on the Combined Code'. In September 2014 this was superseded by the FRC's Risk Guidance. See, generally, ICAEW, Internal Control: Turnbull Report, 1999.
27 Derek Higgs, *Review of the Role and Effectiveness of Non-Executive Directors* (London: Department of Trade and Investment Publications 2003).
28 See <www.frc.org.uk/getattachment/88bd8c45-50ea-4841-95b0-d2f4f48069a2/2018-UKCorporate-Governance-Code-FINAL.PDF> accessed 24 October 2019.
29 Hampel Committee Report (n 25) para 1.3.
30 Ibid, supporting principles A.1. It is interesting to also note that the word *stakeholder* was only mentioned in the Preface section and not in any Main or Supporting Principles of the code.
31 Three generational stages of CSR were identified by Zadek. See generally, Simon Zadek, *The Civil Corporation: The New Economy of Corporate Citizenship* (London: Earthscan 2001).
32 Jason Prno, 'An Analysis of Factors Leading to the Establishment of a Social Licence to Operate in the Mining Industry' (2013) 38 *Resources Policy* 577–590.
33 Bryan Horrigan, *Corporate Social Responsibility in the 21st Century: Debates, Models and Practices Across Government, Law and Business* (Cheltenham: Edward Elgar 2010) 4.
34 Adolf Berle, 'Corporate Powers as Powers in Trust' (1931) 44 *Harvard Law Review* 1049.

34 Background, theories and global outlook

35 Merrick Dodd, 'For Whom Are Corporate Managers Trustees?' (1932) 45 *Harvard Law Review* 1145.

36 Ibid. 1148.

37 See, generally, Edward Freeman and others, 'Stakeholder Theory and "The Corporate Objective Revisited"' (2004) 15 *Organization Science* 364; see also Edward Freeman and others, *Stakeholder Theory: The State of the Art* (Cambridge: Cambridge University Press 2010).

38 See for instance the arguments and underpinning assumptions of theories such as 'the Team Production Theory' canvassed by Professors Margaret Blair and Lynn Stout in Margaret Blair and Lynn Stout, 'A Team Production Theory of Corporate Law' (1999) 85 *Virginia Law Review* 247 and 'the Entity Maximisation and Sustainability Model' (EMS) canvassed by Professor Andrew Keay in Andrew Keay, 'Ascertaining the Corporate Objective: An Entity Maximisation and Sustainability Model' (2008) 71 *Modern Law Review* 663. These theories are discussed in Chapter 2; they are compared and contrasted with another stakeholder-inspired model (the Responsible Stakeholder Model, RSM), a formulation of this author.

39 Tom Campbell, 'The Normative Grounding of Corporate Social Responsibility: A Human Rights Approach' in Doreen McBarnet, Aurora Voiculescu and Tom Campbell (eds.), *The New Corporate Accountability: Corporate Social Responsibility and the Law* (Cambridge: Cambridge University Press 2007) 529–564, 532.

40 David Engel, 'An Approach to Corporate Social Responsibility' (1979) 32 *Stanford Law Review* 1, 5, 6.

41 John Edward Parkinson, 'Models of the Company and the Employment Relationship' (2003) *British Journal of Industrial Relations* 481–509, 498.

42 Gabriel Eweje, 'Multinational Oil Companies' CSR Initiatives in Nigeria: The Scepticism of Stakeholders in Host Communities' (2007) 49 *Managerial Law* 218–235 citing Marydee Ojala, 'Finding Socially Responsible Companies' (1994) 17 (5) *Database*, October/November, 86–89.

43 Horrigan (n 33) 34.

44 Archie B. Carroll, 'A Three-Dimensional Conceptual Model of Corporate Performances' (1979) 4 *Academy of Management Review* 499 (Hereinafter simply 'Carroll 3 Dimensional Model'); see also Archie B. Carroll, 'The Pyramid of Corporate Social Responsibility: Toward the Moral Management of Organizational Stakeholders' (1991) 34 *Business Horizons* 39, reprinted in Andrew Craine, Dirk Matten and Laura Spence (eds.), *Corporate Social Responsibility: Readings and Cases in a Global Context* (Abington: Routledge 2008) 64.

45 Carroll 3 Dimensional Model (n 44) 500.

46 Andrew Zur and Jody Evans, 'Corporate Social Responsibility Orientation and Organizational Performance in the Australian Retail Industry' (2008) *Melbourne Business School* 5, 2.

47 Ibid. 608.

48 Ibid. 5.

49 Mark S. Schwarz and Archie B. Carroll, 'Corporate Social Responsibility: A Three-Domain Approach' (2003) 13 *Business Ethics Quarterly* 503, 505–507.

50 Ibid. 505–507.

51 Thomas Kimeli Cheruiyot and Patrick Onsando, 'Corporate Social Responsibility in Africa: Context, Paradoxes, Stakeholder Orientations, Contestations and Reflections' in A Stachowicz-Stanusch (ed.), *Corporate Social Performance in the Age of Irresponsibility: Cross National Perspective* (Charlotte: Information Age Publishing Inc 2016) 91. Idemudia (n 7) 425; Peter Raynard and Maya Forstater, *Corporate Social Responsibility: Implications for Small and Medium Enterprises in Developing Countries* (Vienna: United Nations Industrial Development Organization 2002) 17; see also Kingsly Awang Ollong, 'Corporate Social Responsibility and Community Development in Cameroon' Conference Paper (12th International Conference on Corporate Social Responsibility, ISSN

2048-0806, Niteroi and Rio de Janeiro, Brazil, June 2013). *Cf.* Interestingly, Nigeria (in recent times) and South Africa are developing economies where this conceptual problem appears fizzling out. CSR and sustainability issues are discussed at an advanced level, devoid of the restrictive corporate charity conception. See the 2018 Nigerian Code of Corporate Governance, issued by the Financial Reporting Council of Nigeria, replacing the controversial National Code of Corporate Governance of 2016; see also, Institute of Directors in Southern Africa, 'King IV Report on Governance for South Africa 2016', replacing the 'King III Report on Corporate Governance for South Africa 2009'; see also, Irene-Marie Esser, 'Corporate Social Responsibility: A Company Law Perspective' (2011) 23 *South African Mercantile Law Journal* 317, 331; Wayne Visser, 'Corporate Citizenship: Is South Africa World Class?' 2005 *The Corporate Citizen* 1–6.

52 See generally Schedule VII of the 2013 Indian Company's Act; Jaheer Mukthar and Sachin Pavithran, 'Corporate Social Responsibility in Birla Group of Companies' Conference Paper (12th International Conference on Corporate Social Responsibility, ISSN 2048-0806, Niteroi and Rio de Janeiro, Brazil, June 2013).

53 Ollong (n 51).

54 Kenneth Amaeshi and others, 'Corporate Social Responsibility in Nigeria: Western Mimicry or Indigenous Influences?' (2006) 24 *JCC* 83–99; see also Hakeem Ijaiya, 'Challenges of Corporate Social Responsibility in the Niger Delta Region of Nigeria' (2014) 1 *Journal of Sustainable Development Law and Policy* 60, 62.

55 Wayne Visser, 'Research on Corporate Citizenship in Africa: A Ten Year Review (1995–2005)' in W. Visser, M. McIntosh and C. Middleton (eds.), *Corporate Citizenship in Africa: Lessons from the Past: Paths to the Future* (Sheffield: Greenleaf Publishing 2006) 18–28.

56 Judy Muthuri, 'Corporate Social Responsibility in Africa: Definition, Issues and Process' in R.T. Lituchy, B.J. Punnett and B.B. Puplampu (eds.), *Management in Africa: Macro and Micro Perspective* (New York and London: Routledge, 2013) 90–111.

57 V.A. Bagire, I. Tusiime, G. Nalweyiso, J.B. Kakooza, 'Contextual Environment and Stakeholder Perception of Corporate Social Responsibility Practices in Uganda' (2013) 18 *Corporate Social Responsibility and Environmental Management* 102–109.

58 Mumo Kivuitu, Kavwanga Yambayamba and Tom Fox, 'How Can Corporate Social Responsibility Deliver in Africa? Insights from Kenya and Zambia' (2005) *Perspectives on Corporate Responsibility for Environment and Development, International Institute for Environment and Development* available at: https://pubs.iied.org/pdfs/16006IIED.pdf accessed 25 October 2019, noting at page 2 in respect to both Kenya and Zambia that: 'in both countries, the activities most commonly identified by companies themselves as CSR could broadly be described as philanthropy. In Kenya, surveys suggest that the cause receiving the highest proportion of corporate donations is health and medical provision, and donations are also directed towards education and training; HIV/AIDS; agriculture and food security; and underprivileged children. The picture in Zambia is similar, with surveys highlighting donations to orphanages as the most common activity identified as CSR, followed by sponsorship of sporting events; cultural ceremonies; education and health provision; and donations to religious and arts organisations'.

59 'Cosgrove Gets NITP, COREN Commendation for CSR' *Thisday*, 2 April, 2019; Raheem Akingbolu, 'CSR as a Launchpad for Development' *Thisday*, 25 October, 2018; FSDH Merchant Bank Limited, 'Corporate Social Responsibility (CSR) Activities in 2015' *The Guardian*, 19 January, 2016; Kaine Agary, 'Is CSR Worth the Trouble for Companies? (1)' *Punch*, 26 July, 2015; see also Raheem Akingbolu, 'Building Equity through CSR: The Grand Oak Example' *Thisday*, 22 March, 2013, 36; Raheem Akingbolu, 'CSR: Groups Hail Nigerite's Efforts' *Thisday*, 14 May 2010. There are many newspaper columns such as the previously mentioned showing the popular conception of CSR in Nigeria, which is still diminished to corporate donations and, at its best, community development projects. *Cf.* Jennifer Abraham, 'Profiting from Corporate Social Responsibility' *Punch*, 27 December, 2018; Nurudeen Oyewole and Omobayo

36 *Background, theories and global outlook*

Azeez, 'Business School Netherlands (BSN) Nigeria Introduces 3 CSR Initiatives' *Daily Trust*, 23 December, 2015 demonstrating a good grasp of the CSR concept 'beyond mere tokenism'.

60 WBCSD, *CSR: Meeting Changing Expectations* (Geneva: WBCSD 2000) 3; see also WBCSD, *Stakeholder Dialogue on CSR* (The Netherlands: WBCSD 1998) 6–8.

61 Organisation for Economic Co-Operation and Development, 'Guidelines for Multinational Enterprises'. The Guidelines were updated in 2011 for the fifth time since they were first adopted in 1976. See Chapter 3 for full discussions on the OECD Guidelines.

62 European Union, 'Communication of European Union Country's Commission Green Paper on Promoting a European Framework for Corporate Social Responsibility' COM (2001) 366 Final (July 18, 2001).

63 Ibid. 6, emphasis added.

64 European Union, Communication from the Commission to the European Parliament, 'The Council, The European Economic and Social Committee and the Committee of the Region: *A Renewed European Union Strategy 2011–14 for Corporate Social Responsibility*' COM (2011) 681 Final 6.

65 Jan Eijsbouts, *Corporate Responsibility, Beyond Voluntarism: Regulatory Options to Reinforce the Licence to Operate* (Inaugural Lecture, Maastricht: Maastricht University 2011) 40; Olufemi Amao, 'Mandating Corporate Social Responsibility: Emerging Trends in Nigeria' (2008) 6 *Journal of Commonwealth Law and Legal Education* 75; Tineke Lambooy, *Corporate Social Responsibility: Legal and Semi-Legal Frameworks Supporting CSR Developments 2000–2010 and Case Studies* (Dissertation and Commercial Edition in IVOR Series, Leiden: Kluwer 2010) 495, 630; also see: UN Global Compact, UN Press Release SG/SM/6881, Secretary-General Proposes Global Compact on Human Rights, Labour, Environment in Address to World Economic Forum in Davos, Text of Speech by Kofi Annan, 1 February 1999, at 1, and see John Ruggie, Final Report of the Special Representative of the Secretary-General on the issue of human rights and transnational corporations and other business enterprises, 'Guiding Principles on Business and Human Rights: Implementing the United Nations' 'Protect, Respect and Remedy Framework,' A/HRC/17/31, 21 March 2011.

66 Dodge *v.* Ford Motor Co. (1919) 204 Mich. 459; see also Martin Wolf, 'Sleep-Walking with the Enemy: Corporate Social Responsibility Distorts the Market by Deflecting Business from Its Primary Role of Profit Generation' *Financial Times* (16 May 2001); see also, Geoffrey Owen, 'Time to Promote Trust, Inside the Company and Out' *Financial Times* (30 August, 2002). *Cf:* It is instructive to note that there are no many corporate statutes around the world specifically stating that the sole purpose of a corporation is to maximize profits for its shareholders. See generally for this position, Section 279 (3) to (5) of Companies and Allied Matters Act, Cap C20, LFN, 2004 (CAMA); William Alan Nelson, II, 'Post-Citizens United: Using Shareholder Derivative Claims of Corporate Waste to Challenge Corporate Independent Political Expenditures' (2012) 13 *Nevada Law Journal* 134, 141.

67 Daniel Franklin, 'Just Good Business: A Special Report on Corporate Social Responsibility' *The Economist* (19 January 2008) 8–9.

68 The famous Enron corporate governance scandal, the British Petroleum oil spill saga in the gulf of Mexico despite its 'green operations' tagged 'Beyond Petroleum' and the popular 2006 'cover-up' involving Cadbury Schweppes, which was forced to recall chocolate bars on a large scale after discovering tiny amounts of undisclosed salmonella, are exemplary in the circumstance; Richard Smerdon, *A Practical Guide to Corporate Governance* (3rd edn, London: Sweet & Maxwell 2007) 441. See also the shocking revelations of Volkswagen's manipulated emission tests just after receiving the Dow Jones Sustainability Indices (DJSI) award as the 'most sustainable automaker'. See, generally, David Guarino, *Volkswagen AG to be Removed from the Dow Jones Sustainability Indices* (New York and Zurich: Standard & Poor's Dow Jones Indices 29 September, 2015).

69 Jennifer Zerk, *Multinational and Corporate Social Responsibilities: Limitations and Opportunities in International Law* (Cambridge: Cambridge University Press 2006) 100, 101; Miriam A. Cherry, 'The Law and Economics of Corporate Social Responsibility and Greenwashing' (2014) 14 *University of California Davis Business Law Journal* 281–303; Miriam A. Cherry and Judy Sneirson, 'Chevron, Greenwashing, and the Myth of "Green Oil Companies"' (2012) 3 *Washington and Lee Journal of Energy, Climate and the Environment* 133, 140–141.

70 Saleem Sheikh, *A Practical Approach to Corporate Governance* (West Sussex: Tottel Publishing 2006) 299.

71 Smerdon (n 68) 431.

72 Horrigan (n 33) 13.

73 Max Clarkson, 'Good Business and the Bottom Line' (1991) *Canadian Business Magazine* 28.

74 For a detailed discussion on the UN Global Compact, see Chapter 3.

75 Robert Monks and Nell Minow, *Corporate Governance* (Cambridge: Blackwell Publishers 1995) 1.

76 OECD, *G20/OECD Principles of Corporate Governance* (Paris: OECD Publishing 2015) 9.

77 Some scholars argue that the discourse on the problems of separation of ownership from control pre-dates the writings of Berle and Means. Adam Smith was reported to have observed that corporate executives do not watch over other people's money with the same vigilance as partners in a private company watch over their own. Smith noted that: 'The directors of such companies, however, being the managers rather of other people's money than of their own, it cannot well be expected, that they should watch over it with the same anxious vigilance with which the partners in a private copartnery frequently watch over their own. . . . Negligence and profusion, therefore, must always prevail, more or less in the management of the affairs of such a company'. Adam Smith, *An Inquiry into the Nature and Causes of the Wealth of Nations* (1776) 741; see also, Bart Schwartz and Amy L. Goodman, *Corporate Governance: Law and Practice* (Vol. 1, Newark: LexisNexis 2005) 2.

78 Branson (n 7) 606.

79 Ige Bolodeoku, 'Corporate Governance: The Law's Response to Agency Costs in Nigeria' (2007) 32 *Brooklyn Journal of International Law* 467, fn 38 citing, Michael C. Jensen and William H. Meckling, 'Theory of the Firm: Managerial Behaviour, Agency Costs and Ownership Structure' (1976) 3 *Journal of Financial Economics* 305, 309.

80 Lambooy (n 65) 50.

81 Sybren Christiaan de Hoo, *In Pursuit of Corporate Sustainability and Responsibility: Past Cracking Perceptions and Creating Codes* (Inaugural Lecture, Maastricht: Maastricht University 2011) 29.

82 Mark Walsh and John Lowry, 'CSR and Corporate Governance' in Ramon Mullerat (ed.), *Corporate Social Responsibility: The Corporate Governance of 21st Century* (The Hague: IBA & Kluwer Law International 2005) 38, 39.

83 Bob Tricker, *Corporate Governance, Principles, Policies and Practices* (Oxford: Oxford University Press 2009) 349.

2 Theoretical underpinnings of CSR practices

2 Background

The ideological foundation of commerce and corporate law focusing on profit maximization for shareholders within the business community, paying little or no regard to the welfare of other constituents of the society, continues to gain ground in many business communities. However, apart from facilitating and reducing the costs for the organization and smooth running of businesses through the corporate form, one other objective of corporate law, as indeed should be any aspect of the law, is the pursuit of overall social welfare,[1] efficiency and accountability to stakeholders. Further to discussions in Chapter 1, the emergence of CSR as a catalyst corporate governance and business management model for furthering such overall social welfare, efficiency and accountability is no longer news. As also earlier discussed in Chapter 1, CSR appears to have won many hearts already as it affects the work of corporate insiders, corporate advisers and all of the communities in which the corporations operate. Therefore, based on the popularity of CSR, almost everyone belongs to one CSR camp or another, whether supporting it, tolerating it or otherwise condemning it.[2] The popularity in the CSR conception has also succeeded in drawing it to a number of theoretical approaches and regulatory and policy questions in relation to the legal and economic justifications for its adoption within any business community. These questions, for instance, include: are there justifications to promoting stakeholder interests and public good objectives even at the expense of shareholders' interests for profits on investment? Assuming but not conceding that companies must be responsible for the social and environmental impact of their operations, under what theoretical (and by extension) regulatory or enforcement framework should companies be held accountable or responsible?

2.1 Theorizing about CSR: a useless waste of time?

A theory is a group of logically organized and deductively related laws.[3] Theoretical models may also be described as searchlights that illuminate particular judgments and show them for what they really are.[4] Theories have also been seen as humanly constructed means by which people make sense of the

Theoretical underpinnings of CSR practices   39

judgments that constitute their ethical and political worlds.[5] Put in other words, theories are constructed principles, guidelines and assumptions aiding deeper interpretations of concepts, ideas, actions and inactions.

Generally speaking, there are different theoretical approaches and models from which corporate actions and CSR may be and have been analyzed.[6] However, whether the theories are on the nature of the corporation or on corporate legal personality, these theories are usually overlapping and interwoven. Most often than not, individual authors adopt different theoretical approaches under disparate categorizations to serve varying purposes depending on the individual theme of research involved. The existence of different theoretical approaches is by no means strange in the present case of CSR given its multi-disciplinary nature and the broad based interactions of companies with political, economic, legal and human elements. Accordingly, effort has therefore been made in this chapter to streamline the ideological analyses with an eye on the target of finding an acceptable yardstick from which corporate behaviour and business decisions may be measured as responsible or not, incentivized or otherwise punished.

Before proceeding, however, it is important to underscore the need for theorizing about CSR in the first place. Within the English corporate legal system, for instance, there appears to be little or no regard for theories. Theories are described as 'interesting philosophical speculations' or 'intellectual games', 'metaphysical' or just bluntly called 'useless waste of time'.[7] While many scholars would object to any philosophical voyage into many conceptions such as CSR, which is supposedly practice-based, this book has come up with a few reasons for theorizing about companies and their CSR practices as adduced in the following:

(i) Theorizing about corporate actions aids the development of a framework within which one can assess the values and assumptions that either unite or divide the plethora of cases, reform proposals, legislative amendments and practices that constitute modern corporate law;[8]

(ii) Theorizing about companies and their CSR practices is also important in making progress in the process of steering companies in a desired direction;[9]

(iii) It also aids an understanding of the raison d'être behind different corporate governance models applicable from one jurisdiction to the other;

(iv) As a corollary of the previous point, an underlying theoretical framework will engender a coherent approach to policy-making, regulation and standard setting initiatives on CSR;[10]

(v) Finally, theories can be used as interpretational answers to the increasingly challenging organizational structure, governance and management of businesses in general and their CSR practices in particular.

The theoretical investigations undertaken in this chapter are targeted at properly situating the nuances of effective and intrinsic CSR implementation

40 *Background, theories and global outlook*

within a body of corporate law theory and towards demonstrating from where the eventual proposals in Chapter 7 of this book originate.

2.2 CSR and theoretical underpinnings of companies

Theories governing company operations or explaining their nature take various shapes including: business models, foundational theories, operational theories, organic theories, instrumental theories, political theories, integrative theories, ownership theories and ethical theories amongst others.[11] As noted earlier, different authors attempt a delimitation of these theories as applicable to his or her CSR perspective or in line with a particular conclusion sought to be achieved. Accordingly, this chapter has categorized the CSR theoretical approaches into the following broad headings viz:

   (i) *The Ideological Corporate Models*;
  (ii) *The Legitimation Theories*;
 (iii) *The CSR Operational Theories.*

The previous categorizations and headings of theories adopted in this chapter are adopted for convenience of discussions only and may not represent any generally accepted headings in any discourse on the theoretical underpinnings of corporations and their CSR practices. Discussions under the heading of Ideological Corporate Models inquire into the existential nature and the purpose of companies themselves while discussions in relation to the Legitimation Theories offer explanations on the possible yardsticks for measuring the responsibility or otherwise of corporate behaviour. The third heading represents operational groupings of CSR theories.

2.3 Ideological corporate models

These Ideological Corporate models characterized the popular debate in the academic circle since the early 1930s as discussed earlier under Section 1.2.1 of Chapter 1. Many ideas and thoughts[12] have sprung up in connection with the said debate amongst different scholars from different fields. As earlier observed, although at the centre of the debate were the arguments of Berle and Dodd, the debate has, however, over time, taken different descriptions and shapes; a few of its popular descriptions are: shareholder primacy model versus stakeholder model, the communitarian versus the contractarian debate, the Berle versus Dodd debate, monotonic versus pluralistic views on corporate objectives. This debate is still relevant to date (and useful for discussions in this book) despite Berle's supposed concession of the outcome of the debate to Dodd. This is because extenuating arguments from both divides of the debate have continued to polarize scholastic thinking on the existential nature of companies and consequently on the responsibility or otherwise of corporate behaviour in any given jurisdiction. The two prominent schools of thought that have emerged from the debate are: (i) the shareholder primacy and (ii) the

Theoretical underpinnings of CSR practices   41

stakeholder school.[13] For the purpose of discussions in this book, these schools are identified as the Ideological Corporate Models and are discussed seriatim in the following sections.

2.3.1 Shareholder primacy model

The model is about the assemblage of rules and regulations towards a quasi-constitutional protection of investments. It assumes that corporations should be run for the sole and exclusive benefit of their owners. The proponents posit that corporate directors have the primary obligation to enhance shareholder value and maximize shareholder wealth.[14] It is based on a fundamental individualistic assumption that whosoever risks investing his funds in doing a business should naturally have such business managed for his/her sole benefit. Further, it centralizes the shareholders of a company at the core of activities and decision-making process of any business concern. The major rationale behind this model is that whoever bears the greatest risks in the operations of a company should naturally have such company run for his/her exclusive benefits; after-all, as residual claimants, if anything goes wrong, others like creditors and employees will have their interests prioritized and settled before theirs. This model may also be described as proceeding on a fundamental assumption that companies and businesses are exclusive private properties[15] of their incorporators and investors, and as such the success of the company must be taken as the success of the shareholders. This assumption is said to have been borne out of the historical development of the body of laws now known as 'company law' out of Joint Stock Company or better still laws governing partnerships.[16]

The shareholder primacy model also underpins decided cases invalidating corporate decisions – however reputable or noble towards other constituents or stakeholders in the society – deemed not taken towards promoting the success of the company (enhancing shareholder value and maximizing their profits).[17] It should be emphasized that besides being authorities on the ultra vires doctrine, these cases also constitute classic authorities equating the success or interest of the company to and in perfect simulacrum with the interest or success of the shareholders as a whole.[18] The submission of Milton Friedman is the most cited academic authority adopting the shareholder primacy model. Friedman had postulated that: 'Few trends could so thoroughly undermine the very foundation of our free society as the acceptance by corporate officials of a social responsibility other than to make as much money for their stockholders as possible'[19] and that

> there is one and only one social responsibility of business – to use its resources and engage in activities designed to increase its profits so long as it stays within the rules of the game, which is to say engages in open and free competition, without deception or fraud.[20]

Corroborating Friedman, Hayek also argued against the use of corporate properties and resources 'for specific ends other than those of a long-run

42 *Background, theories and global outlook*

maximization of the return on the capital placed under their control' and further warned that the fashionable doctrine that their policy should be guided by 'social consideration' is likely to produce most undesirable results.[21]

The shareholder primacy model essentially sees corporate governance from the prism of the agency problem. Therefore, corporate governance is a simple agency problem. Having placed the shareholders at the centre of corporate governance discourse and in whose interests the companies must be exclusively managed, the only relevant corporate governance question is, how can directors (as agents) act in the best interests of their principals (the shareholders)? Said differently, the argument is that corporate managers are employed by the shareholders to manage the company on their behalf as they (shareholders) do not have the time and/or competence to manage the businesses themselves, the corporate fiduciary duty automatically ought to be enforced to the benefits of the principals (shareholders) of the agents. The argument concludes that without the shareholder primacy model, corporate executives will be encouraged to engage in opportunistic behaviour ('shirking'), which will only add on to the agency cost – the cost resulting from corporate managers' opportunistic behaviour and the costs expended in monitoring the managers in order to prevent them from abusing their positions.[22]

The 21st-century representation of the shareholder primacy model by neoclassical economics has no doubt been succinctly captured by Henry Hansmann and Reinier Kraakman. They contended that:

> The triumph of the shareholder-oriented model of the corporation over its principal competitors is now assured, even if it was problematic as recently as twenty-five years ago. . . . We predict, therefore, that as European equity markets develop, the ideological and competitive attractions of the standard model will become indisputable, even among legal academics. And as the goal of shareholder primacy becomes second nature even to politicians, convergence in most aspects of the law and practice of corporate governance is sure to follow.[23]

They also contended that:

> the ultimate control over the corporation should be in the hands of the shareholder class . . . the managers of the corporation should be charged with the obligation to manage the corporation in the interest of its shareholders . . . other corporate constituencies, such as creditors, employees, suppliers and customers should have their interests protected by contractual and regulatory means rather than through participation in corporate governance.[24]

The shareholder primacy model appears to have gained so much dominance as a corporate culture, particularly in the Anglo-American jurisdictions, and almost all corporate governance mechanisms and activisms in the Anglo-American

Theoretical underpinnings of CSR practices 43

jurisdiction are geared towards only enhancing returns on investment for shareholders.[25] In fact, corporate governance activists in the USA in particular have been arguably concerned overwhelmingly with financial performance rather than long term productive investment.[26] In the UK, despite the conscious effort[27] at whittling down the dominance of the shareholder primacy or attempting to promote a seeming third way model in between shareholder primacy model and stakeholder model called the 'Enlightened Shareholder Value'[28] (ESV) – where extraneous competing interests of certain stakeholders are supposedly balanced but for the long term benefits of the shareholders – it is rather clear that the ideological foundation of the ESV is deeply rooted in the shareholder primacy model having not given the stakeholders any real justiciable rights enforceable in courts.[29] To start with, corporate executives are statutorily required to 'promote the success of the company for the benefit of its members as a whole'.[30] Further, shareholders still retain the ultimate control of the corporate executives with the power of hire and fire;[31] the business 'owners' have several participatory rights in corporate governance; the investors are specifically promised returns and benefits from the company's profits;[32] the minority shareholders are also assured of statutory protection;[33] the legislative and regulatory framework for mergers and takeovers of companies still largely prioritizes shareholders' interests as opposed to other stakeholders such as employees. It is seriously doubted if those on the other side of the spectrum – the stakeholders – other constituents of the company – such as the employees and their families, the creditors, the suppliers, business partners, the local community, the society and any other group with which the company may interact in the course of its business – have similar benefits, especially beyond contractual stipulations.

The dominance of the shareholder primacy model appears to have also encouraged what Peter Muchlinski and Paddy Ireland, following Gerald Epstein, have called 'financialization' of the global economy. This simply refers to the increasing role of profits motives, financial incentives and motives, financial markets, financial actors and financial institutions in the operations of the world economies.[34] The shareholder primacy has indeed encouraged the rise of the shareholder value companies around the world, which has in turn not only contributed to the global growth in income and wealth inequality but also welded these corporate groups into a new aristocracy of finance.[35] One of the most noteworthy features of financialization has been the growth in rentier incomes – in the incomes accruing to capital (interest, dividends and so on), while those accruing to labour, the other legitimate stakeholders or available to the wider society appear to have stagnated.

Africa is not spared of the influence of the shareholder primacy model. For instance, the provisions of Section 76(3)(b) of the 2008 South African Companies Act No. 71 still enjoin corporate executives and directors to perform their functions in the best interests of the company (largely interpreted as the shareholders as a whole), suggesting that the shareholder primacy model still largely underpins the provisions.[36] Similarly, in Nigeria, the shareholder

44 *Background, theories and global outlook*

primacy model appears statutorily embedded in the duties of corporate executives under Section 283. The relevant section provides:

> Directors are trustees of the company's moneys, properties and their powers and as such must account for all the moneys over which they exercise control and shall refund any moneys improperly paid away, and shall exercise their powers honestly in the interest of the company and all the shareholders, and not in their own or sectional interests.[37]

In summary, the shareholder primacy model can thus be seen as a business model, which gives very little or no support to any wider stakeholder considerations outside the interest of the business owners. It is assumed that such wider stakeholders' interests are different from the interests of those considered owners of the business.

Clearly, a major advantage of this model is that it absorbs the management of the company from undue distractions and external pressures.[38] The argument is that this will in turn prevent abuse of corporate powers by corporate executives who are 'forced' to one – and just one – goal in running the company: maximizing returns for the business owners. From the previous analysis, it is not surprising that the proponents of the shareholder primacy model will pay little or no attention to encouraging board room consideration of CSR matters relating to the wider society, the labour, creditors or environmental concerns. As far as these theorists are concerned, wealth maximization for the shareholders is tantamount to effective economic distribution of resources in the society. It will simply be unacceptable for corporate executives to sacrifice profits that would otherwise have been available for sharing by the shareholders on the altar of some grandiose ethical, social, or environmental considerations. This attitude should not be strange at all; the whole idea here is that the business itself is a private property of the investors who should operate in a free and perfect market as the incorporators and their agents (corporate managers) may deem fit. After all, as they say, he who pays the piper dictates the tune. The implication for CSR can also be summed to mean that corporate executives will not need to care about social obligations, and shareholders can hold claims against executives who do, as this would amount to a breach of duties to the company and indirectly to the shareholders.

2.3.1.1 Critique of the shareholder primacy model

But unlike the assertions of Hansmann and Kraakman, is it really the end of history? Is the debate over in respect of the monotonic shareholder primacy versus the pluralist stakeholder views of corporate governance? A few criticisms and queries have continued to trail the fundamental assumptions underlying the shareholder primacy model and are highlighted in the following list:

(i) The first criticism is that the protagonists of the shareholder primacy model appear to have adopted a zero-sum mentality whereby it is assumed that an adoption of a pluralist corporate governance view, which encourages consideration of wider stakeholder interests and CSR practices, will be suicidal to the company and those considered to be its owners. The fact, however, is that there is no credible evidence anywhere to the effect that corporate executives have automatically chosen corporate suicide whenever they decide to act socially responsibly.[39] Further, a fallacious premise on which the shareholder primacy model is based is the assumption that the interest of the shareholders is always at variance with the interests of relevant stakeholders on issues. Sometimes, however few such situations may be, pluralist views regarding corporate decisions are actually aligned. No constituents in a company, for instance, would argue against such a company operating within legal and regulatory bounds;

(ii) Historically speaking, the adequacy of the shareholder primacy model to justify the existential nature of modern day businesses has also been queried. The argument is that, in the past, there were factory-like companies (whereby the business owners essentially provided the whole capital and assembled all the factors of production and therefore should have the business primarily run to maximize their profits). In modern day companies, however, companies are rather organized by professionals, managed using the skills and knowledge of employees and operated on huge risks undertaken by creditors and leveraging the well-being and peaceful co-existence with the local communities. Under this sort of modern arrangement, it is illogical and, quite frankly, irrational, to insist on the advocacy that the business of companies should primarily be managed for the wealth maximization of the shareholders alone.[40] The point made here is that modern day businesses and corporations exist— and to a very large extent it can be argued, are not capable of successful operation and long term survival – but for the wider recognition, support, cooperation, dependence and interaction with relevant stakeholders in the society. How truly successful can a company be without the peaceful co-existence with its local community? How profitable can a business get without the cooperation of competent, hardworking and loyal employees? Regardless of the risks business owners are willing to take, how successful can the business really get without support from mortgagors, creditors and debenture holders? How effectively or efficiently can a company operate without the support, cooperation and sometimes guidance of regulators? In summation, as it is important to appreciate the contribution of business owners to the success or profitability of the business, so is it crucial not to underrate the contributions of other stakeholders;

(iii) The concept of CSR cannot receive positive evaluation under the shareholder primacy model or even the ESV for that matter, as the directive to corporate executives under this regime to only have 'regard to' the interests of stakeholders seems to only constitute a means of ensuring better returns for the business owners. The principle of law enunciated in cases such as *Hutton v. West Cork Railway Co*,[41] *Greenhalgh v. Ardene Cinemas Ltd*[42] or *Parke v. Daily News Ltd*[43] that 'the law does not say that there are to be no cakes and ale, but that there are to be no cakes and ale except such as are required for the benefit of the company'[44] and equating the success of the company to the success of the shareholders largely undermines the interests of other stakeholder groups and jeopardizes corporate responsibility and accountability. In other words, by the shareholder primacy model, it appears corporate executives can legitimately engage in CSR practices only where a CSR business case can be established towards ultimately enhancing shareholders' wealth. This criticism was echoed by Pennington thus:

> The other question of policy is whether it is satisfactory that directors should be required by law to manage the company's affairs solely with a view to the financial benefit of the shareholders . . . it would, surely, be more in accordance with modern views about the functions of business enterprises in society to relieve directors from this myopia which the law forces on law.[45]

In conclusion, in view of the modern realities in the business community, the previously enunciated principles in the Hutton case amongst others in relation to corporate responsibility and accountability is not only unsatisfactory as it is limiting CSR to corporate charity and donations but also portends serious injustice to legitimate stakeholders' interests in companies;

(iv) The communitarian team production theorists have also identified a crack in the shareholder primacy model. Margaret Blair and Lynn Stout maintained that the appropriate normative goal for a board of directors is to build and protect the wealth-creating potential of the entire corporate team – 'wealth' that is reflected not only in dividends and share appreciation for shareholders but also in reduced risk for creditors, better health benefits for employees, promotional opportunities and perks for executives, better production support for customers and good 'corporate citizenship' in the community;[46]

(v) The shareholder primacy model has also been described by Jack Welch, former CEO of General Electric, as a 'dumb idea'.[47] Further, it has been criticized as not only morally untenable but also out of line with prevailing social norms.[48] How really sane or tenable is the view that the success of the company is equal to the success of the shareholders with little regard for balancing the ratio of returns on investment and each shareholder equity contribution? If the preceding question could be answered in the affirmative by the shareholder primacist can it be argued that the failure, liability or debts of the company are equal to (in perfect simulacrum to) the failure, liability and debts of the shareholders? The point this book is making here is that, while there is no limit to the amount of returns on shareholders' investment, (the bigger the profit, the higher his returns without any form of limitation), morally (and logically) speaking, there should not have been a limitation as to the amount of liability on

Theoretical underpinnings of CSR practices 47

shareholders' investments. The reality, however, is different, as the liability of shareholders is clearly limited even at the level of their investment;

(vi) The dominance claim of the shareholder primacy model also received some jurisdictional queries. Corporate governance in the United Kingdom, for instance, appears rather more in a state of flux than of being dominated by the shareholder-oriented model.[49] The reason for this assertion is not far-fetched. There are a number of principles and provisions in the 2018 UK Corporate Governance Code and the Companies Act of 2006 still enjoining corporate executives to balance competing stakeholder interests in running the companies. For instance, the provisions of Section 172 of the UK Companies Act 2006 enjoins corporate managers to have regard to the interests of employees, local communities, customers, suppliers and other related stakeholder concerns in working for the success of the company. Such wider stakeholder interest considerations are also contained in Principle D (paragraph 5) of the 2018 UK Corporate Governance Code;

(vii) It can also be argued that there is no reason to isolate corporate law from obligations of other areas of law[50] — such as human rights law, environmental law, labour law and others — all areas of law, including corporate law, should be instrumental to moving our society closer to what we want — social efficiency.[51] The mainstream claim that corporate law should serve only the interests of the shareholder and managerial elite only encourages global financialization and is highly suspect, especially if we believe that the purpose of corporations is to serve society as a whole rather than a small, wealthy minority;[52]

(viii) The shareholder primacy model can also be criticized and perhaps rendered ideologically baseless on the ground that its fundamental assumption of taking the shareholders as the 'owners' of the businesses is after all not unassailable.[53] While John Parkinson characterized such assumption as a 'technical error' and invincibly circular as it assumes the very point it seeks to prove,[54] Paddy Ireland demonstrated with the aid of historical evidence on the meaning of 'shares' that it is not correct to state that businesses are 'owned' by shareholders.[55] It has also been argued that the idea that the shareholders own the company does not sit well with the concept of the company being a separate legal entity. Shareholders actually own 'shares' as their private properties and cannot claim to own the company itself. Corporate properties belong to the company itself as a separate legal personality.[56] In the locus classicus case of *Bligh v. Brent* (1837) 2 Y & C Ex. 268, for instance, joint stock companies' shares were held to be intangible rights to profit, not equitable interests in the company's assets. Shareholders were therefore portrayed not as asset-owners but as providers of money, ownership of which they transferred to the company;

(ix) Finally, it is also arguable that the shareholder primacy model, having unduly focused the entire resources of the company on the shareholders,

48 *Background, theories and global outlook*

appears a dangerous model. Its principles are not only dangerous to the continued existence of the human society as we presently know it but also dangerous to the long-term survival of the company itself. First, its encouragement of global financialization appears intrinsically antithetical to progressive calls for companies to be mindful of the negative societal and environmental impacts of their activities. If the justifications for the shareholder-oriented corporate model are not intellectually challenged and its fundamental assumptions duly queried, the model has the capacity (and some would contend has started) to breed new financial aristocrats, extremely profitable and humongous companies with dangerous influences and powers to revolutionize human societies and with very weak or no legal ideology to checkmate such powers. Instances of modern day corporations' and cartels' complicity in drug trafficking, money laundering, terrorism and illegal international gun trades appears exemplary.[57] Second, the idea is also dangerous to the continued existence of the company itself as such other excluded wider stakeholders have been shown to have the capacity of engineering the 'sudden death' of such companies in reaction to the company's exclusionary policy and stakeholder mismanagement. The eventual forced business shut down by Shell Petroleum Development Company of Nigeria in the wake of Ken Saro-wiwa's activism era in the oil rich Niger-Delta region of Nigeria is instructive.

2.3.2 Stakeholder model

It is settled that the landmark article[58] of Merrick E. Dodd entitled him to be the father of the stakeholder model although organized thinking about the stakeholder model only began with Edward Freeman,[59] while the classical work of Adolf Berle and Gardiner Means[60] had also made references to 'a group far wider than either the owners or the control'.[61] The stakeholder model is a business management model that assumes that companies ought to exist for the mutual benefit of those with relevant 'stakes' or 'interests' in or against the corporation as a going concern.[62] While the shareholder primacy model is prevalent in Anglo-Saxon jurisdictions such as the United Kingdom, Australia, the United States of America, Canada and New Zealand amongst others, the stakeholder model has been mostly adopted in East Asia and continental Europe, The Netherlands and Germany[63] in particular. The group of stakeholders of a business is usually a large one, although traditionally there were just six stakeholder groups, namely: shareholders, employees, customers, managers, suppliers and the local community. The group may change over time due to changes in business operations, and the list of a company's stakeholders cannot be easily closed. The usual suspects in the stakeholder groups now include, apart from the business owners, creditors, suppliers, consumers, employees, local communities, society, and the environment amongst others.

Theoretical underpinnings of CSR practices 49

The stakeholder group also represents the various *constituents* of the business or company.

The Stanford Research Institute in 1963 defined *stakeholders* as 'those groups without whose support the organization would cease to exist'.[64] In 1999, Edward Freeman, who made the stakeholder model most popular in the *Strategic Management: A Stakeholder Approach*,[65] also defined the term *stakeholder* as the 'groups and individuals who benefit from or are harmed by, and whose rights are violated or respected by, corporate actions'.[66] In 2002, Post and others defined stakeholders in relation to a company as 'individuals and constituencies that contribute, either voluntarily or involuntarily, to its wealth-creating capacity and activities, and who are therefore its potential beneficiaries and/or risk bearers'.[67]

The stakeholder groups could be primary or secondary stakeholders.[68] The primary stakeholders include the shareholders, employees, customers and others, who ensure the continuity of the company as a going concern.[69] The secondary stakeholders are those who influence or affect – or are influenced or affected by – the company but are not in transaction with the company or essential for its survival.[70] Although the stakeholders of a company exist in large numbers independent of any recognition by the business or companies involved, the stakeholder group is, however, not unrestricted. It will be sheer absurdity to assert that anybody or entity who considers himself a stakeholder can be regarded as a legitimate stakeholder of a business. Although Freeman is quoted to have also defined stakeholders as 'any group or individual who can affect or is affected by the achievement of the firms objectives',[71] an important yardstick to identifying legitimate stakeholders appears to have been provided by Donaldson and Preston who enjoined drawing a distinction between 'stakeholders' and 'influencers' of a company.[72] The point made here is that the stakeholder group does not extend to such broad group of anything influencing or influenced by the operations of the company. Influencers of corporate decisions such as the media should not be categorized as stakeholders as they have no stakes or interests in or against the company. Sometimes, even some legitimate stakeholders of a corporation may be unable to influence corporate actions. Example of such are job seekers who are said to have an interest in ensuring that their job applications are considered by the companies involved (not that they should be hired, however).[73] Another probable example will be the natural environment. Even the environment in almost every situation is a stakeholder in the wake of ever increasing concerns for climate change and global warming and their numerous social, economic and environmental effects resulting from emissions and wastes from industrial activities of companies. Edward Freeman, Andrew Wicks and Bidham Parmar summarized the rationale behind the stakeholder theory as follows:

> Business is about putting together a deal so that suppliers, customers, employees, communities, managers and shareholders all win continuously

50 *Background, theories and global outlook*

over time. In short, at some level, stakeholder interests have to be joint – they must be travelling in the same direction – or else there will be exit, and a new collaboration formed.[74]

In a nutshell, the stakeholder model is the ideological business model underlying the arguments that corporate decisions, actions and inactions must demonstrate due consideration of multiple stakeholder interests including shareholder interests. Therefore, within the ambits of this model, no singular interest of any stakeholder is particularly ranked higher than the other. All such interests from different constituents must be balanced in determining the success of the company.[75]

It should be noted that the stakeholder theory is an evolving model, and, just like the concept of CSR itself, it also has been plagued by the problems of definitions, pluralism in conception and backgrounds of views amongst others, especially in the business management field. Due to these pluralistic definitional problems, Donaldson and Preston gave a classical synthesis of the stakeholder theory and identified four key ideas (contents) of the theory, namely: normative, descriptive, instrumental and managerial contents. Since Donaldson and Preston's categorization, different perspectives[76] have since been canvassed as to the best suitable content (normative, instrumental, descriptive or managerial) by many writers, others arguing for a rather convergent theory.[77]

Compared with the shareholder primacy model, this book considers this model more favourably disposed to embedding the core values of corporate social and environmental responsibility and sustainable development in companies as more businesses can act or choose not to act in the interest of not just the business investors (today's needs) but also in the interest of all stakeholders including the environment and the needs of future generations. However, the biggest shortcoming of the stakeholder model lies in its assumption that shareholder interests and other stakeholder rights should be equated.[78] Further, the stakeholder model also lags in the provision of practicable paradigm with which corporate executives can actually or effectively balance the so-called equal interests of all stakeholders and in the best interest of the company.

Despite of the previous shortcomings, the stakeholder model is important to the eventual recommendations in this book, and it is imperative to enumerate its usefulness and rationale behind its consideration as follows:

2.3.2.1 Justifications for the stakeholder model

(i) This model questions the argument that businesses are absolute private properties of their owners, and, as such, businesses ought to be managed solely for them. It is reasonably impossible to claim absolute ownership of any property in a modern sense without restrictions, hence, it is unreasonable to assert that businesses are absolute private properties of investors.[79] More so, the idea of shareholders being referred to as 'owners' has also been historically and logically dislodged in a few decided cases and

Theoretical underpinnings of CSR practices 51

by Paddy Ireland[80] as shareholders are, at best, stockholders or owners of 'shares' in the business rather than owners of the business itself;

(ii) Further, the stakeholder model can also be justified on the strength of its wide adoption in modern legal principles,[81] codes of corporate governance,[82] (business conducts) court judgments[83] and legislations[84] around the world. It can even be argued that an ideological shift (or an attempt thereof) towards adopting the stakeholder model may be found in the ESV adopted under Section 172 of the English Companies Act 2006 or under Section 72(4) of the South African Companies Act 2008, which talks about a social and ethics committee and under Sections 134(3)(o) and 135 of the 2013 Indian Companies Act also requiring, inter alia, the constitution of a corporate social responsibility committee on the board of directors of qualified Indian companies;

(iii) Another justification for the theory is rooted in deontological ethics. It has been noted as fair a business model that takes into consideration the interests of people with stakes in the company before most of its corporate decisions.[85] But the question may be asked, what is fair? Is fairness a universal or neutral concept? Is it possible for a fair scenario to A to be at the same time and in similar circumstances unfair to B? Who determines fairness?

(iv) The socio-economic realities of modern times where the companies can no longer exist in isolation but naturally depend on material contributions from non-shareholder stakeholders such as creditors and employees also offers ample justification to consider such wider stakeholder interests in determining what is in the best interests of such companies.

(v) Finally, against the backdrop of the imminent threat of climate change and undue influences of the very large transnational or multinational corporations (TNCs or MNCs), the need for sustainable development in both the society and within the business community has become imperative. The targets of sustainable development are better fostered by a stakeholder model under which more companies and businesses can act and/or omit to act more responsibly in the interest of not just business investors (today's needs) but also in the interest of all relevant and legitimate stakeholders including the environment.

2.4 The legitimation theories

Having considered the Ideological Corporate Models, the legitimation theories[86] are hereafter discussed with a focus on finding appropriate theoretical undercurrents to legitimize CSR practices. For emphasis, the theories discussed here can be (and are being) employed as microscopic theoretical lenses through which corporate behaviour may be measured or categorized as either responsible or otherwise, incentivized or punished. As will be demonstrated later, it is not impossible that the previously discussed ideological models may overlap the present legitimation theories. Some would argue, for instance, that

52   *Background, theories and global outlook*

the shareholder primacy model is more attributable to the contractarians while the stakeholder model is more readily canvassed by the communitarians. Having said this, there appear to be some thin lines separating these ideas and theories, and for the purposes of clarity they have been discussed under distinct headings.

2.4.1 The contractarian theories

Two major theories can be distilled from the philosophical approach that a company is a web of contractual interrelation; the contractarian theories are analyzed from the perspective that business organizations or companies are platforms through which groups of two or more contractors conduct business operations. The theories are: (i) Legal Contractarianism and (ii) Nexus of Contract Theory (Economic Contractualism).

2.4.1.1 Legal contractarianism

The legal contractarian takes a company as the product of private contracts freely entered into between or amongst its incorporators or 'owners'. The company is said to be efficient as a result of the freedom of the contractors to determine the terms and conditions of their relationship, the contract. A company is born when two or more parties are said to have come together to form a pact to carry on commercial activity.[87] If the whole company is one huge interconnection of contracts, it would appear justified to take the articles (and memorandum) of the association of companies as the ultimate contract or, better still, the constitution or *grundnorm* of the contractors. This view seems approved in a number of corporate law provisions around the world.[88] As Janet Dine pointed out, this theory is largely foundational[89] as opposed to an operational theory and will therefore offer little or no assistance for our analytical purposes in this book. Further, rendering this theory of little significance are historical facts confirming that a company cannot simply be reduced to a contract since, for a long time now, companies have primarily and largely come into existence not by means of contract but by means of positive concession of state or registration.[90] What implication will this legal contractarianism have on the CSR concept? A line of thought reducing a company to a contractual relationship between the owners of the company inter se on the one hand and possibly between the owners and other constituents such as the employees, creditors and suppliers on the other hand will create a number of problems for effective CSR practices. For instance, while it may be possible to legitimately justify the interests of creditors and employees in a company under this model as having a contractual relationship with the business, it is doubtful if the same can be said of the interests of the natural environment or the host and local communities or any other non-directly influencing constituents of the company that may not have a signed contract with the business.

2.4.1.2 The nexus of contracts theory/economic contractualism/contractarianism

While Michael Jensen and William Meckling could be regarded as the foremost protagonists of this theory,[91] the primary expositors of the Nexus of Contracts theory include Eugene Fama[92] and more especially Frank Easterbrook and Daniel Fischel.[93] This theory appears to represent the extremist thinking of the contractarian theories and has been described as the classical foundation on which companies in the USA and the UK operate. The theory brings to bear the voluntary, market-oriented nature of the company or firm and dismisses the notion that companies or firms owe their existence and operations to states creation.[94] It states that a firm or any business corporation is a mere central hub for series of contractual relationships.[95] Easterbrook and Fischel described the nexus of contract theory as 'a short hand for the complex arrangements of many sorts that those who associate voluntarily in the corporation will work out among themselves'.[96] Accordingly, the firm or company itself is taken as a mere fiction,[97] a mere nexus or link for contractual relationships involving the business owners, the creditors, corporate managers, customers, suppliers and employees amongst other constituents. Therefore, corporate law is taken only as an extension of contract law and whose business really should be focusing on facilitating the contractual interrelationships in the most efficient manner.[98] This theory is hinged on the fundamental notions of 'rational actors' and 'efficiency'. It is argued that a combination of the nexus of contracts framework and the freedom of individual contractors acting accordingly in a rational manner can only result in an effective and efficient allocation of resources in the society.[99] In other words, high value use of resources and, therefore, efficient allocation of resources in society, is guaranteed in an economy where rational actors[100] as individuals exchange assets and resources rationally and each derive utility and welfare therefrom.[101] Cheffins explained that 'rational actors under economic theory, make decisions so as to improve their personal well-being, frequently referred to as their utility, welfare or wealth'.[102] There is need for some clarifications on the doctrine of 'efficiency'. Efficiency is usually measured using two standards as gauges on whether or not a change, transaction, or business decision has been efficient, having increased or capable of increasing the aggregate social welfare.[103] First, Pareto Efficiency was developed by an Italian economist, Mr Vilfredo Pareto, and it is to the effect that a decision or transaction can be said to be *Pareto-efficient* if it will make someone better off without making anyone else worse off. This has received criticisms because hardly will any decision or transaction make all parties to the transaction feel better-placed without producing losers.[104] Second, the British duo of Professors Nicholas Kaldor and John R. Hicks also developed another test. A transaction or law is *Kaldor-Hicks efficient* if, on the aggregate and on the whole, the benefits, social welfare or utility derivable from it outweigh the associated cost. Under this test, rational actors who benefit and are made better off are said to obtain enough to compensate fully those who lose (in the long run). Obviously, as the Pareto efficiency is almost impossible to attain, Kaldor-Hicks

54 *Background, theories and global outlook*

efficiency is usually adopted as it not only promotes social welfare but also creates some soft landing for losers. This nexus of contract theory provides notional foundation for the shareholder primacy model since the sole purpose of the company, according to the contractarians, is to maximize shareholders' profits and that the wider stakeholder groups are protected to the extent of the provisions of their contracts with the company.

2.4.1.3 *The nexus of contract theory critique*

From the original proponents of the nexus of contracts theory to its recent expositors, contractarianism has been attended by a number of critical antagonisms including:

(i) This theoretical approach is not only difficult to defend[105] but also appears not to correspond with a realistic picture of the corporation, even on a metaphorical level;[106]

(ii) Jensen and Meckling's approach to economic contractarianism is also challenged in that, despite the title of their work, a full-fledged theory of corporation or the firm (as they call it) has perhaps not been really offered as they appear to have only offered a theory of agency cost. Their theory seems to leave corporate law focused entirely on financial transactions that are cut off from the primary strategic operating transactions of the corporation. In other words, they are said to have assumed in their analysis of the nexus of contracts that a firm or company already exists, and the authors have only gone ahead to tackle a problem within the corporate model;

(iii) Contractarianism appears to have also missed the whole point about the essence of a company; rather than being a nexus 'of' contracts, a company is in reality a nexus 'for' contracts as it provides the platform through which series of contractual interrelations involving the company, the 'owners', the employees and other constituents are formed;

(iv) Another criticism of the nexus of contracts theory is the relegation of the role played by corporate law and the state to the background gap-filling function. Easterbrook and Fischel had argued:

> Why not just abolish corporate law and let people negotiate whatever contracts they please? The short but not entirely satisfactory answer is that corporate law is a set of terms available off-the-rack so that participants in corporate ventures can save the cost of contracting. There are lots of terms, such as rules for voting, establishing quorum, and so on, that almost everyone will want to adopt. Corporate codes and existing judicial decisions supply these terms 'for free' to every corporation, enabling the venturers to concentrate on matters that are specific to their operations.[107]

(v) The theory also appears fundamentally questionable against the background of the pseudo-scientific notion of 'efficiency' (whether Pareto-Efficiency or Kaldor-Hick's), and the claim that creating wealth is beneficial to society as a whole means that the end result is a picture where interference with the freedom of markets needs to be justified by anyone who argues for any regulation of corporate behaviour;[108]

(vi) Just like the shareholder primacy model, the nexus of contract theory also focuses too much attention on the present contractors of a company – the present so-called owners of the company and, perhaps, present creditors and employees – without much consideration for the long term[109] interests of future generations of contractors who, unfortunately, are not present to negotiate favourable contractual terms and conditions for themselves.

(vii) Further, the economic contractualism analysis of Jensen and Meckling whereby companies are pure inanimate contracts and incapable of social and moral obligations is a misconception;[110] there is a difference between the ideas of having social responsibilities and having social conscience;

(viii) Just as the shareholder primacy model, this ideological stance also appears dangerous to maintaining a healthy balance between economic growth for the business community and sustainable development for the society; shunning CSR, relegating all forms of state regulation and corporate law in the scheme of business affairs, can only mean one thing: creation of global aristocrats of finances, asocial companies and global monsters.[111]

The implication of testing corporate actions and CSR practices against the assumptions of this theory cannot be far-fetched. As identified in the discussions under the legal contractarian theory, this theory is a clear limitation on the capability of businesses to demonstrate corporate responsibility and accountability towards many a constituent of the business, especially those without 'contract' with the business. It will justify the wealth maximization drive of the corporate executives for their appointers, almost at all costs and usually at the expense of the wider non-contracting stakeholders who may not even be influencers of the corporate decisions.

2.4.2 The communitarian theory

The leading exponents of the communitarian approach to corporate law include Lawrence E. Mitchell, William Bratton Jnr and David Millon, and the theory seeks to regulate and define the legal institution of property and contract in service of social values.[112] The communitarian theory appears to represent an extremist thinking in corporate governance discourse away from the individualistic contractarian approach of the nexus of contract theory. Here, a company is not only taken as a concessionary creation of the state but also a veritable state instrument for driving social cohesion, social inclusion and

56 *Background, theories and global outlook*

public welfare. Communitarians regard a company as a 'community of interdependence, mutual trust and reciprocal benefit' whereby corporate executives must ensure the company is managed for the benefit of any and all present or potential stakeholders of the company such as creditors, employees, suppliers, customers and local communities where such a company operates.[113] The communitarian theorists would measure the economic success of businesses by how far such businesses can demonstrate commitment to social responsibilities and providing social goods and public services. Therefore, this theory has the following implications:

(i) The company has no strong commercial identity because it has largely become a political tool with diffused goals;
(ii) The company's diffused goals remove its commercial focus;[114]
(iii) The interests of other constituents and wider stakeholders in the scheme of business affairs are easily justifiable for corporate executives.

Corporate socially responsible and accountable practices can easily be justified hereunder, although how effective or efficient such CSR practices will be appears to be a different question. A necessary conclusion from the previous points may therefore be that the communitarian theorists are more likely to hold the interests of the corporate body to be in perfect simulacrum with the objectives of state institutions and the government in the provision of public goods and social services. Many companies from the former communist countries and fascist Italy were modelled on the assumptions of this theory.

The major argument against the communitarian theory is the risk of complete loss of the commercial focus of businesses; its diffusion of goals is more often than not inefficient as it would only confirm Friedman's argument that where profit maximization for shareholders ceases to be the narrow focus of companies, corporate executives are most likely to be confused as to determining in whose interests the company's affairs are being run. It is therefore doubtful if this theory can foster effective CSR practices, as even the notion of CSR does not seek a complete removal of the commercial focus of the business as this theory tends to.

2.4.3 The state concession theory

The concession theory holds the view that companies owe the state their existence and should be gratified for such privilege even in their governance by tolerating state interference. State concession theorists argue that such state interferences are needed in ensuring that companies remain useful socioeconomic vehicles for development. While the theory is not as extreme as the communitarian in seeking to align the interests of both the state and the business community in perfect simulacrum, however, it shares in the view that the existence and operation of companies is a concession by the state, which grants the ability to trade using the corporate tool, particularly where they operate

Theoretical underpinnings of CSR practices   57

with limited liability.[115] Two forms of the theory were identified by William Bratton Junior[116] namely:

(i) A strong version that attributes the company's very existence to state sponsorship;
(ii) A weaker version that sets up state permission as a regulatory prerequisite to doing business.

Under the state concession theory, the businesses and companies do not exist in reality but are mere fictional creations of the state, enjoying the privileges of delegated powers to operate commercially within the bounds[117] granted[118] by the state. Popular exponents of this include Von Savigny, Albert Venn Dicey and John Austin amongst others. Against the backdrop of its origins within the state authority, other leading academic proponents of this theory include Kent Greenfield and Stephen Bottomley who argued for the introduction of public law principles such as constitutionalism, citizenship, legitimacy and separation of powers into corporate governance discourse.[119] Against this backdrop, this book finds this model very useful in justifying the CSR construct, since, as a creation of the state, companies are political animals and must owe duties to the public.[120]

The major undoing of the state concession theory appears to be its association with the fiction theory. If the company is taken as a mere fiction, not existing in reality, how exactly then do we explain its de facto operational existence? It has even been said that just 'like the fiction theory, the concession theory is not a theory (as it practically explains nothing). It is no more than an idea, an idea which is used to justify state interference in groupings other than the state.'[121] While the theory can be easily dissociated from the extremist ideology of the communitarian, it has, however, created the problem of justifying state interference in corporate governance and management without specifying to what extent such interference is permissible to guarantee the commercial focus of companies. Further, under the regulatory and policy making discourse on CSR, the state concession theory would justify externalized state prescription of CSR-inspired corporate principles and rules to guide corporate executives in taking into consideration the interests of other constituents apart from the shareholders in corporate decision making.

Notwithstanding the previous criticisms, the central idea of the state concession theory justifying prescription of corporate law and business rules by the state in deserving circumstances appeals to this book, hence its consideration in the formulation of the responsible stakeholder model (RSM) in the later part of this chapter.

2.5 The CSR operational theories

The CSR Operational Theories are the four CSR theories categorized by Elisabet Garriga and Domenec Mêlê[122] and are accepted as representing a successful and brilliant account of foremost academic debates on the CSR subject. The general mapping of the operational theories is designed to situate ideological assumptions about CSR within relevant political, social and economic topics. Garriga and Mêlé classified the theories as follows:[123]

(i) Instrumental theories;
(ii) Political theories;
(iii) Integrative theories;
(iv) Ethical theories.

The instrumental theories view CSR as instruments of achieving economic objectives of the business. The social responsibility of the corporations under these theories is wealth creation for shareholders. This group of theories is labelled 'instrumental' because under such theories CSR is perceived as a mere means to the end of profit for businesses. Put differently, CSR is just a potent tool for wealth maximization for companies. They also discuss CSR as marketing and a method of building a brand for improved bottom line and an instrument for long-term wealth creation.[124]

The political theories highlight the notion of corporate power and its relationship with responsibility within the society. This is the grouping of theories where the social power of the corporation is emphasized, specifically in its relationship with society and its responsibility in the political arena associated with this power. Under these theories, CSR is also adopted using the corporate citizenship perspective. This is the viewpoint of running a corporation as a political citizen within rights and responsibilities, be it social, economic, civic or political.[125]

The integrative theories examine how businesses integrate social demands.[126] It is usually argued under these theories that businesses depend on society for their continuity and growth and even for the existence of businesses themselves.[127] The theories synthesize other categories of theories to provide a framework for gauging corporate response, analysis and developing corporate policy. Some basic assumptions of this theoretical approach have been adopted in Section 2.8 of this chapter.

The ethical theories are the moralistic and normative focus of running businesses with a constant recourse to some higher standard of what is fair, right and just for the society. To the author, these theories lead to a vision of CSR from an ethical perspective and, as a consequence, corporations ought to accept social responsibilities as an ethical obligation above any other consideration. It incorporates other theories such as stakeholder theories, sustainable development and the common good approach. Therefore, these theories will enjoin the adoption of CSR practices with due regard and fairness to all necessary constituents of the corporation.

While it is important to note the convenience of justifying CSR practices using pure moral persuasions[128] as their normative base, this book has been written on – and proceeds on the basis of – an exclusion of morality or similar or related concepts such as fairness in justifying or measuring what corporate actions may be considered responsible or not. Accordingly, the analyses in the succeeding section are undertaken with the consciousness of excluding such moral considerations (as far as possible) from seeking theoretical justifications for CSR within corporate law. This is deliberately done to dissociate the findings and recommendations in this book from the idea of pure morality.

2.6 Analyzing the theories in terms of CSR practices

Following the previous discussions, a pertinent question appears to be: by what policy framework and underpinned by what corporate law theoretical approach can effective and efficient CSR practices be embedded in companies for the sustainable development of both the business community and society alike? Answers to the previous questions appear not clearly discernible within any one of the existing theoretical corporate models, especially as they have been described in the earlier part of this chapter.

Therefore, the objective of this section of the chapter is to attempt an answer from a careful consideration and sifting through the body of the previously discussed corporate law theories and their synthesis into some inevitable conclusion. Having discussed a few models, it should be noted that this book proposes a synthetic theory: a synthesis of the shareholder primacy, stakeholder, contractarian, communitarian, state concession and integrative theories as discussed in parts 2.3 to 2.5.

One thing is clear to the author, whether or not the phenomenon of CSR can be justified under any individual corporate law theory, the models and theories can surely be collectively utilized to provide some useful insights into effective CSR practices in the business community. For instance, CSR may not thrive very well under the shareholder primacy model or the contractarian theories. Many objective minds will find unpalatable the idea that companies should be taken as absolute or exclusive private properties of investors on which basis companies ought to be managed for the sole and exclusive benefits of the investors. As a matter of fact, the concept of private ownership of properties itself admits of several exceptions for reasons of public safety and welfare. The idea of absolute ownership without any considerations of non-owners of such properties (outside contractual relations) may not even exist in any jurisdiction any longer. Private property exceptions admitted for public interest purposes is a realization of the constant interaction and interdependence between individualism and collectivism. Therefore, it is seriously doubted if any company or business corporation anywhere in the world can operationally exist and survive without recognition, cooperation and interaction with stakeholders. Besides, as earlier explained in 2.4, the idea of businesses constituting the private properties of shareholders has also been sufficiently dislodged by Paddy Ireland, Andrew Keay and Irene Lynch-Fannon amongst others. This appears to be a cogent justification for societal expectations from companies and legal obligation on such companies to respect the interests of other constituents and

60   *Background, theories and global outlook*

stakeholder groups. Consequently, investors must accept the reality of stakeholder recognition and engagement in corporate management even as they may seek wealth maximization from their investments.

However, it should be clarified that there may be nothing intrinsically wrong in the wealth maximization for shareholders per se. It is crucial to draw a distinction between the implications of the arguments that companies 'exist' for the sole purpose of shareholders on one hand and that companies should be 'managed' for the sole purpose of the shareholders on the other hand. It is arguable that the shareholders bring the entity into existence, give it life in reality as the realist scholars would argue (or at least provide the platform on which the state/crown could grant concession to exist, as the state concession theorists may argue); they have obviously sown seeds and should legitimately be allowed to reap therefrom by participating in the profit and final assets sharing (as residual claimants) in the final hours of the entity. Therefore, it seems not totally incorrect to maintain that the company exists 'but for' the initial financial commitment and investments of the shareholders, and conscious efforts can therefore be deployed by the corporate executives towards enhancing shareholder wealth. However, away from corporate existence and into corporate governance and management, it appears legitimate to assert that 'but for' the 'wide recognition, constant interaction and concession of the state and society' – society comprising of other constituents of the company including the creditors, the employees, the customers, the host and impacted communities, even arguably the natural environment – the company may just be unable to survive, operate, function or otherwise achieve any economic gains, growth or development.

Further, against the backdrop of the constant and inevitable interaction and interdependence between business and society – and since one other goal of corporate law, presumably as any aspect of the law, is to serve the public interest and ensure overall social efficiency – it is only reasonable to legally enshrine some corporate responsibility towards the society. It would follow therefore that it is rather fictional, unrealistic and unjustifiably restrictive to claim that corporate law ought not to be deployed towards protection against unfair labour practices of companies or against any other irresponsible corporate behaviour in their operations. It could be argued that assuming but not conceding that corporate law should not be made to perform the roles of other aspects of the law such as environmental law, human rights law and industrial law, the relevant question is, should corporate law be so ideologically poised to jeopardize the protections already guaranteed or sought to be guaranteed under other aspects of the law? Shouldn't the roles of different aspects of the laws be complementary rather than antithetical? Many corporate law commentators would object to the suggested notion of aligning in perfect simulacrum the interests of companies and that of state institutions to provide public goods and social services. The primary focus of putting together resources to organize companies and other business entities must be appreciated; whether as a real or fictive entity, companies do exist and they exist for commercial purposes and economic gains, growth and development. However, what will remain untenable and constitute sheer surrealism is insistence that for some economic efficiency to be guaranteed in the society companies shall be owned and operated freely as absolute and exclusive private properties (of the shareholders) under some invisible hand of a free (and perfect) market with as little as possible state intervention in rare cases of market failures. The author submits that this argument is weakened by the incidences of societal recognition of companies and the state concessions of separate legal personality, limited liability and perpetual succession amongst other state privileges to companies. It is seriously doubted if indeed shareholders can functionally solely operate companies with their funds for economic gains in any society independent of the wide recognition, inevitable interaction and concession of the society and state institutions. History, especially in the Anglo-American jurisdiction, has it that the state developed concepts, doctrines and principles in order to make the corporate form more efficient within the business community. An exemplar is the limited liability (see, for instance, the Limited Liability Act 1855 in the UK) concept introduced by the state to foster investment and afford the shareholders some protection where an ordinarily profitable business venture turns sour. In fact, the best-known changes underlying the transformation of the legal rules that were applied to joint stock companies (JSCs) and the gradual emergence of what we now call 'company law' were purely legislative. The pertinent question therefore is, if the state is justified in doing this in order to promote the overall social efficiency, on what basis should the state not be justified to intervene with legal cum economic interventions towards embedding corporate, social, environmental responsibility and accountability within the business community in modern history? Finally, consequent upon the foregoing, postulations attempting to condition the efficiency of CSR practices on eventual benefit to the shareholders seem misplaced, to say the least. It would seem, as a matter of fact, that the efficiency of CSR practices does not lie within the exclusive purview of any single theoretical model discussed previously. In light of the forgoing, this chapter seeks to develop an alternative corporate law theoretical model that synthesizes the relevant assumptions in existing models with a view to propose a corporate objective, which should underlie corporate operations and effective CSR practices within the business community.

2.7 Regulatory consequences of theoretical approaches

In order to understand the rationale behind specific regulatory initiatives of corporate law as shall be later discussed in this book, it is important to highlight the regulatory consequences of a few corporate law models and theories. For writing convenience and in consideration of their relevance to the recommendations in this book, the author focuses on the shareholder primacy, contractarian, communitarian and the state concession theories. This part appraises the regulatory implications of adopting the assumptions of the different corporate law models. For instance, what will be the implications of holding a

62 *Background, theories and global outlook*

contractarian view within the context of a CSR regulatory framework? How does a state concessionist react to the regulation and enforcement of responsible corporate behaviour using the invisible hand of the free market?

For proponents of the shareholder primacy model, where the existential purpose of running a corporate entity is tied to profit maximization for shareholders, the shareholder has been raised to the single most important regulator over the management power.[129] Hence, the general meeting of the body of shareholders is usually afforded various controlling and safeguarding governance mechanisms by the internal instruments such as the Articles of Association, the external statutory legislations towards ensuring corporate powers wielded by corporate executives are not abused and the success and interest of the company (which is usually interpreted to be the success and interest of all the entire shareholders as a whole[130]) is protected at all times. But in reality, shareholders no longer constitute an effective corporate governance control mechanism.[131] The shareholders rather have little financial incentive to ensure that corporate executives behave legally, ethically or decently because, in law, they are personally untouchable. In the 2007 to 2008 economic crash, for instance, the shareholders of the companies concerned neither have to worry about being held liable for the losses incurred because the shares were fully paid-up, nor did anyone consider them in any way morally responsible for what had happened, even though they had happily accepted regular and substantial dividends from the corporate executives responsible for the crash.[132] But even where shareholders are motivated to ensure corporate executives behave responsibly, the shareholder primacy model appears to be of very little real practical relevance or use to unhappy shareholders in public companies as they are probably better advised to 'exit' than to try to hold corporate executives to account using company law.

What will be the regulatory consequences of the contractarian theory? The contractarian states that a corporate entity is a mere central hub for series of contractual relationships, and the voluntary, market-oriented nature of the company is brought to the fore while dismissing the notion that companies owe their existence and operations to state creation. Therefore, in terms of regulatory features, the *laissez-faire* market system is assumed to constitute an effective regulator of corporate behaviour. By way of example, the idea of hostile takeovers has been argued as evidence of effectiveness of the free market as a tool of corporate regulation in reducing monitoring costs. Dine had explained that:

> if a wealthy company's assets are not being fully utilized by lazy and inefficient managers, then the company presents a tempting target for a predator company, which may make an offer for the shares (which will be undervalued because of the poor performance of management) acquire control of the company, put in an efficient management and restore the efficiency and profitability of the company.[133]

Theoretical underpinnings of CSR practices   63

This was put differently by Cheffins that:

> executives fear takeover bids since they usually lose their jobs after a successful offer. This anxiety has, however, a beneficial by-product: managers, with their jobs potentially on the line, have an incentive to run their companies in a manner which maximizes shareholders wealth.[134]

However, evidence concerning post-bid performance also casts doubt on the disciplinary hypothesis. Several studies have identified long-term share-price declines following mergers, whether resulting from a hostile or an agreed bid, and the most comprehensive study has found that this negative effect intensifies over time, and companies that were acquired by tender offers had slightly below industry-average cash flow and sales performance both before and after takeover. Therefore, to Cheffins, the hypothesis that takeovers improve performance is not supported.

Under the communitarian framework where the corporate entity itself is considered a public agency in a planned economy, the company becomes a veritable state tool for driving social cohesion, social inclusion and public welfare. In this circumstance, not only does the state assume the role of the regulator, but the consequential stultification and bureaucracy in corporate governance and business management occasioned by heavy government interferences may after all be legendary.

A state concessionist takes the existence of the corporate entity to be the result of state concession, and companies should be gratified for such state privilege even in their governance by tolerating state interference in order to keep business operations within the ambits of public policy and implant notions such as fairness or equity in the business community. The attitude of the state concessionist to regulation is therefore permissive of government interference and intervention as may be necessary; this marks the slight difference between this model and the communitarian's position because the economy does not have to be holistically planned as advocated under the communitarian theory. Therefore, these state concession theorists will view regulations in terms of injection of more public law concepts such as the doctrine of ultra vires and citizenship into corporate law discussions.

The shareholder primacy and contractarian neo–classical economics approaches are de-regulatory in nature and have been rejected in this book (in their strict sense), having discarded regulations attempting to enforce social values on companies. The regulatory consequences of the shareholder primacy approach are also criticized and therefore rejected in this book because the underlying social relations which underpin economic transactions appear undervalued, particularly by the contractarians, and the attempt to justify regulation only to restore a free market (following market failures) seems wholly incorrect. Further, it is also evident that the communitarian, with the assumption that the corporate entity has a social conscience, embeds the company in a social environment

64   Background, theories and global outlook

and will regulate businesses behaviour with public, social and moral norms. Therefore, if not revisited and re-theorized as shall be done in the succeeding section in this chapter, the communitarian approach to regulation may not be very useful as it will only constitute a potential source of distraction and incoherence[135] for businesses.

Consequent upon the previous, it is submitted that the regulatory consequences of a model to be proposed in Section 2.8 are preferable as theoretical foundations of measuring corporate actions as responsible or otherwise. Under such a model, whether or not there is market failure, it is understood that without the recognition of the state, the support and cooperation of employees and creditors and the peaceable and inevitable interaction with host communities and other stakeholders, the survival of companies in the long term is jeopardized.

In the final analysis on this, it should be noted that, in spite of the marked differences in the theoretical regulatory approaches adopted by corporate law theorists, the dividing lines are actually getting blurred,[136] as there is usually a constant interplay and interconnectedness in the varying theoretical assumptions in the process of making regulations. Sometimes such interplay leads to inevitable confusion in identifying which theoretical model actually underlies individual regulations.

2.8 The proposed synthesis – responsible stakeholder model (RSM)

The question of determining corporate purpose is a varied, inclusive and open-ended discourse,[137] and many theoretical models have been analyzed earlier. It is important to emphasize that the ideological corporate models were discussed first because they were considered central to the general theme resonating throughout this book. A little more clarification is provided about these two dominant models later. While it is imperative to recognize and adopt some of their respective assumptions, some other arguments embedded in these theories have been simply found to be unacceptable. In fact, Professor Andrew Keay, in establishing the need for an alternative corporate law model, had noted that many of the existing traditional and dominant corporate law theories were devised in old societal contexts, and that new ones are required in response to the ever changing nature of the firm and commerce.[138] He further noted that:

> Arguably, shareholder primacy is not as attractive from a normative perspective, although it might be regarded as more pragmatic and workable. While stakeholder theory has attractions, normatively speaking, it is not practical, and it has been argued that stakeholder theory, while solving the problem of shareholder opportunism, leads to a more serious problem of stakeholder opportunism [footnotes excluded].

Theoretical underpinnings of CSR practices 65

As earlier shown in 2.3, while the shareholder primacy model appears both normatively indefensible and morally untenable, the stakeholder theory in trying to provide solutions to the criticisms of the shareholder primacy model presents an unworkable and impractical framework. Put differently, in spite of the attraction of the stakeholder theory in not discounting the important contributions of other constituents in the promotion of the success of the company in the long run, it can nonetheless be criticized for, amongst others things: its lack of clarity on who stakeholders are, its normative basis in morality, lack of clarity in implementation and enforcement formula to effectively balance the stakeholder stakes or interests.[139] In fact, while Andrew Keay had described the enforcement challenges with the stakeholder theory in respect of how to effectively balance competing stakeholder interests as a 'tricky issue,'[140] John Parkinson concluded that it is tantamount to imposition on directors and courts a near-impossible task.[141] Therefore, the primary objective of this section of the chapter is to develop and canvass arguments for a new and alternative corporate law model as a normative theoretical underpinning for measuring corporate social responsibility and accountability within the business community. By way of emphasis, as advocated by economic contractualism, the notions of rational actors and efficiency need revisiting and re-theorizing in such a way that the corporate form would adequately advance the aggregate welfare of all whose legitimate stakes may be genuinely affected by corporate activities. The overall welfare to be guaranteed by the state will extend to shareholders, employees, suppliers, creditors, customers, local communities and the natural environment. The need therefore to balance the varying interests of all constituents/stakeholders including the shareholders' interests in corporate decision making becomes only a logical conclusion as another important target of corporate law. But then, how exactly and under what suitable assumptions and principles of corporate law should corporate executives be guided in effectively balancing the interests of the companies together with those of the shareholders and other stakeholders? Following the inability of existing theories (especially the stakeholder model) to provide a workable formula for achieving such effective balancing of stakeholder interests, scholars have called for reforms in corporate law policies. Frynas summarized that:

> Policy makers should make a concerted effort to re-write company law and other regulatory instruments to increase the power of 'non-traditional stakeholders' and to require companies to become more transparent about all of their activities. Corporate governance reforms will help companies to make better social and environmental choices in front of shareholders.[142]

In light of the previous quote, this author submits that simply prescribing external regulatory minimum standards or drawing up voluntary guidelines and codes of conduct under a CSR framework and expecting corporate executives to fall in line in balancing the varying stakeholder interests and demonstrating

66 *Background, theories and global outlook*

responsibility would probably be an exercise in futility;[143] indeed many efforts have been committed to this in the past – at national, regional or multinational levels – but with very little success.[144] Every company seeks economic gains, growth and development; the manner in which each company seeks to achieve such gains, growth and development (through its operations) will differ, depending on the line of business involved and the management idiosyncrasies of the corporate executives (board of directors) involved. Therefore, in order to safeguard the commercial focus of companies and guarantee economic efficiency, this author concurs that corporate law may not necessarily descend into the arena to prescribe specific internal corporate governance rules for businesses to adopt with a view to ensuring a balanced and responsible consideration of stakeholder interests by corporate executives; such attempt would actually constitute a tall order. Therefore, with a view to avoiding falling prey to having a corporate model where CSR practices would only constitute undue detraction from serious corporate activities, this author proposes a corporate law model that, though it assumes the need to enhance shareholder value (wealth creation for shareholders), conjunctively ensures social efficiency through the employment of the principles of corporate law to advance the aggregate welfare of stakeholders; these stakeholders may be without contract with the company but will have stakes genuinely affected by corporate decisions and relevant to the long term survival of the company. This proposed model is called the responsible stakeholder model (RSM).[145]

Further to earlier discussions, the stakeholder theorists already confirmed the importance of the recognition, interaction and concession of both the state and society for the smooth operations and survival of businesses in the long run. Accordingly, in recognition of this crucial contribution of other constituents to the long term success or survival of the business, this author proposes a corporate law theory, which assigns extra corporate governance 'presumptive duty' to companies to self-develop appropriate and suitable technique towards responsibly balancing stakeholder interests. Further to the prevalence of soft law enforcement and self-regulatory CSR regime (as shall be discussed in Chapter 4), this proposed theoretical model assumes that companies exist for shareholders' wealth maximization, to be fundamentally conditioned by another assumption that the legitimate stakes of other constituents must be safeguarded in the course of the said wealth maximization for shareholders. The understanding of a conditional assumption for shareholder wealth maximization informs the proposal for a default obligation to ensure the safeguard of relevant stakes in the company. Whenever any qualified[146] stakeholder with the legitimate interest (be it employees, creditors, financiers, suppliers, contractors, customers, local communities et cetera) alleges oppression, injury, maltreatment, violation or disregard to its stake/interests as relevant to the success of the company, (disregard to employee rights for instance, in takeover bids or in the process of dividend declaration or in the determination of directors remuneration or in cases of environmental degradation of local community infrastructure in business operations or violations of executed agreements with

Theoretical underpinnings of CSR practices 67

local communities) then, in addition to (or as an alternative to) any other remedy or respite afforded in other aspects of the law, recourse should be had to this corporate law 'presumptive duty to balance interests' for redress. It is important to note that in measuring the relevance and legitimacy of a stakeholder's interest as against a particular corporate decision or action, the success of the company from such corporate action would be interpreted in terms of the survival of the company as a pluralist whole (shareholders and stakeholders alike) in the long run and not the myopic, short-term interests of the residual claimants (shareholders) for immediate return on investments.

The RSM proposes an obligation on the corporate form itself (the company, as opposed to an obligation owed by the corporate executives or the shareholders which for instance appears under Section 172 of the English Companies Act 2006 and Section 279 (4) of the Nigerian Companies and Allied Matters Act, 1990). Under this model, therefore, all a particular stakeholder – who may not have a binding or subsisting and enforceable contract (whether originating contract or operational contract) with the company – needs to show is a resultant and 'verifiable' damage or injury to its established (legitimate) stake. The major hurdle to cross (which will prevent unnecessary opening of floodgates to meddlesome interlopers) by a stakeholder is the establishment (to the reasonable satisfaction of the judicial authority involved) of its qualification to petition as a legitimate stakeholder whose interest is relevant and tied to the long term survival of the company involved. This is better explained. This proposed model appreciates the important contribution of individual stakes from respective stakeholders and therefore safeguards the fulfilment of the reasonable and legitimate expectations of these stakeholders at the time of making such contribution for the long term survival of the company.

As a corollary to the foregoing and in terms of CSR regulation and enforcement, RSM also proposes a policy imposition by corporate law of a presumption of corporate irresponsibility on companies, such that, whenever an infringement of the duty to balance competing interests is alleged by a legitimate stakeholder that had resulted in some verifiable damage or injury, the onus should lie on the company to prove, on a scale of probability, that it acted responsibly and accountably in due regard to the stakeholder and having effectively balanced all other relevant stakeholders' interests in the circumstance. Very importantly, in contrast to a mandatory or permissive rule, RSM is proposing a default and presumptive[147] rule, which automatically applies to companies regardless of the contents of their memorandum or articles of association and may only be avoided by discharging the duty to the reasonable satisfaction of the judicial or quasi-judicial authorities involved. From the foregoing, this proposed theory labelled RSM embodies these two key notions:

(i) A default legal duty to balance stakeholder interests;
(ii) A presumption of verifiable corporate irresponsibility whenever alleged by a qualified stakeholder.

68   Background, theories and global outlook

It should be noted that RSM does not really see anything intrinsically inaccurate about wealth maximization for shareholders *simpliciter*. RSM, however, draws a distinction between the arguments that companies 'exist' for the sole purpose of shareholders on one hand and that companies should be 'managed' for the sole purpose of the shareholders on the other hand. The shareholders bring the entity into existence, give it life in reality as some scholars would argue (or at least provide the platform on which the state/crown could grant concession to exist, as the *state concession* theorists may argue); they have obviously sown seeds and should therefore legitimately be allowed to reap therefrom by participating in the profit and assets sharing (as residual claimants) in the final hours of the entity. In fact, if some contractarian assumptions are applied, shareholders appear to take the greatest risks as they have no contractual guarantee of a return on their investment, unlike voluntary creditors who have entered into contracts with the company. Therefore, it seems not totally incorrect to maintain that the company exists but for their investments, and conscious efforts can be deployed by the corporate managers towards maximizing shareholders' wealth. RSM is based on the assumption that it appears legitimate to assert that but for the constant recognition, interaction and concession of the state and society, the company may be unable to survive, operate, function or otherwise achieve any economic gains. Therefore, while profit creation may be encouraged, however, such drive for wealth maximization for shareholders cannot justifiably be done at all costs (for instance, treating corporate compliance with laws as a mere cost element or otherwise engaging in externalizing[148]) at the expense of the key constituents of the company. Finally, therefore, the notion that business organizations *exist* for the sole purpose of their incorporators and shareholders may after all be unassailable. Further, in balancing competing interests, where ranking (consideration of) shareholder interests higher may result in injury to other stakeholders (from which the corporate entity may be affected in the long run), only then should such interest be reviewed, reconsidered and balanced to avoid such injury to the company (stakeholders) as a whole.

An example appears useful in the circumstance, using the facts of the popular American case of *Shlensky v. Wrigley*.[149] In this case, the corporate executives of a company running a baseball team refused to install lights at the stadium to permit night games (which would ordinarily translate to more profits available to the shareholders) because of the deleterious effect of such light on the lives of local people in the surrounding community. The shareholders had brought a claim to declare such corporate action as irresponsible and without due regard for shareholders rights for returns on investment (hinged on the assumptions of the shareholder primacy model). The court held that the corporate executives' actions were valid. This case shows that the RSM would provide a workable normative *impetus* for holding such executives' acts as valid. It is a clear instance of situations where, although the shareholders' interests may be ranked important in day to day corporate activities, there should be instances where such must be balanced against non-violation of any relevant and legitimate constituent interests. Another instance is where corporate managers are desirous of declaring dividends to shareholders as a result of high profits secured on a project in a particular financial year, but there are outstanding terminal benefits of dead former employees remaining unpaid as a result of delays in securing proper probate documents for the same; it would be commercially unreasonable and illegitimate to so declare such dividend without due regard for such unpaid employment benefits. The interests of the shareholders on such occasion should be down-played, otherwise the other stakeholders (and indeed the company as an entity) may suffer an injury to its financials (wasting corporate time and financial resources defending resulting litigations) or reputational damage for insensitivity and irresponsibility towards an important stakeholder group such as former employees.

Despite the foregoing, it is important to clarify that, unlike the stakeholder theorists contend, other constituents of businesses such as employees, creditors and customers should not legitimately claim to be on the same pedestal as the interests of the shareholders. The shareholders are the investors; without the shareholders who took the huge risks of setting up the company, which could collapse and be tragically wound up shortly after commencement, there may not really be other constituents. Therefore, rather than see shareholders as merely part of the stakeholder group (constituents) of the business, the interest of the shareholders may need to be ranked important in balancing competing interests in a company. We must add that such shareholder interest may be upheld as crucial enough as to legitimize corporate behaviour that enhances shareholder value but never crucial enough to be upheld as inalienable, unassailable or in absolution from any competition from other constituents where necessary.

At this juncture, it is useful to distinguish the policy ramifications of the RSM from some similar propositions such as the team production theory of Professors Margaret Blair and Lynn Stout.[150] The team production theorists perceive the company as a nexus of investments where several groups contribute unique and essential resources to the corporate enterprise, each of which defines its contribution through explicit contract.[151] The RSM also takes the company as a web (in a very limited guise) of investment requiring the contribution of stakeholders for its survival and smooth running. However, unlike the team production theorists,[152] RSM does not discuss companies in terms of a contract (whether legally originating contracts or operational contracts) and, to this extent, so deviates from the team production theorists. RSM is proposed in terms of a company being an entity whose existence and survival are tied state privileges. Further, the team production theory does not only take issue with maximizing shareholder wealth but also describes an independent board of directors in terms of a 'mediating hierarchy', which is insulated from the control of shareholders in the course of balancing competing interests of team members.[153] In the case of RSM, it does not only assume the need to enhance

70 *Background, theories and global outlook*

shareholder value (maximizing shareholder wealth, subject to the condition of corporate law presumption of corporate irresponsibility) but also subjects the board of directors to the control of the shareholders (as far as possible) in the course of balancing competing stakeholder interests. RSM adopts some elements of the traditional agency theory conception, with the recognition that corporate executives remain agents of the shareholders, and as such, maintaining that the ultimate power of control resides in the principal.

It is also necessary to distinguish the RSM from the Entity Maximization and Sustainability Model (EMS)[154] of Professor Andrew Keay. The EMS assumes the need to foster the wealth of the entity (business or company itself, as opposed to maximizing shareholder wealth), which will entail directors endeavouring to increase the overall long-run market value of the company as a whole, taking into account the investment made by various people and groups.[155] In other words, while the EMS may be beneficial to shareholders and stakeholders alike, the emphasis is on the success and sustainability of company (the entity) towards enhancing its position in the long run. Again, EMS enjoins balancing of 'courses of action' by directors towards enhancing entity wealth as opposed to shareholder wealth.[156] From the foregoing, both RSM and EMS appear to share certain similarities: both appear to build on the stakeholder model by the recognition of the important contribution of different 'investors' or stakeholders to the overall long term survival of the firm, and both seem favourably disposed to respecting the fulfilment of the reasonable and legitimate expectations of stakeholders at the time making contributions to the firm (the company). However, RSM is distinguishable from the EMS on a few grounds.

First, while the goal prescribed by the EMS to corporate executives in the course of balancing competing stakes in the company is entity wealth maximization, RSM, on the other hand, prescribes the target of ensuring non-violation of relevant legitimate interests of other constituents in the course of enhancing shareholder wealth maximization. Second, the notion of the 'Entity' under the EMS appears to assume that the shareholders do not control the directors, hence treating shareholders just like other stakeholders like the employees, creditors or financiers who are all categorized as 'investors'. RSM differs; while shareholders are also taken as part of the stakeholder group, RSM assumes shareholders may not be treated equally as other 'investors'. Slight priority is afforded the shareholders to, for instance, appoint directors or remove non-performing ones. Third, RSM may also be distinguished in light of some 'hard decisions'[157] noted by Keay whereby some long-term reasonable and legitimate expectations of certain stakeholders may be sacrificed for the good of entity maximization. This is perhaps explained better in terms of CSR and painting a similar scenario as used by Keay in his analysis of the EMS. Under the EMS, a corporate action to relocate the business to another jurisdiction (probably with weaker regulatory framework) to enable more profits for the entity is accommodated and justifiable within the EMS, even though such corporate decision may violate the reasonable and legitimate expectation of some stakeholders such as employees and host communities. Under the RSM, however, such a corporate action is likely to be deemed as corporate social irresponsibility being deleterious to the stakes of employees who, having contributed and invested important skills towards the enhancement of both the entity and the shareholder wealth, get expectations of a continued employment (all things being equal) simply dashed. RSM therefore does not accommodate such corporate action, and, adopting the assumptions of the RSM, such an act would be measured irresponsible.

Further, Dine has suggested that the promotion of CSR and its principles such as accountability are probably best served at the national level rather than by the international law.[158] This author aligns with this view, and against this background it is recommended that the RSM be adapted and codified with variations to suit individual national legislations in different jurisdictions across the African continent. It is important to reiterate that the RSM, in its explanation of the nature and purpose of companies in the society, is a synthesis of existing assumptions, drawing insights from shareholder primacy model, the stakeholder model, state concession theory and Garriga and Mêlé's integrative theory. Within the RSM framework, the business of business may still be business, only that the meaning of business itself will have to be redefined and qualified by the need to strategically implant CSR values in the business community; the business of business has to now be responsible business!

For some time now, corporate law has imposed a duty on corporate managers to promote the financial interests and assets of the corporations (using their discretion and expanding business judgment rule as far as possible) without specifying how exactly they should do this. Similarly, it is submitted that, against prevailing modern socio-economic, political and environmental realities, corporate law can justifiably impose a duty on companies for their corporate executives to act responsibly in the exercise of their discretions and balance competing interests of constituents without specifying guidelines or codes through which these may be achieved. Therefore, RSM recognizes that companies may be managed for the ultimate benefit of the shareholders only in the sense that they constitute the residual risk bearers or claimants. For such residual risk, shareholders have the privilege of appointing competent and responsible managers who shall ensure that the business of the business is a responsible business and not involved in opportunism or shirking performance. The previous analysis only describes the formulation and delineation of the theoretical and policy ramifications of the RSM at this stage. The meta-regulatory, operational and enforcement features of the RSM as an alternative CSR regulatory framework especially in application to the case study economies in Africa will be further espoused in Chapter 7. The following diagram summarizes the key elements of the RSM in terms of its theoretical formulation and policy components.

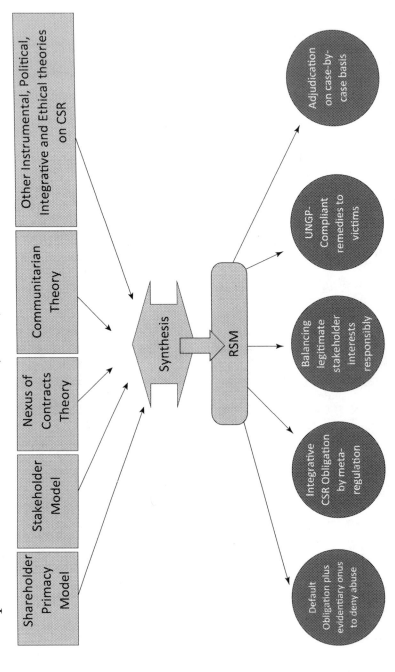

Figure 2.1 Illustration of RSM formulation

2.9 Chapter summary

This chapter underscored the need to examine corporate law theoretical models towards an understanding of different assumptions underpinning corporate actions and CSR practices. It accordingly investigated and assessed relevant corporate law theories in CSR discourse; the established, though highly debated, corporate law models of shareholder primacy, stakeholder, economic contractarian, communitarian and the state concession models were respectively appraised with a view to finding acceptable corporate objective and ideological foundation for efficient CSR implementation within the business community. The chapter also discussed CSR theoretical groupings by Garriga and Mêlê into the instrumental theories, political theories, integrative theories and ethical theories. This chapter explained that despite some useful insights individually offered by many of the discussed theories, many scholars have been unable to unreservedly adopt any of them or otherwise situate effective CSR practices within any one of these extant theoretical models. For instance, although the stakeholder and the state concession theories have been useful in explaining CSR and its significance within business and society, neither of them has so far particularly provided generally acceptable answers to the fundamental questions generated in the society as a result of the CSR construct. Accordingly, the chapter enumerated the key weaknesses in the examined theories and confirmed the difficulties associated with working with any particular one of them in providing answers to the questions sought to be addressed in this book. Although the author synthesized an alternative corporate law model within which framework effective CSR practices may be conceptualized and better embedded in the business community, further arguments supporting the synthesized model's normative, theoretical underpinnings and regulatory consequences were reserved for inclusion in Chapter 7.

Notes

1 John Armour, Henry Hansmann and Reinier Kraakman, *The Essential Elements of Corporate Law: What Is Corporate Law?* (Harvard John M. Olin Discussion Paper Series, No. 643, Cambridge, MA: ISSN 1936-5357, ZDB-ID 2551889-6 2009) 25.
2 Bryan Horrigan, *Corporate Social Responsibility in the 21st Century: Debates, Models and Practices Across Government, Law and Business* (Cheltenham: Edward Elgar 2010) 4.
3 Karl Marx, *Early Writings*, T. Bottomore, trans. and ed. (New York: McGraw-Hill 1963) 52.
4 Cass Sunstein, *Legal Reasoning and Political Conflict* (Oxford: Oxford University Press 1996) 52.
5 Ibid.
6 Thomas Kimeli Cheruiyot and Patrick Onsando, 'Corporate Social Responsibility in Africa: Context, Paradoxes, Stakeholder Orientations, Contestations and Reflections' in A. Stachowicz-Stanusch (ed.), *Corporate Social Performance in the Age of Irresponsibility: Cross National Perspective* (Charlotte: Information Age Publishing Inc 2016) 95, 96, *et seq.*; see also, Elisabet Garriga and Domenec Mele, 'Corporate Social Responsibility Theories: Mapping the Territory' (2004) *Journal of Business Ethics* 53, 65; John Parkinson, 'Models of the Company and the Employment Relationship' (2003) *British Journal of Industrial Relations* 481–509.

74 *Background, theories and global outlook*

7 Nicholas H.D. Foster, 'Company Law Theory in Comparative Perspective: England and France' (2000) 48 *American Journal of Comparative Law* 573, 588.

8 Janet Dine, *The Governance of Corporate Groups* (New York: Cambridge University Press 2000) 1.

9 Ibid. 2.

10 Horrigan (n 2) 73, 76. Horrigan submits that corporate theorizing is the bedrock of normative justifications that inform corporate law making, law reform and practice.

11 Colin Marks and Paul S. Miller, 'Plato, The Prince and Corporate Virtue: Philosophical Approaches to Corporate Social Responsibility' (2010) 45 *University of San Francisco Law Review* 1–46, 1; Dine (n 8) 1, 2; see also, Garriga and Mêlé (n 6) 52–53; Olufemi Amao, 'Reconstructing the Role of the Corporation: Multinational Corporations as Public Actors in Nigeria' (2007) 29 *Dublin University Law Journal* 312–320; Duane Windsor, 'Corporate Social Responsibility: Three Key Approaches' (2006) 43 *Journal of Management Studies* 93–114; Richard J Klonoski, 'Foundational Considerations in the Corporate Social Responsibility Debate' (1991) 34 (4) *Business Horizons* 9–18.

12 Horrigan (n 2) 17–25, 97. Such related ideas appear to focus on any one or more of the following ideas: the standard shareholder-oriented model, state-oriented model, stakeholder-oriented model, manager-oriented model, voluntary 'do-gooderism' model, higher-order society-oriented model.

13 William Bratton and Michael Wachter argued, however, that the generally accepted historical picture putting Berle in the position of being the grandfather of shareholder primacy and Dodd cast as the grandfather of pluralist *stakeholderism*, as done in this book, is mistaken. To the author, it appears the two learned professors Berle and Dodd appeared to be discussing other corporate law topics and not the origins of shareholder primacy, or even CSR for that matter. See, generally, William W. Bratton and Michael L. Wachter, 'Shareholder Primacy's Corporatist Origins: Adolf Berle and the Modern Corporation' (2008) 34 *Journal of Corporate Law* 99, 101, 103.

14 Parkinson (n 6) 482. It is useful to clarify that profit maximization constitutes an assumption as there are not many corporate statutes around the world specifically stating that the sole purpose of companies shall be to maximize profits for its shareholders. See generally for this position, William Alan Nelson, II, 'Post-Citizens United: Using Shareholder Derivative Claims of Corporate Waste to Challenge Corporate Independent Political Expenditures' (2012) 13 *Nevada Law Journal* 134, 141 citing Einer Elhauge, 'Sacrificing Corporate Profits in the Public Interest' (2005) 80 *New York University Law Review* 733, 763.

15 Lisa Whitehouse, 'Corporate Social Responsibility as Regulation: The Argument from Democracy' in Justin O'Brien (ed.), *Governing the Corporation, Regulation and Corporate Governance in an Age of Scandal and Global Market* (West Sussex: John Wiley & Sons 2005) 156.

16 Joseph Abugu, *Principles of Corporate Law in Nigeria* (Lagos: MIJ Professional Publishers 2014) 45–65; Paddy Ireland, 'Capitalism without the Capitalist: The Joint Stock Company Share and the Emergence of the Modern Doctrine of Separate Corporate Personality' (1996) 17 *Journal of Legal History* 40; Paddy Ireland, 'Company Law and the Myth of Shareholder Ownership' (1999) 62 *Modern Law Review* 32–57 footnotes 40–52, 164–168 (hereinafter simply 'Ireland').

17 *Hutton v. West Cork Railway Co.* (1883) 23 Ch.D., 654; *Lee v. Chou Wen Hsien* [1985] BCLC 45 (PC); *Item Software (UK) Ltd v. Fassihi* (2004) EWCA Civ 1244 (CA); Re *Smith & Fawcett* [1942] Ch 304; *Brady v. Brady* [1988] BCLC 20; *Peskin v. Anderson* [2000] All ER (D) 2278; *Dawson International Plc v. Coats Paton Plc* [1989] BCLC 233; *Percival v. Wright* (1902) 2 Ch 421; *Dodge v. Ford Motor Co.* (1919) 204 Mich. 459, 170 N.W. 668; Re *Lee, Behrens & Co Ltd* (1932) *Ch 46; Rogers v. Hill* 289 U.S. 582 (1933); *McQuillen v. National Cash Register Co.*, 27 F. Supp. 639 (D. Md. 1939); *Greenhalgh v. Arderne Cinemas Ltd* (1951) Ch. 286, 291; *Gottlieb v. Heyden Chemical Corp.*, 90 A. 2d 660 (Del. 1952); *Parke v. Daily News Ltd* (1962) 3 WLR 566; *Amalgamated Society of*

Theoretical underpinnings of CSR practices 75

Woodworkers of South Africa v. Die 1963 Ambagsaa Wereniging (1967) 1 SA 586 (T); *Michelson v. Duncan* 407 A. 2d 211 (Del 1979); *Katz v. Oak Industries, Inc.* 508 A-2d 873, 878 (Del. Ch. 1986). These cases also constitute good authorities that although directors are given wide latitude in exercising 'business judgement', however, the law (Business Judgment Rule) still binds them to act out of fidelity and honesty in their roles as fiduciaries. Increase in director liabilities as a result of challenges on director's business judgments was recently empirically established in Andrew Keay, Joan Loughrey, Terry McNulty, Francis Okanigbuan and Abigail Stewart, 'Business Judgment and Director Accountability: A Study of Case-Law Over Time' (2019) *Journal of Corporate Law Studies* 1, 27.

18 Ibid. See this principle codified under Section 172 of the UK Companies Act 2006; Section 76(3) (b) of the 2008 South African Companies Act No. 71; and Section 283 of the Nigerian Companies and Allied Matters Act, 1990, as amended.

19 Milton Friedman, *Capitalism and Freedom* (Chicago: University of Chicago Press 1962) 133.

20 Milton Friedman, *Capitalism and Freedom* (40th anniversary edn, Chicago: University of Chicago Press 2002) 133. While the pursuit of wealth maximization for shareholders is entrenched in this model, such drive for profit, as advocated by Friedman at least, appears not to be at all costs. Friedman still recognizes certain restrictions to act within the limits of the law and play 'within the rules of the game'. Friedman's views are only classic however; more recent exponents of the shareholder primacy model argue that in the drive for profit maximization for shareholders, corporate executives may simply treat statutory laws and regulations as mere cost of operation and may willingly flout them if, despite paying penalties for non-compliance or violation, there will in the end be a result for more profits for shareholders. Judd F. Sneirson, 'Shareholder Primacy and Corporate Compliance' (2015) 26 *Fordham Environmental Law Journal* 1, 4, 5 *et seq.*

21 Friedrich Hayek, 'The Corporation in a Democratic Society: In Whose Interest Ought It and Will It Be Run?' in M. Anshen and G. Bach (eds.), *Management and Corporations* (New York: McGraw-Hill 1985) 100.

22 Michael C. Jensen and William H. Meckling, 'Theory of the Firm: Managerial Behaviour, Agency Costs and Ownership Structure' (1976) 3 *Journal of Financial Economics* 305. Perhaps the arguments of Michael Jensen at the Harvard Business School together with William Meckling, a graduate student of Milton Friedman, remain crucial to ending almost any debates or doubts that shareholder primacy and agency theory hold supreme in corporate law discourse. See Duff McDonald, 'Harvard Business School and the Propagation of Immoral Profit Strategies' *Newsweek* (14 April, 2017) 7; see also, Andrew Keay, 'Tackling the Issue of the Corporate Objective: An Analysis of the United Kingdom's Enlightened Shareholder Value Approach' (2007) 29 *Sydney Law Review* 577, 583. *Cf:* However, Michael Jensen later in 2011 attempted to alter his argument for a strict shareholder value by advocating 'integrity' in the course of profit maximization. Notwithstanding this turn by Jensen, Duff McDonald noted that such attempt has been largely unsuccessful as the harm, if any, appeared to have been done already. To McDonald, Jensen's propagation of the agency theory and shareholder primacy theory at the Harvard Business School helped in the creation of Frankenstein monster companies, which no one knows how to kill. McDonald also noted that Jensen's ideas may even be linked to the Enron scandal and collapse. See Duff McDonald, 'Harvard Business School and the Propagation of Immoral Profit Strategies' *Newsweek* (14 April, 2017) 11, 12, 13.

23 Henry Hansmann and Reinier Kraakman, 'The End of History for Corporate Law' in Jeffrey N. Gordon and Mark J. Roe (eds.), *Convergence and Persistence in Corporate Governance* (Cambridge: Cambridge University Press 2004) 67–68.

24 Ibid. 35.

25 United Kingdom's Company Law Review Steering Group, Department of Trade and Industry, 'Modern Company Law for a Competitive Economy: The Strategic

76 *Background, theories and global outlook*

Framework' (1999) 37; Janet Dine, 'Jurisdictional Arbitrage by Multinational Companies: A National Law Solution?' (2012) 3 *Journal of Human Rights and the Environment* 44, 57; Charles Craypo, 'The Impact of Changing Corporate Governance Strategies on Communities, Unions and Workers in the U.S.A.' (1997) 24 *JLS* 10; and Teresa Ghilarducci and others, 'Labour's Paradoxical Interests and the Evolution of Corporate Governance' (1997) 24 *JLS* 26; Paul Davies, 'Enlightened Shareholder Value and the New Responsibilities of Directors' (Inaugural W E Hearn Lecture, University of Melbourne Law School 2005) 5.

26 Andrew Keay, 'Stakeholder Theory in Corporate Law: Has It Got What It Takes?' (2010) 3 *Rich. J. Global L. & Bus.* 249 (hereinafter simply 'Keay Stakeholder Theory').

27 Cynthia Williams and John Conley, 'An Emerging Third Way? The Erosion of the Anglo-American Shareholder Value Construct' (2005) 38 *Cornell International Law Journal* 493–551.

28 Enlightened shareholder value is similar to the Australian 'Business Approach to Corporate Responsibility' and justifies making a 'business case' for CSR by enjoining corporate executives to consider stakeholder interests and report on non-financial matters of CSR like employee or environmental matters so long as it will make *business sense* (cost-benefit implications) to so do, and such considerations promote the overall economic performance of the company, without prejudice to enhancing shareholder value; see Charlotte Villiers, 'Corporate Law Corporate Power and Corporate Social Responsibility' in Nina Boeger, Rachel Murray and Charlotte Villiers (eds.), *Perspectives on Corporate Social Responsibility* (Cheltenham: Edward Elgar 2008) 85, 97, 98 *et seq.*

29 Richard Williams, 'Enlightened Shareholder Value in UK Company Law' (2012) 35 *UNSW Law Journal* 360–377, 376; Jan Eijsbouts, *Corporate Responsibility, Beyond Voluntarism: Regulatory Options to Reinforce the Licence to Operate* (Inaugural Lecture, Maastricht: Maastricht University 2011) 51.

30 The English Companies Act, 2006, Section 172. The provisions of the USA Sarbanes-Oxley Act of 2002 have also confirmed the shareholder-oriented corporate culture of corporate America; see also Section 181 of the Australian Corporations Act, 2001. *Cf.* As an attempt to enjoin corporate executives to have regard to (other than shareholders) wider stakeholder interests although still largely shareholder primacy model based, see Principle D in the latest version of the UK Corporate Governance Code. See www.frc.org.uk/getattachment/88bd8c45-50ea-4841-95b0-d2f4f48069a2/2018-UKCorporate-Governance-Code-FINAL.PDF accessed 27 October 2019.

31 The shareholders may remove directors with unsatisfactory performance. English Companies Act 2006, Section 168 thereof.

32 English Companies Act 2006, Section 581.

33 There are provisions for derivative claims and petitions for unfairly prejudicial conducts. See the English Companies Act, 2006, Sections 260 and 994.

34 Gerald Epstein (ed.), *Financialization and the World Economy* (Cheltenham: Edward Elgar 2005) 3; Peter Muchlinski, 'The Changing Face of Transnational Business Governance: Private Corporate Law Liability and Accountability of Transnational Groups in a Post-Financial Crisis World' (2011) 18 *Indiana Journal of Global Legal Studies* 665, 678. On page 670, Muchlinski described the term 'financialization' as the rise of financial markets over traditional bank lending as the main source of investment capital; the seeking of profits through financial transactions as opposed to more traditional forms of manufacturing, services or primary goods industries, as well as the changes in corporate governance theory that place enhanced shareholder value at its heart.

35 Paddy Ireland, 'Making Sense of Contemporary Capitalism Using Company Law' (2018) 33 *Australian Journal of Corporate Law* 379–401 (hereinafter simply 'Ireland Making Sense'.

36 Irene-Marie Esser, 'Corporate Social Responsibility: A Company Law Perspective' (2011) 23 *South African Mercantile Law journal* 317, 324.

37 The Nigerian Companies and Allied Matters Act, 1990 as amended (CAMA), Section 283 (1).

38 David Henderson, 'Misguided Virtue: False Notions of Corporate Social Responsibility' (2001) cited in Robert T. Miller, 'The Coasean Dissolution of Corporate Social Responsibility' (2014) 17 *Chapman Law Review* 1, 2.

39 Horrigan (n 2) 94; Edward Freeman, Jeffrey Harrison, Andrew Wicks, Bidhan Parmer and Simone de Cole, *Stakeholder Theory: The State of the Art* (New York: Cambridge University Press 2010) 209.

40 Roberta S. Karmel, 'Implications of the Stakeholder Model' (1993) 61 *The George Washington Law Review* 1156, 1171; Lyman Johnson and David Millon, 'Corporate Takeovers and Corporate Law: Who's in Control?' (1993) 61 *The George Washington Law Review* 1177, 1197–1207.

41 Above (n 17).

42 Ibid.

43 Ibid.

44 Dictum per Bowen LJ in Hutton's case at 672. Although this dictum appears dated, the introduction of Section 172 in the latest company legislation in the United Kingdom (Companies Act 2006) has not changed much. See Andrew Keay and Taskin Iqbal, 'The Impact of Enlightened Shareholder Value' (2019) 4 *Journal of Business Law* 303, 326; and *Re West Coast Capital (LIOS) Ltd* (2008) CSOH 72; *Cobden Investments Ltd v. RWM Langport Ltd* (2008) EWHC 2810 (Ch); *Madoff Securities International Ltd (in liq) v. Raven* (2013) EWHC 3147 (Comm); *Re HLC Environmental Projects Ltd* (2013) EWHC 2876 (Ch).

45 Robert R. Pennington, 'Terminal Compensation for Employees of Companies in Liquidation' (1962) 25 *Modern Law Review* 715, 719.

46 Margaret M. Blair and Lynn A. Stout, 'Specific Investment: Explaining Anomalies in Corporate Law' (2006) 31 *Journal of Corporate Law* 719; Ige O. Bolodeoku, 'Economic Theories of the Corporation and Corporate Governance: A Critique' (2002) *Journal of Business Law* 420, 420, 421.

47 Francesco Guerrera, 'Welch Condemns Share Price Focus' *Financial Times* (12 March, 2009), saying 'The idea that shareholder value is a strategy is insane. It is the product of your combined efforts – from the management to the employees'; see also, Paddy Ireland, 'Corporate Schizophrenia: The Institutional Origins of Corporate Social Irresponsibility' in Nina Boeger and Charlotte Villiers (eds.), *Shaping the Corporate Landscape: Towards Corporate Reform and Enterprise Diversity* (Oxford: Hart 2018); Duff McDonald, 'Harvard Business School and the Propagation of Immoral Profit Strategies' *Newsweek* (14 April, 2017) 11, 12, 13.

48 Thomas Donaldson and Lee E. Preston, 'The Stakeholder Theory of the Corporation: Concepts, Evidence and Implications' (1995) 20 *The Academy of Management Review* 65, 88; Lyman Johnson, 'The Delaware Judiciary and the Meaning of Corporate Life and Corporate Law' (1990) 68 *Texas Law Review* 865, 934.

49 Klaus J. Hopt, 'Comparative Corporate Governance: The State of the Art and International Regulation' (2011) 59 *American Journal of Comparative Law* 1–74, 7.

50 There are indeed instances where the shareholder primacy model may encourage noncompliance with legal obligations if such may increase the earnings of shareholders in the long run. For instance, under the shareholders primacy regime, corporate executives may deliberately evade tax obligations if calculations suggest that penalty for such evasion is lesser than the tax obligation itself, thereby saving a few company funds to be made available for distribution to the shareholders as dividends. After all, it is all about profit maximization almost at any cost.

51 Social efficiency denotes the employment of the principles of corporate law to promote public interest and advance the aggregate welfare of all who are affected by a company's activities, including the shareholders, employees, suppliers, and customers, as well as third parties such as local communities and beneficiaries of the natural environment.

Background, theories and global outlook

See John Armour and others (n 1) 25. In fact, using the words of the former CEO of General Electric, Jack Welch, 'on the face of it, shareholder value is the dumbest idea in the world. Shareholder value is a result, not a strategy. . . . Your main constituencies are your employees, your customers and your products' Duff McDonald, 'Harvard Business School and the Propagation of Immoral Profit Strategies' *Newsweek* (14 April, 2017) 9.

52 Muchlinski (n 34) 667, 668.

53 Assuming the private property argument is valid, there is really hardly any absolute right to private ownership of property. See limitation to land ownership rights for instance under Sections 43 and 44 of the Constitution of the Federal Republic of Nigeria Cap C23 Laws of the Federation of Nigeria (LFN) 2004; see also Sections 28 and 29 of the Land Use Act Cap L5 LFN 2004.

54 Parkinson (n 6) 483, 484.

55 Ireland (n 16) footnotes 40–52, 164–168. In fact, there is also the argument that as the proponents of the shareholder primacy may contend that shareholders have private ownership of the company because of their investment, so can, as stakeholder theorists would argue, other stakeholders lay similar ownership claim to the company having also invested their skills and monies. Steve Letza, Sun Xiuping and James Kirkbride, 'Shareholding versus Stakeholding: A Critical Review of Corporate Governance' (2004) 12 *Corporate Governance: An International Review* 242, 251.

56 As held in plethora of cases such as *Bligh v. Brent* (1837) 2 Y & C Ex. 268, *Salomon v. Salomon* (1897) AC 22, *Short v. Treasury Commissioners* (1948) 1 KB 116; *Fulham Football Club Ltd v. Cabra Estates Plc* (1994) 1 B. C. L. C. 363, 379; *Marina Nominees Ltd. v. Federal Board of Inland Revenue* (1986) 2 N.W.L.R. 48; *Habib Nigeria Bank Limited v. Ochete* (2001) FWLR (Pt. 54) 384; *CDBI v. COBEC* (Nigeria) Ltd (2004) 13 NWLR (Pt. 948) 376; *Mezu v. Co-operative Commerce Bank & Anor* (2013) 12 W.R.N. 1, 4; shareholders have no proprietary interest in the company but in shares, as the company has a separate personality of its own with which it can sue or be sued. Irene Lynch-Fannon, *Working within Two Kind of Capitalism: Corporate Governance and Employee Stakeholding: US and EU Perspectives* (Oxford: Hart Publishing 2003) 82.

57 Ole Kristian Fauchald and Jo Stigen, 'Corporate Responsibility Before International Institutions' (2009) 40 *The Geo. Wash. Int'l L. Rev.* 1027, 1034; Charlotte Villiers, 'Corporate Law Corporate Power and Corporate Social Responsibility' in Nina Boeger, Rachel Murray and Charlotte Villiers (eds.), *Perspectives on Corporate Social Responsibility* (Cheltenham: Edward Elgar 2008) 85, 86.

58 Merrick E. Dodd, 'For Whom Are Corporate Managers Trustees?' (1932) 45 *Harvard Law Review* 1145.

59 See Edward Freeman, *Strategic Management: A Stakeholder Approach* (Boston: Pitman 1984).

60 Adolf Berle, Jr. and Gardiner Means, *The Modern Corporation and Private Property* (New York: The Macmillan Company 1932).

61 Thomas M. Jones, Andrew C. Wicks and Edward Freeman, 'Stakeholder Theory: The State of the Art' in Norman E. Bowie (ed.), *The Blackwell Guide to Business Ethics* (Oxford: Wiley-Blackwell 2001) 20, 21 *et seq.*

62 John Parkinson, *Corporate Power and Responsibility* (Oxford: Clarendon Press 1993) 310 (hereinafter simply 'Parkinson CP').

63 Confirming Germany as the cradle of codetermination, *industrial democracy* and other stakeholder-oriented doctrines, see, Klaus Hopt and Patrick C. Leyens, 'Board Models in Europe: Recent Developments of Internal Corporate Governance Structures in Germany, the United Kingdom, France, and Italy' (2004) 2 *European Company and Financial Law Review* 135, 141.

64 Donaldson and Preston (n 48) 72.

65 Freeman (n 59) 31, 46.

66 Edward Freeman, 'A Stakeholder Theory of the Modern Corporation' in L.B. Pincus (ed.), *Perspectives in Business Ethics* (Singapore: McGraw-Hill 1998) 171–181, 174.

67 James Post, Lee E. Preston and Sybille Sachs, 'Managing the Extended Enterprise: The New Stakeholder View' (2002) 45 *California Management Review* 6–28, 8.

68 Max B.E. Clarkson, 'A Stakeholder Framework for Analyzing and Evaluating Corporate Social Performance' (1995) 20 *Academy of Management Review* 92.

69 Amao (n 11) 312.

70 Lance Moir, 'What Do We Mean by Corporate Social Responsibility?' (2001) 1 *Corporate Governance* 16 cited in Amao (n 11) 320.

71 Freeman (n 59) 46.

72 Donaldson and Preston (n 48) 85, 86.

73 Ibid.

74 Edward Freeman, Andrew Wicks and Bidham Parmar, 'Stakeholder Theory and "The Corporate Objective Revisited"' (2004) 15 *Organization Science* 364, 365.

75 John Farrar, *Company Law* (2nd edn, London and Edinburgh: Butterworths 1988) 12.

76 Christopher Stoney and Diana Winstanley, 'Stakeholding: Confusing or Utopia? Mapping the Conceptual Terrain' (2001) 38 *Journal of Management Studies* 603–626; Pursey P.M.A.R. Heugens and Hans (Johannes) van Oosterhout, 'The Confines of Stakeholder Management: Evidence from the Dutch Manufacturing Sector' (2002) 40 *Journal of Business Ethics* 387–403; Eric Orts and Alan Strudler, 'The Ethical and Environmental Limits of Stakeholder Theory' (2002) 12 *Business Ethics Quarterly, Philosophical Documentation Centre* 215.

77 Thomas Michael Jones and Andrew C. Wicks, 'Convergent Stakeholder Theory' (1999) 24 *Academy of Management Review* 206–221; Thomas M. Jones, 'Instrumental Stakeholder Theory: A Synthesis of Ethics and Economics' (1995) 20 *Academy of Management Review* 92–117, where Jones essentially argued that companies whose managers are able to create and sustain mutually trusting and cooperative relationships with their stakeholders will achieve competitive advantage over companies whose managers cannot.

78 Parkinson (n 6) 495; the stakeholder theorists argue that all interests, shareholders' and stakeholders alike, are to be managed, preserved and protected equally, and the protection of stakeholder interests should be seen as an end in itself, not a means towards protection of shareholders' interests.

79 Donaldson and Preston (n 48) 65–91.

80 Ireland (n 16) footnotes 40–52, 161–163; see also *Bligh v. Brent* (1837) 2 Y & C Ex. 268.

81 For instance the weakening of the hitherto supreme principle of Business Judgment Rule such that some form of protection is afforded stakeholders in what is considered legitimate management of a business enterprise; corporate executives may now legitimately increase wages of employees rather than declare profits for the shareholders; also, the definition of a 'reasonable takeover' now involves consideration of the impact of such takeover on employees, suppliers, local communities and creditors in determining how reasonable or not a takeover may be permitted. See, amongst others: *Hampson v. Price's Patent Candle Co* (1876) 45 LJ Ch. 437; *Shlensky v. Wrigley* (237 N.E 2d 776 ill. App 1968); *Harlowe's Nominees Pty Ltd v. Woodside Lakes Entrance)* Oil NL (1968) 121 CLR 483, 493; *Teck Corporation Ltd v. Millar* (1973) 33 DLR (3d) 288 (BCSC); *People's Department Stores Inc v. Wise* (2004) 3 S. C. R. 461; *Lonrho Ltd v. Shell Petroleum Co. Ltd* (1980) 1 WLR 627 (HL); *Unocal Corporation v. Mesa Petro Co.* (1985) Del. Supr. 493 A.2d 946; see also Horrigan (n 2) 108 citing Lynn Stout, 'Bad and Not-So-Bad Arguments for Shareholder Primacy' (2002) 75 *Southern California Law Review* 1189, 1202–1203.

82 See Principle 16 of the King IV. Institute of Directors in Southern Africa, "King IV Report on Governance for South Africa 2016" replacing the "King III Report on Corporate Governance for South Africa 2009. See also, Part 5.5 of King IV, embodying the stakeholder-inclusive approach towards getting businesses to behave responsibly to stakeholders; see also, Principle 4 of the 2014 *Central Bank of Nigeria Code of*

80 *Background, theories and global outlook*

Corporate Governance (Nigeria); Part D, Principle 28 of the 2011 Nigerian *Securities and Exchange Commission Code of Corporate Governance for Public Companies*; Principle 10 of the 2014 *Nigerian Communication Commission Code of Corporate Governance for the Telecommunications Industry*; see also, Principle D of the 2018 UK *Corporate Governance Code*.

83 Even courts within the Anglo-American jurisdiction have stated that corporate executives may take into account, instead of short term benefits of maximizing profits for the shareholders, the long term well-being of a company. See, for instance, Provident *International Corporation v. International Leasing Corp Limited* (1969) 1 NSWR 424, 440; *Paramount Communications Inc v. Time Inc* 571 A. 2d 1140 (Del, 1989); *People's Department Stores v. Wise* (2004) 3 S. C. R. 461; *BCE Inc. v. 1976 Debentureholder* (2008) 3. S. C. R.560; see also, Keay Stakeholder Theory (n 26) 250.

84 Section 7(d) and (k) of the South African Companies Act No. 71 of 2008; Section 279 of the Nigerian Companies and Allied Matters Act, 1990 as amended; Section 166 of the Indian Companies Act, 2013; and Section 172 of the English Companies Act 2006, among others.

85 See generally, Donaldson and Preston (n 48).

86 As earlier hinted, discussions on the contractarian and the communitarian theories as Operational Legitimation theories are only for argumentative convenience. Other writers such as Lynch-Fannon, for instance, may otherwise in the context of this chapter discuss the contractarian and the communitarian theories as Ideological Corporate Models. See Lynch-Fannon (n 56) 77, 78.

87 Stephen Bottomley, 'Taking Corporations Seriously: Some Consideration for Corporate Regulation' (1990) 19 *Federal Law Review* 203, 208.

88 A crude adoption of the nexus of contract view appears under Section 41 of the Nigerian Companies and Allied Matters Act 1990 as amended. Refined adoption of the legal contractarianism can be garnered from the provisions of Section 15(6) and (7) of the South African Companies Act No. 71 2008 and the combined effect of Sections 17 and 33 of the 2006 English Companies Act to the effect that the articles of a company shall have the effect of binding covenants between the company and members. See also Section 10 of the Indian Companies Act, 2013 with similar provisions.

89 Dine (n 8) 1.

90 In the history of the UK company law and practice, this is courtesy the 1844 Joint Stock Companies Act.

91 Michael C. Jensen and William H. Meckling, 'Theory of the Firm: Managerial Behaviour, Agency Costs and Ownership Structure' (1976) 3 *Journal of Financial Economics* 305, who appeared to build on the work of Armen Alchian, Harold Demsetz, 'Production, Information Costs, and Economic Organization' (1972) 62 *America Economic Review* 777. It is not impossible also that Meckling would be influenced in his writings by the assertions of Milton Friedman in criticism of CSR. Meckling was actually a graduate student of Milton Friedman. See Duff McDonald, 'Harvard Business School and the Propagation of Immoral Profit Strategies' *Newsweek* (14 April, 2017) 5, 10.

92 Eugene Fama, 'Agency Problems and the Theory of the Firm' (1980) 99 *Journal of Political Economy* 288, 290.

93 Frank Easterbrook and Daniel Fischel, *The Economic Structure of Corporate Law* (Cambridge, MA: Harvard University Press 1991); see also Daniel Fischel, 'The Corporate Governance Movement' (1982) 35 *Vanderbilt Law Review* 1259.

94 Grant M. Hayden and Matthew T. Bodie, 'The Uncorporation and the Unraveling of the "Nexus of Contracts" Theory' (2011) 109 *Michigan Law Review* 1127.

95 Ibid. 1129.

96 Frank Easterbrook and Daniel Fischel, 'The Corporate Contract' (1989) 89 *Columbia Law Review* 1416, 1426.

97 Fama (n 92) 290.

98 Henry N. Butler and Larry E. Ribstein, 'Opting Out of Fiduciary Duties: A Response to the Anti-Contractarians' (1990) 65 *Washington Law Review* 1, 7.

99 Paddy Ireland and Renginee G. Pillay, 'Corporate Social Responsibility in a Neoliberal Age' in Peter Utting and J.C. Marques (eds.), *Corporate Social Responsibility and Regulatory Governance Towards Inclusive Development?* (Basingstoke: Palgrave Macmillan 2010) 85; Brian R. Cheffins, *Company Law: Theory, Structure and Operation* (Oxford: Clarendon Press 1996) 4, 5, *et seq.*

100 Rational actors are described in terms of having necessary information about products and services they are interested in, can at little cost have sufficient financial resources to transact, can enter and leave the market or bargain with little difficulty and can carry out obligations that they agree to perform. See Cheffins (n 99) 6.

101 Cheffins (n 99) 6.

102 Ibid. 4.

103 Ibid. 14.

104 Ibid.

105 Foster (n 7) 587; Ige O. Bolodeoku, 'Contractarianism and Corporate Law: Alternative Explanations to the Law's Mandatory and Enabling/Default Contents' (2005) 13 *Cardozo Journal of International and Comparative Law* 433, 437, 438, *et seq.*

106 Hayden and Bodie (n 94) 1134; see also William W. Bratton, Jr, 'The "Nexus of Contracts" Corporation: A Critical Appraisal' (1989) 74 *Cornel Law Review* 407, 445, noting that: 'If the corporation really is contract, as the new economic theory tells us, then the last doctrinal vestiges of state interference should have withered away by now . . . but the sovereign presence persists'.

107 Easterbrook and Fischel (n 96) 1444.

108 Dine (n 8) 13.

109 Research has also shown the dangers associated with the pre-occupation of corporate executives with short term values such as share price as undermining conditions for innovation and human capital development and the long term competitive strength of such companies and of the economy as a whole. Parkinson (n 6) 50.

110 Dine (n 8) 16.

111 Muchlinski (n 34) 668; Dine (n 8) 17; Lawrence E. Mitchell, *Corporate Irresponsibility: America's Newest Export* (New Haven, CT: Yale University Press 2001) 28; Bolodeoku (n 105) 418, noting that: 'Because there are differences in rights, responsibilities and expectations of each corporate constituent in relation to a corporation, it is crucial to investigate the contents of the various jural relationships within the corporation. The nexus of contract theoretical approach does not favour such investigation'.

112 David K. Millon, 'New Directions in Corporate Law Communitarians, Contractarians, and the Crisis in Corporate Law' (1993) 50 *The Washington and Lee Law Review* 1373.

113 David K. Millon, 'Communitarianism in Corporate Law: Foundations and Law Reform Strategies' in L.E. Mitchell (ed.), *Progressive Corporate Law: New Perspectives on Law, Culture and Society* (Boulder, Colorado: Westview Press 1995) 10.

114 Dine (n 8) 17.

115 Ibid. 21.

116 William W. Bratton, Jr., 'The New Economic Theory of the Firm: Critical Perspectives from History' (1989) 41 *Stanford Law Review* 1471, 1475.

117 Such bounds can be exemplified in the many rules, whether default, permissive or mandatory, in statutory company laws in many jurisdictions around the world.

118 Concession was first granted to religious orders, local authorities and guild of merchants and later extended to a point of introducing incorporation by registration and limited liability. See the UK Joint Stock Companies Act 1844 and the UK Limited Liability Act 1855.

119 Thomas Hobbes, *Leviathan* (Oxford: Blackwell 1960) chapter 22, 146; see also Stephen Bottomley, 'From Contractualism to Constitutionalism: A Framework for Corporate Governance' (1997) 19 *Sydney Law Review* 277; Kent Greenfield, *The Failure of Corporate Law: Fundamental Flaws and Progressive Possibilities* (Chicago: University of Chicago Press 2006).

82 Background, theories and global outlook

120 Daniel Campbell, 'Why Regulate the Modern Corporation? The Failure of "Market Failure"' in J. McCahery, S. Picciotto and C. Scott (eds.), *Corporate Control and Accountability* (Oxford: Clarendon 1993) 103.

121 Foster (n 7) 582.

122 Garriga and Mêlé (n 6).

123 Ibid.

124 Ada Okoye, *Legal Approaches and Corporate Social Responsibility: Towards a Llewellyn's Law-Jobs Approach* (Abingdon, UK: Routledge 2017) 74.

125 Jörg Andriof and Malcolm McIntosh (eds.), *Perspectives of Corporate Citizen* (Sheffield: Greenleaf 2001). See also the US landmark case of *Burwell v. Hobby Lobby Stores*, Inc. 134 S. Ct. 2751, 2781 (2014) where the United States Supreme Court allowed closely held for-profit corporations to be exempt from a regulation its owners religiously object to if there is a less restrictive means of furthering the law's interest, according to the provisions of the Religious Freedom Restoration Act (RFRA). Tenth Circuit Judge Neil Gorsuch testifying before the Senate Judiciary Committee on Tuesday, March 21, 2017 in respect of his confirmation as judge of the US Supreme Court also confirmed the holding in this case as correct interpretation of corporate law in the US. See www.washingtontimes.com/news/2017/mar/28/why-religious-freedom-is-important-to-both-dems-an/ accessed 29 October 2019. In Nigeria, it is codified that companies have all the power of a natural person with full capacity but expressly prohibited from making any political donations and otherwise gifting its properties for any political purposes. See Section 38, CAMA.

126 Lee E. Preston and James E. Post, *Private Management and Public Policy: The Principle of Public Responsibility* (Englewood Cliffs: Prentice-Hall 1975).

127 Garriga and Mêlé (n 6) 52.

128 Miller (n 38) 1–28. *Cf:* Duff McDonald, *The Golden Passport: Harvard Business School, the Limits of Capitalism, and the Moral Failure of the MBA Elite* (New York: HarperCollins Publishers 2017); Duff McDonald, 'Harvard Business School and the Propagation of Immoral Profit Strategies' *Newsweek* (14 April, 2017) 1–13. Uwafiokun Idemudia, 'Corporate Social Responsibility and Development in Africa: Issues and Possibilities' (2014) 8/7 *Geography Compass* 421.

129 Dine (n 8) 118; see generally, Section 63 (5) of CAMA.

130 The UK Companies Act 2006, Section 172 thereof; see also CAMA, Sections 283 (1), 303 (2) (d) and 390 (2) (b) thereof; see generally decided cases also to this effect: *Hutton v. West Cork Railway Co.* (1883) 23 Ch.D., 654; *Percival v. Wright* (1902) 2 Ch 421; *Dodge v. Ford Motor Co.* (1919) 204 Mich. 459, 170 N.W. 668; Re Lee, Behrens & Co Ltd (1932) Ch 46; *Rogers v. Hill 289* U.S. 582 (1933); *McQuillen v. National Cash Register Co.*, 27 F. Supp. 639 (D. Md. 1939); *Greenhalgh v. Arderne Cinemas Ltd* (1951) Ch. 286, 291; *Gottlieb v. Heyden Chemical Corp.*, 90 A. 2d 660 (Del. 1952); *Parke v. Daily News Ltd* (1962) 3 WLR 566; *Amalgamated Society of Woodworkers of South Africa v. Die 1963* AmbagsaaWereniging (1967) 1 SA 586 (T); *Michelson v. Duncan* 407 A. 2d 211 (Del 1979).

131 Violet Aigbokhaevbo, 'Evaluation of Corporate Governance in Nigeria and Directors Liability' (1997) *Nigerian Contemporary Law Journal Uniben* 82–102, 83. Violet explained, for instance, that corporate governance and disclosure mechanisms hinged on shareholders are only effective when the shareholders are sufficiently knowledgeable to understand the information disclosed, have requisite shareholding to influence decisions and the shareholders not only willing but also able to resort to litigation if necessary.

132 Ireland Making Sense (n 35) footnote 64 and surrounding texts.

133 Dine (n 8) 120.

134 Cheffins (n 99) 119.

135 Philip Selznick, 'Self-Regulation and the Theory of Institutions' in G. Farmer and E. Murphy (eds.), *Environmental Law and Ecological Responsibility* (Chichester: Wiley 1994) 398.

Theoretical underpinnings of CSR practices 83

136 Tom Hadden, *Company Law and Capitalism* (2nd edn, London: Weidenfeld and Nicolson 1977) 496, 497.

137 Andrew Keay, 'Ascertaining the Corporate Objective: An Entity Maximisation and Sustainability Model' (2008) 71 *Modern Law Review* 663.

138 Ibid. 666.

139 Keay Stakeholder Theory (n 26) 270–298. *Balancing* of stakeholder interest means assessing, weighing and addressing the competing claims of those who have a stake in the actions of the organization, while *stake* means an asserted or real interest, claim or right, whether legal or moral or an ownership share in an undertaking. Scott Reynolds, Frank Schultz and David Hekman, 'Stakeholder Theory as Managerial Decision-Making: Constraints and Implications of Balancing Stakeholder Interests' (2006) 64 *Journal of Business Ethics* 285, 286; Leo V. Ryan, 'The Evolution of Stakeholder Management: Challenges at Potential Conflict' (1990) 3 *International Journal of Value Based Management* 105, 108 respectively for these definitions.

140 Keay Stakeholder Theory (n 26) 300.

141 Parkinson C.P. (n 62) 86.

142 Jedrzej G. Frynas, *Beyond Corporate Social Responsibility* (Cambridge: Cambridge University Press, 2009) 175–176. See similar call for alternative corporate law policies by Professors Margaret Blair, Lynn Stout and Andrew Keay respectively in Margaret Blair and Lynn Stout, 'A Team Production Theory of Corporate Law' (1999) 85 *Virginia Law Review* 247; Keay (n 137).

143 Parkinson (n 6) 494.

144 See *Norms on the Responsibilities of Transnational Corporations and Other Business Enterprises with Regard to Human Rights* (2003) UN Doc. E/CN.4/Sub.2/2003/12 Rev.; 'Commentary on the Norms on the Responsibilities of Transnational Corporations and Other Business Enterprises with Regard to Human Rights', UN Doc. E/CN.4/Sub.2/2003/ 38/Rev.2 (2003); Sub-Commission Res. 2003/16, UN Doc. E/CN.4/Sub.2/2003/L.11, 52, 2003; OECD, *Guidelines for Multinational Enterprises*; *Tripartite Declaration of Principles concerning Multinational Enterprises and Social Policy*, adopted by the Governing Body of the International Labour Office at its 204th Session (Geneva, November 1977), as amended at its 279th Session, Geneva, November 2000; the 2000 *UN Global Compact*; see also UN Human Rights Council (General Assembly), Promotion and Protection of all Human Rights, Civil, Political, Economic, Social, and Cultural Rights, including the right to Development. Report of the Special Representative of the Secretary General on the issue of Human Rights and Transnational Corporations and Other Business Enterprises, "Protect, Respect and Remedy: A Framework for Business and Human Rights", 7th April, 2008, UN Doc. A/HRC/8/5. These amongst others are individually examined and discussed in detail in Chapter 3.

145 For some foundational arguments leading to this theoretical approach, see Nojeem Amodu, 'The Responsible Stakeholder Model: An Alternative Theory of Corporate Law' (2018) 5 *Journal of Comparative Law in Africa* 1.

146 Within the framework of this theoretical approach, a stakeholder capable of maintaining a petition has to be qualified to avoid a needless open-ended floodgate of litigations by meddlesome interlopers and busy-bodies. Such qualified stakeholders will have a genuine and legitimate interest or stake, which is crucial to the success and long term survival of the company. While qualification determination will have to be on a case-by-case basis, stakeholders like shareholders, employees, creditors and host communities are likely to easily establish their qualification and legitimate interests. Despite the pointers suggested in this book, the author appreciates the anticipated difficulty that may be encountered by the judiciary in determining legitimacy or genuineness in stakeholders' interests to the long term survival of the company in view of the decisions in *O'Neill & Anor v. Phillips & Anor* (1999) 2 B.C.L.C. 1 HL, *Re Saul D Harrison & Sons Plc* (1995) 1 B.C.L.C. 14 at 19 and *Ebrahimi v. Westbourne Galleries* (1973) AC 360 at 379 amongst others showing that the determination of legitimacy or otherwise of interests are wide or vague considerations, which may be very difficult to assess even

84 *Background, theories and global outlook*

using the objective test of a hypothetical reasonable bystander. Professors Gower and Davies had noticed similar difficulties in determining fairness or otherwise of directors' actions in cases of unfair prejudice remedy. See Paul L. Davies, *Gower and Davies' Principles of Modern Company Law* (8th edn, London: Sweet & Maxwell 2008) 691.

147 For detailed discussions on the three forms of corporate rules, see, generally, Cheffins (n 99) 218, 219 *et seq.*; John H. Farrar and others, *Farrar's Company Law* (3rd edn, London: Butterworths 1991) 96.

148 Externalizing is said to be the practice of directors holding the interests of the shareholders to be paramount against the interests of other constituents. An instance of this externalizing was given by Keay citing that Shell, in late 2009, despite fall in corporate profits, decided to increase dividend value by simply axing 5,000 jobs. Keay Stakeholder Theory (n 26) 256.

149 *Shlensky v. Wrigley* 237 N. E. 2d 776 (ill. App. 1968).

150 Blair and Stout (n 142) 247.

151 Bolodeoku (n 105) 426, 437, 438 *et seq.*

152 Blair and Stout (n 142) 254.

153 Ibid. 255; see also Keay (n 137) 696.

154 See generally, Keay (n 137).

155 Ibid. 685.

156 Ibid. 696.

157 Ibid. 690.

158 Dine (n 8) 44–69.

3 CSR implementation and international regulatory framework

3 Background

Globalization has not only brought markets closer and increased economic prosperity but has also heightened the rate of exporting high risk business activities to weak and mostly less-industrialized societies in Africa. In order to combat recurring cases of corporate irresponsibility in terms of human rights abuses and environmental degradation amongst others, several international regulatory dialogues have been undertaken; various domestic regulatory measures have been proposed and are being implemented in different countries, and a few corporate social responsibility and accountability (CSR)[1] scholars have also suggested some regulatory proposals. In the face of the suggested framework – which is largely market-driven – and on a voluntary basis, rogue companies (with the target of profit maximisation at all costs) continue to behave irresponsibly, and corporate executives remain complicit in the infringements of many stakeholder rights and occasioning harm on the society.

With cross-border operations of many companies, a sizeable number of companies has become so large,[2] powerful and influential (making their behaviour affect so many in the society) that the law should properly regulate their activities, whether or not they are notionally viewed as either financialized[3] private economic property of shareholders or as social institutions promoting aggregate social welfare and efficiency.[4] However, the initial reaction of the business community to any regulatory and enforcement attempts towards societal concerns has been probably cooperative on the surface but rather antagonistic[5] in reality. This reality to maintain the pure commercial focus of businesses and probably insulate the business community from regulation appears confirmed by *The Economist* as follows:

> It is indeed desirable to establish a clear division of duties between business and government. Governments, which are accountable to their electorates, should decide matters of public policy. Managers, who are accountable to their shareholders, should run their business . . . businesses should not try to do the work of governments . . . the proper guardians of the public interest are governments, which are accountable to all citizens . . . the proper business of business is business. No apology required.[6]

The implication of the previous quote is that businesses (and corporate law) should remain insulated from government interferences, and it further asserts that businesses should not be made to assume the functions and responsibilities of states and governments in the provision of public goods and social services. But this author wishes to clarify that the argument for proper regulation of the business community was never about businesses taking over state functions but, rather, about the modern reality of the world economy, which warrants that businesses must own up to the negative impacts of their operations on stakeholders in the wider society.

Since it is settled that companies cannot simply operate and maximize profits at all costs,[7] even capitalist corporate executives appear to have now realized that maintaining such an antagonistic stance is no longer sustainable in view of the recurring cases of corporate irresponsibility and violations of the interests of other stakeholders in the process of doing business and making profits at all costs. Following such realization, in fear of the possibility of hard law mandatory government regulations, the business community has adjusted its stance to accepting at least minimalist voluntarist regulations in the form of self-regulation.[8] The argument, therefore, in recent times is that, while some level of regulation may be permissible, purely externalized government interventionist regulation of business operations is inappropriate and unsuitable for smooth business operations.[9] Hence, the regime of self-regulatory framework, whereby businesses themselves (based on the laissez-faire market model) work out internal rules and principles to regulate their business conducts, have become entrenched. This internalized self-regulatory framework has heralded a number of international regulatory dialogues and the emergence of a code of conduct mania[10] in corporate governance and CSR discussions with very little done to verify claims in such codes. By this internalization of the regulatory regime, the business community originated, sponsored and participated in different guidelines, rules and principles but in many cases with poor monitoring or enforcement mechanisms. These business codes of conducts abound in many jurisdictions around the world. Exemplified in Africa are the 2018 Nigerian Code of Corporate Governance, issued by the Financial Reporting Council of Nigeria, replacing the National Code of Corporate Governance 2016 and the Institute of Directors in Southern Africa, King IV Report on Governance for South Africa 2016, replacing the King III Report on Corporate Governance for South Africa 2009. Self-regulatory initiatives have also been dominant features at the inter-governmental and international law levels, and such initiatives include the United Nations Global Compact[11] (UNGC), the UN Guiding Principles on Business and Human Rights: Implementing the United Nations' Protect, Respect and Remedy Framework[12] (UNGPs) and the Organisation for Economic Cooperation and Development Guidelines for Multinational Enterprises[13] (OECD Guidelines for MNEs), amongst others. In this regard, Bryan Horrigan notes that their (the self-regulatory initiatives) existence and prominence are a testament to the new reality and that the 'civil society organisations have managed to implant elements of public account-ability into the private transactional spaces of transnational firms'.[14] However, despite the attitudinal change and increase in codes of conduct and other self-regulatory guidelines, violations of human rights, environmental degradation and other stakeholder rights infractions have not ceased and appear to consti-tute an irresistible implication of the inadequacies[15] (if not outright failure[16]) of self-regulation. Many more discoveries are made about businesses participating in the self-regulatory framework of corporate social responsibility only to legit-imize their operations and that are greenwashing[17] and paying mere lip service to effective CSR practices such as found in the humungous accounting scandal leading to the Enron collapse.[18] John Farrar had lamented:

> The Enron case demonstrates that a company can be widely respected for CSR in its environmental record, triple bottom line reporting, code of conduct respecting human rights and philanthropic contributions and yet have gross breaches of fiduciary duties by its key executives.[19]

It seems therefore that the search for the anticipated solution to recurring cases of irresponsible corporate behaviour may not be strictly within the self-regulatory regimes. There is a clear need to rethink strategies towards regulat-ing and enforcing effective CSR practices within business communities.

3.1 Methods of CSR regulation

Just before specific consideration of individual CSR implementation initia-tives both at intergovernmental and domestic levels, it appears useful to high-light the different policy framework and regulatory methods adopted across different jurisdictions towards embedding corporate social and environmental responsibility and accountability in the business community.[20] Regulation is an intentional activity of attempting to control, order or influence the behav-iour of others. Regulation can include law, but it is not limited to law as the concept of regulation is broader than law itself. Law can be an instrument of regulation, which is the ultimate target of this book: to use the instrumentality of law, amongst others, to design and proffer a suitable regulatory and enforce-ment system for corporate social responsibility for business communities in Africa. Regulation is not governance, per se. While regulation concerns how and why behaviour relating to the conduct of affairs of an entity is directed, steered and otherwise guided, governance concerns how and why an entity or system structures and conducts its affairs.[21] The goal of enforcement is compli-ance with regulations and the achievement of the underlying goals of regula-tions;[22] hence, enforcement is a means to an end and not an end in itself.[23] As a result of the different theoretical approaches to corporate actions and the dif-ferent CSR regulatory consequences about the theoretical models highlighted in Chapter 2, implementation of CSR or embedding of corporate social and

88   *Background, theories and global outlook*

environmental responsibility and accountability have taken varying methods.[24] The following features and methods of regulations have been identified and are discussed seriatim:[25]

1 Formal versus informal regulations;
2 Soft law versus hard law regulations;
3 Private versus public regulations;
4 International versus domestic regulations;
5 Principle-based versus rule-based regulations;
6 Voluntary versus mandatory regulations;
7 Internal versus external regulations.

3.1.1 *Formal versus informal regulations*

Formal regulations refer to regulations deliberately instituted to order a particular behaviour and are backed by established and mostly binding enforcement mechanisms. Informal regulations, on the other hand, occur through other informal means such as policies and guidelines. They may not be enforced in any formal way, but relevant actors may nevertheless feel compelled to comply with them in the interests, say, of remaining in good standing with different stakeholders.[26] Instances of the formal regulation will include duly enacted statutory laws guiding particular corporate behaviour in different jurisdictions. This will include the 2008 South African Companies Act No. 71; the 1990 Nigerian Companies and Allied Matters Act, as amended (CAMA) and the 2006 UK 2006 Companies Act; the 2002 US Sarbanes-Oxley Act among others. On the other hand, the informal regulations will include the UN Global Compact, Guiding Principles on Business and Human Rights: Implementing the United Nations 'Protect, Respect and Remedy' Framework and the OECD Guidelines for MNEs, amongst others.

3.1.2 *Soft law versus hard law regulations*

Soft law regulations can be described as non-legally binding regulations usually containing the aspirational goals, lofty ideals and other best practices expected to govern or regulate certain behaviours. The importance of soft law non-legally binding regulations is underscored at international law given its state-centeredness.[27] In other words, since international law is usually seen in terms of a law of nations, with its rules and regulations only applicable to state actors (as distinct from private individuals and companies), regulations to order corporate behaviour at an international level usually take the shape of soft laws. These soft law instruments do not have the status of international treaties that are ratified by states; they include guidelines, declarations, recommendations and resolutions. Although soft law regulations are non-binding, they are particularly useful in the following ways:

CSR international implementation 89

(i) Soft laws provide official credibility and impetus for the development of complementary multi-stakeholder CSR initiatives at industry, regional or wider levels;[28]

(ii) They help to galvanize support for a particular programme or policy and can help to focus thinking about certain issues to clarify positions and to develop understanding between states;[29]

(iii) Sometimes, soft laws may harden into positive law, where they are seen as evidence of emergent new standards of international law;[30]

(iv) Soft laws also provide a quick and flexible response to contemporary challenges and allow non-state actors to participate in international law where they cannot in traditional international law making processes.[31]

On the other hand, hard law regulations are positive and legally binding regulations, with a clear and predictable enforcement mechanism, usually in domestic legislation. This regulatory method has not enjoyed wide adoption across jurisdictions in the discourse of embedding corporate social responsibility. The provisions of Section 72(4) of the South African Companies Act No. 71 of 2008 about a social and ethics committee looks promising in this regard, but its exact usefulness towards proper CSR regulation and implementation appears doubtful. Another example of hard law CSR regulation can also be made of Section 135 of the Indian Companies Act 2013 (Indian Companies Act), which requires, inter alia, the constitution of a CSR committee at the level of the board of directors of qualified Indian companies. The UK in 2002 attempted to harden CSR regulation[32] by the introduction of a Private Member sponsored bill on the subject of CSR, but it never saw the light of day. Nigeria also attempted in March 2007 to harden CSR enforcement through a bill,[33] which also never saw the light of day. The reasons for this will be addressed in Chapter 4. There is yet another pending proposed legislation before the Nigerian National Assembly that also seeks hard law regulation of CSR in Nigeria. The bill is known as the Petroleum Host and Impacted Communities Development Trust Bill, introduced in 2018 following the unbundling of the notorious Petroleum Industry Bill by the 8th National Assembly of the Federal Republic of Nigeria.

3.1.3 Private versus public regulations

Private regulation is defined as a set of norms regulating individual (corporate) conduct that did not – or at least did not originally – stem from public authorities' formal legislative powers.[34] Even from the definition, the connection with earlier-discussed soft law regulation and informal regulation becomes obvious. The concept of de-regulation, which blossomed in the 1980s fed by the belief that too much regulation affects the smooth operation of the laissez-faire market (which can self-regulate), accounts for increase in the private soft law and self-regulatory CSR regime.[35] The growing CSR private regulations (or

90   *Background, theories and global outlook*

dialogues) excluding (at least directly) state/government actors are reflexive of the increased legitimacy of private business community and actors in the global economy.[36] The regulatory initiatives under this method of regulation differ in their objectives, origins, areas covered and implementation mechanisms. For instance, some focus on general issues of human rights, labour issues, corruption, environment et cetera like the UNGC and the OECD MNE guidelines, while others focus on a particular and single aspect, say investment,[37] security[38] or forest conservation.[39] On the flip side, public regulatory regime involves governments, public and state authorities enacting formal regulations or legislations (whether domestically or with cross-border extraterritorial implications). This includes initiatives at the EU, as such initiatives usually entail participation of government representatives and the passing of resolutions and directives that member states are to adopt. For instance, the 2003 Accounts Modernization Directive[40] of the EU imposes an obligation on companies to consider non-financial matters (social and environmental matters) in the preparation of their annual reports. Another example is the Conflict Minerals Regulation 2017/821 of the European Parliament and of the Council of 17 May 2017, laying down supply chain due diligence obligations for the EU importers of tin, tantalum and tungsten, their ores and gold (3TG) originating from conflict-affected and high-risk areas and ensuring such imports meet international responsible sourcing standards, set by the OECD.

3.1.4 *International versus domestic regulations*

International regulatory initiatives are regulations operational at an intergovernmental level of international law and therefore mostly applicable (though not necessarily only) to nation states.[41] It must be appreciated at this stage that while there seems to be an international consensus for the need to regulate the businesses, queries have arisen however from using less well-recognized or road-tested mechanisms.[42] It has therefore remained difficult[43] for international law to achieve a global consensus and thus legally binding CSR regulatory and enforcement regime owing to a number of issues[44] such as national interests' considerations, the sovereign equality of states doctrine[45] and the fear of over-regulation.[46] The fear of over-regulation amongst others has resulted in the current resort to a widespread, looser regime of soft law, private initiatives and transnational regulatory dialogues to combat corporate irresponsibility and has also made the achievement of an overarching treaty almost impossible.[47] Jennifer Zerk's concern in terms of securities regulations applies in this circumstance:

> The main focus of international efforts . . . at present is on achieving greater convergence of regulatory approaches and standards and better cooperation and consultation between states to deal more effectively with cross-border regulatory problems. While no internationally binding framework is likely in the near future, international . . . organisations seem to be gaining in international standing and influence.[48]

Domestic regulations are local, municipal or national regulations based on the territorial jurisdiction of a state over people or activities located/domicile within its own territorial boundaries.[49] Jennifer Zerk drew an important distinction between cases of direct assertion of jurisdiction over the foreign conduct of individuals and companies (for instance the US Sarbanes-Oxley Act) – which represents extraterritorial jurisdiction on the one hand – and control over the conduct of foreign actors within the territory of the regulating state, which is still strictly domestic/territorial jurisdiction. In other words, where domestic and national regulatory initiatives have, geographically speaking, far reaching effects, they are still domestic measures but with extraterritorial implications.[50]

3.1.5 Principle-based versus rule-based regulations

Principle-based regulations usually contain non-prescriptive guidelines and principles. Examples are the OECD Guidelines for MNE, the UNGC et cetera. The regulatory philosophy behind many business codes of conduct and many corporate governance codes are principle-based. This also includes the 2018 Nigerian Code of Corporate Governance, issued by the Financial Reporting Council of Nigeria, to the Institute of Directors in Southern Africa, King IV Report on Governance for South Africa 2016. The rule-based regulations are the prescriptive regulatory methods containing clearly defined enforcement mechanisms and predictable remedies for victims in cases of violations. Domestic legislations with positive rules and regulations include the US 2002 Sarbanes-Oxley Act, the UK 2006 Companies Act, Indian 2013 Companies Act; the South African Companies Act No. 71 of 2008 and the Nigerian Companies and Allied Matters Act, Cap C20 Laws of Federation of Nigeria 2004. It should be noted that while principle-based regulations may be common at international regulatory dialogues for reasons explained earlier, there is nothing intrinsically connecting principle-based regime and international regulations together. Rule-based regulations contain positive rules and regulations backed by predictable enforcement mechanisms. Rule-based regulations are said to provide guidance for desired conduct in a clearer way than principle-based regulation.[51] One major reason for less adoption of and the shunning by the business community of rule-based regulatory framework such as the Sarbanes-Oxley Act in the US is the accusation that they are over-regulative, too prescriptive, intrusive, and frankly sometimes a disrespect of the other regulatory initiatives of other countries.[52]

3.1.6 Voluntary versus mandatory regulations

Voluntary regulations are optional in terms of compliance. Under CSR discussions, voluntariness appears to have been informed by two phenomena: First, the false notion that CSR is synonymous with corporate charity and second, the 'business case' argument in the CSR discourse. The idea that CSR is corporate gift or donation or representing something beyond the requirements of the law has been shown earlier[53] to be faulty, and such idea has been jettisoned in this book. This faulty notion constitutes a major factor behind the popular belief that CSR or its regulation must be on a voluntary basis. This has been, until recently, the stance of the EU on CSR and its regulatory or enforcement regimes. In 2001, the European Commission[54] defined CSR as 'a concept whereby companies integrate social and environmental concerns in their business operations and in their interaction with their stakeholders on a voluntary basis' and clarifying further that 'being socially responsible means not only fulfilling legal expectations, but also going beyond compliance and investing "more" into human capital, the environment and the relations with stakeholders'.[55] Further, the 'business case' argument of CSR appears to be the official CSR policy stance amongst many EU member states. It is argued that CSR is a voluntary concept and must be strategically shown to have some positive values, benefits and other company (shareholder)-success-related attributes before it may be embraced by the business community.[56] As a corollary of the former statement, it is also argued that the normal interplay of free market forces is the best method to regulate CSR and therefore there is no need for any hard law externalized or mandatory CSR rules. Arguably, this is the most significant disservice to the CSR conception and implementation in the world. This is partly because it appears to represent the official position of the EU (the largest economy in the world and the host community of the majority of the largest multinational enterprises in the world) and has provided the nest for the nefarious activities of many a rogue[57] company who will only fly below the radar of self-regulation and greenwash CSR. It is the submission of this author that voluntarism will likely breed mere brush-stroking and surface scratching regulatory initiatives at best, good enough only to regulate the activities of Thomas McInerney's Group A or B businesses as analyzed in the following:

> Many regulatory scholars recognize that there are four types of companies with which regulators have to deal. These four types include: those who know the law and are willing to follow it (Group A); those who do not know the law but would like to be law abiding (Group B); those who know the law and do not want to follow it (Group C); and those who do not know the law and do not wish to be law abiding (Group D). Most CSR literature does not even reflect these basics. As this analysis suggests, Group A firms are willing to comply on intrinsic grounds.[58]

From the previous quote, the relevant question is, how effective and efficient are the voluntary initiatives against Groups C and D businesses? Howsoever convincing the business case argument, together with the inherently voluntary CSR approach and the free (perfect) market forces argument may be, the voluntary regulatory initiatives will never be strong enough to secure responsible corporate behaviour.[59]

Mandatory CSR regulatory initiatives are not optional and must be complied with.

3.1.7 Internal versus external regulations

Internal regulations are insider regulations, self-generated, self-developed and self-enforced by corporate entities involved. Instances of internal regulations are systems of control in banks and insurance companies that identify transactions that are likely to be money laundering transactions. Internal regulations are said to be effective because the regulator is an insider who truly understands the exact regulatory need, and such regulations will likely not be resented by the regulated. However, it is usually advised that mere internal regulation without more – or any – recourse to any external control system hardly ever really works. It seems a smart admixture of the two or more methods (co-regulation) is usually the way to go. External regulations are regulations that are prescribed by an external body such as the state authorities and usually outside the direct fold of the business community. Externalized punitive regulations that impose penal or quasi-penal rules in order to prevent a particular aspect of behaviour, especially when used in isolation, are, however, an ineffective way of regulation. Therefore, a regulator with both degree of discretion (externalized) and with some good relationship and understanding of the business operations being regulated (insider regulator) is usually preferred by regulatory experts.

Despite the previous identification and discussions of the different regulatory methods, it is instructive to note that the usefulness of the previous categorizations in modern regulatory discourse, especially in the CSR domain, appears to be gradually whittling down; for instance, the lines between the hitherto strictly polarized voluntary and mandatory spheres are getting blurred.[60] This may not be unconnected with the discussion in Chapter 2 of the book confirming that no theoretical approach or its regulatory consequences to CSR is hardly ever perfect, completely cast in concrete. In reality, a regulatory initiative can therefore be internal, private, soft law, domestic, voluntary and principle-based all at the same time. Further, Jennifer Zerk had relatedly noted that: 'in short, the "voluntary versus mandatory" debate is based on the mistaken impression that CSR and the law are somehow separate, whereas in reality they are intertwined' and 'the crucial question is not whether CSR should be "voluntary" or "mandatory" but in light of a particular problem, what is the best regulatory response?'[61] Bryan Horrigan also confirmed that the voluntary–mandatory dichotomy is of limited use, even in accounting for how business responds to multi-order regulation, let alone understanding the 21st-century environment for CSR.[62] More often than not in recent times, therefore, regulatory initiatives indirectly combine one or more of the methods using lighter and more subtle mechanisms to demand compliance. Parker explained this using the following words:

> Meta-regulation should be about requiring organisations to implement processes . . . that are aimed at making sure they reach right results in terms of actions that impact on the world. . . . It recognises, however, that lawmakers and regulators may not know exactly what the 'right' processes, and even the right results, will look like in each situation. The people who

94 *Background, theories and global outlook*

are involved in the situation are best placed to work out the details in their own circumstances, if they can be motivated to do so responsibly.[63]

From the previous analysis, in light of the continuous blurring of traditional lines separating the various forms and methods of CSR implementation and regulation, CSR regulation in the 21st century therefore appears to thrive under both co-regulation and meta-regulatory regimes. There have been a few CSR implementation initiatives including:

(i)   Draft Code of the UN Commission on Transactional Corporations;
(ii)   UN Sub-Commission on the Protection and Promotion of Human Rights' Norms;
(iii) United Nations Global Compact;
(iv)   Organisation for Economic Cooperation and Development Guidelines for Multinational Enterprises;
(v)   Organisation for Economic Cooperation and Development Declaration on International Investment and Multinational Enterprises;
(vi)   Global Reporting Initiative;
(vii) Guiding Principles on Business and Human Rights: Implementing the United Nations 'Protect, Respect and Remedy' Framework;
(viii) International Labour Organisation Tripartite Declaration of Principles concerning Multinational Enterprises and Social Policy;
(ix)   International Standard Organisation 26000 Social Responsibility Standard;
(x)   Voluntary Principles on Security and Human Rights;
(xi)   Transparency International's Anti-Corruption Handbook amongst others;
(xii) CSR regulatory initiatives and directives at the European Union level;
(xiii) United Nations Principles for Responsible Investment.

The previously listed initiatives at the international level constitute only but a few; myriad other initiatives exist or are currently in the process of being developed. Some of these initiatives address general issues of labour rights, human rights, anti-bribery and corruption and deforestation amongst other issues,[64] and some other are more narrowly issue-specific.[65] The succeeding sections will now consider a few of these CSR implementation initiatives operated both at the intergovernmental and domestic levels. These selected initiatives are singled out and discussed in this book principally owing to their overarching nature in addressing many issues in which the business community is involved as opposed to regulatory initiatives targeted at a single matter and are considered more relevant to the corporate law perspective from which the CSR implementation is discussed in this book.

3.2 United Nations Global Compact (UNGC)

3.2.1 Background to the UNGC

The UNGC is one of the UN's galaxy of agencies with direct interest in the activities of transnational or multinational business actors.[66] UNGC is a

CSR international implementation   95

strategic policy initiative for businesses that are committed to aligning their operations and strategies with ten universally accepted principles in the area of human rights, labour, environment and anti-corruption.[67] The UNGC has the mandate of mobilizing a global movement of sustainable companies and stakeholders to create the world we want. The principles of the UNGC are as follows:

(i)   Businesses should support and respect the protection of internationally proclaimed human rights within their sphere of influence;
(ii) Make sure that they are not complicit in human rights abuses;
(iii) Businesses should uphold the freedom of association and the effective recognition of the right to collective bargaining;
(iv) The elimination of all forms of forced and compulsory labour;
(v)   The effective abolition of child labour;
(vi) Elimination of discrimination in respect of employment and occupation;
(vii) Businesses should support a precautionary approach to environmental challenges;
(viii) Undertake initiatives to promote greater environmental responsibility;
(ix) Encourage the development and diffusion of environmentally friendly technologies;
(x)   Business should work against corruption in all its forms, including extortion and bribery.

By way of history, the previously highlighted ten UNGC principles are traceable to the speech of the then Secretary-General of the United Nations, the late Kofi Annan, addressing the Davos World Economic Forum in January 2009 where he challenged the business community 'to give a human face to the global market'[68] and join a 'global compact of shared values and principles' in response to global economic unease as a result of an increasingly borderless nature of doing business. Annan argued that shared values provide a stable environment for a world market and that without these explicit values business could expect backlashes from protectionism, populism, fanaticism and terrorism.[69] Following the 1999 Davos meeting, Annan and a group of business leaders formulated nine principles, which have come to be known as the UN Global Compact. After lengthy consultation, a tenth principle against corruption was added in June 2004.[70] The ten principles of the Global Compact focus on human rights, labour rights, concern for the environment and corruption and are taken directly from commitments made by governments at the UN: the Universal Declaration of Human Rights (1948), the Rio Declaration on Environment and Development (1992), the International Labour Organization's Fundamental Principles and Rights at Work (1998) and the UN Convention Against Corruption (2003).[71]

In his speech, Annan had noted that:

The global economy will remain fragile and vulnerable – vulnerable to backlash from all the 'isms' of our post-cold-war world: protectionism;

96 *Background, theories and global outlook*

populism; nationalism; ethnic chauvinism; fanaticism; and terrorism. What all those 'isms' have in common is that they exploit the insecurity and misery of people who feel threatened or victimized by the global market. The more wretched and insecure people there are, the more those 'isms' will continue to gain ground.[72]

. . .

Many of you are big investors, employers and producers in dozens of different countries across the world. That power brings with it great opportunities – and great responsibilities. You can uphold human rights and decent labour and environmental standards directly, by your own conduct of your own business.[73]

Therefore, the UNGC principles originated as 'social safety nets'[74] in reaction to the socio-economic and political imbalances underpinning 'the new global economy'.[75] CSR within the UNGC framework is often referred to as corporate sustainability and defined as the as a company's delivery of long-term value in financial, social, environmental and ethical terms.

3.2.2 Structure of the UNGC

Unlike earlier UN attempts at regulating corporate behaviour such as the Draft Code and the Sub-Commission Norms, which were said to be rather confrontational in their approach and probably the cause of their collapse, the 2000 UNGC represents a shift that emphasizes 'cooperation' as opposed to 'confrontation' by reflecting a global public policy network and bringing together UN agencies, corporations, NGOs and labour representatives from all over the world.[76] Following the expulsion of 2,048 participants in 2011 for noncompliance with the UNGC rules, the total number of active business participants in the UNGC as of 2011 was 6,066 companies in 132 countries.[77] This number has grown, as of 30 October 2019, to 9,953 companies in 161 countries. There are 8,000 business and 4,000 non-business participants in the UNGC.[78] Therefore, UNGC provides the largest international regulatory platform for corporate responsibility in the world. The UNGC principles are a voluntary initiative based on CEO commitments to implement universal sustainability principles and to take steps to support UN goals.[79] The UNGC principles require participating businesses to communicate every year with stakeholders on their progress in integrating the ten principles. Companies that do not issue a Communication on Progress (COP) for two consecutive years face expulsion and must reapply for participation in the initiative.[80] The intention is that, through leading by the power of good example, member companies will set a high moral tone operating throughout the world.[81] Interestingly, however, the custodians of the UNGC principles state that the principles are neither a 'regulatory instrument' nor do they 'police, enforce or measure the behavior or actions of companies'.[82] According to the then Executive Director of the UNGC, Georg Kell:

The Global Compact is neither a seal of approval, nor a certification. In fact, if things go wrong and a company stands accused of violating work ers' rights or damaging the environment, their participation in the Global Compact puts arguably even more pressure on them. Because joining the Global Compact requires a public commitment, we don't hide it. And it requires follow-up, transparency, and disclosure.[83]

Therefore, perhaps, the major argument for the UNGC is its creation of a platform for consensus on what the moral and corporate responsibility should be, and participation by any corporate entity would definitely expose such business to added criticism and perhaps legal action from critics in the event of non-compliance.

3.2.3 The critique of the UNGC

An irresistible criticism of the UNGC is its so-called cooperative approach with the business community without any concrete verifiable mechanism of measuring actual compliance with the principles.[84] Although others have argued that one should not criticize the UNGC for something it never pretended or intended to be (that is, a compliance-based regulatory mechanism[85]), it is nonetheless arguable that the UNGC is tantamount to hobnobbing with corporate actors, some of which are only rogue companies with little or no intention for corporate social and environmental responsibility and accountability but only motivated by profit maximization and self-interest. How does one really explain the UNGC release of instruments with which CSR should be embedded within the business community through the activities of legal professionals such as the 2019 *Guide for General Counsel on Corporate Sustainability* Version 2.0 and yet sustain the argument that the UNGC principles do not constitute a regulatory instrument nor do they police, enforce or measure the behaviour or actions of companies? What exactly are they and of what real benefits to the sustainability discourse? In this light, Nader also noted:

> An effective United Nations must be free of corporate encumbrances. Its agencies should be the leading critics of the many ways that corporate globalization is functioning to undermine the U.N. missions to advance ecological sustainability, human rights, and global economic justice – not apologists and collaborators with the dominant corporate order.[86]

Further, the voluntary compliance and self-regulatory and self-policing nature of the UNGC without concrete mechanisms of external monitoring, verification or sanctioning[87] in its structure appears to have rendered the UNGC an 'exercise in futility' that 'provides a venue for opportunistic companies to make grandiose statements of corporate citizenship without worrying about being called to account for their actions'.[88] These opportunistic companies (willing and ready to do business regardless of elements of unlawfulness and irregularities

98 *Background, theories and global outlook*

involved) are only involved in mere participation or implementation of voluntary CSR initiatives and framework for public relations and marketing purposes as opposed to more altruistic reasons and are therefore said to be engaged in bluewashing.[89] Therefore, this kind of voluntary or self-regulatory initiative to address corporate irresponsibility will definitely provide the nest for the nefarious activities of many a rogue company who will likely fly below the radar of self-regulation. This regime will constitute mere brush-stroking and surface scratching regulatory initiatives at best, good enough only for Thomas McInerney's Group A or B businesses. In the final analysis on the subject, the fact that the UNGC is expelling companies for non-compliance is an empirical testament that a lot of rogue companies are only interested in hiding behind the blue logo of the UN and wallowing in irresponsible corporate behaviour. This is indeed what is commonly referred to as 'bluewashing'. Therefore, as a result of its wholly voluntary regime at the moment, it is not totally out of place to describe the UNGC as another mere talking shop with no capacity to provide real remedy or redress in cases of violations of stakeholder rights arising from corporate irresponsibility. The Promoters of the UNGC should consider more seriously the advice of prominent scholars and NGO leaders contained in a letter dated 20 July 2010 to Mr Annan:

> We recognize that corporate-driven globalization has significant support among governments and business. However, that support is far from universal. Your support for this ideology, as official UN policy, has the effect of delegitimizing the work and aspirations of those sectors that believe that an unregulated market is incompatible with equity and environmental sustainability. . . . Many do not agree with the assumption of the Global Compact that globalization in its current form can be made sustainable and equitable, even if accompanied by the implementation of standards for human rights, labor, and the environment. . . . We are well aware that many corporations would like nothing better than to wrap themselves in the flag of the United Nations in order to "bluewash" their public image, while at the same time avoiding significant changes to their behavior. . . . Without monitoring, the public will be no better able to assess the behavior, as opposed to the rhetoric, of corporations.[90]

3.3 The United Nations 'protect, respect and remedy' framework

3.3.1 Background to the framework

In 2005, the then-UN Secretary-General, the late Kofi Annan, appointed Professor John Ruggie of Harvard University as the Secretary-General's Special Representative on Business and Human Rights with a mandate to identify and find solutions to issues surrounding the chaotic and polarized[91] discussions about states[92] not only failing in their fundamental responsibility to protect their subjects and citizens from corporate-related human rights abuses but companies[93] also paying lip service to being responsible corporate citizens while continuing to violate human rights. Hence, Professor John Ruggie was appointed with a view to identify the issues and come up with some solutions.[94] The present framework endorsed by the Human Rights Council on 16 June 16 2011 and titled the *Guiding Principles on Business and Human Rights: Implementing the United Nations 'Protect, Respect and Remedy' Framework* (hereinafter simply called 'UNGPs')[95] is the final report of the Special Representative, Ruggie, to the Human Rights Council. The 2011 UNGPs are a culmination of the works of Ruggie from 2005 to 2011; his work evolved in three phases. Reflecting the mandate's origins in controversy, its initial duration was only two years, and it was intended mainly to 'identify and clarify' existing standards and practices.[96] In 2005, there was little that counted as shared knowledge across different stakeholder groups in the business and human rights domain. Thus, the special representative began an extensive programme of systematic research that has continued to the present. His research has been actively disseminated, including to the Human Rights Council itself. Marking phase 2, in 2007, the Human Rights Council renewed Ruggie's mandate for an additional year, inviting him to submit recommendations. The special representative observed that there were many initiatives, public and private, which touched on business and human rights. But none had reached sufficient scale to truly move markets; they existed as separate fragments that did not add up to a coherent or complementary system. One major reason has been the lack of an authoritative focal point around which the expectations and actions of relevant stakeholders could converge. Marking the third phase, in its resolution 8/7, welcoming the 'Protect, Respect and Remedy' framework, the Human Rights Council also extended Ruggie's mandate until June 2011, asking him to 'operationalize' the framework through concrete and practical implementation recommendations and leading to the 2011 UNGPs.[97] Beyond the Human Rights Council, the UNGPs have been endorsed or employed by individual governments, business enterprises and associations, civil society and workers' organizations, national human rights institutions and investors. It has been drawn upon by such multilateral institutions as the International Organization for Standardization (ISO) and the Organization for Economic Cooperation and Development (OECD) in developing their own initiatives in the business and human rights domain.[98] Apart from the intrinsic utility of the UNGPs, the large number and inclusive character of stakeholder consultations convened by and for the mandate no doubt have contributed to its widespread positive reception. Indeed, by January 2011 the mandate had held 47 international consultations, on all continents, and the Special Representative and his team had made site visits to business operations and their local stakeholders in more than 20 countries.[99]

3.3.2 Structure of the UNGPs

A succinct background of the framework is contained in the Introduction to the Guiding Principles in the 2011 final report, while the actual UNGPs are annexed to the report and contain 31 principles divided into three pillars,

100　*Background, theories and global outlook*

which are explained next. The regulatory framework of the UNGPs is embedded in and rests on the three pillars of 'Protect, Respect and Remedy' framework. These pillars appear to contribute to the debate in terms of who has what roles in the society. The UNGPs are an acknowledgement by the international community that businesses can and do in fact violate human rights either by themselves or in complicity with states. The principles are also a clarification of the relationship and respective roles played between states and the business community in promoting corporate social and environmental responsibility, sustainability and accountability. The pillars are examined in turn in the following list:

(i) *States Duty to Protect*

States must protect against human rights abuses within their territory and/or jurisdiction by third parties, including business enterprises. This requires taking appropriate steps to prevent, investigate, punish and redress such abuse through effective policies, legislation, regulations and adjudication.[100] Hence, regardless of where the injury to any stakeholder occurred, whether domestically or abroad, the state must enact policies and rules to hold violators accountable. Further, as part of the operational principles of the UNGPs and in meeting their duty to protect, states should ensure that other laws and policies governing the creation and ongoing operation of business enterprises, such as corporate law, do not constrain but enable business respect for human rights. A logical deduction from the previous is that the UNGPs clarified that there is no basis for the continued isolation of corporate law from the legal benefits derivable from other aspects of the law. Corporate law systems in different jurisdictions must be employed by states forestall cases of human rights abuses using the corporate form;

(ii) *Corporate Responsibility to Respect*

The business community should respect human rights. This means that companies should avoid infringing on the human rights of others and should address adverse human rights impacts with which they are involved. This obligation to respect human rights is applicable to all business enterprises regardless of their size, sector, operational context, ownership and structure. Nevertheless, the scale and complexity of the means through which enterprises meet that responsibility may vary according to these factors and with the severity of the enterprise's adverse human rights impacts;[101]

(iii) *Victim's Access to Remedy*

In addition to their duty to protect against corporate-related human rights abuse, states must take appropriate steps to ensure that when such abuses occur within their territory and/or jurisdiction those affected have access to effective remedy.[102] Measures towards providing remedies to victims could be judicial, administrative, legislative or other appropriate means, and the remedies may include apologies, restitution, rehabilitation, financial or non-financial compensation and punitive sanctions (whether criminal or administrative, such as fines), as well as the prevention of harm through, for example, injunctions or guarantees of non-repetition. The UNGPs also provide that, with a view to making it possible for grievances to be addressed early and remediated directly, business enterprises should establish or participate in effective operational-level grievance mechanisms for individuals and communities who may be adversely impacted.[103] This aspect of the third pillar is useful as it demonstrates that stakeholder engagement is an important element of CSR implementation.

Although the UNGPs do not explicitly require states to develop national action plans (NAPs), there is a broad agreement that NAPs, which are the government-led policy strategies outlining strategic orientation and concrete activities to address specific policy issues, comprise the key policy tool for states that want to honour their duty to protect against adverse human rights impacts by business enterprises in line with the UNGPs.[104] The UN Working Group on Business and Human Rights[105] encourages states parties to develop, enact and update an NAP on business and human rights as part of the state responsibility to disseminate and implement the principles. Therefore, while the UNGPs pillars implicitly provide guidance, the NAPs provide the mechanisms for states on how to support business in fulfilling their responsibility to protect human rights. As of September 2019, the UN Human Rights Office of the High Commissioner website[106] confirms that 22 states[107] have produced NAPs, Kenya being the latest to join in June 2019,[108] and it remains the only African country on the list. States that are in the process of or committed to developing an NAP include Argentina, Australia, Azerbaijan, Guatemala, Greece, India, Japan, Jordan, Latvia, Malaysia, Mauritius, Mexico, Mongolia, Morocco, Mozambique, Myanmar, Nicaragua, Peru, Portugal, Thailand, Uganda, Ukraine and Zambia. There is also a third category of states[109] where either their national human rights institutions (NHRIs) or civil society organizations have begun steps in the development of NAPs. The two biggest economies in Africa, South Africa[110] and Nigeria, fall within this third category.

Generally, the UNGP have been 'road-tested'[111] and are intended to constitute a 'single, logically coherent and comprehensive template' to guide the operations and activities of both the state and the business community.[112] The framework appreciates that 'one size does not fit all'[113] and therefore expects states to adopt a 'smart-mix of measures'[114] in adapting the initiatives and a due diligence exercise from the business community whereby they, on an individual basis, 'identify, prevent, mitigate and account for how'[115] they address the adverse impacts of their operations. According to Ruggie all of these three

102 *Background, theories and global outlook*

principles together 'form a complementary whole in that each supports the others in achieving sustainable progress'.[116]

3.3.3 Critique of the UNGPs

The UNGPs have clarified that:

> Nothing in these Guiding Principles should be read as creating new international law obligations, or as limiting or undermining any legal obligations a State may have undertaken or be subject to under international law with regard to human rights.[117]

The UNGPs are an overarching regulatory initiative; they have tactically stayed away from constituting a binding international regulatory mechanism and therefore will not, at least by themselves, bring corporate irresponsibility to an end.[118] For this, Sorcha MacLeod lamented that the UNGPs constitute a 'weak and disappointing culmination' of eight years of extensive research and wide multi-stakeholder consultation and are reduced only to a 'useful template'.[119] The weak nature of the UNGPs using words like 'should respect', 'should avoid' or 'should address' was berated in strong words by Amnesty International's Senior Director for International Law and Policy, Widney Brown:

> We do not believe the draft guiding principles effectively protect victims' rights or ensure their access to reparations. . . . Let's be frank – the real opposition to effective guiding principles does not come from Amnesty International but from business interests. The draft guiding principles enjoy broad support from business, precisely because they require little meaningful action by business.[120]

The UNGPs are also criticized for their categorical statement that states actually owe the primary duty to protect rights and not the business community, which is only enjoined to respect them. The statement is said to have fallen short in reality, having proceeded on a faulty assumption that all states can actually protect. As mentioned in the background section of this chapter, many companies have become more powerful and influential than groups of states put together, and advantage is usually taken by the large companies to influence and lobby weak CSR regulations, especially in less industrialized society. There are different factors responsible for the inability or reluctance of state authorities to actually protect stakeholder rights. It could be complicity of the government, such as in Burma/Myanmar where the government was instrumental in the provision of forced labour for the construction of infrastructure for a gas pipeline.[121] Also in Ecuador, a state-owned company had further compounded human rights abuses after some oil concessions were granted to US oil companies such as Texaco whose operations ravaged the environment as a result of sub-standard technology, which caused untold damage to the indigenous population.[122] Similar state complicity played out in Nigeria over the involvement of Shell in human rights abuses in the oil rich Niger-Delta region of the country.[123] There are other factors why states may not be in the position to protect rights. Especially in less industrialized economies, antipathy towards implementing what is considered 'Western ideas' and economic pressures and fear[124] of losing out on foreign investments are also responsible for states' reluctance sometimes.[125] In reality, however, the fear and predictions of capital flight do not always come true. Jennifer Zerk gave an example of the fear and predictions trailing the introduction of the 2002 US Sarbanes-Oxley Act where people had thought such would lead to massive avoidance of the US capital market, but instead investors were quoted to have only ended up just gritting their teeth and getting on with it. It can be concluded that the seemingly wide reception afforded by the UNGPs by many companies within the business community, the OECD or even the EU, should not be considered as any positive signal as a successful CSR regulatory or implementation initiative. It simply probably confirms early fears that businesses will associate their businesses with such largely voluntary soft law framework while in deeds they continue with reckless business operations with an eye on profit maximization at all costs. Despite its wide adoption, the inability of the Human Rights Council to get the business community and stakeholders to adopt the UNGPs as a binding international law instrument in form of a treaty may not be unconnected to the satisfaction of the business community and the reduction of the UNGPs to their present global template status.

3.4 OECD Guidelines for Multinational Enterprises

The Guidelines for Multinational Enterprises by the Organisation for Economic Cooperation and Development, OECD, (hereinafter simply called 'the OECD Guidelines') aim to promote the positive contributions that multinational enterprises (MNEs) can make to economic, environmental and social progress. They are an overarching cooperative agreement amongst adhering states and set out principles of globally acceptable behaviour for transnational business actors in the social and environmental sphere (such as abstaining from any improper local politics or bribery and corruption) with a view to facilitating transnational business.[126] Under the guidelines, MNEs should take fully into account established policies in the countries in which they operate and consider the views of other stakeholders.[127] In this regard, they should strive for sustainable development, encourage employment creation in the local community where it operates, uphold good governance principles, engage in stakeholder management and develop self-regulatory policies to foster good relations with stakeholders and ensure it, its supply chain, contractors and subcontractors comply with the Guidelines.[128] It is an interestingly unique corporate social responsibility and accountability implementation initiative and can be differentiated in a number of ways from counterparts at the UN level. Highlights of the background to the Guidelines are given in the following section.

104 *Background, theories and global outlook*

3.4.1 Background to the OECD Guidelines

The Guidelines were originally drafted in 1976 with two revisions, first in 2000 and then in 2011 in 'response to strategic challenges for enterprises and their stakeholders'.[129] It was reported that one major reason for the OECD Ministers creating the Guidelines was to hinder the development of stronger regulation by the developing nations and a few developed member governments – such as Canada, The Netherlands and the Scandinavian nations – and in this regard the OECD Ministers were successful, given the subsequent failure of the UN Draft Code to deliver a universally agreed binding regulatory initiative.[130] Muchlinski noted that:

> To counter these developments the OECD ministers, urged on by the US government, decided to adopt their own policy on MNEs, which it was hoped would influence the UN's attempts at 'codification' to move away from a highly regulatory position of MNE control.[131]

3.4.2 The structure of the OECD Guidelines

The Guidelines in their most current form are an element of the OECD Declaration on International Investment and Multinational Enterprises.[132] The Guidelines are unique in different respects to the UN initiatives, one such difference being that it adopts a top-down and at the same time bottom-up approach. Unlike the UNGC, for instance, which can be reduced to a mere international regulatory dialogue not requiring state participation, the Guidelines operate as a cooperative document between and amongst subscribing (adhering) states at the international level, hence top-bottom – but at the same time also encouraging and enabling domestic measures as regulatory initiatives, therefore, bottom-up approach. It is also unique because although the Guidelines are addressed to the business community, it is however the responsibility of the adhering states and governments to comply with them and therefore 'observance . . . by the enterprises is voluntary and not legally enforceable'.[133] Therefore, the Guidelines are recommendations addressed by governments to MNEs.[134] The Guidelines are

> to ensure that the operation of these enterprises are in harmony with government policies, to strengthen the basis of mutual confidence between enterprises and the societies in which they operate, to help improve the foreign investment climate and to enhance the contribution to sustainable development.[135]

It is important to note that although the Guidelines are said to be addressed to multinational enterprises (MNEs), the term 'MNE' was, however, carefully not given a specific definition and would thus generally include private, state or mixed enterprises established in more than one country and so linked that

CSR international implementation   105

they may co-ordinate their operations in various ways. While one or more of these entities may be able to exercise a significant influence over the activities of others, their degree of autonomy within the enterprise may vary widely from one multinational enterprise to another.[136]

Further, a unique procedural form of implementation is observed in the Guidelines in terms of the National Contact Points (NCPs) and the Specific Instance Procedure. In other words, the implementation of the Guidelines relies on NCPs, which are government offices (often tri-partite in structure) located in each of the 36 adhering countries (the 30 OECD member countries plus Argentina, Brazil, Chile, Estonia, Lithuania and Slovenia). The NCPs are charged with promoting the Guidelines in the national context. Following the 2000 revision, each member state was required to create an NCP for the purpose of, inter alia, monitoring the implementation of the Guidelines, promoting the Guidelines among all MNEs operating in or from its territory and contributing to the resolution of complaints. However, an NCP cannot initiate an investigation but may only mediate a resolution in response to a complaint and may only make recommendations.[137] In addition to their monitoring function, the NCPs play a crucial role in contributing to the 'resolution of issues that arise relating to implementation of the Guidelines in specific instances'[138] and this 'specific instance' grievance mechanism of the Guidelines is where their unique added value lies and a key determinant of the positive impact they can have.[139] Hence, unlike the other initiatives, the Guidelines appear to have some predictable enforcement mechanism.

3.4.3 Critique of the OECD Guidelines

The very first criticism lies in its so-called unique style. As earlier noted, the Guidelines operate within member (adhering) states, whereas the entirety of the directives and guidelines – covering varying issues including labour issues, environmental protection, taxation and human rights – which are rather vaguely couched, are directed at the business community who are non-members. In this regard, Stephen Tully noted that:

> The Guidelines endeavour to achieve an atmosphere of confidence and predictability between business, labour, governments and society. Such objectives are ill-satisfied by jargon such as 'local capacity building,' 'individual human development' and good corporate governance which are evidently directed at non-participating addressees.[140]

Second, although the Guidelines might be promising in enforcement as they encourage domestic legislations for corporate social and environmental responsibility and generally protect stakeholder rights, however, the reality is that many member states have only not lived up to the expectations of the Guidelines by passing national laws with enforceable provisions to punish corporate irresponsibility,[141] but, even where they have, the local NCPs and the Specific

106 *Background, theories and global outlook*

Instance Procedure are grossly deficient[142] as decisions from the specific instance procedures are unenforceable against defaulting companies. It would appear therefore that the real CSR implementation and regulatory mechanism of the Guidelines is probably to embarrass the defaulting company (by naming and shaming it) before its customers and stakeholders.[143]

Finally, just like the initiatives at the UN level, the OECD Guidelines constitute another soft law, self-regulatory and voluntary regulatory and enforcement initiative. Therefore, almost all the criticisms afforded under the previous headings of the UNGC and the UNGPs are applicable mutatis mutandis here. In conclusion, when compared to the CSR implementation attempts of the UN and within the EU for instance, the Guidelines seem to provide a measure of public accountability. However, the bottom line is just that the current soft law approach appears ineffective in view of resistant and recalcitrant business actors, and, without the requisite stick, it is difficult to imagine rogue companies voluntarily demonstrating and genuinely adhering to the non-legally binding declarations and directives of the OECD Guidelines.

3.5 CSR regulation in the European Union

The EU originally conceptualized CSR as essentially and inherently a voluntary idea of which regulatory and enforcement features, if at all necessary, must also be dominated by voluntarism. In 2001, the European Commission[144] defined CSR as a:

> concept whereby companies integrate social and environmental concerns in their business operations and in their interaction with their stakeholders on a voluntary basis.

further noting that:

> Being socially responsible means not only fulfilling legal expectations, but also going beyond compliance and investing 'more' into human capital, the environment and the relations with stakeholders.[145]

The previous CSR definition on a voluntary basis has been faulted on many grounds and fora. During the handover of the EU Presidency from Sweden to Spain in 2010, the following Declaration was issued:

> The European Union and its Member States should take a global lead and serve as a good example on CSR when building markets, combating corruption, safe- guarding the environment and ensuring human dignity and human rights in the workplace. The European Union is the largest economy in the world and the largest development cooperation partner. Europe hosts many of the multinational enterprises in the world. We

welcome that European employers consider it an important task to promote and take a global lead on CSR.[146]

Probably owing to the criticism of its CSR definition in 2001 in terms of a voluntary CSR, the European Parliament attempted to redeem its image by asserting the commitment of the EU to be the global 'pole of excellence' in CSR discourse:

> Due to its ambition to become a 'pole of excellence' for CSR, to its human rights tradition and commitment, its economic and moral influence, and its large network of external relations, the EU is certainly one of the best positioned actors to make a true difference in the field of business and human rights.[147]

In 2011, the Commission appreciated the need to improve its regime for undertakings' disclosure of social and environmental information and also improved its CSR conception and gave a modernized definition of CSR as 'the responsibility of enterprises for their impacts on society'.[148] Further, in 2014, as if in constant realization of its slow progression in regulating CR, the EU acknowledged the importance of businesses divulging information on sustainability such as social and environmental factors, with a view to identifying sustainability risks and increasing investor and consumer trust and adopted the Directive 2014/95/EU of the European Parliament and of the Council of 22 October 2014 amending Directive 2013/34/EU as regards disclosure of nonfinancial and diversity information by certain large undertakings and groups.[149] Legal transposition amongst member states in the EU is not expected until 2017, and the directive is clear in its adoption of the 'comply or explain' compliance mechanism.[150] It is expected that the disclosure requirements within the locally transposed laws amongst member states will play an important role in boosting private sector action and commitment towards meeting the sustainable development goals (SDGs) and the Paris Climate Agreement.[151] Much improved CSR implementation regime is indeed noticeable within the EU. As part of efforts to checking, monitoring and promoting responsible corporate social and environmental responsibility throughout global value chain system of EU companies, the EU published the text of a 'Conflict Minerals' Regulation (2017/821)[152] on 19 May 2017 in the Official Journal of the EU and entering into force 20 days after publication. The Conflict Minerals Regulation, which is applicable across the EU from 1 January 2021 and was largely inspired by the US Dodd – Frank Act (2010), aims to help stem the trade in four minerals – tin, tantalum, tungsten and gold – (otherwise referred to as the '3TG'). These minerals are particularly selected because they sometimes finance armed conflict or have been established to be subject to illegal mining or mining using forced labour. The EU Regulation therefore basically requires that affected EU importers of the respective minerals (the 3TG, whether these are in the form

108 *Background, theories and global outlook*

of mineral ores, concentrates or processed metals), need to comply with – and report on – supply chain due diligence obligations if the minerals originate (even potentially) from conflict–affected and high–risk areas. The regulation, as agreed by the EU Institutions, will ensure sustainable sourcing for more than 95% of all EU imports of the minerals, as will be covered by due diligence provisions as of 1 January 2021. Although it directly applies only to EU-established importers of the targeted minerals but companies from outside the EU will also be impacted, EU-companies will need to make sure that:

(i) The imports meet international responsible sourcing standards, set by the OECD;
(ii) Global and EU smelters and refiners of 3TG source responsibly;
(iii) The link between conflict and the illegal exploitation of minerals is broken;
(iv) An end is put to the exploitation and abuse of local communities, including mine workers and local development is supported.

The EU Commission will publish white-lists of companies that fulfil requirements set out by the Regulation, and importers that do not reach the volume-thresholds set out in Annex I of the Regulation will be exempt from due-diligence obligations.

Further improvements have also been seen in the EU CSR implementation framework as it mainstreams in its trade agreements with partners' CSR[153] together with its core values of human rights protection and consideration of (business) trade impacts on the society and the environment. Therefore, prior to concluding trade agreements, the sustainability impact assessments (SIAs) of such agreements – which would give robust analysis of the potential economic, social, human rights and environmental impacts on society, the environment, and the economy of the negotiating parties – are finalized, and complementary measures towards mitigating any negative effects are identified.[154] However, as commendable as this improved framework is, the EU policy directives and guidelines do not impose any mandatory disclosure of comprehensive information on CSR matters, nor does it give a clear guidance on the specific non-financial information to be disclosed. Therefore, beyond this disclosure, there are no known concrete monitoring or enforcement mechanisms at the level of EU to verify that the actual operations of the companies indeed comply with what has been disclosed in their annual reports. There also appears to be no clearly defined and effective monitoring or enforcement mechanism of Regulation (2017/821) such that where a member state finds an EU importer has not complied with the regulation it can indeed order the business to address the problem within a given deadline and with clearly defined consequences in the event non-compliance persists.

Therefore, despite all the lofty initiatives at the EU, especially considering the level of developments at other international and intergovernmental initiatives on CSR implementation such as the UNGPs and the OECD Guidelines, it seems that the EU may after all only be playing catch up as opposed to being a front-runner or a global pole of excellence for CSR as the European Parliament had insinuated. Further, it may also be necessary to monitor and hope that the promising resolutions of the 2014 Directive will not end up effectively abandoned like some previous EU directives such as the 5th Directive requiring member states to adopt the German two-tier board structure.[155] In any event, the EU's claim to any pole of excellence is also suspect in view of statements contained on page 6, paragraph 3.2 of its 2011 communication. In the said communication, the EU rather referred companies in member states seeking formal adoption of a CSR framework to other initiatives such the UNGC, UNGPs and ISO 26000 amongst others rather than creating a robust, effective and enforceable CSR implementation framework of its own.[156] The EU's engagement in a wholehearted adoption of the business case argument of CSR[157] remains a concern. It must be reiterated that this business case adoption is a major disservice to the CSR concept within the EU, which happens to host the largest MNEs and TNCs in the world. This impedes an effective and efficient CSR regulatory framework at the global level, and such stance will only further nest the nefarious activities of rogue companies and other companies in Groups C and D as categorized by McInerney.[158]

3.6 Domestic measures and other instances of CSR regulations

3.6.1 The United Kingdom and other EU members

The UK Corporate Responsibility Bill sought to create a government agency that will be directly and primarily responsible for coordination, regulations and enforcement of corporate sustainability activities within the UK business community and thereby institutionalize the CSR concept by way of hard law and mandatory regulation in the UK.[159] Although this bill appears abandoned now, it is still useful as there is a marked difference in approach when compared to African countries like Nigeria who also sought hard law enforcement approach to CSR.

The bill was introduced into the English Parliament in 2002 and sought to create a government agency, which will be directly and primarily responsible for coordination, regulations and enforcement of CSR activities within the UK business community and thereby institutionalize the CSR concept by way of hard law. This bill has not become legislation and appears unlikely to become one anytime soon. This would seem a demonstration that the UK has rejected any attempt to institutionalize CSR as a mandatory phenomenon within the English corporate law system. As a member of the EU, this is not a surprising development in view of the largely voluntary CSR conception at the EU. It can therefore be concluded that the UK expectedly opted for a principle-based (rather than rule-based) system of regulating corporate behaviour. The regulatory approach is based on the popular compliance or explanation doctrine[160]

110   *Background, theories and global outlook*

(comply with the rule or make an explanation for why not). The emphasis is on identifying a system that works for individual companies, rather than imposing a standard formula of corporate governance structure externally.[161]

Although its CSR framework is principle-based, on soft law basis and largely aligns with the EU strategy, the UK is nonetheless still considered a global CSR leader because of its engaging and participatory approach to CSR.[162] The UK government facilitates CSR through a distinct government department headed by designated ministry-level officials which department is known as the UK Department for Business Innovation and Skills.[163] Still a member of the EU, the UK system, in the provisions of Sections 417 and 423 amongst others of the English Companies Act 2006, is a clear implementation of the earlier mentioned Accounts Modernisation Directive[164] of the EU. There are also CSR-related provisions in other legislations in the UK. For instance, in 2000, pension funds were required to state whether and how they took account of social, environmental and ethical considerations[165] in their investment decisions. However, there was no mandatory legal obligation on them to so disclose, the requirement was merely to disclose whether they did so or not (comply or explain doctrine). Furthermore, it is interesting to note that the UK government is improving on the non-financial-matter disclosure requirements through its 2013 amendment of the 2006 English Companies Act expecting qualified companies to produce a strategic report informing their shareholders and helping them assess how the directors have discharged their duty under Section 172 of the Companies Act in actually promoting the success of the company.[166]

The previous paragraph probably also confirms that the 2002 proposed Corporate Responsibility Bill still at the House of Commons will probably never become legislation, especially if the UK remains within the EU. It is safe to summarize that the UK government encourages its business community to be involved in stakeholder engagement and to disclose on non-financial matters in statutory documents such as the strategic report. It is therefore arguable that the combined effect of: the provisions of Sections 172 and 417 (5) of the 2006 English Companies Act; the expanded non-financial matters disclosures in the strategic report from the 2013 amendment and the adoption of the enlightened shareholder value (that directors and corporate executives are enjoined to have regard to the interests of employees, local communities, customers, suppliers and other related stakeholder concerns in working for the success of the company) all appear to lead to the irresistible conclusion that the UK system is essentially principle-based and adopts a voluntary regulatory CSR approach. Expectedly, just as under the previously mentioned pension funds regime, compliance with the requirements is not mandatory but on a 'comply or explain' basis.[167]

In summing up, it is instructive to note that appearing in line with the general EU policy framework on corporate social and environmental responsibility, countries such as Denmark,[168] Sweden,[169] France and Germany[170] have enacted local legislations towards requiring non-financial reporting on CSR and integrating corporate sustainability matters within the business community. However, it should be noted that although these are domestic measures towards regulating CSR by positive local laws, the legislatures in these countries in line with the EU approach have maintained the use of general, loose and vague terms and expressions without any concrete or mandatory enforcement or other mechanisms to keep companies bound by anything they have disclosed.[171] It is observed that whilst the quantity of CSR narrative in annual reports across many jurisdictions in Europe may have increased, the quality and usefulness of information disclosed is in doubt as most companies tailor their disclosures towards enhancing shareholder value and do not demonstrate how effective CSR forms an integral part of the businesses. Further, the majority of the CSR reporting is a list of boilerplate disclosures that do not provide a meaningful discussion of potential impacts or mitigation strategies and that most companies still approach the way they communicate on governance as a box-ticking exercise.[172]

3.6.2 The United States of America (US)

The US CSR regulatory landscape is an example of effective combination of principle-based, rule-based, voluntary, mandatory, hard law and soft law regulatory methods. The regulation of corporate behaviour is largely through voluntary codes of ethical conducts and often in response to laissez-faire market forces and pressures from investors, consumers and NGOs.[173] Together with the free market regulation, CSR is facilitated by state/government agencies using enforcement strategies.[174] Against human rights abuses, CSR regulation is usually discussed in terms of the Alien Tort Claims Act.[175] While a full scale appraisal of this law is outside the corporate law purview of this book, it suffices to say that the efficacy of ATCA has been grossly undermined by recent interpretations of its ambits.[176] Therefore, the ATCA does not constitute any real succour for victims of corporate irresponsibility even in the realm of human rights. Further, enforcing the codes of conducts introduced by the 2002 Sarbanes-Oxley Act, agencies such as the US Sentencing Commission foster CSR by making evidence of a corporate 'culture of integrity' a mitigating factor in sentencing corporate crime.[177]

Further, after the financial crisis of 2007–2008, the US in 2010 passed the legislation known as the Dodd – Frank Wall Street Reform and Consumer Protection Act (commonly called 'Dodd – Frank Act') towards, inter alia, the promotion of the financial stability of the US by improving accountability and transparency in the financial system, together with ending 'too big to fail', protecting the American taxpayer by ending bailouts and requiring US-listed companies to, for instance, carry out due diligence on minerals sourced from the Democratic Republic of Congo and neighbouring countries. Section 1502 of the Dodd – Frank Wall Street Reform and Consumer Protection Act has proved a major source of inspiration for implementation of CSR regulation in other jurisdictions including within the EU. The Dodd – Frank Act

112 *Background, theories and global outlook*

actually inspired the Conflict Minerals Regulation (2017/821) in the European Union. Specifically, Section 1502 requires US stock exchange-listed companies that manufacture – or contract to manufacture – products containing conflict minerals in their supply chain to disclose annually whether any of said minerals originated in the Democratic Republic of Congo (DRC) or an adjacent country ('covered countries'). If so, reporting obligations apply, including a description of measures taken to exercise due diligence.

Accordingly, government agencies such as the Environmental Protection Agency are said to take account of internal policies in deciding on penalties;[178] the Securities and Exchange Commission (SEC) also requires the codes of ethics and evidence of implementation procedures;[179] in fact, the SEC also requires listed companies to disclose financial and non-financial information in their annual reports known as Management's Discussion and Analysis of Financial Condition and Results of Operations (MDA), and the MDA should identify and discuss key performance indicators, including non-financial performance indicators like requirements under Section 1502 of the Dodd – Frank Act, which their management uses to manage the business and which would be material to investors. Furthermore, several federal agencies including the Department of Commerce, the Department of State and the Department of Energy also endorse and facilitate CSR through explicit CSR award and training programs.[180]

As a result of the foregoing level of implementation across different government agencies and commissions, some US scholars have argued that, especially for public companies operating in the US, the codes of conduct have become 'arguably a legal necessity'.[181] Therefore, as earlier mentioned, the US framework is a smart mix of both principle-based regulatory method (free market-driven system) and at the same time rule-based method (government agencies' CSR endorsing and facilitating requirements sometimes pursuant to enactments such as the 2010 Dodd – Frank Act and the Sarbanes-Oxley Act of 2002). It could be concluded that in the US, although CSR and ethical codes are upheld as a voluntary business practice and largely regulated by the laissez-faire market forces,[182] at the same time, CSR is actively endorsed, facilitated and fostered by state authorities and agencies through indirect hard law regulatory and enforcement mechanism.[183]

3.6.3 The Indian CSR regulatory and enforcement regime

The conception of CSR under the 2013 Indian Companies Act[184] and its regulatory approach appear a little confusing. In India, it is also unclear whether or not a co-regulatory or meta-regulatory approach is intended by the drafters of the relevant CSR provisions in the Indian companies' legislation. In order to put the point in proper perspective, the relevant provisions are reproduced in the following list.

Section 135 provides:

CSR international implementation 113

135. (1) Every company having net worth of rupees five hundred crore or more or turnover of rupees one thousand crore or more or a net profit of rupees five crore or more during any financial year shall constitute a Corporate Social Responsibility Committee of the Board consisting of three or more directors, out of which at least one director shall be an independent director.

(2) the Board's report under sub-section (3) of section 134 shall disclose the composition of the Corporate Social Responsibility Committee.

(3) The Corporate Social Responsibility Committee shall,

(a) formulate and recommend to the Board, a Corporate Social Responsibility Policy which shall indicate the activities to be undertaken by the company as specified in Schedule VII;[185]

. . .

(5) The Board of every company referred to in sub-section (1) shall ensure that the company spends, in every financial year, at least two per cent of the average net profits of the company made during the three immediately preceding financial years, in pursuance of its Corporate Social Responsibility Policy:

Provided that the company shall give preference to the local area and areas around it where it operates, for spending the amount earmarked for Corporate Social Responsibility activities:

Provided further that if the company fails to spend such amount, the Board shall, in its report made under clause (o) of sub-section (3) of section 134, specify the reasons for not spending the amount.

The Indian framework appears to have adopted a CSR that focuses on corporate charity and community development (as evidenced in the 7th Schedule), and it must be noted that this is a disservice to modern conception of CSR especially as conceptualized in book.[186] As shown earlier, even within the EU where CSR implementation is still playing catch up to developments at the UN and the OECD, such a narrow definition and conception of the CSR subject has long been discarded and improved upon. Within the Indian corporate law system, it is equally interesting to note a mandatory[187] requirement and compulsory expenditure of some 2% of the company profit on some charity. Following recent international trends, one would expect that the Indian CSR initiative, having adopted a narrow conception of CSR, would only justify CSR within the Indian business community using the 'business case' argument. That is to say that CSR is voluntary and should be strategically shown to have some positive value, benefits and other company-success–related attributes before it may be embraced by the business community. Therefore, mandating CSR on one hand and insisting its practice be based on corporate charity

114 *Background, theories and global outlook*

appears incoherent and, frankly, confusing. Further, in spite of the supposed compulsory 2% spent on CSR, the Indian regime in the proviso to sub-section 5 of Section 135 of the 2013 Indian Companies Act gave an escape route for non-compliance. Therefore, the 'comply or explain' approach is accommodated as well within the system. The earlier noted incoherence has largely informed the author's conclusion that the Indian CSR regulatory and enforcement lacks a clear, consistent policy framework grounded in a clearly ascertainable ideological basis. The regime is relatively new and yet to be properly tested for success in promoting sustainable development and effective corporate responsibility practice in India. Very importantly, it must be noted from the previous that the Indian CSR regulatory approach has a similarity with regulatory approach under an aborted 2007 Nigerian CSR bill; they both specify that a certain percentage of the corporate revenue be spent on CSR activities. However, there are a few differences, which will be considered in Chapter 4.

3.6.4 Indirect contractual CSR enforcement

Finally, in concluding domestic measures at enforcing CSR, a trend has also been observed for enlightened governments and companies alike to incorporate CSR commitments in contractual terms and conditions they set out for their contractors and suppliers similar to the practice as discussed within the EU.[188] These corporate social and environmental responsibility contractual clauses are provisions in business contracts that cover social and environmental issues that are not directly connected to the subject matter of the specific contract.[189] Hence the clauses may not specify the physical quality of goods to be delivered or describe the nature the service to be rendered but rather prescribe how parties should generally behave when conducting business.[190] This indirect CSR enforcement has become widespread and quite effective,[191] but the ready criticism of the trend is that it is too soft and may only be useful within a set of enlightened business communities and governments.[192] Will rogue business actors willingly subscribe to such commitment on a voluntary basis?

3.7 Chapter summary

This chapter gave a background to the problem of corporate irresponsibility within the business community and underscored the perceived antagonism of the business community to CSR implementation largely labelling such attempts as over-regulation. It explained that, at some point, CSR was taken as a mere conception to manage reputation in the public sphere without real or genuine corresponding commitment to CSR values. It further explained that while CSR might have begun in terms of humanitarian gestures and ad hoc community development, corporate failures and scandals such as the Enron collapse raised the bar of societal expectations from businesses. Therefore, CSR activities hinged on corporate philanthropy or 'giving back to the society' or other activities done 'beyond the requirements of the law' became suspect.

CSR international implementation 115

Corporate greenwashing and bluewashing became rampant. When it became clear that the bar had been raised and that NGOs like Amnesty International had become effective watchdogs, the business community, on its own, – in fear of possibility of strong, mandatory hard law regulations from governments – came up with self-regulatory CSR initiatives. This also increased the number of governance codes, international regulatory dialogues, several guidelines, and other soft law initiatives. The chapter examined various CSR implementation attempts at the global (the United Nations, Organisation for Economic Cooperation and Development and the European Union) and domestic (UK, USA and India) levels. The recurring themes of voluntarism, self-regulation and soft law approach to CSR regulation were highlighted and, in many instances, lamented. Many CSR implementation attempts at the international level ended up being exercises in futility, mere talking shops (such as the Draft Code of the UN Commission on Transnational Corporations and the UN Sub-Commission on the Protection and Promotion of Human Rights' Norms) or otherwise simply reduced to avoidable business templates (the UNGPs). The chapter underscored a few policy innovations and advancements recorded at the level of the EU yet was very critical about the undue and unwarranted voluntarist CSR approach at the EU level, which was considered dangerous in light of how important the EU is to the world economy, being the host to the largest corporations of the world. While relevant lessons are extracted in a subsequent chapter in this book, especially in relation to the policy innovations, this chapter nonetheless lamented the recurrent theme of soft law, self-regulatory and voluntarist strategies adopted for CSR implementation within the examined international regulatory dialogues.

Notes

1 It has been shown in Chapter 1 that CSR is not about how surplus profit is given away as corporate charity but rather how profit is made responsibly in the course of business operations, having properly managed the social, economic, legal and environmental impacts involved in the process of making such profit. See, generally, Doreen McBarnet, 'Corporate Social Responsibility, Beyond Law, through Law, For Law: The New Corporate Accountability' in Doreen McBarnet, Aurora Voiculescu and Tom Campbell (eds.), *The New Corporate Accountability: Corporate Social Responsibility and the Law* (Cambridge: Cambridge University Press 2007).

2 Stephen Tully, *International Corporate Legal Responsibility* (Alphen aan de Rijn: Wolters Kluwer 2012) 13; Sorcha MacLeod, *Towards Normative Transformation: Reconceptualising Business and Human Rights* (Unpublished, PhD thesis submitted to the University of Glasgow, UK, 2012) 48 available at: http://theses.gla.ac.uk/3714/1/2012macleodphd.pdf accessed 31 October 2019.

3 See discussions in Section 2.3.1 of Chapter 2.

4 See discussions in Section 2.3.2 of Chapter 2.

5 MacLeod (n 2) 79.

6 Clive Crook, 'The Good Company: A Survey of Corporate Social Responsibility' *The Economist* (22 January, 2005) 14, 16.

7 Even foremost advocates of the shareholder primacy model such as Milton Friedman advocate that businesses must operate 'within the rules of the game'. See Milton

116 *Background, theories and global outlook*

Friedman, *Capitalism and Freedom* (40th anniversary edn, Chicago: University of Chicago Press 2002) 133; Judd F. Sneirson, 'Shareholder Primacy and Corporate Compliance' (2015) 26 *Fordham Environmental Law Journal* 1, 4, 5 *et seq*.

8 Tineke Lambooy, *Corporate Social Responsibility: Legal and Semi-Legal Frameworks Supporting CSR Developments 2000–2010 and Case Studies* (Dissertation and Commercial Edition in IVOR Series, Leiden: Kluwer 2010) 251 fn 93.

9 Janet Dine, *The Governance of Corporate Groups* (New York: Cambridge University Press, 2000) 129; see also Ian Ayres and John Braithwaite, *Responsive Regulation* (Oxford: Oxford University Press 1992) 25; see also Bryan Horrigan, *Corporate Social Responsibility in the 21st Century: Debates, Models and Practices across Government, Law and Business* (Cheltenham, UK: Edward Elgar 2010) 65.

10 MacLeod (n 2) 62.

11 UN Press Release SG/SM/6881, Secretary-General Proposes Global Compact on Human Rights, Labour, Environment in Address to World Economic Forum in Davos, Text of Speech by Kofi Annan, 1 February 1999, 1 available at: www.un.org/News/Press/docs/1999/19990201.sgsm6881.html last accessed 28 October 2019.

12 John Ruggie, Final Report of the Special Representative of the Secretary-General on the issue of human rights and transnational corporations and other business enterprises, 'Guiding Principles on Business and Human Rights: Implementing the United Nations' 'Protect, Respect and Remedy ' Framework,' A/HRC/17/31, 21 March 2011 available at: www.ohchr.org/documents/issues/business/A.HRC.17.31.pdf accessed 28 October 2019.

13 OECD, *OECD Guidelines for Multinational Enterprises* (Paris: OECD Publishing 2011) available at: http://dx.doi.org/10.1787/9789264115415-en and also www.oecd.org/corporate/mne/48004323.pdf accessed 28 October 2019.

14 John Ruggie, 'Reconstituting the Global Public Domain: Issues, Actors, and Practices' (2004) 10 (4) *European Journal of International Relations* 499.

15 Brian Cheffins, *Company Law* (Oxford: Clarendon Press 1997) 125; see also Horrigan (n 9) 65; see also generally, MacLeod (n 2).

16 MacLeod (n 2) 75.

17 This occurs where the business community appears only to be complying with the codes, just for the sake of compliance, without embedding code requirements as a corporate culture or making them part of the so-called DNA of the company. This would entail fake integrated reporting, faux CSR and empty stakeholder protection activities. See Miriam Cherry, 'The Law and Economics of Corporate Social Responsibility and Greenwashing' (2014) 14 *University of California Davis Business Law Journal* 281–303; Miriam A.M. Cherry and Judd F. Sneirson, 'Chevron, Greenwashing, and the Myth of "Green Oil Companies"' (2012) 3 *Washington and Lee Journal of Energy, Climate and the Environment* 133–140, 141.

18 McBarnet (n 1) 15.

19 John Farrar, *Corporate Governance: Theories, Principles and Practice* (3rd edn, Melbourne: Oxford University Press 2008) 502; see also Andrew Keay, 'Stakeholder Theory in Corporate Law: Has It Got What It Takes?' (2010) 9 *Richmond Journal of Global Law and Business* 249, 251 (hereinafter simply 'Keay Stakeholder Theory').

20 For earlier arguments, see Nojeem Amodu, 'Regulation and Enforcement of Corporate Social Responsibility in Corporate Nigeria' (2017) 61 *Journal of African Law* 105.

21 Horrigan (n 9) 60.

22 Ibid.

23 Lambooy (n 8) 260.

24 Jennifer Zerk, 'Extraterritorial Jurisdiction: Lessons for Business and Human Rights Sphere from Six Regulatory Areas' (Corporate Social Responsibility Initiative Working Paper No. 59, Cambridge, MA: John F Kennedy School of Government, Harvard University 2010) 82.

25 The list provided is far from exhaustive because there are other methods. For instance, see the categorization of Jennifer Zerk into: Direct Extraterritorial Jurisdictional Regulations and Domestic Measures with Extraterritorial Implications.

26 Zerk (n 24) 16.

27 Horrigan (n 9) 169.

28 Ibid.

29 Jennifer Zerk, *Multinationals and Corporate Social Responsibility: Limitations and Opportunities in International Law* (Cambridge: Cambridge University Press 2006) 70–71.

30 Peter Muchlinski, 'Corporate Social Responsibility and International Law: The Case of Human Rights and Multinational Enterprises' in D. McBarnet, A. Voiculescu and T. Campbell (eds.), *The New Corporate Accountability: Corporate Social Responsibility and The Law* (Cambridge: Cambridge University Press 2007) 431, 456–458.

31 Charlotte Villiers, 'Corporate Law, Corporate Power and Corporate Social Responsibility' in Nina Boeger, Rachel Murray and Charlotte Villiers (eds.), *Perspectives on Corporate Social Responsibility* (Cheltenham: Edward Elgar 2008) 101.

32 See the English Corporate Responsibility Act 2002, A bill to make provision for certain companies to produce and publish reports on environmental, social and economic and financial matters; to require those companies to consult on certain proposed operations; to specify certain duties and liabilities of directors; to establish and provide for the functions of the Corporate Responsibility Board; to provide for remedies for aggrieved persons and for related purposes. It was presented by Linda Perham, supported by Mr Barry Sheerman, Mr Tony Colman, Mr Frank Field, Mr Martin O'Neill, Mr Tony Banks, Sue Doughty, Mr Simon Thomas, Glenda Jackson, Mrs Jackie Lawrence, Sir Teddy Taylor and Mr John Horam available at: https://publications.parliament.uk/pa/cm200102/cmbills/145/2002145.pdf accessed 31 October 2019.

33 A bill for an act to provide for the Establishment of the Corporate Social Responsibility Commission, introduced by the late Senator Uche Chwukwumerije.

34 Lambooy (n 8) 229.

35 Ibid. 234.

36 Ibid.

37 United Nations Principles for Responsible Investment, available at: www.unpri.org accessed 31 October 2019.

38 The Voluntary Principles on Security and Human Rights developed by the governments, NGOs and companies operating in the extractive and energy sector; see available at: www.voluntaryprinciples.org accessed 31 October 2019.

39 The Forest Stewardship Council set up a sustainably harvested timber certification programme, see available at: https://us.fsc.org/en-us accessed 31 October 2019.

40 Council Directive, 2003/51/EC, 18 June 2003 amending Directives 78/660/EEC, 83/635/EEC and 91/674/EEC on the annual and consolidated accounts of certain types of companies, banks and other financial institutions and insurance undertakings, OJ L178/16, 2003; see also The Directive 2014/95/EU on Disclosure of Non-Financial and Diversity Information by Certain Large Undertakings and Groups, available at: http://eur-lex.europa.eu/legal-content/EN/TXT/?uri=CELEX:32014L0095 accessed 31 October 2019.

41 MacLeod (n 2) 127; see also Horrigan (n 9) 168, 169.

42 See for instance, the Obama administration's 'Brief for the United States as Amicus Curiae' filed in the case of *Morrison v. National Australia Bank*, 547 F 3d 167 (2d Cir.2008) cited by Zerk (n 24) 71.

43 For instance, earlier CSR regulatory attempts by the United Nations with the aim of producing an international legally binding treaty through the instrumentality of the Draft Code of the UN Commission on Transactional Corporations (hereinafter simply 'UN Draft Code') and the UN Sub-Commission on the Protection and Promotion of Human Rights' Norms (hereinafter simply 'UN Sub-Commission Norms') both

118 *Background, theories and global outlook*

resulted in a failure to agree on a unified approach to CSR standards, and ultimately the two projects collapsed, although for different reasons. The Draft code was said to have collapsed for political reasons as developing countries played the card of their fledging sovereignty while the UN Sub-Commission Norms were said to have proposed a regulatory regime contrary to international law. For further discussions, see MacLeod (n 2) Chapter 3 thereof.

44 Because of the interplay of these issues, some of the earlier regulatory attempts at international law level were turned into 'a forum for a shouting match'. See Seymour J. Rubin, 'Transnational Corporations and International Codes of Conduct: A Study of the Relationship between International Legal Cooperation and Economic Development' (1995) 10 (4) *America University Journal of International Law and Policy* 1275, 1276; Seymour J. Rubin, 'Transnational Corporations and International Codes of Conduct: A Study of the Relationship between International Legal Cooperation and Economic Development' (Symposium: Codes of Conduct for Transnational Corporations)' (1981) 30 *American University Law Review* 903–921.

45 See the Charter of the United Nations, Article 2(1) and a corollary principle that no state may interfere in the domestic affairs of another state. See, generally, the Declaration on Principles of International Law Concerning Friendly Relations and Cooperation Among States in Accordance with the Charter of the United Nations, UNGA/Res/2625/(XXV): 'No State or group of States has the right to intervene, directly or indirectly, for any reason whatever, in the internal or external affairs of any other state'.

46 Zerk (n 24) 67, 68.

47 Nicola Jagers, 'Access to Justice for Victims of Corporate-Related Human Rights Abuse: An Echternach-Procession' (2015) 33 *Netherlands Quarterly of Human Rights* 269–273.

48 Zerk (n 24) 75.

49 Ibid. 26.

50 Ibid. 15. After the Enron collapse, the US regulatory regime has been more inclined towards a rule-based approach (e.g., the introduction of the pro-active 2002 Sarbanes-Oxley Act), which is not only highly prescriptive but also has far-reaching extraterritorial implications. This has been criticized as overregulating the American regulatory framework. The fine distinction captured in this section is significant to the book, especially in relation to the proposals in Chapter 7.

51 Lambooy (n 8) 261.

52 Zerk (n 24) 66, 67.

53 McBarnet (n 1) 1, 18.

54 European Union, 'Communication of European Union Country's Commission Green Paper on Promoting a European Framework for Corporate Social Responsibility' COM (2001) 366 Final (July 18, 2001).

55 Ibid. 6; in 2011, the Commission appreciated the need to improve its regime for undertaking disclosure of social and environmental information and also improved its CSR conception and therefore gave a modernized definition of CSR as 'the responsibility of enterprises for their impacts on society'. See European Commission, Communication from the Commission to the European Parliament, the Council, the European Economic and Social Committee and the Committee of Regions, A Renewed EU strategy 2011–14 for Corporate Social Responsibility, COM (2011) 681 final (Brussels 25th October, 2011).

56 MacLeod (n 2) 257; Richard Smerdon, *A Practical Guide to Corporate Governance* (3rd edn, London: Sweet & Maxwell 2007) 436.

57 Towards maximizing shareholder wealth, many rogue businesses (regardless of where they are domiciled anywhere in the world) are willing and ready to do business regardless of elements of unlawfulness and irregularities involved. See, for instance, Report of the Panel of Experts on the Illegal Exploitation of Natural Resources and other Forms of Wealth of the Democratic Republic of Congo, 12 April 2001, S/2001/357 available

at: www.natural-resources.org/minerals/CD/docs/other/357e.pdf at 42, para.215 accessed 6 July 2015.

58 Thomas McInerney, 'Putting Regulation before Responsibility: Towards Binding Norms of Corporate Social Responsibility' (2007) 40 *Cornell International Law Journal* 171–200, 185.

59 Olivier de Schutter, 'Corporate Social Responsibility European Style' (2008) 14 *European Law Journal* 203–236.

60 Horrigan (n 9) 57; Tom Hadden, *Company Law and Capitalism* (2nd edn, London: Weidenfeld and Nicolson 1977) 496, 497.

61 Zerk (n 24) 34–36.

62 Horrigan (n 9) 66; see also MacLeod (n 2) 302.

63 Olufemi Amao, 'Mandating Corporate Social Responsibility: Emerging Trends in Nigeria' (2008) 6 *Journal of Commonwealth Law and Legal Education* 75, 79 citing Christine Parker, 'Meta-Regulation: Legal Accountability for Corporate Social Responsibility?' in Doreen McBarnet, Aurora Voiculescu and Tom Campbell (eds.), *The New Corporate Accountability: Corporate Social Responsibility and the Law* (Cambridge: Cambridge University Press 2007) 207–237.

64 For instance, the UN Global Compact and the OECD Guidelines for MNEs.

65 For instance, Voluntary Principles on Security and Human Rights.

66 Tagi Sagafi-nejad and John H. Dunning, *The UN and Transnational Corporations* (Bloomington: Indiana University Press 2008) 175; Smerdon (n 56) 464.

67 United Nations Global Compact available at: www.unglobalcompact.org accessed 31 October 2019.

68 UN Press Release SG/SM/6881, Secretary-General Proposes Global Compact on Human Rights, Labour, Environment in Address to World Economic Forum in Davos, Text of Speech by Kofi Annan, 1 February 1999, at 1 available at: www.un.org/News/Press/docs/1999/19990201.sgsm6881.html accessed 31 October 2019.

69 Kofi Annan, 'Business and the UN: A Global Compact of Shared Values and Principles' 31 January 1999, World Economic Forum, Davos, Switzerland, Reprinted in *Vital Speeches of the Day* 65(9) (15 February 1999) 260–261; Sandrine Tester and Georg Kell, *The United Nations and Business* (New York: St. Martin's Press 2000) 51.

70 Annan (n 69) 260–261.

71 Ibid.

72 Annan (n 68) 4.

73 Ibid. 3, 4.

74 Ibid. 1

75 Ibid. 1, 2.

76 Andreas Rasche, 'Toward a Model to Compare and Analyze Accountability Standards: The Case of the UN Global Compact' (2009) 16 *Corporate Social Responsibility and Environmental Management* 192–205, 200.

77 UNGC, Number of Expelled Companies Reaches 2,000 as Global Compact Strengthens Disclosure Framework' (New York, 20 January 2011) available at: www.unglobalcompact.org/news/95-01-20-2011 last accessed 29 June 2015.

78 UNGC website, www.unglobalcompact.org/what-is-gc/participants last accessed 29 June 2015.

79 UNGC website, www.unglobalcompact.org/about/governance last accessed 29 June 2015.

80 UNGC, 'Number of Expelled Companies Reaches 2,000 as Global Compact Strengthens Disclosure Framework' (New York, 20 January 2011) available at: www.unglobalcompact.org/news/95-01-20-2011 accessed 29 June 2015.

81 See also, for instance, the 2019 *Guide for General Counsel on Corporate Sustainability* Version 2.0 designed to help legal professionals drive change and become leaders in embedding sustainability into their companies' strategies and operations. The guidance issued by the UNGC basically helps general counsel to advance the CSR agenda and

120   *Background, theories and global outlook*

make their companies behave responsibly. This latest 2019 version replaces the 2015 version available at: www.unglobalcompact.org/library/1351 last accessed 9 November 2019.

82 UN Global Compact, 'The UN Global Compact Operational Guide for Medium-Scale Enterprises,' July 2007 available at: www.unglobalcompact.org/docs/news_events/8.1/Operational_guide_ME.pdf at 3 accessed 29 June 2015.

83 Thalif Deen, 'Q & A: Bluewashing Has Become a Very Risky Business' *Inter Press Service* (3 June 2010) Thalif Deen interviews Georg Kell available at: www.unglobalcompact. org/docs/news_events/in_the_media/IPS_3.6.10.pdf accessed 31 October 2019.

84 MacLeod (n 2) 194.

85 Andreas Rasche, 'A Necessary Supplement': What the United Nations Global Compact Is and Is Not' (2009) 48 *Business & Society* 511–537, 524.

86 Ralph Nader, 'Corporations and The UN: Nike and Others "Bluewash" Their Images' *San Francisco Bay Guardian* (18 September, 2000) cited in MacLeod (n 2) 190.

87 MacLeod (n 2) 262.

88 Interview with S. Prakash Sethi, 'Global Compact Is Another Exercise in Futility' *Financial Express* (7 September 2003) available at: www.financialexpress.com/news/global-compact-is-another-exercise-in-futility/91447/0 accessed 31 October 2019; see also, Charlotte Villiers, 'Corporate Law, Corporate Power and Corporate Social Responsibility' in Nina Boeger, Rachel Murray and Charlotte Villiers (eds.), *Perspectives on Corporate Social Responsibility* (Cheltenham: Edward Elgar 2008) 101.

89 MacLeod (n 2) 64; see also Smerdon (n 56) 441. To this end, Richard anticipated that in the near future relevant organizations and governments will eventually impose on companies concrete and verifiable action that matches many of their publicized words.

90 Letter to Kofi Annan, Secretary-General, United Nations, 20 July 2000, from: Upendra Baxi, Professor of Law, University of Warwick, UK, and former Vice Chancellor University of Delhi (India): Roberto Bissio, Third World Institute (Uruguay): Thilo Bode, Executive Director, Greenpeace International (Netherlands); Walden Bello, Director, Focus on the Global South (Thailand); John Cavanach, Director, Institute for Policy Studies (US); Susan George, Associate Director, Transnational Institute (Netherlands); Oliver Hoedeman, Corporate Europe Observatory (Netherlands); Joshua Karliner, Executive Director, Transnational Resources and Action Center (US); Martin Khor, Director, Third World Network (Malaysia); Miloon Kothari, Coordinator International NGO Committee on Human Rights in Trade and Investment (India); Smitu Kothari, President, International Group for Grassroots Initiatives (India); Sara Larrain, Coordinator, Chile Sustentable (Chile); Jerry Mander, Director, International Forum on Globalization (US); Ward Morehouse, Director, Program on Corporations, Law and Democracy (US); Atila Roque, Programme Coordinator, Brazilian Institute of Economic and Social Analysis (Brazil); Elisabeth Sterken, National Director INFACT Canada/IBFAN North America; Yash Tandon, Director, International South Group Network (Zimbabwe); Vickey Tauli-Corpuz, Coordinator, Tebtebba (Indigenous Peoples' International Centre for Policy Research and Education), and Asia Indigenous Women's Network (Philippines); Etienne Vernet, Food and Agriculture Campaigner Ecoropa (France).

91 See for instance, David Kinley and Rachel Chambers, 'The UN Human Rights Norms for Corporations: The Private Implications of Public International Law' (2006) 6 (3) *Human Rights Law Review* 447–497 available at: http://hrlr.oxfordjournals.org/content/6/3/447.abstract accessed 24 September 2019.

92 In *Velasquez Rodriguez v. Honduras* (1988) Inter-Am Court HR (Ser. C) No. 4, the Inter-American Court of Human Rights ('IACHR') found as a fact that the Government of Honduras had a policy of carrying out or tolerating disappearances of more than 100 persons between 1981 and 1984, and therefore held that the Honduran Government was liable for a human rights violation that is initially not directly imputable to a state but can lead to international responsibility of the state 'not because of the act

itself, but because of the lack of due diligence to prevent the violation or to respond to it'.

93 See, for instance, the case of Blackwater USA, which was caught in a scandal of egregious human rights violations by its operatives involved in a massacre of civilians in Nisour Square in Iraq. Blackwater was a member of the International Peace Operators Association, IPOA (later known as the International Stability Operations Association) and subject to that organization's internal code of conduct. Despite its so-called commitment to due process and diligence, the company simply refused to submit to scrutiny processes. The company instead left IPOA, changed its name to Xe and continues to win US government contracts to operate in Iraq. See A. Cole, 'Blackwater Quits Security Association' *Wall Street Journal* (11 October 2007) available at: http://online. wsj.com/article/ SB119207104012555696.html accessed 15 September 2019; see also, Sorcha MacLeod, 'The Role of International Regulatory Initiatives on Business and Human Rights for Holding Private Military and Security Companies to Account' in F. Francioni and N. Ronzitti (eds.), *War By Contract: Human Rights, Humanitarian Law and Private Contractors* (Oxford: Oxford University Press 2011) 343–361. See also the matter involving Afrimex UK Limited who was not only found complicit (within its supply chain system) in the use of child labour and forced labour in mines within the Congo conflict zone but also could not controvert allegations that the company (Afrimex) spurred tensions in the Congo conflict by paying 'taxes' to rebel forces. See generally, *Final Statement by the UK National Contact Point for the OECD Guidelines for Multinational Enterprises: Afrimex (UK) Ltd, 28 August 2008.*

94 Human Rights Council Resolution 2005/69, Human rights and transnational corporations and other business enterprises, 20 April 2005.

95 John Ruggie, 'Report of the Special Representative of the Secretary General on the Issue of Human Rights and Transnational Corporations and Other Business Enterprises: Guiding Principles on Business and Human Rights: Implementing the United Nations' Protect, Respect and Remedy Framework' A/HRC/17/31, 21 March 2011 ('UNGPs').

96 OECD, *OECD Guidelines for Multinational Enterprises* (Paris: OECD Publishing 2011); see Introduction to the UNGPs, para 4.

97 Introduction to UNGPs para 9.

98 Introduction to the UNGPs, para 7.

99 Introduction to UNGPs para 8.

100 UNGPs Principle 1.

101 Ibid. 14.

102 Ibid. 25.

103 Ibid. 29.

104 Beata Faracik, *Implementation of the UN Guiding Principles on Business and Human Rights* (Policy Department, Directorate-General for External Policies, Belgium: European Union 2017) 21. However, the Human Rights Council in its Resolution 26/22 adopted at the 39th meeting of 27 June 2014 encouraged all states to take steps to implement the Guiding Principles, including to develop national action plans on business and human rights or other frameworks and to submit annual reports on the implementation of their commitments. Available at: www.right-docs.org/doc/a-hrc-res-26-22/ accessed 31 October 2019.

105 In its Resolution 17/4 (2011), the Hunan Rights Council created and mandated the UN Working Group on the issue of human rights and transnational corporations and other business enterprises (UN Working Group) to, inter alia identify, exchange and promote good practices and lessons learned on the implementation of the Guiding Principles and to assess and make recommendations thereon. The group should also provide support for efforts to promote capacity-building and the use of the Guiding Principles, as well as, upon request, to provide advice and recommendations regarding the development of domestic legislation and policies relating to business and human rights.

122 Background, theories and global outlook

See generally, the UN Working Group on the issue of human rights and transnational corporations and other business enterprises website available at: www.ohchr.org/EN/Issues/Business/Pages/WGHRandtransnationalcorporationsandotherbusiness.asp accessed 31 October 2019.

106 See The Office of the High Commissioner for Human Rights website, www.ohchr.org/EN/Issues/Business/Pages/NationalActionPlans.aspx accessed 31 October 2019.

107 The UK – launched September 2013, updated May 2016; The Netherlands – launched December 2013; Denmark – launched April 2014; Finland – launched October 2014; Lithuania – launched February 2015; Sweden – launched August 2015; Norway – launched October 2015; Colombia – launched December 2015; Switzerland – launched December 2016; Italy – launched December 2016; USA – launched December 2016; Germany – launched December 2016; France – launched April 2017; Poland – launched May 2017; Spain – launched July 2017; Belgium – July 2017; Chile – July 2017; Czech Republic – launched October 2017; Ireland – launched November 2017; Luxembourg; Republic of Slovenia – launched November 2018; Kenya – launched June 2019.

108 The Kenyan National Action Plan Is available at: http://nap.knchr.org/Portals/0/2019%20FINAL%20BHR%20NAP%20JUNE%20PDF.pdf accessed 31 October 2019.

109 They include: Ghana, Indonesia, Kazakhstan, Nigeria, Republic of Korea, South Africa, Tanzania, and The Philippines.

110 The national human rights institution (NHRI) in South Africa, the South African Human Rights Commission (SAHRC), adopted the programmatic theme of business and human rights as its key strategic focus area in the 2014/15 financial year. Since then, the Commission has undertaken several capacity building programmes in an attempt to ensure that adequate legal frameworks in respect to human rights in business activities exist. For instance, in March 2015, the Commission launched a Human Rights and Business Country Guide on South Africa to sensitize business to key human rights shortcomings in South Africa.

111 Introduction to the UNGPs para 11.

112 Introduction to UNGPs para 14.

113 Ibid. para 15.

114 Commentary to Principle 3 of the UNGPs.

115 UNGPs Principle 17.

116 John Gerrard Ruggie, 'Protect, Respect, and Remedy: The UN Framework for Business and Human Rights' in Mashood A. Baderin and Manisuli Ssenyonjo (eds.), *International Human Rights Law: Six Decades after the UDHR and Beyond* (Surrey: Ashgate 2010) 528.

117 UNGPs, General Principles.

118 General Principles UNGPs at 5 para. 13.

119 MacLeod (n 2) 142; see also Ole Kristian Fauchald and Jo Stigen, 'Corporate Responsibility before International Institutions' (2009) 40 *The George Washington International Law Review* 1025, 1027.

120 See the robust exchange between Ruggie and Widney Brown: JG Ruggie, Letter to the *Financial Times*, 'Bizarre Response by Human Rights Groups to UN Framework Plan' *Financial Times* (19 January 2011); Widney Brown, Letter to the *Financial Times*, 'Stronger UN Draft on Human Rights Abuses Needed' *Financial Times* (20 January 2011).

121 UNOCAL litigation, California, USA: *John Doe et al. v. Unocal Corp et al.* 963 F. Supp. 880 (March 25 1997); 27 F. Supp. 2d 1174 (November 18 1998); *Doe v. Unocal* 963 F. Supp. 880 (C.D. Cal. 1997) (Unocal I), 110 F. Supp. 2d 1294 (C.D. Cal 2000) (Unocal II), on appeal, 2002 WL 31063976 (9th Cir. 2002).

122 Sorcha MacLeod, 'Maria Aguinda v. Texaco Inc.: Defining the Limits of Liability for Human Rights Violations Resulting from Environmental Degradation' (1999) 2 *Contemporary Issues in Law* 189–209.

123 McBarnet (n 1) 7, 8, 9 *et seq*; see also, US District Court, New York, *Wiwa v. Royal Dutch Petroleum (Shell)*, 28 February 2002, LEXIS 3293.

124 Zerk (n 24) 88 citing A. Giles, 'SOX: What Does It Mean for UK Companies?' quoting the Chairman of UK telecommunications firm BT.

125 MacLeod (n 2) 167; see also Lambooy (n 8) 233.

126 Organization for Economic Co-Operation and Development, Declaration on International Investment and Multinational Enterprises (1979), Cmnd. 6525.

127 OECD, *OECD Guidelines for Multinational Enterprises* (Paris: OECD Publishing 2011) (hereinafter simply 'OECD Guidelines').

128 OECD Guidelines II (1–15).

129 OECD Guidelines, Preface at para 5.

130 Muchlinski (n 30) 578.

131 Ibid.

132 OECD, OECD Declaration on International Investment and Multinational Enterprises, of 21 June 1976, C (76)99(Final) (OECD, Paris, 1976) as amended in 2000: The OECD Guidelines for Multinational Enterprises: Text, Commentary and Clarifications DAFFE/IME/WPG (2000)15/FINAL, 31st October 2001; as amended in 2011: OECD Guidelines for Multinational Enterprises: Recommendations for Responsible Business Conduct in a Global Context, 25 May 2011, cited in MacLeod (n 2) 18.

133 OECD Guidelines Guideline I (1).

134 OECD Guidelines Preface, 13.

135 Ibid.

136 Ibid. Guideline I (4).

137 MacLeod (n 2) 213.

138 OECD Guidelines, para 1.

139 OECD Watch, '10 Years On: Assessing the Contribution of the OECD Guidelines for Multinational Enterprises to Responsible Business Conduct' *OECD Watch*, June 2010, 6 available at: http://oecdwatch.org/publicationsen/Publication_3550 accessed 1 July 2015 at 21.

140 Stephen Tully, 'The 2000 Review of the OECD Guidelines for Multinational Enterprises' (2001) 50 *ICLQ* 394–404, 403.

141 MacLeod (n 2) 213.

142 Ibid parts 5.4, 5.5 and 5.6 of chapter 5; see also Hadden (n 60) 511.

143 See generally, Robert McCorquodale, 'Corporate Social Responsibility and International Human Rights Law' (2009) 87 *Journal of Business Ethics* 385–400.

144 European Union, 'Communication of European Union Country's Commission Green Paper on Promoting a European Framework for Corporate Social Responsibility' COM (2001) 366 Final (July 18, 2001). For previous documents and actions at the EU towards CSR, see Tully (n 140) 24, 25.

145 European Union (n 144) 6.

146 Swedish Presidency of the European Union, 'Protect, Respect, Remedy: Making the European Union Take a Lead in Promoting Corporate Social Responsibility,' Declaration, November 2009 available at: http://ec.europa.eu/enterprise/policies/sustainable-business/files/deklaration_engelska_en.pdf accessed 1 July 2015.

147 MacLeod (n 2) 261.

148 European Commission, 'Communication from the Commission to the European Parliament, the Council, the European Economic and Social Committee and the Committee of Regions, A Renewed EU strategy 2011–14 for Corporate Social Responsibility' COM (2011) 681 final (Brussels 25 October 2011).

149 The Directive 2014/95/EU on Disclosure of Non-Financial and Diversity Information by Certain Large Undertakings and Groups, available at: http://eur-lex.europa.eu/legal-content/EN/TXT/?uri=CELEX:32014L0095 accessed 3 September 2015. Earlier in 2003, EU adopted the disclosure regime whereby it enjoins companies in member states to consider and report on non-financial (social, environmental

124　*Background, theories and global outlook*

and employee-related) matters in their annual reports (popularly referred to as the Accounts Modernisation Directive). Council Directive (EC) 2003/51/EC, 18 June 2003 amended Directives 78/660/EEC, 83/635/EEC and 91/674/EEC on the annual and consolidated accounts of certain types of companies, banks and other financial institutions and insurance undertakings, OJ L178/16, 2003. Based on this, many member states have introduced non-financial disclosure requirements including France, UK, Spain, Germany, Sweden, Denmark and Norway amongst others.

150 Ibid. resolution 19 for instance.

151 Global Reporting Initiative and CSR Europe, *Member State Implementation of Directive 2014/95/EU: A Comprehensive Overview of How Member States Are Implementing the EU Directive on Non-Financial and Diversity Information* (GRI & CSR Europe 2017) 4 available at: www.globalreporting.org/resourcelibrary/nfrpublication%20online_version. pdf accessed 31 October 2019.

152 See Europa website, available at: https://eur-lex.europa.eu/legal-content/EN/TXT/ PDF/?uri=OJ:L:2017:130:FULL&from=EN accessed 31 October 2019.

153 CSR inspired clauses are now specifically added to EU trade agreements such as in Article 13.6 of the EU-Korea Free Trade Agreement; see also Article 271 (3) of the EU Columbia/Peru Free Trade Agreement.

154 Materials on both ongoing assessments and completed impact assessments are contained at: http://ec.europa.eu/trade/policy/policy-making/analysis/policy-evaluation/ sustainability-impact-assessments/index_en.htm accessed 31 October 2019.

155 Hadden (n 60) 508.

156 European Commission 2011 COM, 13–15.

157 Jan Wouters and Leen Chanet, 'Corporate Human Rights Responsibilities: A European Perspective' (2008) 6 *Northwestern University Journal of International Human Rights* 262, 266–267 paras 26, 27; The CSR 'Business Case' argument enjoins corporate managers to consider stakeholder interests and report on non-financial matters of CSR like employee or environmental matters so long as it will make business sense (cost-benefit implications) to so do and such considerations are in relation to the overall economic performance of the company and without prejudice to enhancing shareholder value; Charlotte Villiers, 'Corporate Law Corporate Power and Corporate Social Responsibility' in Nina Boeger, Rachel Murray and Charlotte Villiers (eds.), *Perspectives on Corporate Social Responsibility* (Cheltenham: Edward Elgar 2008) 85, 97, 98 *et seq.*

158 McInerney (n 58).

159 Section 9 of the English Corporate Responsibility Act 2002.

160 Dine (n 9) 135.

161 Ibid. 136.

162 Virginia Harper Ho, 'Beyond Regulation: A Comparative Look at State-Centric Corporate Social Responsibility and the Law in China' (2013) 46 *Vanderbilt Journal of Transnational Law* 375, 394.

163 Smerdon (n 56) 462; Department of Business Innovation and Skills available at: www. bis.gov.uk accessed 31 October 2019. This department has been merged with the Department for Energy and Climate Change and is now called the Department for Business, Energy and Industrial Strategy (BEIS). See generally available at: www. gov.uk/government/organisations/department-for-business-innovations-skills/about accessed 31 October 2019.

164 Council Directive, 2003/51/EC, 18th June, 2003 amending Directives 78/660/EEC, 83/635/EEC and 91/674/EEC on the annual and consolidated accounts of certain types of companies, banks and other financial institutions and insurance undertakings, OJ L178/16, 2003.

165 Occupational Pension Schemes (Investment, and Assignment, Forfeiture, Bankruptcy etc.) (Amendment) Regulations 1999, S.I. 1999/1849.

166 See Section 414C, the Companies Act 2006 (Strategic Report and Directors' Report) Regulations 2013, Statutory Instrument 2013 No. 1970, available at: www.legislation. gov.uk/uksi/2013/1970/pdfs/uksi_20131970_en.pdf accessed 27 October 2016.

CSR international implementation 125

167 Section 417 (5), (10) and (11) of the 2006 English Companies Act; see also Section 414C (7) of the Companies Act 2006 (Strategic Report and Directors' Report) Regulations 2013.

168 2008 Danish Financial Statements Act effective on 1 January 2009. The aim of the law is to inspire businesses to take an active position on CSR and communicate this to the outside world. The statutory requirement is part of the first National Action Plan for Corporate Social Responsibility (May 2008) and is intended to improve the international competitiveness of Danish businesses. The law requires large businesses in Denmark to account for their work on Corporate Social Responsibility (CSR). In 2013 a new requirement was introduced into the law, making it mandatory for businesses to also expressly account for their policies for respecting human rights and for reducing their climate impact. Danish businesses are free to choose whether or not they wish to work on CSR. However, the statutory requirement means that the businesses must account for their policies on CSR or state that they do not have any (comply or explain principle); see http://csrgov.dk/legislation last accessed 17th November, 2015; see also, GRI, 'New Danish Law Requires CSR Disclosures' available at: www.globalreporting. org/News-EventsPress/LatestNews/2009/NewsJanuary09DanishLaw.html; Lambooy (n 8) fn 38.

169 Swedish Annual Reports Act available at http://ec.europa.eu/enterprise/policies/sme/business environment/files/annexes_accounting_report_2011/sweden_en.pdf accessed 3 July 2015.

170 See the *Nouvelles Regulations Economiques* adopted by the French Parliament in 2001, which requires all companies listed on the French stock market to publish social and environmental information in their annual reports. Also, see the Law on Retirement Savings of 2001 imposed by the German government, obligating pension fund managers to disclose the extent to which they consider the social and environmental records of the companies they invest in.

171 McBarnet (n 1) 31, 32.

172 Financial Reporting Council, *Effective Company Stewardship: Enhancing Corporate Reporting and Audit* available at: www.frc.org.uk/consultation-list/2011/effective-company-stewardship-enhanc accessed 31 October 2019.

173 Larry Ribstein, 'Accountability and Responsibility in Corporate Governance' (2006) 81 *Notre Dame Law Review* 1431, 1444–1447; see also McBarnet (n 1) 36.

174 Ho (162) 385.

175 Alien Tort Claims Act, codified at 28 USC § 1350. It dates back to 1789 and grants extraterritorial jurisdiction to the US District Court in respect of 'any civil action by an alien for a tort only, committed in violation of the law of nations or a treaty of the United States'.

176 The US Alien Tort Claims Act (ATCA), codified at 28 USC § 1350, which is otherwise thought to be effective across borders in extraterritorial application, has been seriously undermined in recent times. In *Bowoto v. Chevron* [F. Supp. 2d 1229 (N.D. Cal. 2004)], which began in 1999, the US court applied the doctrine of forum non conveniens and declined jurisdiction under the ATCA having found that there existed a better and more adequate forum to determine the case outside the jurisdiction of the United States of America. See also the recent judgment of the Supreme Court of the United Kingdom in *Vedanta Resources Plc v. Lungowe* [2019] UKSC 20.

177 In the USA, for instance, evidence of effective ethics and CSR practices constitutes a mitigating factor in sentencing corporate crime. See Chapter 8 of the 2018 United States Sentencing Commission Guidelines Manual available at: https://www.ussc.gov/sites/default/files/pdf/guidelines-manual/2018/CHAPTER_8.pdf accessed 31 October 2019; see also Section 12.3 of the Criminal Code Act 1995 (Australia) and Article 102 of the Criminal Code of the Swiss Federation (1937, amended 2019).

178 McBarnet (n 1) 36.

179 Ibid.

180 Ho (n 162) 390.

181 McBarnet (n 1) 37.

182 Susan Ariel Aaronson, 'Corporate Responsibility in the Global Village: The British Role Model and the American Laggard' (2003) 108 *Business and Society Review* 309, 318–329.

183 Ho (n 162) 391; see also McBarnet (n 1) 37.

184 2013 Indian Companies Act available at: www.mca.gov.in/Ministry/pdf/Companies Act2013.pdf accessed 31 October 2019.

185 Activities that may be included by companies in their Corporate Social Responsibility Policies Activities relating to: – (i) eradicating extreme hunger and poverty; (ii) promotion of education; (iii) promoting gender equality and empowering women; (iv) reducing child mortality and improving maternal health; (v) combating human immunodeficiency virus, acquired immune deficiency syndrome, malaria and other diseases; (vi) ensuring environmental sustainability; (vii) employment enhancing vocational skills; (viii) social business projects; (ix) contribution to the Prime Minister's National Relief Fund or any other fund set up by the Central Government or the State Governments for socio-economic development and relief and funds for the welfare of the Scheduled Castes, the Scheduled Tribes, other backward classes, minorities and women and (x) such other matters as may be prescribed.

186 McBarnet (n 1) 1, 18.

187 Another mandatory CSR regime can be found in the Indonesian Investment Law No. 25 of 2007 and the Limited Liability Company Law No. 40 of 2007.

188 McBarnet (n 1) 45.

189 Katerina Peterkova Mitkidis, 'Sustainability Clauses in International Supply Chain Contracts: Regulation, Enforceability and Effects of Ethical Requirement' (2014) *Nordic Journal of Commercial Law* 1, 5.

190 Ibid.

191 Ibid. 10.

192 McBarnet (n 1) 47.

Part II

CSR conceptual and regulatory framework in Africa

4 CSR in Nigeria

4 Background

Although the concept of corporate social and environmental responsibility and accountability (CSR) is not strange within the Nigerian business community, there has, however, been paucity of standard legal texts and materials on the subject, especially from a corporate law perspective. While corporate (business) law and corporate governance are widely taught subjects in tertiary institutions across Africa, together with discussions on CSR and business sustainability, not very many authors have extensively written about the subject in standard legal texts in Africa and using business law or company law perspectives. Literature, for instance, reveals works like Joseph Abugu's *Principles of Corporate Law in Nigeria*,[1] which highlights CSR in one chapter of the book; Adaeze Okoye's *Legal Approaches and Corporate Social Responsibility: Towards a Llewellyn's Law-Jobs Approach*,[2] which also provided some CSR discussions around law's potential role and interaction with the concept and Olufemi Amao's *Corporate Social Responsibility, Human Rights and the Law: Multinational Corporations in Developing Countries*[3] with interesting human rights protection discussion on the subject. As shall be discussed later in this chapter, many leading authors and reputed standard texts and materials on corporate law and practice appear rather silent on the CSR subject, while others rather confine their CSR discourse within the ambits of moralistic corporate philanthropy, charity and voluntary community development projects, beyond legal requirements.

Talking about CSR in corporate Nigeria without focusing on the particular perspective from which it is being appraised, a few authors including Uwafio-kun Idemudia, Uwem Ite, Felix Tuodolo and Olufemi Amao,[4] among others, traced CSR to the practices of foreign-owned[5] multinational enterprises (MNEs) operating in the oil and gas sector.[6] However, it is perhaps useful to quickly note that companies had played a major role in the historical development of Nigeria and that the administration of law and justice generally in the whole of what is now called Nigeria began through the activities of a (foreign-owned) company, the Royal Niger Company.[7] In terms of British colonial rule and administration of justice, Lagos was annexed in 1861, when the then King of Lagos, King Docemo,[8] 'in order that the Queen of England may be the better enabled to assist, defend and protect the inhabitants of Lagos, and to put an end to the slave trade in this and the neighbouring countries', entered into a treaty with the British, and the Port and Island of Lagos were ceded to Great Britain. The bulk of the former colony, protectorate and mandated territories as we now know as Nigeria was first administered in in terms of law and justice by the Royal Niger Company under a charter granted to the company in 1886. In relation to the activities of the foreign-owned MNEs in Nigeria in recent history, their corporate social responsibility activities were focused on corporate charity and undertaking community development projects such as the building of schools, providing scholarships, constructing roads, providing health care facilities and services and water supply amongst other infrastructure ordinarily provided by state institutions and governments. The reason why the MNEs' CSR activities were largely characterized by corporate gifts, philanthropy and community development projects will be later clarified in Section 4.1.

4.1 CSR conception and practices

CSR appears restrictively conceptualized in Nigeria, if at all recognized as an important construct for discussions in corporate law and corporate governance discourse. Literature reveals that, but for the publication of Joseph Abugu in his *Principles of Corporate Law in Nigeria*,[9] which discusses CSR in its modern conception, many leading authors and reputed standard texts and materials on Nigerian corporate law and governance, including from Olakunle Orojo,[10] Fabian Ajogwu[11] and KD Barnes[12] amongst others appear rather silent on the CSR subject. Emeka Chianu and[13] Emmanuel Okon,[14] amongst some others,[15] instead restrictively conceptualized CSR in terms of corporate gifting and community development projects beyond legal requirements. In light of these community development projects, Hakeem Ijaiya defined CSR in terms of obligations on companies to consider the interests of the communities by providing social infrastructure such as schools, hospitals, roads and water supply in their area of operation.[16] Rebecca Enuoh and Sunday Eneh also defined CSR as 'an obligatory move by MNCs to address the challenges in the society, technologically and financially, in order to benefit the society at large'.[17] Although Kenneth Amaeshi and others noted that CSR is a socially embedded construct and practice they also confine the CSR subject to largely community development projects by maintaining that:

> CSR in Nigeria would be aimed towards addressing the peculiarity of the socio-economic development challenges of the country (e.g. Poverty alleviation, health care provision, infrastructure development, education, etc) and would be informed by socio-cultural influences (e.g. communalism and charity). They might not necessarily reflect the popular western standard/expectations of CSR (e.g. consumer protection, fair trade green marketing, climate change concerns, social responsible investments, etc).[18]

In Chapters 1, 2 and 3 of this book, CSR discussions apparently transcended philanthropy and were shown to constitute a comprehensive corporate governance and business management model through which the economic, legal, ethical and discretionary responsibilities of a company may be balanced for the sustainable development of both the business community and society. It was also shown to mean a construct that broadens the responsibility of companies in an attempt to align the interests of corporate executives and the interest of not only the shareholders but also that of a stakeholder group within the environment of such companies. The said earlier discussion clearly demonstrated that CSR is a subject far beyond voluntary tokenism of companies or corporate philanthropy or community development projects, per se. However, discussions about CSR conception in Nigeria in this chapter are rather testamentary that what is conceptualized as CSR in Nigeria is still largely corporate philanthropy, charity and community development projects of companies. The CSR conception in corporate Nigeria appears at the atavistic stage of noblesse oblige and non-strategic short-term gifts. It is largely confined to just giving back to the society. Little wonder therefore that many businesses in Nigeria still brag about being good corporate citizens or champions of CSR on their websites and in newspapers because of their corporate charity and provision of pipe-borne water, hospitals, schools, scholarships et cetera. The necessary implication of this restrictive conception is the reduction of CSR in Nigeria to gratuitous activities of the business community beyond the requirements of the law.[19]

The previous conception is so deeply rooted in Nigeria that almost every policy and legislative attempt by the government to promote corporate social and environmental responsibility and accountability within the business community has been underpinned by tokenism (whether voluntary or mandatory) and/or companies undertaking community development projects in communities. This was the case in 2007 when the (now abandoned) CSR Bill[20] was presented before the Nigerian National Assembly. The bill primarily sought to, inter alia, establish a CSR Commission to collect some 'CSR contribution' or levy from companies for the purpose of executing community development projects for the citizenry. This approach simply reduces CSR to just some levy or some further corporate tax. The same approach was adopted in the (abandoned) Petroleum Industry Bill (PIB), and following the unbundling of the PIB by the 8th National Assembly of Nigeria and the introduction of the Petroleum Host and Impacted Communities Development Trust Bill in 2018, a somewhat similar approach could also be seen. This will be discussed further in the latter part of this chapter.

Actually, linking CSR to corporate gifting and community development projects in Nigeria may not be unconnected to how it was introduced and by what agents. It can be argued that it was not until the peak of corporate irresponsibility amongst the then-existing MNEs in the extractive industry in the early 1990s, which had culminated in the death of environmentalists and human rights activists such as the Ogoni Nine, that attention was drawn to

132 *CSR conceptual and regulatory framework in Africa*

the social and environmental responsibility and accountability of the business community. Apparently, discussions on CSR started against the background of poor community development policies of these MNEs in the extractive industry, and this continues to dominate CSR discussions to date in Nigeria. Almost every company still conceives of CSR in terms of what efforts the business community takes towards donating to the society or developing the local communities where they operate. For instance, Statoil once stated that:

> Because of past and present experiences with petroleum activities in the Niger-Delta with widespread environment destruction and little or no economic development, the population is deeply suspicious towards oil companies. Because of this, Statoil has to prove itself when it comes to corporate social responsibility in Nigeria.[21]

While it may be correct that the socio-cultural, economic and political environment of a country should condition the CSR issues in such a country,[22] however, the core elements, values, categories or components of the CSR conception remain largely similar everywhere. No company should claim to be engaged in the vein CSR of corporate donations or charity without ensuring, for instance, compliance with legal requirements guiding its operations or considering the welfare of its workforce. Perhaps Freeland has succinctly summarized the issue at hand:

> The Gulf oil spill and the financial crisis have taught us, rather brutally, that the heart of the relationship between business and society doesn't lie with the charitable deeds companies do in their off-hours but whether they are doing their day jobs that help – or hurt the rest of us.[23]

Again, as shown in Chapters 1 and 3, corporate social and environmental responsibility and accountability is a global phenomenon whose elements and values are similar everywhere. While corporate charity or undertaking community development projects may sometimes (not all the time) be justifiable within the CSR framework, CSR is certainly much broader in scope than just corporate charity, corporate culture or some simple call for business ethics that is concerned with moral dilemmas.

Corporate Nigeria must consolidate on the fact that CSR, all over the world, is evolving. CSR in Nigeria cannot and should not be defined by corporate charity. CSR has at least four elements or components and several core values and issues. Philanthropy is at best only a component of CSR. Proper engagement in effective and efficient CSR by any business association will see such business obeying all relevant laws governing its operations, being ethical, socially responsive and responsible in its wealth creation for its so-called owners. In other words, effective and intrinsic CSR will also entail simultaneous but balanced consideration of: economic profit maximization; ethical responsibilities towards employees; environmental responsibility in operations and, not to say the least, constantly ensuring compliance with all legal rules and regulations governing their operational activities. It is also part of CSR in modern times to show the company activities in the areas of consumer protection, human rights protection, concerns for global warming and biodiversity among others. The modern practice by ethically conscious corporate executives is to balance out all these interests one way or the other. This is the intrinsic and effective CSR practice, which ought to be the practice within the Nigerian business community. In closing on this, while CSR practices in Nigeria may not have gotten to such an advanced stage when compared to developed economies, the narratives on the continent are, however, gradually changing; CSR has started evolving beyond mere tokenism, many organizations and institutions have now paid requisite attention to the subject matter as a comprehensive corporate governance and business management strategy, and some changes have been noticed in this regard in the national codes of corporate governance in Nigeria.[24] Specialized departments and teams are being created in Nigerian companies to handle CSR and business sustainability issues and, sometimes, the heads of such departments made to sit on the corporate boards of such companies.[25]

4.2 Theoretical underpinning of CSR in Nigeria

Of the two dominant Ideological Corporate Models (shareholder primacy and the stakeholder models) already discussed in Chapter 2, the objectives of corporate activities including CSR in Nigeria are underpinned by the shareholder primacy model, although there are a few interesting primary legislations[26] enjoining corporate executives to safeguard stakeholder interests. To confirm this underlying dominance of the shareholder primacy model, the following sections of the Companies and Allied Matters Act (CAMA) appear useful. Section 279 (1) and (3) provide:

(1) A director of a company stands in a fiduciary relationship towards the company and shall observe the utmost good faith towards the company in any transaction with it or on its behalf.
(3) A director shall act at all times in what he believes to be the best interests of the company as a whole so as to preserve its assets, further its business, and promote the purposes for which it was formed, and in such manner as a faithful, diligent, careful and ordinarily skillful director would act in the circumstances.

Section 282 (1) also provides:

(1) Every director of a company shall exercise the powers and discharge the duties of his office honestly, in good faith and in the best interests of the company, and shall exercise that degree of care, diligence and skill which a reasonably prudent director would exercise in comparable circumstances.

134 CSR conceptual and regulatory framework in Africa

Section 283 (1) equally provides:

(1) Directors are trustees of the company's moneys, properties and their powers and as such must account for all the moneys over which they exercise control and shall refund any moneys improperly paid away, and shall exercise their powers honestly in the interest of the company and all the shareholders, and not in their own or sectional interests.

The cumulative effect of the foregoing provisions is that corporate executives are enjoined to act in the best interests of the company as a whole. The problem is that these sections are a clear adoption of the common law position of what is considered to be the 'company' or the 'interest of the company as a whole' in circumstances such as this. The 'company' is assumed to mean members or shareholders as a whole, and the best interest or success of the company is therefore taken to mean what is beneficial to the (economic) interests of the shareholders as a whole.[27]

It is also useful to clarify that, although there are clear references to consideration of other interests apart from shareholder interests in the previous list showing the Nigerian primary corporate law takes cognizance of stakeholder protection, the value to be derived from these sections by stakeholders in relation to safeguarding their interests in the running of the company is suspect. For instance, having sought to protect an important stakeholder group such as employees at Section 279 (3) and (4),[28] the same legislation in the same section immediately weakens the efficacy of such provision (as least in the eyes of any victim employee stakeholder) under sub-section (9)[29] to the effect that, even if the corporate executives do not behave responsibly in safeguarding stakeholder interests, only the 'company' can complain.[30]

In further confirmation of the shareholder primacy model in corporate Nigeria, especially in relation to corporate disclosures in financial statements, the Nigerian primary corporate legislation is focused on the shareholder primacy model with no provisions for consideration of important stakeholder interests (such as impacts on community life or the environment) as there are no provisions for non-financial corporate disclosures[31] or integrated reporting[32] as otherwise known in jurisdictions such as South Africa (where corporate disclosures and statements of corporate accounts and affairs integrate and combine both financial matters and non-financial matters, like social and environmental issues). Although there is an ongoing legislative process to amend the CAMA in a proposed 2016 Companies and Allied Act, the author's review of relevant provisions on corporate objectives and the duties of corporate executives shows there are no significant changes to the status quo.

4.3 Legal, regulatory and enforcement framework

This section of the chapter discusses CSR regulatory and enforcement attempts in the Nigerian business community generally. It highlights a few regulatory mechanisms contained in hard law instruments such as: the aborted Corporate Social Responsibility Bill 2007 (Nigerian CSR Bill); the proposed 2012 Petroleum Industry Bill (PIB); and, following the unbundling of the PIB, the newly proposed 2018 Petroleum Host and Impacted Communities Development Trust Bill; the primary corporate law legislation in Nigeria – Companies and Allied Matters Act 1990 as amended (CAMA); the Investments and Securities Act 2007 (ISA); the Nigerian Extractive Industries Transparency Initiative Act 2007 (NEITI) and the Nigerian Minerals and Mining Act 2007. This segment also appraises CSR enforcement regime using soft law instruments within corporate Nigeria by examining enforcement mechanisms in relevant ethical codes of conducts of organizations across industries including: the Central Bank of Nigeria (CBN) Code of Corporate Governance, May 2014; the Nigerian Securities and Exchange Commission (SEC) Code of Corporate Governance for Public Companies, 2011 and the Nigerian Communication Commission (NCC) Code of Corporate Governance for the Telecommunications Industry, 2014; the National Pension Commission (PENCOM) Code of Corporate Governance for Licensed Pension Operators, June, 2008; the National Insurance Commission (NAICOM) Code of Corporate Governance for Insurance Companies 2009; the abandoned 2016 National Code of Corporate Governance by the Financial Reporting Council and finally the 2018 Nigerian Code of Corporate Governance (the Nigerian Code).

4.3.1 Aborted Corporate Social Responsibility Bill 2007

With a view to providing a comprehensive and adequate relief to host communities suffering the negative consequences of the industrial and commercial activities of companies operating in their areas,[33] a Corporate Social Responsibility Bill was introduced to the Nigerian National Assembly in 2007.[34] The attempted CSR legislation sought to be the direct primary legislation in Nigeria and establish a CSR Commission, which shall ensure a compulsory 3.5% of company's gross annual profit as CSR spent for the purpose of executing community development projects for the citizenry.[35] The bill received very strong criticisms for its attempt to introduce another form of corporate tax and for its rather atavistic conception of CSR as just some corporate gift or charity[36] and therefore never became law and probably was condemned to the archives of the National Assembly bills. However, for the purpose of necessary lessons, the bill is nonetheless juxtaposed against earlier discussed CSR conception in UK, USA and India[37] later, showing marked differences in approach and conception. First, the UK in 2002 also attempted a comprehensive CSR law called the 'Corporate Responsibility Bill'. It sought to create a government agency, which will be primarily responsible for coordination, regulations and enforcement of CSR activities within the UK business community and thereby institutionalize the CSR concept by way of hard law and mandatory regulation in the UK.[38] Although this UK bill shares the fact of abandonment with the Nigerian 2007 CSR bill, in the UK, unlike in Nigeria, CSR issues and

136 *CSR conceptual and regulatory framework in Africa*

disclosures on non-financial social and environmental matters are a matter of aligned requirements in primary company legislation (Sections 172, 417 and 423(5) of the 2006 English Companies Act) in compliance with relevant EU directives, together with subsidiary enactment requirements such as expecting qualified companies to produce a Strategic Report informing their shareholders and helping them assess how the directors have discharged their duty under Section 172.[39] It is difficult to find the aligned primary company law provisions on which basis the seeming extra taxes under the aborted Nigerian CSR bill were based. Further, in comparison with CSR implementation strategy in the USA, unlike passing a comprehensive hard law creating a specific government agency coordinating CSR, measures adopted in the USA towards regulating corporate behaviour include requiring compliance with codes of business conducts often in response to laissez-faire market forces and pressures from investors, consumers and NGOs,[40] together with conscious CSR facilitation by government agencies and departments requiring demonstration of responsible corporate behaviours.[41] Third and lastly, in comparison with the approach in 2013 Indian Companies Act,[42] while the two models specify that a certain percentage of the corporate revenue be spent on CSR activities, there are a few differences nonetheless: first, the Nigerian CSR bill had sought to establish a CSR Commission to regulate CSR activities. The Indian regime, however, seeks some form of self-regulatory approach to CSR by creating a CSR Committee from the company's Board of Directors. Second, the Indian regime creates a form of internalized self-regulatory regulation (in the CSR Committee of the Board of Directors); the Nigerian system rather chose an externalized regulator in the CSR Commission, which would prescribe laws and regulations for the coordination and monitoring of corporate responsibility from outside the business community. In concluding discussions on the aborted Nigerian CSR Bill, it is instructive to reiterate the following perceived misgivings: (i) the reduction of a comprehensive business management and corporate governance model of CSR to some corporate donation and corporate tax and (ii) the proposal for CSR implementation through the unfashionable externalized[43] CSR Commission, with the attendant little knowledge of the internal workings of the business community together with attendant regulatory inefficiencies.

4.3.2 Companies and Allied Matters Act and other enactments

CSR conception under the CAMA has perhaps been of tremendous influence on the nature of CSR practices in Nigeria. The earlier noted restrictive CSR conception amongst Nigerian corporate executives in terms of gifting or philanthropy may after all be directly attributable to CAMA provisions. Businesses can engage in charity and philanthropy only if the same would benefit the company in the long run and promote the interests and success of the shareholders as a whole. Otherwise, corporate law abhors corporate gifting, which is taken as undue depletion of capital and monies, which will be otherwise available as profits for shareholders. Bowen L. J. in *Hutton v. West Cork Railway Co.* put it succinctly as follows:

> the law does not say that there are to be no cakes and ale, but that there are to be no cakes and ale except such as are required for the benefit of the company . . . charity has no business to sit at the board of directors qua charity. There is, however, a kind of charitable dealing which is for the interest of those who practice it, and to that extent and in that garb . . . charity may sit at the board, but for no other purpose.[44]

In this regard, by virtue of Section 38 of CAMA, all companies are said to have the powers of a natural person of full capacity including powers to make donations. Section 38 (1) and (2) provides:

(1) Except to the extent that the company's memorandum or any enactment otherwise provides, every company shall, for the furtherance of its authorized business or objects, have all the powers of a natural person of full capacity.
(2) A company shall not have or exercise power either directly or indirectly to make a donation or gift of any of its property or funds to a political party or political association, or for any political purpose; and if any company, in breach of this subsection makes any donation or gift of its property to a political party or political association, or for any political purpose, the officers in default and any member who voted for the breach shall be jointly and severally liable to refund to the company the sum or value of the donation or gift and in addition, the company and every such officer or member shall be guilty of an offence and liable to a fine equal to the amount or value of the donation or gift.

From the previous points, it logically follows that having the powers of a natural person portends that any incorporated business will therefore be able to engage in corporate gifting provided no contrary provisions exist in its memorandum and articles of association. Further, sub-section (2) only contains a prohibition of corporate gifts to political parties or to fund political associations or any other political purposes. This, again, can only mean that if such corporate donation is not towards any political ends or purposes and not otherwise prohibited by the company's constitution (memorandum and articles of association), such corporate gifts will be intra vires, lawful and legitimate. However, although it will be lawful for corporate executives to engage in such corporate gifting from corporate funds, where such is done randomly purely in the name of corporate charity or philanthropy and not under an efficient and effective CSR framework as described in this book, such will constitute not only a disservice to the true meaning and imports of CSR but will also provide justifications for commentators who claim that CSR is just another detraction

138   *CSR conceptual and regulatory framework in Africa*

from serious business, a ridiculous idea and undue depletion of capital and monies that would otherwise have been available to shareholders as profits.

Further, as earlier observed in Section 4.2, CAMA has not provided a conducive ideological support for effective CSR practices in Nigeria as it is underlain by the shareholder primacy model. It was also mentioned earlier that, in terms of corporate statement reporting and disclosures, CAMA strictly focuses on the shareholder primacy model with no provisions for corporate disclosures or integrated reporting on non-financial (social and environmental) matters.[45] Everything towards accountability, transparency and corporate responsibility under CAMA has been geared towards shareholder protection with little or no protection afforded other constituents such as the local community, suppliers, employees, contractors, the government, the environments and other relevant stakeholders. It is interesting to add that even the Corporate Responsibility Part VIII of the Nigerian 2007 Investments and Securities Act (ISA), which established the Securities and Exchange Commission (SEC) and regulates the activities of public liability and quoted companies in Nigeria, fails to also provide for corporate reporting on non-financial matters.[46]

4.3.2.1 Nigeria Extractive Industries Transparency Initiative (NEITI) Act 2007

Towards promoting CSR in the extractive industry, the Nigerian government bought into the idea of a UK-led Extractive Industries Transparency Initiative (EITI), which is targeted at creating accountability and transparency in the management of oil, gas and mining resources in resource-rich countries such as Nigeria.[47] A diverse group of countries, companies and civil society organizations attended a Lancaster House Conference in London (in 2003) hosted by the UK government, at which certain Statement of Principles for transparency over payments in the extractive industry were agreed.[48] The Nigerian Extractive Industries Transparency Initiative (NEITI) was inaugurated in February 2004 by former president Olusegun Obasanjo when he set up the National Stakeholders Working Group (NSWG) under the leadership of Mrs Obiageli Ezekwesili, who was at that time Senior Special Assistant to the president on budget monitoring and price intelligence BMPIU located with its office inside the Presidential Villa, Aso Rock,[49] and upon the presidential assent on 28 May 2007 of the Nigeria Extractive Industries Transparency Initiative (NEITI) Act 2007, Nigeria became the first EITI-implementing country with a statutory backing for its operations.[50] NEITI introduced the framework for transparency and accountability in the reporting and disclosure by all extractive companies of revenue due to or paid to the Federal Government of Nigeria.[51] It is to ensure the transparency through publication of company accounts and through regular audits and tax returns on payments. NEITI commissioned the first comprehensive audit of Nigeria's petroleum industry for the period 1999 to 2004 and has been working with various stakeholders to build national consensus on the need for extractive revenue transparency in Nigeria.[52] NEITI appears, however, not to be living up to expectations in CSR implementation in the Nigerian extractive industry for a few reasons. Key among this is the seeming superficial power to monitor payments to the government from the companies and publicize defaults without relevant authority to enforce any defaults or violations of its mandate and having to rely on other government agencies in this regard. Further, there are other inherent hindrances to the NEITI Act itself as contained in Sections 3 (d), (e) and 14 (1) of NEITI Act.

Section 3 (d) provides

Obtain, as may be deemed necessary, from any extractive industry company an accurate record of the cost of production and volume of state of oil, gas or other minerals extracted by the company at any period, provided that such information shall not be used in any manner prejudicial to the contractual obligation or proprietary interests of the extractive industry company.

Section 3 (e)

Request from any company in the extractive industry or from any relevant organ of the Federal, State or Local Government, an accurate account of any money paid by and received from the company at any period, as revenue accruing to the Federal Government from such company for that period, provided that such information shall not be used in a manner prejudicial to contractual obligations or proprietary interests of the extractive industry company or sovereign obligations of Government.

Section 14 (1)

The NEITI shall cause the account of total revenue which accrued to the Federal Government from all extractive industry accompanies, its receipts, payments, assets and liabilities to be audited . . . the independent auditor shall submit the report with comments of the audited entity to the NEITI which shall cause same to be published for the information of the public, provided that the contents of such report shall not be published in a manner prejudicial to the contractual obligations or proprietary interests of the audited entity.

The previous provisions, especially in the underlined and italicized portions, show that NEITI is inherently and fundamentally hindered in its CSR implementation mandate as it cannot utilize or otherwise publish reports considered prejudicial to a company's contractual obligations or proprietary interests (as there is no clear definition of what is prejudicial or highlighting its indicia). These provisions would appear to have precluded any hope of successful realization of NEITI's mandate from the onset. This development appears to be bordering on legislative rascality, that intentions of private parties to contracts in the extractive industry – however crooked or dodgy such intentions might

140   *CSR conceptual and regulatory framework in Africa*

be – should be made to override the national interest (captured in the legislation). One wonders if this can be attributed to the fact that NEITI Act was not assented to until the very last day of former President Obasanjo's administration.

In summation, there is no gainsaying that the legal transplantation[53] of the EITI Standards into the 2007 NEITI Act is fundamentally faulty. Legal transplantation is a process of moving a rule or a system of law from one system or country to another. It is not a new phenomenon but involves a careful process of copying principles of laws and rules with sufficient understanding of the comparative laws involved and adequate consideration for the local (corporate) culture of the target country. It would appear that the drafters of the NEITI either feigned denial of prevailing domestic systems or had very little consideration for the existing legal, institutional and socio-economic realities of the recipient Nigerian system in the process of adopting the EITI principles. It would appear that the NEITI Act attempts to put a square peg in a round whole. The majority of jurisdictions where transparency and accountability standards or requirements are intended, such as the EITI principles, ensure that the adopted framework fits into the general corporate law model of such countries. To this end, for instance, the USA adopts a smart mix of hard law and soft law regulations on any of its critical economic issues such as corporate reporting, disclosure and accountability and, as such, passed laws like the Foreign Corrupt Practices Act (FCPA),[54] the Sarbanes-Oxley Act of 2002, and the Dodd – Frank Wall Street Reform and Consumer Protection Act of 2010 towards promoting the core values of CSR and providing a coherent and properly aligned regulatory framework with which government agencies such the SEC and courts facilitate CSR. Similarly, in the UK, there is also a coherent model; the UK CSR implementation framework is dependent on the disclosure regime and social reporting on non-financial matters as contained in Section 417 (5) of the 2006 English Companies Act, which aligns with, inter alia, the EU 2003 Accounts Modernisation Directive[55] and the Directive 2014/95/EU[56] of the European Parliament and of the Council of 22 October 2014 amending Directive 2013/34/EU as regards disclosure of non-financial and diversity information by certain large undertakings and groups. Therefore, there is coherence in the legal instruments through which the UK authorities and agencies such as the FRC facilitate, endorse and encourage effective CSR practices within the UK business community. The irresistible questions for corporate Nigeria are: on what properly aligned (corporate) legislative framework are the principles or the requirements of the NEITI Act based? On what corporate law model does the NEITI seeks to effectively implement CSR in the Nigerian extractive industry? The reality is simply that the CAMA and ISA do not support or contain provisions justifying or facilitating non-financial CSR disclosures to stakeholders on which principle, inter alia, the EITI Standards are premised.[57] Consequently, proper legal transplantation, which considers and aligns all relevant legislative enactments in the circumstance, is required towards effective CSR implementation within the NEITI framework.

CSR in Nigeria 141

4.3.2.2 Petroleum Industry Bill, and the Petroleum Host and Impacted Communities Development Trust Bill

The Petroleum Industry Bill (PIB) has evolved from the year 2000 when the Oil and Gas Sector Reform Implementation Committee was inaugurated by the Federal Government of Nigeria to carry out holistic reforms of the oil and gas industry covering the upstream, midstream and downstream sectors of the industry. PIB has accordingly been touted as the Nigerian oil and gas industry messiah legislation and is much awaited by all stakeholders to solve the myriad problems and challenges in the oil and gas industry including entrenching the principles of good governance, transparency and sustainable development in the petroleum sector. PIB proposes to carry out an overarching regulatory and enforcement reform in the Nigerian upstream, midstream, downstream and natural gas industries. Such reforms include the unbundling of the national oil company, Nigerian National Petroleum Corporation (NNPC), in order to make it more effective, efficient, transparent, accountable and responsible. PIB has 362 Sections of 223 pages and supported by five schedules. While there appeared to be many versions[58] of PIB, and several provisions therein are controversial, this chapter appraises its provisions relating to CSR implementation. For the purpose of this chapter, the version available on the Nigeria-Law website[59] is adopted. In this regard, Sections 4, 116, 190 and 290 will be examined.

Section 4 provides

In achieving their functions and objectives under this Act, the institutions and the companies established in pursuance of this Act shall be bound by the principles of the Nigerian Extractive Industries Transparency Initiative Act LFN 2007.

Section 190 (6) provides

All bids received based on the bid parameters established in subsection (2) of this section shall be handled in accordance with the published guidelines and monitored by the Nigeria Extractive Industries Transparency Initiative (NEITI).

The previous provisions demonstrate that the PIB relies on the CSR framework under the NEITI Act of 2007. The NNPC's 2009 PIB Inter-Agency Project Team Report confirms this development of ensuring full compliance with the NEITI Act, 2007 by all the institutions.[60] As a result of this, all the criticisms noted under the NEITI discourse are applicable, mutatis mutandis, to the PIB. Further, Section 116 of the PIB provides for the establishment of a fund to be known as the Petroleum Host Communities Fund (PHCF). PIB provides that each upstream petroleum company shall remit to the PHCF, on a monthly basis, 10% of its net profit, which shall be utilized for the development of the economic and social infrastructure of the communities within the

142 *CSR conceptual and regulatory framework in Africa*

petroleum-producing communities.[61] This provision is interesting because it appears to adopt the same CSR conception as did the aborted 2007 CSR Bill demanding contribution of a percentage of corporate revenue to a fund.[62] As a result of its noted qualification, though this extra corporate taxation may not really receive criticisms, unlike the 2007 CSR Bill, the capacity to effectively channel such funds to the local/host community developmental project remained suspect. The fact that the PIB cannot define how the PHCF shall be effectively administered, managed and by what agency to achieve its objectives provides a recipe for further corrupt practices in the oil and gas operations and its attendant further impoverishment of the same host communities intended to be salvaged; the reasoning here is that oil and gas companies then get under the impression of effective CSR practices once the remittance to the fund has been done without any concomitant efforts to minimize any other negative socio-economic and environmental impacts of business operations. Based on the previous analysis, it is little wonder that the PIB CSR implementation strategy did not receive wide acceptance and is now abandoned. Towards achieving what its predecessors were unable to achieve, the 8th National Assembly of the Federal Republic of Nigeria decided to unbundle the PIB by dividing it into the four different but interrelated bills, namely: the Petroleum Industry Governance Bill, the Petroleum Industry Administration Bill, the Petroleum Industry Fiscal Bill, and the Petroleum Host and Impacted Communities Development Trust Bill (hereinafter the '2018 Bill').[63]

The 2018 Bill was proposed towards fostering sustainable shared prosperity amongst host and impacted communities, providing direct social and economic benefits from petroleum operations and enhancing peaceful and harmonious coexistence between settlor and host and impacted communities, among others. Although a full analysis of the 2018 Bill has been done in the referenced article, it suffices to note here that the bill in its current form may be unable to achieve its target of promoting and enhancing peaceful and harmonious coexistence between the business community (settlor companies) and host and impacted communities if the drafters do not pay requisite attention towards addressing a few issues. These issues include: the seeming negligence by the government of its fundamental role of providing social services and public goods and shifting such responsibilities to the settlors; the classic reduction or confinement of the CSR subject to the undertaking of community development projects and finally, the absence of useful definition or description of what areas should constitute host and impacted communities in relation to settlor operations in the oil and gas industry.

4.3.2.3 Nigerian Minerals and Mining Act 2007

The Nigerian Minerals and Mining Act No. 20 of 2007 (hereinafter simply 'the NMMA') repealed the 1999 Minerals and Mining Act and vests the ownership, control and regulation of mineral resources in the extractive industry in the Federal Government of Nigeria.[64] In terms of administration, the NMMA provides for a Mining Cadastre Office[65] (MCO), a Mines Environmental

Compliance Department (MECD)[66] and a Mineral Resources and Environmental Management Committee (MREMC)[67] amongst others and charges them with complementary regulatory responsibilities in their respective locations, levels and jurisdictions. In relation to CSR implementation, NMMA enjoins every holder of mineral title to be responsible by minimizing, managing and mitigating any environmental impact resulting from their activities.[68] For instance, Section 61 (1) (a) and (b) provides:

Every holder of an exploration licence shall

(a) conduct exploration activities in a safe, friendly, skilful, efficient, and workmanlike manner in accordance with the regulations;
(b) conduct exploration activities in an environmentally and socially responsible manner.

Further, Section 116 of the NMMA states that holders of mining lease shall not commence development activities within any lease area until they finalize a community development agreement[69] (CDA) with the host communities towards transferring social and economic benefits to the communities. Section 116 (3) provides for matters it envisages the CDA will address as follows:

(i) educational scholarship, apprenticeship, technical training and employment opportunities for indigenes of the communities;
(ii) financial or other forms of contributory support for infrastructural development and maintenance such as education, health or other community services, roads, water and power;
(iii) assistance with the creation, development and support for small scale and micro enterprises;
(iv) agricultural product marketing;
(v) methods and procedures of environment and socio-economic management and local governance enhancement.

While there are many useful provisions in the NMMA in relation to CSR implementation as highlighted previously, some improvements may be required towards an effective safeguard for stakeholder interest or advancing effective CSR practices with this law. To start with, issues that the CDA are supposed to resolve between the extractive companies and their host communities appear limited to community development activities with host communities. CSR transcends such projects. Further, assuming but not conceding to the efficacy of the CDA per se, the host communities cannot be said to constitute the only stakeholder group whose interests require state protection. What happens to the interests of the employees of the companies? What happens to corporate responsibility of the companies involved towards their clients, consumers, creditors and even the government? In other words, how responsible are the companies behaving generally beyond the CDA signed with the host and impacted communities? Moreover, in the absence of a definition of 'host

144   *CSR conceptual and regulatory framework in Africa*

communities' in the NMMA, who determines which local groups are entitled to negotiate a CDA with the extractive companies?[70] Will such negotiations with different communities not rather detract such extractive companies from their commercial focus? In the event no agreement is reached and matters to be addressed by the CDA are referred to the Minister, what model will the Minister utilize in his resolution and balancing of conflicting interests (which will not prejudice the companies as profitable ventures nor prejudice effective protection of the legitimate interests of the host communities)? How useful will revocation (or threat thereof) of granted licenses be in embedding responsible minerals mining activities? If licenses are constantly revoked for breaches as conceivable under Section 151 of the NMMA, what impacts will this have on efforts at encouraging FDI in this sector? What assurances are there that the next grantee of the mining lease or any other holder of licenses will not behave irresponsibly towards relevant stakeholders also? Has the NMMA made the extractive companies instruments and tools of state control? Is the government, through the instrumentality of the NMMA, shirking its primary responsibilities of providing social services and public goods and rather shifting some to the business community? These uncertainties and issues posed earlier are likely to contribute to, if not result in, the inefficiency of the CDA as a CSR implementation strategy. While it is not the argument that the idea behind the CDA is totally worthless as a CSR regulatory technique rather than mandating the signing of such CDA or even making it a condition precedent to operations, such a CDA may only be encouraged to be signed and utilized by regulators within the ambits of a regulatory framework called the Responsible Stakeholder Model (RSM) as proposed in Chapter 2 and whose regulatory framework will be further delineated in Chapter 7; in other words, the author will argue in Chapter 7 that credible answers to the previously raised questions surrounding the implementation of the CDA and other related issues bordering on effective CSR implementation are perhaps best situated within the RSM. For instance, under the regulatory framework of the RSM, as shall be expatiated in Chapter 7, the business community will not necessarily view the CDA as some herculean task to be accomplished before operations (and even after commencement of operations), but it will rather be viewed in terms of normal corporate operational requirements towards promoting the success of all relevant interests of the company. Invariably therefore, the ease of doing business in this industry may be seen to have been improved through the instrumentality of the CDA and further seen in light of encouraging FDI accordingly.

4.4 CSR and corporate governance codes in Nigeria

Corporate governance is often discussed in relation to codes of conduct and governance that usually give effect to legislated provisions. In other words, in further discussions in Chapter 1 of this book, corporate governance codes give effect to and complement the primary corporate legislations.[71] While industry players in many jurisdictions such as in South Africa have one comprehensive code of corporate governance in the King IV,[72] the Nigerian business community appears not so lucky. Nigeria has the following:

(i)   The Code of Corporate Governance for the Telecommunication Industry 2016, issued by the Nigerian Communications Commission (NCC) (replaced 2014 NCC Code);
(ii) The Code of Corporate Governance for Banks and Discount Houses in Nigeria 2014 issued by the Central Bank of Nigeria (CBN) (replaced 2006 CBN Code);
(iii) The Code of Corporate Governance for Public Companies in Nigeria 2011 issued by the Securities and Exchange Commission (SEC) (replaced 2003 SEC Code);
(iv) The Code of Good Corporate Governance for Insurance Industry in Nigeria 2009 issued by the National Insurance Commission (NAICOM);
(v)   The Code of Corporate Governance for Licensed Pension Fund Operators 2008 issued by the National Pension Commission (PENCOM).

The previous list is often referred to as the sectoral codes, and they have their respective CSR implementation requirements.[73] Following complaints about the multiplicity of codes in Nigeria and recommendation for one comprehensive document,[74] the Financial Reporting Council of Nigeria[75] issued the 2018 Nigerian Code of Corporate Governance,[76] replacing a controversial 2016 National Code of Corporate Governance (the 'Nigerian Code'). The CSR implementation framework in the 2018 Nigerian Code is impressive.[77] For instance, the following provisions appear useful:

Principle 1 provides:

> A successful Company is headed by an effective Board which is responsible for providing entrepreneurial and strategic leadership as well as promoting ethical culture and responsible corporate citizenship. As a link between stakeholders and the Company, the Board is to exercise oversight and control to ensure that management acts in the best interest of the shareholders and other stakeholders while sustaining the prosperity of the Company.

Principle 26 reads:

> Paying adequate attention to sustainability issues including environment, social, occupational and community health and safety ensures successful long term business performance and projects the Company as a responsible corporate citizen contributing to economic development.

Principle 27 states:

> Communicating and interacting with stakeholders keeps them conversant with the activities of the Company and assists them in making informed decisions.

146 *CSR conceptual and regulatory framework in Africa*

Principle 28 provides:

> Full and comprehensive disclosure of all matters material to investors and stakeholders, and of matters set out in this Code, ensures proper monitoring of its implementation which engenders good corporate governance practice.

These provisions are indeed impressive as they confirm an appreciation by the drafters of the importance of corporate executives, as an effective CSR implementation strategy, properly managing the social, economic and environmental impacts of the company's operations on the stakeholders. The provisions also confirm that effective engagement with, and management of stakeholders has direct implications on the overall success of the company in the long run.

From the previously highlighted principles, it would seem that corporate social and environmental responsibility and accountability to both shareholders and stakeholder groups is encouraged and really not strange to CSR implementation attempts in the Nigerian business community, especially at the level of codes of corporate governance. Although these, on the surface, appear impressive, the relevant question is, how effective can they really be? The provisions, most of the time, use the word 'should' instead of 'shall', demonstrating their lack of hard law bite. In the wake of these soft law approaches and voluntary application[78] of these codes, how efficient can the provisions be in enforcing responsible and accountable corporate behaviour in Nigeria? It has been discussed in Chapter 3, and relevant lessons have been learnt to the effect that soft law CSR implementation initiatives are generally only useful against law-abiding corporate entities and will become grossly inadequate and inefficient against rogue corporate entities in the society who are simply within the business community to maximize profits at all costs.

Second, although it would be incorrect to state that the Nigerian Code together with the sectoral codes are utterly useless towards implementing CSR, these codes, as they are, are inadequate and will remain inefficient as a result of what appears to be a faulty legal transplantation process involved in their establishment. While it is evident that some international best practices and codes were adopted in incorporating CSR requirements in many codes,[79] it is nonetheless arguable that their implementation will be largely lax and, frankly speaking, unenforceable against companies because such social reporting or stakeholder engagement provisions therein are not only incoherent with primary legislations but probably also ultra vires the powers of the agencies prescribing them. For instance, as earlier noted, throughout the length and breadth of both CAMA and ISA, there is no positive obligation on any companies and their corporate executives 'to balance the interests of the shareholders and other stakeholders' as otherwise required, for instance, by Principle 10 of the NCC Code. Similarly, while the disclosure requirements in the primary enactments within the corporate law system of Nigeria are primarily financial disclosures and targeted at shareholders and investors, the requirement in the

Nigerian Code for companies to engage in 'full and comprehensive disclosure of all matters material to investors and stakeholders, and of matters set out in this Code' under its Principle 28[80] appears misaligned. Therefore, regardless of any provisions in the codes attempting to ensure compliance with such a requirement, they may simply just be unenforceable as the agencies prescribing would have acted ultra vires.[81] In summation, the incoherence between the provisions of the primary corporate law legislations and the ethical codes is the strongest pointer to the argument of faulty legal transplantation of the codes and perhaps some consequence of what Abugu termed 'error in scholarship'[82] in this area.

4.5 Factors militating effective CSR in Nigeria

Discussions in this chapter have already shown a few factors militating against effective CSR implementation in corporate Nigeria. These include:

(i) The restrictive conceptualization of the CSR to corporate charity and undertaking community development projects;
(ii) Poor legal transplantation involved in laws such as the NEITI Act, the codes of corporate governance;
(iii) The dominance of shareholder primacy model underlying the objectives of corporate actions and CSR activities in Nigeria;
(iv) Government's Regulatory Chill Syndrome with Large Companies.

While almost all other points have been discussed in other sections of this chapter or in other chapters of the book, the last point on the previous list appears deserving of further clarification. Literature reveals that a fundamental issue for consideration in proper CSR implementation across Africa, Nigeria not an exception, is the 'regulatory chill' syndrome. This syndrome occurs where there is government reluctance to undertake legitimate CSR implementation through appropriate regulations for fear of lawsuits from investors or withdrawal of investment. The author has some first-hand experience working in the Nigerian extractive industry and has seen this syndrome play out in, for instance, the interaction of the Nigerian government (including its legislature and agencies such as the Nigerian National Petroleum Corporation) with the MNEs in their oil exploration joint venture discussions. This also plays out in the negotiation, preparation and interpretation of private investment contracts, trade agreements and investment treaties involving the MNEs and developing host states. For fear of losing out on critical investment opportunities, the host states claim to encourage investment by affording a strong regime of legal and contractual protection to the investors (MNEs) which are guaranteed in a number of bilateral investment treaty (BIT) provisions under international investment law. The actual concern is with the use of the so-called stabilization clauses in such contracts, which create obstacles to the countries like Nigeria applying new social and environmental legislation to investment projects in

148 *CSR conceptual and regulatory framework in Africa*

the state. According to Leyla Davarnejad, such clauses are so carefully worded and will usually be interpreted in favour of the MNEs to the detriment of the developing countries.[83] Faith Stevelman appears to better summarize this issue in the following words:

> Too often, host states have been so needful of financing and assistance in project development that they have agreed to halt social welfare regulation during the pendency of such a project of financing (or to pay damages if they do enact such regulations). These BITs have thus too often stymied host governments from enacting new regulations essential to social welfare. Indeed, in a given country, such a privately enforced 'hiatus' in social welfare regulation may persist for decades.[84]

From the previous quote, it seems that the challenge centres around the non-integration of core CSR values of environmental protection, human rights and other similar corporate social responsibility and accountability obligations in the investment contracts leading to their disregard by MNEs in the decision-making and consequently by international arbitral tribunals.[85] As earlier hinted, at the receiving end of this scourge are developing countries who most times, in order to attract FDI, give concessions to MNEs allowing these companies to 'skirt labour and environmental regulations' amongst other irresponsible corporate practices.[86] The growing body of jurisprudence of the International Centre for Settlement of Investment Disputes (ICSID) also attests to this point.[87] The United Nations summarized the helplessness of most governments especially in the developing economies in addressing this problem as follows:

> The major difficulty . . . is how to identify the point at which a process of governmental action changes to an incremental deprivation of an owner's rights, such that the deprivation becomes the subject of a duty to compensate. If that definition is drawn too widely it will catch entirely legitimate regulatory and administrative action. . . . So an extensive interpretation of regulatory takings can limit the national policy space by hindering a government's right to regulate, creating the risk of regulatory chill, with governments unwilling to undertake legitimate regulation for fear of lawsuits from investors.[88]

In conclusion, the words of Charlotte Villiers perhaps succinctly sum up the challenge noting that the fear of capital flight by investors in many developing countries appears to suppress the regulatory powers of government legislators for effective CSR practices even in BITs.[89]

4.6 Chapter summary

This chapter assessed the prospects and challenges of CSR conceptualization and implementation, first generally within the Nigerian corporate law system,

CSR in Nigeria 149

then specifically in relation to the extractive industry in Nigeria. While the Nigerian business climate is often quoted as having sufficient legislative solutions to many of its problems and that the challenge had been that of weak or lackadaisical enforcement, this assumption was queried, and the chapter clarified that the challenges for effective CSR implementation in Nigeria include: (i) a bouquet of otherwise impressive legislative and regulatory initiatives grossly undermined by faulty legal transplantation processes; (ii) the confinement of CSR conception and philanthropy practices and undertaking community development projects; (iii) incoherence and policy misalignment between CSR implementation provisions in primary legislations on the one hand and their subsidiary laws on the other and (iv) government regulatory chill syndrome to properly implement CSR against multinational enterprises (MNEs). In order to strike a balance between, for instance, preventing double operational CSR standards of MNEs within the Nigerian extractive industry on the one hand and allaying the fears of capital flight or jurisdictional arbitrage from perceived over-regulation, this chapter recommends proper legal transplantation and harmonization of the different and incoherent hard and soft law CSR implementation framework. The harmonization will involve, just as in the USA discussed in Chapter 3, a smart-mix of different regulatory methods also discussed in that chapter. This will include amendment of relevant provisions of the primary company legislation and the Companies and Allied Matters Act 1990 as amended (CAMA) to expand its requirements on financial statements and annual reporting to accommodate integrated reporting. It may also be necessary to amend the relevant reporting or disclosure provisions in the Investments and Securities Act 2007 (ISA) to also integrate non-financial CSR reporting on issues of the environment, employees, social matters et cetera for public liability and quoted companies. Further, the provisions of NEITI also require amendments to secure the independence and integrity of the NSWG, and the provisions of Sections 3 and 14 of the NEITI Act – undermining the ability of NEITI to use or publish audited reports considered prejudicial to some signed contracts of the business community in the Nigerian extractive industries or the government – should be revisited. If these recommendations are favourably considered, the risk of the otherwise impressive CSR implementation provisions in the sectoral codes and the Nigeria Code being *ultra vires* of primary enactments become eliminated. Against the backdrop of the perception of soft law, self-regulatory voluntary CSR regulatory regimes being generally inadequate and inefficient, Nigeria should consider the proposal made in Chapter 7. Proper formulation, delineation and elucidation of the normative framework and the regulatory implications of the said proposal are outside the scope of this chapter and are accordingly addressed in Chapter 7.

Notes

1 Joseph Abugu, *Principles of Corporate Law in Nigeria* (Lagos: MIJ Professional Publishers 2014); see chapter 15 thereof dedicated to CSR. Other works containing highlight

150 *CSR conceptual and regulatory framework in Africa*

discussions about the CSR subject include: John W. Hendrikse and Leigh Hefer-Hendrikse, *Corporate Governance Handbook: Principles and Practice* (2nd edn, Cape Town: JUTA 2012) chapters 30 and 41; Jean Jacques Du Plessis, Anil Hargovan and Mirko Bagaric, *Principles of Contemporary Corporate Governance* (2nd edn, Cambridge: Cambridge University Press 2011) 51, 52; Farouk H.I. Cassim and others, *Contemporary Company Law* (Cape Town: JUTA 2011) 435–437.

2 Adaeze Okoye, *Legal Approaches and Corporate Social Responsibility: Towards a Llewellyn's Law-Jobs Approach* (Abingdon, UK: Routledge 2017); see also, Adefolake O. Adeyeye, *Corporate Social Responsibility of Multinational Corporations in Developing Countries: Perspectives on Anti-Corruption* (Cambridge: Cambridge University Press 2012).

3 Olufemi Amao, *Corporate Social Responsibility, Human Rights and the Law: Multinational Corporations in Developing Countries* (Abingdon, UK: Routledge 2011).

4 For a brief history of company law development in Nigeria, see Olufemi Amao, 'Corporate Social Responsibility, Multinational Corporations and the Law in Nigeria: Controlling Multinationals in Host States' (2008) *Journal of African Law* 89–113, 94, 95, *et seq.*

5 The administration of law and justice generally in the whole of what is now called Nigeria began through the activities of a foreign owned company, the Royal Niger Company. Olufemi R. Ekundare, *An Economic History of Nigeria 1860–1960* (London: Methuen & Co Ltd 1973) 60.

6 Felix Tuodolo, 'Corporate Social Responsibility: Between Civil Society and Oil Industry in the Developing World' (2009) 8 *ACME: International E-Journal for Critical Geographies* 530–541, 531; Amao (n 4) 89; Uwafiokun Idemudia and Uwem E. Ite, 'Corporate-Community Relations in Nigeria's Oil Industry: Challenges and Imperatives' (2006) 13 *Corporate Social Responsibility and Environmental Management* 194, 195.

7 For an account of how the Royal Niger Company was established and metamorphosed into the currently existing United Africa Company (UAC) of Nigeria Limited, see George Nwangwu, 'The Influence of Companies on the Legal, Political and Economic History of Nigeria' (2018) 12 *Journal of Economics and Sustainable Development* 115, 117–119.

8 King Docemo received 1,200 bags of cowries as annual pension calculated as of 1861 to amount to £1,030 sterling. Relevant parts of the 1861 treaty between King Docemo and the British Government concerning the Port and Island of Lagos reads: 'I, Docemo, do, with the consent and advice of my council, give, transfer, and by these presents grant and confirm unto the Queen of Great Britain, her heirs and successors forever . . . full and absolute dominion and sovereignty of the said port, island, and premises . . . freely, fully, entirely, and absolutely'. UO Umozurike, *International Law and Colonialism in Africa* (Enugu: Nwamife Publishers 1979) 40.

9 Abugu (n 1); see Chapter 15 thereof dedicated to CSR; see also, Imran O. Smith, 'Corporate Social Responsibility towards a Healthier Environment' (2000) 4 Modern Practice Journal of Finance and Investment Law 22–40 for another succinct discussion of CSR as conceptualized in this book but from an environmental management perspective.

10 Olakunle J. Orojo, *Company Law and Practice in Nigeria* (5th edn, Durban: LexisNexis 2008).

11 Fabian Ajogwu, *Corporate Governance in Nigeria: Law and Practice* (Lagos: Centre for Commercial Law Development 2007).

12 Kiser D. Barnes, *Cases and Materials on Nigerian Company Law* (Ibadan: Samadex Printing Works 1992).

13 Emeka Chianu, *Company Law* (Abuja: LawLords Publications 2012) 236.

14 Emmanuel Okon, 'Corporate Social Responsibility by Companies: The Liberal Perspective' (1997) *Nigerian Current Law Review* 193, 201.

15 See, Abiola Odutola, 'GTBank, Zenith, Access, FBN, 10 Others Spend over N8 Billion on CSR' *Nairametrics* (3 November 2019) available at: https://nairametrics.com/2019/11/03/gtbank-zenith-access-fbn-10-others-spend-over-n8-billion-on-csr/

accessed 3 November 2019; also see the CSR affiliate of Aliko Dangote, the richest man in Africa. On its website, it notes that the Aliko Dangote 'Foundation is the Corporate Social Responsibility arm of Dangote Group' (and) 'responsible for contributing over $100 million in charitable funds to several causes in Nigeria and Africa over the past four years.' See available at: www.devex.com/organizations/dangote-foundation-8101 accessed 3 November 2019; see also, FSDH Merchant Bank Limited, 'Corporate Social Responsibility (CSR) Activities in 2015' *The Guardian* (19 January 2016); Kaine Agary, 'Is CSR Worth the Trouble for Companies? (1)' *Punch* (26 July 2015); Raheem Akingbolu, 'Building Equity through CSR: The Grand Oak Example' *Thisday* (22 March 2013) 36; Raheem Akingbolu, 'CSR: Groups Hail Nigerite's Efforts' *Thisday* (14 May 2010); see also, Kenneth Amaeshi, Bongo Adi, Chris Ogbechie and Olufemi Amao, 'Corporate Social Responsibility in Nigeria: Western Mimicry or Indigenous Influences?' (2006) 24 *The Journal of Corporate Citizenship* 83–99; Hakeem Ijaiya, 'Challenges of Corporate Social Responsibility in the Niger Delta Region of Nigeria' (2014) 1 *Journal of Sustainable Development Law and Policy* 60–71; Lukman Raimi and others, 'How Adequate and Efficient Are Regulations on Corporate Social Responsibility and Social Reporting? Evidence from the Nigeria Telecommunication Industry' (2014) 4 *Asian Journal of Empirical Research* 315, 318.

16 Ijaiya (n 15) 62.

17 Rebecca Enuoh and Sunday Eneh, 'Corporate Social Responsibility in the Niger Delta Region of Nigeria: In Who's Interest' (2015) 5 *Journal of Management and Sustainability* 74, 75.

18 Amaeshi and others (n 15) 89.

19 David Vogel, *The Market for Virtue: The Potential and Limits of Corporate Social Responsibility* (Washington: Brooking Institution Press 2005); Keith Davis, 'The Case for and against the Assumption of Social Responsibilities' (1973) 16 (2) *Academy of Management Journal* 312–322; Keith Davis and others, *Business and Society: Concepts and Policy Issues* (4th edn, New York: McGraw-Hill 1980) 50–57.

20 It had the title: 'A Bill for an Act to Provide for the Establishment of the Corporate Social Responsibility Commission'. Although the bill passed the second reading in the National Assembly, legislative actions were subsequently discontinued as a result of public outcry about its obvious shortcomings. While one must commend the introduction of this bill for legislation showing awareness to CSR related issues, however, some if not most of its provisions, such as Section 5 thereof in respect to a mandatory 3.5 % contribution of each and every firm, are far from demonstrating proper grasp of the concept of CSR or its role in promoting sustainable development for both the business community and the society.

21 Stella Amadi, Mekonen Germiso and Asle Henriksen, 'Staoil in Nigeria: Transparency and Local Content Report' Report number 1/2006 Supported by The Norwegian Council for Africa and The Future in our Hands Research Institute (FIFI). Center for Democracy and Development, Nigeria (Framtiden, Ivare hender, No 1/2006) 19.

22 Uwafiokun Idemudia, 'Corporate Social Responsibility and Development in Africa: Issues and Possibilities' (2014) 8/7 *Geography Compass* 421–435, 426.

23 Chrystia Freeland, 'What's BP's Social Responsibility?' 19 July 2010, Reuters online available at: http://blog.reuters.com/chrystia-freeland/2010/07/19/whats-bps-social-responsibility/ accessed 24 October 2016.

24 See, for instance, the 2018 Nigerian Code of Corporate Governance, issued by the Financial Reporting Council of Nigeria effective January, 2019 and replacing the National Code of Corporate Governance 2016. This will be discussed in more detail later.

25 For instance, see the latest Social Responsibility and Sustainability Report of one of the leading financial institutions in Nigeria, First Bank of Nigeria Plc, showing better appreciation of the subject matter available at: www.firstbanknigeria.com/wp-content/uploads/2017/03/sustainabilitypolicystatementFBN1.pdf accessed 2 November 2019. Further, the Nigerian Stock Exchange recently advertised vacancies to fill a CSR

152 *CSR conceptual and regulatory framework in Africa*

position, see available at: https://ngcareers.com/job/2019-01/team-lead-corporate-social-responsibility-at-nigerian-stock-exchange-nse-917 accessed 2 November 2019. The Nigerian Stock Exchange services the largest economy in Africa (Nigeria) and is championing the development of Africa's financial markets. The NSE, a registered company limited by guarantee, was founded in 1960, and it is licensed under the Investments and Securities Act (ISA) and is regulated by the Securities and Exchange Commission (SEC) of Nigeria.

26 See for instance the provisions of Sections 11 (a) and 50 of the Financial Reporting Council of Nigeria Act 2011; Section 166 of 2007 Nigerian Minerals and Mining Act No. 20; the 2007 Nigeria Extractive Industries Transparency Initiative (NEITI) Act, the 2007 National Environmental Standards and Regulations Enforcement Agency (NES-REA) Act, among others.

27 See, generally, *Hutton v. West Cork Railway Co.* (1883) 23 Ch.D., 654; *Percival v. Wright* (1902) 2 Ch 421; *Dodge v. Ford Motor Co.* (1919) 204 Mich. 459, 170 N.W. 668; *Evans v. Brunner, Mond & Co.* (1921) 1 Ch. 359, Re Lee, Behrens & Co Ltd (1932) Ch 46; *Rogers v. Hill* 289 U.S. 582 (1933); *McQuillen v. National Cash Register Co.,* 27 F. Supp. 639 (D. Md. 1939); *Greenhalgh v. Arderne Cinemas Ltd* (1951) Ch. 286, 291; *Gottlieb v. Heyden Chemical Corp.*, 90 A. 2d 660 (Del. 1952); *Parke v. Daily News Ltd* (1962) 3 WLR 566; *Amalgamated Society of Woodworkers of South Africa v. Die 1963* AmbagsaaWereniging (1967) 1 SA 586 (T); *Michelson v. Duncan* 407 A. 2d 211 (Del 1979). See also Section 172 of Companies Act, 2006 (England).

28 Subsection (4) provides that 'the matters to which the director of a company is to have regard in the performance of his functions include the interests of the company's employees in general, as well as the interests of its members'.

29 See also Sections 314 and 315 of CAMA showing its shareholder primacy orientation, with little or no real value addition to stakeholder protection.

30 This is a confirmation of Section 299 of CAMA and codification of the long standing common law principle established in the case of *Foss v. Harbottle* (1943) 2 Hare 461, 69 E. R. 199 Ch; see also generally, *Edwards v. Halliwell* (1950)2 All E.R. 1064; *Alex Oladele Elufioye & Ors v. Ibrahim Halilu & Ors* (1990) LPELR-20126(CA); *Abubakari v. Smith* (1973) 6 S.C. 24.

31 CAMA Sections 331, 332 et seq. and schedule 2.*Cf.* Section 334(2) (h) in relation to financial statements containing a 'value-added statement for the year', which content at Section 335(4) is a report of 'the wealth created by the company during the year and its distribution among various interest groups such as the employees, the government, creditors, proprietors and the company'. This has been interpreted in terms of stakeholder protection provision. Joseph Olakunle Orojo, *Company Law in Nigeria* (3rd edn, Lagos: Mbeyi & Associates 1992) 37. Interestingly, the Nigerian 2007 Investments and Securities Act (ISA), which established the Securities and Exchange Commission (SEC) and regulates the activities of public liability and quoted companies in Nigeria, also made no provision for integrated corporate reporting (on non-financial matters). Further, while Sections 11 (a) and 50 of the Financial Reporting Council of Nigeria Act 2011 may contain promising provisions for stakeholder protection, the definition of 'financial statements' under Section 77 of the act linking the same to the purely shareholder-primacy oriented statements of CAMA and with no reference to stakeholder integrated reporting has undermined, in my view, any stakeholder safeguards Sections 11 and 50 might otherwise afford.

32 Integrated reporting shows that the differentiating line between the so-called financial and non-financial matters of a company is getting blurred and that the dimensions of the economy, the society and the natural environment are all intertwined and not separate.

33 Explanatory notes to the Corporate Social Responsibility Bill; see Corporate Social Responsibility Commission (Establishment, etc.) Bill, 2007, C1239-1244 available at: www.nassnig.org/document/download/1 accessed 28 October 2016, (hereinafter simply 'Nigerian CSR Bill').

34 The Private Member bill was sponsored by the late senator Uche Chwukwumerije (Abia North).
35 Nigerian CSR Bill, 2007, Section 5 thereof.
36 Amao (n 3) 167–169.
37 See generally, Section 3.6 of Chapter 3.
38 See Section 9 of the English Corporate Responsibility Act 2002.
39 See Section 414C, the Companies Act 2006 (Strategic Report and Directors' Report) Regulations 2013, Statutory Instrument 2013 No. 1970 available at: www.legislation.gov.uk/uksi/2013/1970/pdfs/uksi_20131970_en.pdf accessed 2 November 2019.
40 Larry E. Ribstein, 'Accountability and Responsibility in Corporate Governance' (2006) 81 *Notre Dame Law Review* 1431, 1444–1447.
41 Virginia Harper Ho, 'Beyond Regulation: A Comparative Look at State-Centric Corporate Social Responsibility and the Law in China' (2013) 46 *Vanderbilt Journal of Transnational Law* 375, 385. See Section 3.6 of Chapter 3.
42 2013 Indian Companies Act available at: www.mca.gov.in/Ministry/pdf/Companies Act2013.pdf accessed 2 November 2019.
43 See Section 3.1.7 of Chapter 3; Joseph Abugu and Nojeem Amodu, 'Regulating Corporate Reporting in Nigeria: The Uncharitable Perception of an Outsider (External) Regulator' (2016) 2 *The Commercial and Industrial Law Review* 64.
44 Dictum per Bowen L.J in Hutton's case (n 27) 672.
45 CAMA Sections 331, 332 *et seq.* and schedule 2.
46 See the Corporate Responsibility provisions of the Investments and Securities Act, 2007 (ISA), Section 60 to 65 of ISA, 2007 available at: www.sec.gov.ng/laws.html accessed 2 November 2019.
47 For earlier discussions about this initiative, see, generally, Nojeem Amodu, 'Regulation and Enforcement of Corporate Social Responsibility in Corporate Nigeria' (2017) 61 *Journal of African Law* 105.
48 See the EITI Standard, Latest Version 2019 available at: https://eiti.org/sites/default/files/documents/eiti_standard_2019_en_a4_web.pdf accessed 2 November 2019 (EITI Standards).
49 For other and current details about the NEITI, see available at: https://neiti.gov.ng/index.php/aboutus/brief-history-of-neiti/ accessed 2 November 2019.
50 NEITI website, www.neiti.org.ng/sites/default/files/documents/uploads/neitiact.pdf accessed 28 October 2016. The EITI Board designated Nigeria as EITI complaint on 1 March 2011; other countries who have also implemented EITI Standards by legislation include Liberia, Tanzania, Ukraine and Peru.
51 Explanatory memorandum to the 2007 NEITI Act.
52 At the point of writing this chapter, the latest published audit report for the Nigerian oil and gas sector is for the year 2016. See NEITI website available at: https://neiti.gov.ng/index.php/neiti-audits/oil-and-gas/category/184-2016-audit-report accessed 2 November 2019.
53 A Legal transplant is simply a domestic copy of a foreign law. Alan Watson, *Legal Transplants: An Approach to Comparative Law* (2nd edn, Edinburgh: Scottish Academic Press 1993); see also Holger Spamann, 'Contemporary Legal Transplants: Legal Families and the Diffusion of (Corporate) Law' (2010) 2009 (6) *Brigham Young University Law Review* 1813–1878; Janet Dine, 'Jurisdictional Arbitrage by Multinational Companies: A National Law Solution?' (2012) 3 (1) *Journal of Human Rights and the Environment* 44–69, 60.
54 The Foreign Corrupt Practices Act of 1977, as amended, 15 U.S.C. §§ 78dd-1, et seq. available at: www.justice.gov/criminal-fraud/foreign-corrupt-practices-act accessed 2 November 2019.
55 Council Directive, 2003/51/EC, 18 June 2003 amending Directives 78/660/EEC, 83/635/EEC and 91/674/EEC on the annual and consolidated accounts of certain types of companies, banks and other financial institutions and insurance undertakings, OJ L178/16, 2003.

154   CSR conceptual and regulatory framework in Africa

56 The Directive 2014/95/EU on Disclosure of Non-Financial and Diversity Information by Certain Large Undertakings and Groups available at: http://eur-lex.europa.eu/legal-content/EN/TXT/?uri=CELEX:32014L0095 accessed 2 November 2019.

57 EITI Standard available at: https://eiti.org/sites/default/files/documents/eiti_standard_2019_en_a4_web.pdf accessed 2 November 2019.

58 For instance, see different versions available at: www.nigeria-law.org and at http://legaloil.com both accessed 28 October 2016.

59 International Centre for Nigerian Law website, www.nigeria-law.org accessed 28 October 2016.

60 NNPC, 'An Overview of the Petroleum Industry Bill' July, 2009 available at: www.nnpcgroup.com/portals/0/pdf/pibconsultativeforum.pdf accessed 28 October 2016.

61 See Sections 116 to 118 of the PIB.

62 This is, however, subject to subsection 2 to the effect that, at the end of the fiscal year, each upstream petroleum company shall reconcile its 10% remittance with its actual filed tax return to the Nigerian tax authorities and settle any differences.

63 Some earlier discussions about this bill may also be found in Nojeem Amodu, 'Sustainable Development and Corporate Social Responsibility under the 2018 Petroleum Host and Impacted Communities Development Trust Bill: Is Nigeria Rehashing Past Mistakes?' (2019) 11 *African Journal of Legal Studies* 319–351.

64 Sections 1 and 161 of the NMMA.

65 By virtue of Section 5 of the NMMA, the MCO is the central agency at the Federal Capital Territory, Abuja involved in the processing of mineral title applications including exploratory licenses, mining licenses, quarrying licenses and small-scale mining licenses.

66 By the combined effect of Sections 16 and 18, the MECD is a department responsible for monitoring and enforcing compliance with environmental requirements and liaising with relevant agencies of government with respect to social and environment issues in mining operations.

67 By Section 19 of the NMMA, the MREMC operates at the state levels to consider and advise the Minister on matters affecting pollution and degradation of any land on which any mineral is being extracted and providing guidance to departments on the implementation of social and environmental protection measures.

68 Sections 56, 61, 70 (f) and 118, NMMA.

69 Under Section 71 (1) (c), a signed CDA as approved by the MECD is a condition precedent to mining activities. The CDA is subject of review every five years. See Section 116 (5), NMMA. This concept of CDA is new as it was not contained in the repealed Minerals and Mining Decree No. 34 of 1999.

70 Despite the provisions of Regulation 193 of the Minerals and Mining Regulation 2011, it is doubtful if the definition of host community in the regulation would be able to actually address this issue.

71 Similarly Irene-Marie Esser and Piet Delport had also noted, in this circumstance, the corporate governance code in South Africa, 'King IV is not law, and does not prescribe, with a primary emphasis not on "what" must be done, but rather "how" it must be done'. Irene-Marie Esser and Piet Delport, 'The South African King IV on Corporate Governance: Is the Crown Shiny Enough?' (2018) 39 (11) *Company Lawyer* 378, 384.

72 Institute of Directors in Southern Africa, 'King IV Report on Governance for South Africa 2016'.

73 See for instance, Principles 2.2, 2.8.1, 28.3, 34.1 of the SEC Code; also see, Principles 6.6., 10.1, and 12 of the NCC Code.

74 Louise Osemeke and Emmanuel Adegbite, 'Regulatory Multiplicity and Conflict: Towards a Combined Code on Corporate Governance in Nigeria' (2016) 133 *Journal of Business Ethics* 431–451, 435.

75 Compare with the Financial Reporting Standards Council in South Africa established under Section 203 of the South African Companies Act No. 71 of 2008. The Financial Reporting Council of Nigeria is a federal government parastatal under the supervision

of the Federal Ministry of Industry, Trade and Investment with the statutory remit to, amongst others, develop and publish corporate governance codes, accounting and financial reporting standards to be observed in the preparation of financial statements of public entities in Nigeria. See Section 8 of the Financial Reporting Council of Nigeria Act, 2011.

76 The code was adopted as part of the Regulation on the Adoption and Compliance with Nigerian Code of Corporate Governance 2018 (Nigerian Code). Companies are mandated to report on the application of the code in their annual reports for financial years ending after 1 January 2020 in the form and manner prescribed by the Financial Reporting Council of Nigeria. These companies include: (i) all public companies (whether a listed company or not); (ii) all private companies that are holding companies of public companies or other regulated entities; (iii) all concessioned or privatized companies and (iv) all regulated private companies being private companies that file returns to any regulatory authority other than the Federal Inland Revenue Service (FIRS) and the Corporate Affairs Commission (CAC). The Nigerian Code is available at: https://drive.google.com/file/d/1_uOzdXFOqexptBQDfDudAvNoI YPjAO27/view accessed 2 November 2019. In any event, other sectoral codes of conduct are still applicable in Nigeria. See paragraph F of the Introduction to the Nigerian Code.

77 References to the 'Code of Business Conduct and Ethics' or the word 'ethics' in Principles 24 and 25 of the Nigerian Code are excluded, as they appear contextualized in terms of morality. See the definition of 'ethics' in paragraph 29.1.9 of the Nigerian Code. Good moral values are generally not enforceable except as they coincide with prescribed legal duty in Nigeria and many jurisdictions therefore. As maintained in other chapters of the book, this author's conception of CSR and discussions in relation thereto are not on the basis of morality.

78 See Principle 1 of both the SEC Code and the NCC Code.

79 Atedo Peterside, *Code of Corporate Governance in Nigeria*, October, 2003 available at: www.ecgi.org/codes/documents/cg_code_nigeria_oct2003_en.pdf accessed 2 November 2019. See the forward by Mr Atedo Peterside in the 2003 code.

80 See similar requirement in under Principle 12 of the NCC Code.

81 See generally, judgment delivered by Justice O.E. Abang on Friday, 21st day of March, 2014 in *Eko Hotels Limited v. Financial Reporting Council of Nigeria* (FHC/L/CS/1430/2012); *NNPC v. Famfa Oil Ltd* (2012) 17 NWLR (Pt. 1328) 148; *Bernard Amasike v. The Registrar General of the Corporate Affairs Commission* (2010) NWLR (Pt. 1211) 337; *Olanrewaju v. Oyeyemi & Ors* (2001) 2 NWLR (Pt. 697) 229; *Din v. A.G. Federation* (1998) 4 NWLR (Pt. 87) 147 at 154; *Adene and Ors v. Dantubu* (1994) 2 NWLR (Part 382) 509; *Gov. Oyo State v. Folayan* (1995) 8 NWLR (Pt.413) 292 at 327. See also the judgment delivered by Salihu Modibbo Alfa Belgore, C.J.N. (as he then was) on Friday, the 22nd Day of September 2006 in the *Attorney General of Lagos State v. Eko Hotels Limited and Oha Limited* (2006) NWLR (Pt. 1011) 3782; *Noble Drilling Nigeria Limited v. Nigerian Maritime Administration and Safety Agency*, (2013) LPELR-22029 (CA); Executive Council, *Western Cape v. Minister for Provincial Affairs and Constitutional Development and Another, Executive Council, KwaZulu-Natal v. President of the Republic of South Africa* 2000 1 SA 661 (CC).

82 Joseph Abugu, 'Issues and Problems in Corporate Governance in Nigeria' (2015) 3 *The Gravitas Review of Business and Property Law* 1, 15.

83 Leyla Davarnejad, 'Strengthening the Social Dimension of International Investment Agreements by Integrating Codes of Conduct for Multinational Enterprises' (OECD Conference Paper, Session 2.2 of the OECD Global Forum on International Investment, 27–28 March, 2008) 10.

84 Faith Stevelman, 'Global Finance, Multinationals and Human Rights: With Commentary on Backer's Critique of the 2008 Report by John Ruggie' (2011) 9 *Santa Clara Journal of International Law* 101, 110.

156   *CSR conceptual and regulatory framework in Africa*

85 See for instance, *Tecnicas Medioambientales Tecmed S.A. v. United Mexican States*, ICSID case No. ARB(AF)/00/2(2003); Compania del DesarrollodeSanta Elena, *S.A. v. Republic of Costa Rica*, ICSID case No. ARB/96/1, 15 ICSID Review- (2000) *Foreign Investment Law Journal* 72, 192.

86 UNCTAD, World Investment Report 2003, 88.

87 Davarnejad (n 83) 8.

88 UNCTAD World Investment Report 2003, 111.

89 Charlotte Villiers, 'Corporate Law, Corporate Power and Corporate Social Responsibility' in Nina Boeger, Rachel Murray and Charlotte Villiers (eds.), *Perspectives on Corporate Social Responsibility* (Cheltenham: Edward Elgar 2008) 88.

5 CSR in South Africa

5 Background

Corporate social responsibility and accountability (CSR) in South Africa is often discussed in terms of good corporate citizenship and corporate social investment (CSI). Before 1994, the CSR construct in South Africa was mainly dominated by the notion of corporate philanthropic responsibility. CSR initiatives in South Africa at such a stage were, just like in Nigeria, about undertaking community development projects and primarily urging the business community to give back to the communities.[1] Evidenced from academic writings and details revealed on relevant corporate websites, this confined conceptualization appears to have changed slightly, however. As shall be explained further in this chapter, unlike in many jurisdictions in Africa where CSR still appears largely conceptualized as simply corporate charity or philanthropy, the business community, the academia and government agencies in South Africa appear to have moved beyond this atavistic CSR conception and have adopted the subject as the comprehensive corporate governance and business management model that it should be. For instance, Henk Kloppers, in describing CSR, adopts the International Organisation for Standardisation (ISO) definition stating that CSR is the responsibility of an organization for the impacts of its decisions and activities on society and the environment, through transparent and ethical behaviour that contributes to sustainable development, health and the welfare of society; takes into account the expectations of stakeholders; is in compliance with applicable law and consistent with international norms of behaviour and is integrated throughout the organization and practised in its relationships.[2] Corporate governance codes also underscore corporate citizenship (CSR) in terms of a tool for managing businesses in a responsible and accountable fashion, showing respect for human rights, environmental responsibility and community engagement through the promotion of collaborative partnerships.[3] Although the government of South Africa has made no direct and formal confirmation of its CSR implementation strategy or CSR conceptualization, the author's conclusion that there is better understanding of the CSR subject in the country (as opposed to the first case study) is borne out of certain legislative advancements especially from corporate law perspective. For instance,

158   *CSR conceptual and regulatory framework in Africa*

the South African Companies Act No. 71 of 2008 together with its subsidiary, the 2011 Companies Regulations, makes provision for a 'social and ethics committee' whose workings appear to implement and monitor a robust CSR framework within the business community. Such CSR framework includes balancing and managing risks involved in complying with CSR-inspired legislations as listed in Section 5.3, together with a few international regulatory initiatives such the United Nations Global Compact as described in Chapter 3. That is definitely a CSR conception beyond corporate philanthropy or charity. This relevance, adequacy or otherwise of the social and ethic committee as an effective CSR implementation strategy is another discussion as reserved for later in this chapter.

5.1 CSR conception and practices

As earlier noted, there appears to be an improved understanding of the subject, and many academics and the business community discuss the subject in terms of a comprehensive governance and management mechanisms towards getting businesses to behave responsibly. Therefore, Kloppers offered a CSR definition in terms of the acceptance by a business that it has a responsibility towards various stakeholders resulting from its business operations and that as a result of this responsibility it can be held accountable if it neglects to act responsibly.[4] While the term CSR in still very popular in corporate Nigeria, CSR is commonly referred to as corporate citizenship or CSI in corporate South Africa. Although a few academics such as Irene-Marie Esser initially conceived of using the terms 'CSR' and 'corporate citizenship' as two distinct terms, this attempt was soon realized to be in futility and the terms were properly adopted as interchangeable.[5] She therefore defined and conceptualized CSR as relating 'to important social, safety, health and environmental factors to which company management must have adequate regard'.[6] Within similar conception, it has also been said that, however one labels CSR, as triple-bottom line reporting, as an inclusive approach or as corporate citizenship, it relates to the intention to link business with wider societal concerns.[7] Further, a good corporate citizen was described by key South African analysts as a business with comprehensive policies and practices in place throughout the business that enable it to make decisions and conduct its operations ethically, meet legal requirements and show consideration for society, communities and the environment.[8]

It was earlier shown in Chapter 1 of this book that CSR is a global concept, similar everywhere in the world; its components and elements are the same, with of course, variations in the CSR 'issues' on which the CSR components in each jurisdiction are premised. Such is the case in South Africa where, despite a good grasp of the subject as a comprehensive corporate governance and business management model, government CSR or corporate citizenship implementation strategies appear focused on addressing the historical issues of economic and social exclusion during the apartheid era.[9] In this regard, Wayne Visser had also noted that corporate citizenship in (South) Africa is a critical area of scholarly enquiry, driven by the legacy of colonialism and apartheid.[10] The apartheid regime in South Africa suppressed wealth and skill endowments among the black communities and had so promoted black population's social and economic exclusion in corporate South Africa that, by the late 1980s, low levels of investments in human capital, racially discriminatory salaries and high levels of unemployment began to take a toll and contributed to a structural divide in the South African economy.[11] Therefore, less attention appears to be paid to other issues such as environmental matters, and government CSR interventionist initiatives have been focused on social transformation and economic inclusion for the majority black population. Consequently, CSR-inspired legislations such as: the Labour Relations Act No. 66 of 1995; the Bill of Rights included in the South African Constitution, 1996; the Employment Equity Act No. 55 of 1998; the Skills Development Act, 1998; the Promotion of Equality and Prevention of Unfair Discrimination Act, 2000; the Broad-Based Black Economic Empowerment (BBBEE) Act No. 53 of 2003 and a Companies Act No. 71 of 2008, which creates a social and ethics committee to monitor CSR implementation were all enacted towards redressing the historic imbalances.[12] With these flagship enactments, South Africa has attracted investments as it manages the transition from a racially skewed to an equitable economy.[13] The country continues to deepen its integration into the world economy through these flagship CSR implementation interventions, and companies in corporate South Africa appear to be adjusting well to complying with the CSR-inspired legislations. For instance, Arya and Bassi reported that some multinationals have chosen to overcome high levels of operational and strategic uncertainty by acquiring stakes in companies that are forerunners in implementing comprehensive CSR programmes in South Africa.[14] For example, in 2005, the South African minister of finance approved the transaction that Barclays Bank Plc (UK) acquired a 56% controlling stake in the ABSA Group Limited, on the key ground that Barclays would further the CSR initiatives within the ABSA Group in line with applicable industry-specific sector charter requirements. Further, towards ensuring that corporate South Africa complies with the CSR implementation strategy of the government, multinational consulting and auditing firms have also improved their services. In this regard, KPMG–South Africa was said to have developed a practice, 'BBBEE Advisory Services', to assist companies in assessing their BBBEE status and developing remedial CSR strategies.

Despite the seemingly improved and impressive conceptualization of CSR and implementation strategy from the government, the proper compliance with the CSR regulatory framework and enforcement of the CSR legislations within the business community may be suspect. While due to the apartheid history of South Africa and an enhancement of the social and economic transformation strategy of the government some businesses and academics still argue for a CSR framework to be undertaken largely as corporate charity and philanthropic contributions,[15] many other businesses appear not interested in any robust adoption of CSR as a comprehensive concept and would rather

160   *CSR conceptual and regulatory framework in Africa*

only pay mere lip service to its implementation. Research has shown that many do implement the government-proposed systems because they are keen to be seen to care for the environment and the social fabric of the country, whereas in reality their CSR activities are only targeted at deflecting criticism of their unsustainable and irresponsible practices.[16] David Fig gave the example of Sappi, a company that grows large tracts of alien eucalyptus and pine plantations for timber or conversion into pulp and paper. Its plantations are monocultures that squeeze out biodiversity, deplete local water resources, alienate land and compromise ecosystems; it pays poverty wages; its paper mills rely on extremely dirty technologies. Yet Sappi has a public reputation as green-oriented, because of the resources it devotes to widely distributed nature publications and numerous other environmental projects. Its rival, Mondi, whose socio-environmental practices are similar, sponsors a major project on wetland protection and rehabilitation.[17] In a call for the business community in South Africa to properly embed effective CSR practices within its operations towards realizing the social transformation and economic inclusion agenda of the CSR-inspired legislations, Fig concludes noting that business usually:

> overemphasizes the extent of its voluntary contribution to socio-economic and environmental progress, while continuing to mask malpractice, and seducing South Africans into forgetting, absolving, effacing old scars, and – most resonant here – reconciling. . . . Firms in South Africa have to first confess and then to set out plans for their own contribution to reconciliation. . . . While business in South Africa uses CSR to manufacture amnesia, the imperative for other sections of civil society remains that of keeping memory alive and continuing to tell the truth.[18]

5.2 Theoretical underpinnings of CSR in South Africa

So, the question is, what theoretical models underpin the CSR conception and practices in corporate South Africa? While there are a few CSR implementation legislations and codes of corporate governance in South Africa suggestive that they are underpinned by the stakeholder Ideological Corporate Model (as discussed in Chapter 2), upon a critical scrutiny, however, at least for the ones examined in this chapter, they are essentially conditioned by the fundamental assumptions of the shareholder primacy model. For instance, Section 7(k) of the primary corporate legislation in South Africa, the Companies Act No. 71 of 2008 (SACA), provides that the SACA is intended to be operated and administered in a manner that balances the rights and interests of all relevant stakeholders. This indicates the intention to accommodate stakeholder interests, which provides a fertile and useful ideological backing for effective CSR implementation. Further, Section 72(4)[19] provides for the minister to release relevant regulations prescribing that qualified businesses must have a 'social and ethics committee'. Such committee shall be established at the level of the board of directors of the company, and, by virtue of the provision of Section 76(3) (a) and (b),[20] such directors are enjoined to act in good faith and in the best interests of the company. Ordinarily, these previously mentioned legislative advancements at Sections 7(k) and 72 of the SACA, together with the complementary Companies Regulations released by the Minister in 2011, are impressive and constitute indications of an effective CSR implementation and protecting stakeholder rights.

This ordinarily also suggests that the SACA is dissociated from the fundamental assumptions of the shareholder primacy model in holding that companies should be managed as exclusive private properties of the shareholders and should therefore be managed to only enhance the shareholder value. This also suggests that the SACA intends that, in relation to corporate activities, the social, economic and environmental impacts of their operations should be effectively managed, providing real benefits to corporate stakeholders such as the employees, customers, host communities, the environment and others. However, the reality is that the CSR implementation provisions as are respectively included in the preliminary sections of the SACA and reduced to board committee considerations are after all not watertight in properly safeguarding stakeholder interests. This is because all the CSR monitoring activities and considerations of the social and ethics committee at the board level are eventually laid before the shareholder group of the company, which group has been shown not to constitute an effective corporate governance mechanism towards stakeholder interests' protection or effective CSR implementation. Apart from the fact that the SACA has not provided very clear terms of reference for the social and ethics committee to operate, the other reality is simply that shareholders are just no longer an effective corporate governance control mechanism.[21] Paddy Ireland has also shown that the shareholder group has rather little financial incentive to ensure that corporate executives (including in the social and ethics committee, this author should add) behave responsibly or are actually performing their job of proper and effective implementation of CSR because, in law, shareholders are simply personally untouchable. An example can be made of the 2007 to 2008 economic crash where the shareholders of the companies concerned did not have to worry about being held liable for the losses incurred because the shares were fully paid-up, and they were only liable (if at all) to the extent of their fully paid-up shares, nor did anyone consider them in any way (morally) responsible for the economic crash, even though they had happily accepted regular and substantial dividends from the corporate executives who were responsible for the crash.[22] So basically, subjecting the monitoring activities of the social and ethics committee to the general meeting of the shareholders as an effective corporate governance and control mechanism simply confirms the primacy of the shareholder interests in the end. Further, despite these innovative Sections 7 and 72(4) of the SACA, the clear provisions of Section 76(3)(b) enjoining corporate executives to perform their functions in the 'best interests of the company' still suggests that shareholder primacy theory, although seemingly disguised, still largely underpins the provisions.[23] In recognition of this entrenchment of the shareholder primacy model, Linda Muswaka has also concluded that, even though efforts appears to have been made in the SACA to ensure that other stakeholders' interests are

162   *CSR conceptual and regulatory framework in Africa*

protected, it seems that legislation is far from effectively safeguarding the rights of stakeholders.[24]

5.3 Legal, regulatory and enforcement framework of CSR

As a result of the imbalances in the South Africa society occasioned by the apartheid policy of the government of the Republic of South Africa pre-1995, so many enactments have been introduced towards ensuring corporate social and environmental responsibility and accountability within the South African business community. These CSR-inspired enactments include:

   (i) Occupational Health and Safety Act No. 85 of 1993;
  (ii) Labour Relations Act No. 66 of 1995;
 (iii) Constitution of the Republic of South Africa (Bill of Rights) 1996;
 (iv) Mine Health and Safety Act No. 29 of 1996.
  (v) Employment Equity Act No. 55 of 1998;
 (vi) Skills Development Act No. 97 of 1998;
 (vii) National Environmental Management Act No. 107 of 1998;
(viii) Promotion of Equality and Prevention of Unfair Discrimination Act, 2000;
 (ix) Promotion of Access to Information Act No. 2 of 2000;
  (x) Mineral and Petroleum Resources Development Act No. 28 of 2002.
 (xi) Broad-Based Black Economic Empowerment Act No. 53 of 2003;
 (xii) Companies Act No. 71 of 2008;
(xiii) King IV Report on Governance for South Africa 2016.[25]

For the purpose of this chapter and in line with the corporate law perspective and theme of the book, although relevant allusions may be made to the other legislations, only the Companies Act and the King Reports are discussed in relation to CSR implementation in corporate South Africa.

5.3.1 The Companies Act

The South African Companies Act No. 71 of 2008 (SACA) repealed the Companies Act No. 61 of 1973 and came into effect on 1 May 2011. Despite the comprehensive changes brought about by the SACA, just like within the Nigeria Companies and Allied Matters Act of 1990 as amended (CAMA), there is no express reference to any responsibility or obligations on companies to integrate CSR issues into their decision-making and corporate governance structures. Although there is no direct and express CSR obligation, the South African government, however, appears to have taken cognizance of the rising public interest in social transformation issues and therefore made an attempt to ensure that CSR is implemented even though indirectly within the legislative framework of the SACA. A few of the relevant sections are examined later. For instance, Section 7(d) and (k) provides:[26]

CSR in South Africa   163

The purposes of this Act are to –

(d) reaffirm the concept of the company as a means of achieving economic and social benefits;
(k) provide for the efficient rescue and recovery of financially distressed companies, in a manner that balances the rights and interests of all relevant stakeholders.

The previous provisions confirm the objectives to accommodate the stakeholder model within the South African corporate law system and thereby provide philosophical foundation for effective CSR implementation. Further, Section 72(4) of the SACA also talks about a 'social and ethics committee' within the board of directors of the company while Section 76(3) (a) and (b)[27] enjoins directors to act in good faith and in the best interests of the company. Section 72(4) provides that:

(4) The Minister may by regulation prescribe that a company or a category of companies must have a social and ethics committee, if it is desirable in the public interest, having regard to – (a) its annual turnover; (b) the size of its workforce; or (c) the nature and extent of its activities.

On the basis of the previous section, the Minister on 26 April 2011, released the 2011 *Companies Regulations*, where state-owned, listed public companies or companies that have in any two of the previous five years scored above 500 points in terms of regulation 26(2)[28] must appoint a social and ethics committee consisting of not less than three directors or prescribed officers of the company, and at least one of these directors or prescribed officers must be a director not involved in the day-to-day management of the company and who has not been so involved in the preceding three financial years.[29] The social and ethics committee monitors CSR implementation matters having regard to any relevant legislation, other legal requirements or prevailing codes of best practice with regard to matters concerning:[30]

(i) social and economic development, including the company's standing in terms of the goals and purposes of –

(aa) the 10 principles set out in the United Nations Global Compact Principles;
(bb) the OECD recommendations regarding corruption;
(cc) the Employment Equity Act;
(dd) the Broad-Based Black Economic Empowerment Act.

(ii) good corporate citizenship, including the company's –

(aa) promotion of equality, prevention of unfair discrimination and reduction of corruption

164   *CSR conceptual and regulatory framework in Africa*

(bb) contribution to the development of communities in which its activities are predominantly conducted or within which its products or services are predominantly marketed;

(cc) record of sponsorship, donations and charitable giving;

(iii) the environment, health and public safety, including the impact of the company's activities and of its products or services;

(iv) consumer relationships, including the company's advertising, public relations and compliance with consumer protection laws;

(v) labour and employment; including –

(aa) the company's standing in terms of the International Labour Organization Protocol on decent work and working conditions;

(bb) the company's employment relationships and its contribution towards the educational development of its employees.

Although there is an ongoing process towards amending the SACA through the 2018 Companies Amendment, the author's review of the relevant parts of the amendment does not show any significant improvements in relation to its CSR implementation strategy, especially regarding the workings of the social and ethics committee. For instance, Amendment 14 essentially seeks to subject the social and ethics committee report to shareholders' discussion at general meetings while Amendment 15, seeking to amend the present Section 72 of SACA, essentially mandates an externally assured social and ethics committee report but as still subjected to the 'politics' of shareholders at general meetings.

The points made earlier in Section 5.2 of this chapter about the foundation of the previous provisions in the shareholder primacy model still hold sway. The effectiveness of the instrumentality of the social and ethics committee creation at the corporate board level to monitor CSR implementation for the benefit of all corporate stakeholders remains doubted. Of what real value to other corporate stakeholders is the laying of the audited reports of the social and ethics committee before general meetings for discussion? Yes, there might be a few shareholders who will be interested in ensuring the approval of a report with concrete benefits to stakeholders beyond just maximizing shareholder wealth. Assuming but not conceding this was always true, this strategy therefore will only be useful to enlightened boards or companies in the Groups A and B of Thomas McInerney[31] as discussed in Chapter 3, being companies 'who know the law and are willing to follow it' (Group A) or 'who do not know the law but would like to be law abiding' (Group B). What happens to the C and D companies within the business community 'who know the law and do not want to follow it' (Group C) or 'who do not know the law and do not wish to be law abiding' (Group D)? Certainly, the control mechanism of getting the reports audited will be bypassed by these rogue companies in groups C and D.

Further, apart from the fact that there are no clear terms of reference for the social and ethics committee to function effectively in CSR implementation towards ensuring the social, economic and environmental risks of the business are properly balanced and managed, the shareholder group itself has been shown not to constitute an effective corporate governance tool insuring the company itself remains accountable. What is more, even where shareholders are motivated to ensure corporate executives in the social and ethics committee behave responsibly and accountably to all affected stakeholders, the neoliberal, open market, contractarianism-backed shareholder primacy model underpinning the SACA will see to it that any unhappy shareholders who may be in the minority in trying to get the company to behave responsibly are probably better advised to 'exit' than to try to hold corporate executives to account using company law.

It is also interesting to note that there are some proponents of an expansive[32] idea that attempts to directly impose a CSR obligation or responsibility on the corporate executives even though the SACA only appears to have done so indirectly. The proponents of this argument rely on inferences or the obiter dicta made by judges in the cases of *Minister of Water Affairs and Forestry v. Stilfontein Gold Mining Co. Ltd,*[33] *De Villiers v. BOE Bank Ltd*[34] and *Mthimunye-Bakoro v. Petroleum Oil and Gas Corporation of South Africa (SOC) Limited*[35] about the importance of corporate executives complying with corporate governance codes like the King IV in running the company. For instance, in the *Minister of Water Affairs and Forestry v. Stilfontein Gold Mining Company,* the court per Justice Hussain, in relation to the 2002 King Report on Corporate Governance (King II), had noted at paragraphs 16.7–16.9 that one of the characteristics of good governance is social responsibility. This particular case dealt with the issue of preventing water pollution in mining operations, and the court came to the conclusion that the relevant respondents acted irresponsibly by not addressing the issue of the water pollution.[36] If relevant allusion can be made to corporate Nigeria, the creative and expansive thinking in this regard may also be extended to saying that since it is the duty of corporate executives to prevent financial loss and avoid unnecessary risks that could affect the company's bottom line or dissipate its assets,[37] it could also be argued that the provisions of Sections 279(3) and 283(1) of the CAMA also allow corporate executives to implement CSR and protect stakeholder interests in avoidance of unnecessary risk to the company's assets.

However, this author submits that while the previous arguments may be considered inspiring, to a judge and/or a regulator they are largely conjectural. Without a clear legislative prescription adopting a stakeholder-oriented model of corporate law such as the RSM earlier proposed in Chapter 2 of this book (and to be further expanded on in Chapter 7), it will be difficult to convince any judge in the two jurisdictions that there is a legal obligation or responsibility on corporate executives to implement CSR or actually safeguard stakeholder interests, on which basis the judges or regulators may hold the company or executives accountably by. In summing up, therefore, the previous creative arguments can offer no real safeguard for the interest of stakeholders or towards effective implementation of corporate social and environmental responsibility and accountability within the South African business community.

166   *CSR conceptual and regulatory framework in Africa*

5.4 King IV Report on Corporate Governance for South Africa 2016

Just as Nigeria has the 2018 Nigerian Code of Corporate Governance, South Africa also has the comprehensive code of corporate governance called the King IV.[38] The King IV[39] has a few interesting provisions on CSR implementation. In terms of a brief historical perspective on the South African 2016 King IV, the 2002 King II replaced the 1994 King I, and this King II was remarkable for acknowledging that there was need for departure from the corporate governance single bottom line approach (shareholder primacy approach) to a triple bottom line, which embraces the economic, environmental and social aspects of a company's activities. The 2009 King III is equally remarkable in refining the triple bottom line concept of King II and used the term 'triple context', which informed the introduction of the concept of integrated reporting, showing that the differentiating line between the so-called financial and non-financial matters of a company are getting blurred and that the dimensions of the economy, the society and the natural environment are all intertwined and not separate.[40] So, rather than corporate disclosure aimed at CSR implementation being referred to as 'non-financial' reporting or disclosure, 'integrated reporting' or disclosure is preferred. Integrated reporting under King III clearly demonstrates improved conceptualization of the CSR construct, especially in relation to stakeholder engagement. Such improved understanding appeared to have prompted independent production of a new form of corporate reporting responsible for the increased number of companies in South Africa compared to Nigeria disclosing on the so-called non-financial matters. After the 2009 King III, King IV was introduced in 2016, effective 2017 and improving on the King III. One of King IV's key objectives is addressing the mindless compliance with corporate governance code.[41] Unlike the Nigerian Code with a seeming tone of mandatory compliance,[42] in its objective of addressing the mindless box-ticking compliance scourge, King IV remains a set of voluntary principles and practices. The phrase 'stakeholder–inclusive approach' appears thematic in King IV and informed its key provisions on CSR implementation and stakeholder protection.[43] A few provisions of the King IV on CSR implementation are highlighted in the following extract:

> Principle 3:
>
>> The governing body should ensure that the organisation is and is seen to be a responsible corporate citizen.
>
> Principle 8, recommended practice 68 provides:
>
>> For some companies, the establishment of a social and ethics committee is a statutory requirement. The governing body of any organisation not so obliged should consider allocating oversight of, and reporting on, organisational ethics, responsible corporate citizenship, sustainable development and stakeholder relationships to a dedicated

CSR in South Africa   167

committee, or adding it to the responsibilities of another committee as is appropriate for the organisation.

Principle 13:

The governing body should govern compliance with applicable laws and adopt, non-binding rules, codes and standards in a way that supports the organisation being ethical and a good corporate citizen.

Principle16:

In the execution of its governance role and responsibilities, the governing body should accept a stakeholder-inclusive approach that balances the needs, interests and expectations of material stakeholders in the best interests of the organisation over time.

While it is obvious that these provisions target CSR implementation, a few questions appear pertinent. What are the primary legislation provisions that these CSR King IV provisions are complementing or are giving effect to? What workable recommendations have been provided to corporate executives to consider and safeguard qualified, material and legitimate stakeholder interests? Analysis done earlier in this chapter shows that the stakeholder-inclusive approach appears enshrined in the primary corporate legislation of South Africa but, upon scrutiny, is essentially shown to be underlain by shareholder primacy. While the policy advancements in King IV must be appreciated in their attempt to address the empty and mindless compliance with integrated reporting requirements, this author nonetheless submits that the corporate governance code is defective;[44] it is a regulatory document meant to complement the primary corporate law enactment and, yet, there are no clear provisions in the primary corporate law regime, which is a definitive adoption of the stakeholder-inclusive approach. The author submits that the impressive and innovative policies of stakeholder-inclusive approach underpinning the integrated reporting in the South Africa King IV do not complement, and as a matter of fact, could be said to have gone on a different trajectory (adopting stakeholder-oriented approach) from the SACA, which is still shareholder primacy-centric.

Further, in relation to the queries of a workable stakeholder management system for effective CSR implementation, this author is of the view that these policy innovations in the voluntary codes may never[45] offer any real protection to stakeholders as cases of CSR greenwash and faux box-ticking integrated reporting will only continue.[46] This is largely because qualified, material and legitimate stakeholders, despite King IV together with any other soft law voluntary codes, will still rely on the company itself (acting through its directors) to protect their interest and, unfortunately for them, the 'company' is still being interpreted to mean the shareholders as a whole and as principals of corporate executives and directors. It is also interesting to note that King IV attempts to extend the meaning of 'company' to other constituents stating that 'the company is represented by several interests and these include the interests of

168   *CSR conceptual and regulatory framework in Africa*

shareholders, employees, consumers, the community and the environment'.[47] The view of the author is that such expansive argument and interpretation in a soft law like King IV is baseless, unsupported and cannot withstand the too many provisions in the harder law SACA with which to hold that the interest of the 'company' remains the interests of the shareholders as a whole in consonance with common law.

5.5 Factors militating against effective CSR in South Africa

Discussions in this chapter have pointed to a few factors militating against effective CSR implementation in corporate South Africa. For the purpose of emphasis, these are enumerated in the following list:

(i)   Corporate greenwashing together with empty and mindless compliance with code requirements just to appear as champions of CSR;

(ii)   The absence of a clear and definitive CSR implementation strategy by the government of South Africa in the Companies Act No. 71 of 2008, (SACA);

(iii) In light of (ii), despite the provisions of Section 7(d), (k) and 72(4) of the Companies Act No. 71 of 2008, the absence of a direct CSR obligation on corporate executives inhibits effective implementation of CSR within corporate South Africa;

(iv)   Just as in corporate Nigeria, poor legal transplantation involved in soft legal instruments such as the King IV, which has misaligned the otherwise impressive CSR implementation provisions in such soft law in relation to the provisions in the primary corporate legislation in South Africa;

(v)   Despite the deliberate attempt to mainstream a stakeholder-inclusive approach within corporate South Africa through soft law, the dominance of shareholder primacy model underlying the objectives of corporate actions and CSR implementation in the SACA still hold sway;

(x)   The last is the absence of a clear term of reference for the social and ethics committee to implement effective CSR policies and with which corporate executives may properly balance competing stakeholder interests and manage the social, economic and environmental impacts of corporate operations.

5.6 Chapter summary

The chapter examined CSR conceptualization, regulation and implementation within corporate South Africa. It also underscored the prevalence of the shareholder primacy model as somewhat disguised within the South African Companies Act No. 71 of 2008 (SACA). While the South African primary corporate law system may be considered improved when compared to Nigeria's, upon scrutiny, however, its stakeholder-inclusive provisions were found to be essentially hinged on the overarching shareholder primacy provisions contained in Section 76(3)(b) of the SACA. The chapter argued that references to stakeholder interests under Section 7(d) and (k) of SACA or even under Section 279 (4) of the Nigerian Companies and Allied Matters Act (CAMA) are insufficient to embed responsible and accountable corporate activities within their respective business communities. The author recommended that the South African government (just as should the Nigerian) should harden its existing largely voluntary, soft law CSR implementation framework, which fosters corporate greenwash and mindless compliance with code requirements. The author also noted that affording real protection to stakeholders' interests against the corporate irresponsibility of McInerney's Group C and D rogue companies would only be afforded where the primary corporate legislation is aligned in philosophy, principle and provisions with the impressive CSR, sustainability and integrated reporting requirements contained in the subsidiary and secondary legal instruments of the corporate governance codes. Against the backdrop that soft law and self-regulatory voluntary CSR regimes are ordinarily inadequate and inefficient, Chapter 7 contains a CSR implementation proposal underpinned by the responsible stakeholder model (RSM), which is commended for adoption not only by corporate South Africa but also other corporate systems on the continent.

Notes

1 Md Humayun Kabir, Janine Mukuddem-Petersen and Mark A. Petersen, 'Corporate Social Responsibility Evolution in South Africa' (2015) 13 *Problems and Perspectives in Management* 281–289, 282.
2 Henk J. Kloppers, 'Driving Corporate Social Responsibility (CSR) through the Companies Act: An Overview of the Role of the Social and Ethics Committee' (2013) 16 *Potchefstroom Electronic Law Journal* 165–199, 166; see also, Wayne Visser, 'Research on Corporate Citizenship in Africa: A Ten Year Review (1995–2005)' in Wayne Visser, Malcolm McIntosh and Charlotte Middleton (eds.), *Corporate Citizenship in Africa: Lessons from the Past; Paths to the Future* (Sheffield: Greenleaf Publishing 2006) 18–28; Lothar Rieth, Melanie Zimmer, Ralph Hamann and Jon Hanks, 'Is Corporate Citizenship Making a Difference?' (2001) 28 *The Journal of Corporate Citizenship* 99–112.
3 Institute of Directors, 'King Report on Corporate Governance for South Africa 2002' (King Report II) 92–93.
4 Kloppers (n 2) 176.
5 Irene-Marie Esser, 'Corporate Social Responsibility: A Company Law Perspective' (2011) 23 *South African Mercantile Law Journal* 317, 319, referring to Ralph Hamann and Nicola Acutt, 'How Should Civil Society (and the Government) Respond to "Corporate Social Responsibility?" A Critique of Business Motivations and the Potential for Partnerships' (2003) 20 *Development Southern Africa* 255 who had noted that '"corporate social responsibility" (CSR) and "corporate citizenship" is meant to link the market economy with sustainable development'.
6 Esser (n 5) 320.
7 Lilian Miles and Mariette Jones, 'The Prospects for Corporate Governance Operating as a Vehicle for Social Change in South Africa' (2009) 14(1) *Deakin Law Review* 71.
8 David Fig, 'Manufacturing Amnesia: Corporate Social Responsibility in South Africa' (2005) 81 *International Affairs* 599–617, 601 citing Trialogue, *The Good Corporate Citizen: Pursuing Sustainable Business in South Africa* (Cape Town: Trialogue 2004) 8.

170   CSR conceptual and regulatory framework in Africa

9 Bindu Arya and Balbir Bassi, 'Corporate Social Responsibility and Broad-Based Black Economic Empowerment Legislation in South Africa: Codes of Good Practice' (2011) 50 (4) *Business & Society* 674–695, 676.

10 Visser (n 2) 18.

11 Arya and Bassi (n 9) 676–677.

12 Wayne Visser, 'Corporate Citizenship in South Africa: A Review of Progress Since Democracy' (2005) 18 *Journal of Corporate Citizenship* 29–38.

13 Arya and Bassi (n 9) 691 and 692.

14 Ibid.

15 Wayne Visser, 'Corporate Social Responsibility in Developing Countries' in Andrew Crane, Abigail McWilliams, Dirk Matten, Jeremy Moon and Donald S. Siegel (eds.), *The Oxford Handbook of Corporate Social Responsibility* (Oxford: Oxford University Press 2008) 473–479.

16 Fig (n 8) 603; also see examples of common CSR practices cited by Irene-Marie Esser, Esser (n 5) 331.

17 Ibid. This is a classic example of corporate 'greenwash', as earlier discussed in Section 1.3 of Chapter 1. This occurs when a company appears to be only complying with the codes, just for the sake of complying, without embedding code requirements as corporate culture or making them part of the so-called DNA of the company. This is faux CSR, empty CSR implementation.

18 Ibid. 617.

19 There is no comparable provision to this one in the Nigerian Companies and Allied Matters Act 1990, as amended (CAMA). There is, however, something similar to the South African framework in Sections 134(3)(o) and 135 of the 2013 Indian Companies Act requiring, inter alia, the constitution of a corporate social responsibility committee on the board of directors of qualified Indian companies.

20 This can be compared to the wording in Section 279 and 283 of the Companies and Allied Matters Act 1990 as amended (CAMA) in Nigeria.

21 Violet Aigbokhaevbo, 'Evaluation of Corporate Governance in Nigeria and Directors Liability' (1997) *Nigerian Contemporary Law Journal Uniben* 82–102, 83. Violet explained, for instance, that corporate governance and disclosure mechanisms hinged on shareholders are only effective when the shareholders are sufficiently knowledgeable to understand the information disclosed, have requisite shareholding to influence decisions and the shareholders not only willing but also able to resort to litigation if necessary.

22 Paddy Ireland, 'Making Sense of Contemporary Capitalism using Company Law' (2018) 33 *Australian Journal of Corporate Law* 379–401, footnote 64 and surrounding texts.

23 Esser (n 5) 324.

24 Linda Muswaka, 'Shareholder Value versus Stakeholders' Interests: A Critical Analysis of Corporate Governance from a South African Perspective' (2015) *Journal of Social Sciences* 217–225.

25 Institute of Directors in Southern Africa, 'King IV Report on Governance for South Africa 2016' replacing the "King III Report on Corporate Governance for South Africa 2009. King III replaced King II of 2002 which had, in turn, replaced King I of 1994.

26 Cf: CAMA Section 7(c); also Section 11(a) of the Financial Reporting Council of Nigeria Act, 2011.

27 This can be compared to the wording in Sections 279 and 283 of the CAMA in Nigeria.

28 Kloppers (n 2) 168. Regulation 26 addresses issues regarding the interpretation of the regulations affecting transparency and accountability, and Regulation 26(2) provides the method to be used to determine a company's 'public interest score' for the purposes of Regulation 43, amongst others. The 500 points referred to in Regulation 43(1) refer to the public interest score, which is calculated as the sum of (i) a number of points equal to the average number of employees of the company during the financial year; (ii) one point for every R1 million (or portion thereof) in third-party liability of the company;

CSR in South Africa 171

(iii) one point for every R1 million (or portion thereof) in turnover during the financial year and (iv) one point for every individual who at the end of the financial year is known by the company to directly or indirectly have a beneficial interest in any of the company's issued securities.

29 Regulation 43(4).

30 Regulation 43(5)

31 Thomas McInerney, 'Putting Regulation Before Responsibility: Towards Binding Norms of Corporate Social Responsibility' (2007) 40 *Cornell International Law Journal* 171–200,185.

32 See, Esser (n 5) for other expansive interpretations of relevant sections in the South Africa Companies Act No. 71 of 2008 towards CSR implementation and stakeholder protection.

33 Although CSR and stakeholder protection were not directly the issues for determination, the allusion to the King Report corporate governance requirements by Justice Hussain in *Minister of Water Affairs and Forestry v. Stilfontein Gold Mining Co. Ltd 2006 5 SA 333 (W)* following the mass resignation of corporate executives involved after an environmental (water) pollution scandal has been argued to be pushing the agenda for CSR implementation in corporate South Africa.

34 [2004] (2) All SA *457* (SCA).

35 [2015] JOL 33744.

36 It should be noted that King II is not a legally enforceable instrument and is replete with voluntary measures, just as even the latest one, King IV.

37 Peter Rott, 'Directors' Duties and Corporate Social Responsibility under German Law: Is Tort Law Litigation Changing the Picture?' (2017) 1 *Nordic Journal of Commercial Law* 9–27, 18.

38 Institute of Directors in Southern Africa, 'King IV Report on Governance for South Africa 2016' replacing the 'King III Report on Corporate Governance for South Africa 2009'.

39 For the general overview of the objective and more historical perspectives on King IV, see Irene-Marie Esser and Piet Delport, 'The South African King IV on Corporate Governance: Is the Crown Shiny Enough?' (2018) 39 (11) *Company Lawyer* 378, 384.

40 See the findings in the empirical research of Grace N Ofoegbu, Ndubuisi Odoemelam and Reginal G. Okafor, 'Corporate Board Characteristics and Environmental Disclosure Quantity: Evidence from South Africa (Integrated Reporting) and Nigeria (Traditional Reporting)' (2018) 5 *Cogent Business & Management* 1–27, 3.

41 Previous note 17.

42 See Regulation 1 of the Regulations on the Adoption and Compliance with Nigerian Code of Corporate Governance 2018. It is interesting to note, however, that, unlike Principle 8 of the Code of Corporate Governance for Banks and Discount Houses in Nigeria 2014 issued by the Central Bank of Nigeria or on page 53 of the 2016 National Code of Corporate Governance, this code has no specific provision categorically stating it is a mandatory code. Explanations in its Introduction coupled with usage of the word 'should' demonstrate that corporate executives are recommended to voluntarily implement it.

43 Part 5.5 of King IV embodies the stakeholder-inclusive approach with recommended practices towards getting businesses to behave responsibly to stakeholders.

44 In this regard, one remembers the lamentation of Ireland Paddy and Renginee Pillay noting that 'The "soft" law of CSR is no match for the "hard(er)" laws protecting shareholder interest'. See Paddy Ireland and Renginee G. Pillay, 'Corporate Social Responsibility in a Neoliberal Age' in Peter Utting and J.C. Marques (eds.), *Corporate Social Responsibility and Regulatory Governance Towards Inclusive Development?* (Basingstoke: Palgrave Macmillan 2010) 79.

45 Ibid. 97.

172 *CSR conceptual and regulatory framework in Africa*

46 Inadequacies or general failure of self-regulatory corporate governance approach and codes around the world and the reduction of compliance requirements of corporate governance codes to box-ticking exercises are no longer news. See: Louise Osemeke and Emmanuel Adegbite, 'Regulatory Multiplicity and Conflict: Towards a Combined Code on Corporate Governance in Nigeria' (2016) 133 *Journal of Business Ethics* 431–445, 438; Anria Sophia van Zyl, 'Sustainability and Integrated Reporting in the South African Corporate Sector' (2013) 8 (12) *International Business & Economics Research Journal* 903–926, 904, 905 *et seq.*; See at footnote 88 and accompanying text in John E. Parkinson, 'Corporate Governance and the Regulation of Business Behaviour' in Sorcha Macleod (ed.), *Global Governance and the Quest for Justice* (Vol. 2, Corporate Governance, Oxford and Portland: Oregon 2006); Robert McCorquodale, 'Corporate Social Responsibility and International Human Rights Law' (2009) 87 *Journal of Business Ethics* 385–400.

47 2016 King IV Report on Governance for South Africa, 26; see also, Irene-Marie Esser and Piet Delport, 'The Protection of Stakeholders: The South African Social and Ethics Committee and the United Kingdom's Enlightened Shareholder Value Approach: Part 1' (2017) 50 *De Jure* 97, 106 and at footnote 33. For similar arguments in Nigeria, see generally, Kunle Aina, 'Board of Directors and Corporate Governance in Nigeria' (2013) 1 *International Journal of Business and Finance Management Research* 21.

Part III

CSR and regionalism in Africa

6 Roadmap to embedding CSR in Africa

6 Background

Trade and investments across borders continue to bring markets closer. While this appears to increase economic prosperity for some, especially in large industrialized economies, it has nonetheless heightened the rate of exporting high risk business activities to weak and mostly less-industrialized societies in Africa. This essentially describes globalization.[1] Apparently, globalization comes with promises, including that countries will attain their full economic potential when trade and investments become liberalized and the strong chains of few 'big men' or individuals holding monopolies in sensitive trade in goods and services in the economies get broken.[2] Consequently, countries in the world have come to the realization of the need to freely trade and take advantage of globalization, and, accordingly, many regional economic integration,[3] trade cooperation and investment facilitation discourses are simultaneously ongoing using different platforms across different regions and at different stages. All types of regional trade arrangements have been finalized ranging from simple free-trade areas, which simply involves reduction in tariffs among integrating countries; customs unions; common markets and economic unions, to the ultimate stage of integration known as a political union where members become one nation all together. Some outcomes of regional integration efforts around the world include:

- (i) North America Free Trade Agreement (NAFTA);[4]
- (ii) European Free Trade Association (EFTA);
- (iii) Association of South-East Asian Nations (ASEAN);
- (iv) Bolivarian Alternative for the Americas (ALBA);
- (v) Andean Community (CAN);
- (vi) South Asian Association for Regional Cooperation (SAARC);
- (vii) Caribbean Community (CARICOM);
- (viii) Australia-New Zealand Closer Economic Relations Agreement (ANZCERTA);
- (ix) European Economic Area (EEC);
- (x) European Union (EU);
- (xi) Economic Community of West African States (ECOWAS);

176 *CSR and regionalism in Africa*

   (xii) Common Market for Eastern and Southern Africa (COMESA);
  (xiii) Southern African Development Community (SADC);
  (xiv) East African Community (EAC);
   (xv) Economic Community of Central African States (ECCAS);
  (xvi) Inter-Governmental Authority on Development (IGAD);
 (xvii) Arab Maghreb Union (AMU);
(xviii) Community of Sahel-Saharan States (CENSAD);
 (xix) Pacific Island Forum (PIF);
  (xx) Trans-Pacific Partnership (TPP);
 (xxi) Southern Common Market (MERCOSUR);
 (xxii) Union of South America Nations (UNASUR);
(xxiii) Gulf Cooperation Council (GCC);
(xxiv) Transatlantic Trade and Investment Partnership – (TTIP), amongst others.

The preceding list is far from exhaustive, and Peter Van den Bossche and Werner Zdouc gave a succinct description and membership account of a few of the previously listed regional integration outcomes.[5] The most successful regional integration outcome in the world so far has been the European Union (EU).[6]

While countries take advantage of globalisation and integration, the renowned American economist and winner of the Nobel Prize in Economic Sciences in 2001, Professor Joseph Stiglitz, cautioned as follows:

> the downside of globalisation is increasingly apparent. Not only do good things go more easily across borders, so do bad. . . . What is remarkable about globalisation is the disparity between the promise and the reality. . . . Unfettered globalisation actually has the potential to make many people in advanced industrial countries worse off, even if economic growth increases.[7]

Further, as cross-border trading and regional integration arrangements proliferate, so have powerful and very influential businesses emerged, and the powers of these corporations have also raised queries on corporate complicity in, for instance, killings, drug trafficking, money laundering, terrorism and illegal international gun trades. As previously mentioned, at the receiving end of the stick appears to be the less industrialized economies (mostly in Africa) to where the highly risky business activities are exported and externalized by the large and developed economies. The negative consequences of globalization have been so significant on Africa as the continent gets further marginalized within the world economy, continually missing global development targets on account of factors including corporate irresponsibility among a few multinational enterprises (MNEs) operating double standards in cross-border activities,[8] of course in complicity with states.[9] This development has led to the call to the business community to embed the principles and core values of CSR.

This will ensure businesses behave more responsibly and give some human face to the global market.[10] In this light, a briefing of the United Nations Research Institute for Social Development also noted that:

> Effective regional mechanisms are no longer confined to trade, finance and labour policy, but have increasingly been able to initiate regional social policies across a wide range of sectors.[11]

While other continents, especially in the industrialized economies, appear to have realized the importance of embedding the core values and principles of CSR within the business community and regional integration discourse, it appears African countries are still thinking about this differently. For instance, while the dangers of an unfettered globalization have been recognized within the EU and steps are taken towards ensuring the core values and principles of CSR are embedded within the Union,[12] not many indications of this realization have been observed within the African regional integration discourse, including within the recent African Continental Free Trade Area (AfCFTA). Among other related undertakings, this chapter will evaluate this geography-wise world's largest regional integration initiative (AfCFTA) in terms of its CSR conception and, as may be found deserving towards avoiding unbridled corporate-driven (and driving) globalization in Africa, propose a policy roadmap towards integrating and mainstreaming effective CSR across corporate systems on the continent.

6.1 CSR antipathies and policy incoherence in Africa

With a view to drawing necessary implications in relation to the African regional agenda and following the discussions in other parts of this book, particularly as identified in Chapters 4 and 5, the seeming antipathy towards corporate social and environmental responsibility and accountability (CSR) in many jurisdictions across Africa is reiterated in this section. By antipathies, the author does not suggest that CSR is shunned or that some 'CSR' is not popular in Africa or that it is a subject alien to practitioners on the continent. The antipathy referred to is this seemingly deliberate CSR conceptualization (or probably more of practices within the business communities) in the atavistic sense of mere tokenism, corporate philanthropy and, at best, undertaking community development projects. Discussions in Chapters 4 and 5 had suggested that there are notable advancements in the conceptual and regulatory framework of the subject beyond charity, following the CSR provisions in legal instruments such as in the corporate governance codes.[13] However, in terms of actual practice of CSR, many business actors across Africa including but not limited to Cameroun,[14] Nigeria,[15] South Africa,[16] Zambia,[17] Uganda[18] and Kenya[19] still regrettably confine their CSR practices to corporate charity, philanthropy, donations and just giving back to the society out of excess

178 *CSR and regionalism in Africa*

profits. Mumo Kivuitu, Kavwanga Yambayamba and Tom Fox actually noted in respect to Kenya and Zambia that:

> In both countries, the activities most commonly identified by companies themselves as CSR could broadly be described as philanthropy. In Kenya, surveys suggest that the cause receiving the highest proportion of corporate donations is health and medical provision, and donations are also directed towards education and training; HIV/AIDS; agriculture and food security; and underprivileged children. The picture in Zambia is similar, with surveys highlighting donations to orphanages as the most common activity identified as CSR, followed by sponsorship of sporting events; cultural ceremonies; education and health provision; and donations to religious and arts organisations.[20]

In situations where the businesses involved do not expressly own up that their CSR is basically about philanthropy, the trend appears to be that, further to the relevant legal instruments enjoining businesses to adopt a CSR regime as a comprehensive corporate governance and business management model – through which the economic, legal, ethical and discretionary responsibilities of a company may be managed and balanced responsibly for the sustainable development of both the business community and society – these businesses simply pay lip service to adopting a robust and comprehensive CSR policy and essentially imbibe CSR practice entrenched in charity. In this regard, for instance, one of the key objectives of the South African King IV introduced in 2016 was to address the empty and mindless compliance with corporate governance codes. The 2009 King III was praised as a remarkable improvement on the King II as it refines the triple bottom-line concept of King II and used the term 'triple context', which informed the introduction of the concept of 'integrated reporting,' which reporting shows that the differentiating line between the so-called financial and non-financial or ESG matters of a company are getting blurred and that the dimensions of the economy, the society and the natural environment are all intertwined and not separate. But despite the impressive CSR requirements in the South African King IV, especially with the deliberate efforts towards addressing empty compliance with code requirements and generally improving a robust CSR practice in corporate South Africa, there is no evidence that the King IV has actually achieved the said objective (but nor that it has not yet), and, frankly speaking, for reasons noted in Chapter 5, King IV as it currently stands with the shareholder primacy-centric provisions of the South African Companies Act, will not address corporate greenwash and lip service to CSR. As David Fig rightly noted, many businesses in South Africa were found to attempt to implement CSR primarily because they are keen to be seen to care for the environment and the social fabric of the country, whereas in reality their CSR activities are confined to mere tokenism and probably only targeted at deflecting criticism of their unsustainable and irresponsible practices.[21] A similar situation presents itself in corporate Nigeria as discussed in Chapter 4; despite the impressive CSR-inspired clauses in the 2018

Nigerian Code of Corporate Governance, such a legal instrument and its provisions are unlikely to embed a robust and comprehensive CSR model within corporate Nigeria. The discussions in Chapter 4 had confirmed that effective and robust CSR practice, together with its values of corporate sustainability, human rights and environmental protection, transparency and accountability together with effective disclosure on non-financial matters found in the subsidiary legal instrument of corporate governance codes, is almost non-existent at the level of primary hard law legislations (CAMA, ISA, NEITI et cetera). The policy incoherence[22] was also shown to be underpinned by a faulty legal transplantation exercise.

It is therefore submitted that the reason why there is (and will continue to be) this disconnect between the identified, isolated, impressive legal instruments in Africa and the actual CSR practices that are still confined to corporate philanthropy (and only box-ticking, paying service to CSR) is not unconnected to policy misalignment and incoherence, underpinned by the absence of proper legal harmonization and integration of CSR-related laws within the respective jurisdictions on the continent. An effective legal harmonization through a legal integration exercise will address this challenge of policy misalignment in the systems (whereby, while primary corporate legislations say one thing about CSR, the subsidiary instruments in the corporate governance codes – which are ordinarily supposed to give effect to and complement[23] the primary legislations – are saying something else completely). The harmonization exercise is expected to entail proper legal transplantation of relevant foreign principles and adopt necessary comparative law approach, which integrates the entire legal system on the CSR subject and ensures any adopted CSR framework not only fits the unique local requirements or demands (such as the social and economic transformation agenda of the South African government in the wake of correcting the injustices of the apartheid regime or the Nigerian government social inclusion and community development undertakings warranted by the long term neglect of extractive industries host and impacted communities) but is also robust enough in outlook to address other CSR core values (of human rights and environmental protection, anti-bribery, information disclosure and employee rights, among others). Such framework must also be aligned with principles and practices within the CSR international regulatory initiatives such as the UNGC, the UNGPs and the OECD Guidelines to MNEs. This legal harmonization and integration at both the domestic jurisdictions across Africa and at the regional level of Africa is not only doable but has also become warranted if: the previously noted policy incoherence and misalignment will be fixed; disconnect between the legislative framework and the actual business CSR practices will be addressed and the double standards operation of multinational enterprises in Africa will be curbed.

6.2 CSR and the World Trade Organization (WTO)

This section of the chapter is aimed at showing that any antipathies towards a robust CSR regime within Africa (as may be imagined a Western or global

180   *CSR and regionalism in Africa*

North concept to which lip service should only be paid) are not sustainable and are, frankly speaking, unjustifiable. The principles and values of CSR are not (necessarily) against the trade liberalization agenda of Africa and are indeed justifiable within the World Trade Organization (WTO) framework. However, before delving into further arguments, a brief historical account of the WTO is provided.

The WTO is an intergovernmental organization that is concerned with the regulation of international trade between nations. The WTO officially commenced on 1 January 1995 under the Marrakesh Agreement, signed by 123 nations on 15 April 1994, replacing the General Agreement on Tariffs and Trade (GATT), which commenced in 1948. It is the largest international economic organization in the world. The global rules that underpin the multilateral economic system of the WTO were a direct reaction to the Second World War, and the WTO is seen by some as part of the 'peace dividend' that came with the end of the Cold War.[24] The whole idea was that such war should never be repeated, and the WTO's creation on 1 January 1995 marked the biggest reform of international trade since the end of the war. Whereas the GATT mainly dealt with trade in goods, the WTO and its agreements also cover trade in services and the Trade-Related Aspects of Intellectual Property Rights (TRIPS).[25] As restrictions can impede the spread of global production chains that may rely on reduced barriers to trade for their continued existence, the WTO seeks to control protectionist tendencies in national trade laws and practices that operate at the border to limit the penetration of the local market by competitive imports of goods and services. The WTO is therefore committed to the promotion of free trade through the obligation not to treat foreign products less favourably than 'like products' of national origin (National Treatment)[26] or less favourably than 'like products' originating from other countries (Most Favoured Nation Treatment),[27] prohibition of unnecessary restrictions to trade[28] and, finally, the requirement to base product regulation, labels and standards on international standards.[29]

The WTO regulates the behaviour of governments, not business in the international trade arena. As a result, it is more concerned with relationships between states than with relationships within states. Thus, the WTO is basically not concerned with how a state treats its own citizens but rather how it treats non-citizens who seek to trade. Further, the WTO has no direct mandate to promote any global CSR agenda, and policy considerations pertaining to CSR issues appear largely futuristic[30] in the WTO's considerations.

Notwithstanding the foregoing – however – and in order to understand in what context CSR issues may be conceptualized within the WTO, it is important to underscore that paragraph 1 in the preamble to the WTO Agreement makes explicit reference to the importance of promoting sustainable development and the preservation of the environment. Therefore, although there is no global agenda to promote CSR or sustainable development properly reflected or mainstreamed within the WTO framework, reference can still be made to provisions supporting CSR values. In this regard, understanding the meanings of 'technical regulation' and 'standard' within the WTO framework appears useful. Technical regulation means a:

> Document which lays down product characteristics or their related processes and production methods, including the applicable administrative provisions, with which compliance is mandatory. It may also include or deal exclusively with terminology, symbols, packaging, marking or labelling requirements as they apply to a product, process or production method.[31]

A standard, on the other, hand is a:

> Document approved by a recognized body, that provides, for common and repeated use, rules, guidelines or characteristics for products or related processes and production methods, with which compliance is not mandatory. It may also include or deal exclusively with terminology, symbols, packaging, marking or labelling requirements as they apply to a product, process or production method.[32]

As a result of CSR regulatory implications on internationally traded products or their market access and competitive opportunities, some scholars insist that CSR is in conflict with WTO agreements and laws.[33] In this light, the previously defined technical regulations and requirements or standards – as imposed by certain states in global trade towards ensuring globally traded goods and services throughout a value chain system have been responsibly produced or provided without violation of CSR – are sometimes interpreted as an undue restriction to freely trade in such goods and services. Therefore, many developing countries of Africa and other less industrialized parts of the world contend that CSR considerations (technical regulations, standards and labelling requirements or labour standards of many large and developed economies inspired by CSR) amount to discrimination of their goods or services, which may not have been so CSR-compliant in production and therefore insist that any rejection of such goods and services on the basis of such CSR standards is a disguised protectionist practice.[34] It is interesting to note that at the heart of the debate about whether CSR standards or values are WTO-laws compatible or not is the question: is the WTO designed for negative rights of states not to be discriminated against by differentiating products on the basis of national origin, or is the WTO framework designed for general positive rights of states to market access, which can only be denied for certain codified or accepted reasons?[35]

Notwithstanding the existence of any contrary viewpoint as highlighted earlier, having clarified CSR in the earlier section of this chapter and in Chapter 1 of this book beyond mere corporate charity, this author is of the view that CSR constitutes a legitimate basis for technical regulations and international standards as may be required by national regulations. In other words, states, including those from developing economies, could leverage the internationally accepted CSR standards as a basis of regional integration of states

182 *CSR and regionalism in Africa*

with commonly acceptable CSR technical regulations and legal standards,[36] ensuring such national regulations meet international standards as permissible under Articles 2.4 and 2.5 of the Agreement on Technical Barriers to Trade.

It is also important to reiterate the argument that CSR and the adoption of CSR values are not anti-trade and constitute an avenue to embed responsible behaviour in corporations[37] driving globalization within the WTO member states. Failure to understand the WTO framework vis-à-vis CSR and sustainable development in this light will make the WTO framework self-contradicting (as the promotion of sustainable development, which is a core element of CSR, is recognized in the preamble to the WTO Agreement); this will also be counter-acting other widely accepted international regulatory framework in the CSR domain (like the UNGC and the UNGPs) and may jeopardize the legitimacy of the WTO itself.[38]

Following from the earlier argument about technical regulation and standards, CSR within the WTO context may also be discussed under Article XX of GATT, which protects the policy space for legitimate regulatory measures under the WTO legal framework. Therefore, Article III: 4 may not be considered violated in relation to National Treatment of foreign goods less favourably than like products of national origin if justifiable under Article XX as a measure necessary to pursue legitimate policy objectives[39] such as: (i) protecting public morals; (ii) protecting human, animal or plant life or health and (iii) conserving exhaustive natural resources.[40]

In order to underscore the points made earlier, the clarificatory language used in the Appellate Body report in the *US – Shrimp* case appears vital:

> The preamble attached to the WTO Agreement shows that signatories to that Agreement were, in 1994, fully aware of the importance and legitimacy of environmental protection as a goal of national and international policy. The preamble of the WTO Agreement – which informs not only the GATT 1994, but also the other covered agreements – explicitly acknowledges the objective of sustainable development. [and] . . . we wish to underscore what we have *not* decided in this appeal. We have *not* decided that protection and preservation of the environment is of no significance to the Members of the WTO. Clearly it is. We have *not* decided that the sovereign nations that are Members of the WTO cannot adopt effective measures to protect endangered species, such as sea turtles. Clearly, they can and should. And we have *not* decided that sovereign states should not act together bilaterally, plurilaterally or multilaterally, either within the WTO or in other international fora, to protect endangered species or to otherwise protect the environment.[41]

The previous quotation, together with arguments canvassed and conclusions reached by the panels and Appellate Body reports in the disputes of the US-Gasoline case of 1996 (*United States – Standards for Reformulated and Conventional Gasoline*, WT/DS2); the EC – Seal Products case of 2014 (*EC – Seal Products,*

Roadmap to embedding CSR in Africa   183

WT/DS/400/AB/R, WT/DS 401/AB/R) and the EC – Sardines case of 2002 (*European Communities – Trade Description of Sardines*, WT/DS231/AB/R) amongst others all have also confirmed the nexus between CSR and trade liberalization and investment facilitation discourse and the usefulness of CSR standards in economic globalization discourse. The Appellate Body's quotation similarly confirms that there is nothing intrinsically incompatible between CSR standards as may be properly designed and applied within the policy space of any WTO member states towards safeguarding social values. In fact, it has been argued that member states of the WTO can and should examine how the WTO system can help members encourage global CSR without necessarily undermining the WTO norms.[42]

6.3 CSR and African regionalism (trade liberalization in Africa)

There is a common realization that, in order to achieve her full economic potential, Africa needs to liberalize its trade in goods and services together with investment. Regional integration means the coming together of countries (usually in the same region) to reduce trade barriers hampering economic growth and development and maximizing general welfare. It involves gradual elimination of trade barriers impeding free flow of goods and services and factors of production from certain sectors. Regionalism encompasses efforts by a group of nations to enhance their economic, political, social or cultural interaction.[43] Such efforts can take on different forms and names including regional cooperation, market integration, development integration and regional integration. African leaders have long envisaged regionalism as a viable strategy to pursue with a view to uniting the continent both politically and economically. Some argue that regional cooperation should be accompanied by a strategy of regional integration, which is a process by which a group of nation states voluntarily and in various degrees have access to each other's markets and establish mechanisms and techniques that minimize conflicts and maximize internal and external economic, political, social and cultural benefits of their interaction.[44] For clarity of terms, although some semantic differences may technically exist among scholars,[45] the words regionalism, regional integration, regional cooperation, economic (market) integration and regional trade arrangements are all used interchangeably in this book to connote arrangement signalling firm commitments among states to take affirmative steps in reducing barriers to trade between the parties involved.

A cursory look at the membership of regional economic communities[46] (RECs) across Africa reveals that an overwhelming majority of African states belongs to two or more sub-regional organizations. This suggests strong acceptance of regional integration as an effective tool for development. The RECs such as the ECOWAS have been and remain central institutional actors in Africa's efforts to resolve its economic development dilemmas.[47] In fact, the RECs are seen by African political leaders as building blocks for an African Economic Community (AEC) in which economic, fiscal, monetary, social and sectoral

184　*CSR and regionalism in Africa*

policies would be harmonized across the continent. Most of the RECs have undergone institutional reforms, but their presence and expansion have been differently interpreted in the African regionalism discourse. Some have seen the co-existence of the RECs on the one hand and the continent-wide international economic organization like the AU on the other as a contradiction; others see them as mutually reinforcing. Some instead see the multiplicity and overlapping memberships in the RECs as barriers to African countries' commitments to treaty compliance and policy implementation generally on the continent. Regardless of the roles played by the RECs, this chapter underscores the point that, although regional integration initiatives in Africa are pervaded by the common motivation for trade liberalization, economic growth and the strengthening of nascent domestic industries in Africa, however, the founding fathers of regional integration in Africa envisioned a continent progressed on the idea of emphasizing the need for trade to serve only as an instrument of accelerated industrialization, structural transformation and development in Africa, rather than as an end in itself.[48] It appears useful to situate the African regional integration agenda within some historical perspectives.

Towards realizing the Pan-Africanist vision of Kwame Nkrumah's 'All Africa People's Conference' as far back as 1958 (Nkrumah is thus regarded as a champion of regional integration in Africa) and following the deteriorating economic crisis in Africa,[49] there were calls for a new world order, and the Economic Commission for Africa (ECA) was instrumental in coming up with three development blueprints for Africa namely:

(i) The 1976 Revised Framework of Principles for the Implementation of the New International Order in Africa;
(ii) Three years later, at the colloquium titled 'Perspectives of Development and Economic Growth in Africa up to the year 2000', convened in Monrovia in 1979 by the Organization of African Unity (now AU), the ECA's 1976 blueprint became the intellectual and theoretical foundation of the AU's Monrovia Declaration;
(iii) One year later in 1980, at the AU's second extraordinary summit in Nigeria, the AU transformed the Monrovia Declaration into the Lagos Plan of Action and the Final Act of Lagos (LPA) and set itself the goal of economic integration of Africa by the year 2000, through the creation of an African Economic Community (AEC).

Rather than focusing purely on economic growth and the strengthening of nascent domestic industries in Africa as an end itself, the ECA attempted crafting an autonomous agenda for Africa founded on developmental regionalism. Professor Adedeji Adebayo, then ECA head, had canvassed four fundamental development principles for Africa as follows:

Self-reliant, self-sustainment, the democratization of the development process, and a fair and just distribution of the fruit of development through the progressive eradication of unemployment and mass poverty.[50]

As interesting as the ECA's developmental agenda for Africa sounds, it did not flourish. The World Bank published a report authored by Elliot Berg (Berg Report) and titled 'Accelerated Development in Sub-Saharan Africa', which turned the intellectual and theoretical foundation of the ECA-proposed LPA on its head. Therefore, the neo-liberalism of the Bretton Woods Institutions (BWI), the orthodoxy that calls for limited governmental intervention in the economy, privatization, the demise of the welfare state and monetary and fiscal discipline (the so-called Washington Consensus) came to the forefront of economic policies in Africa in the guise of BWI's Structural Adjustment Programmes (SAPs). Relatedly, it has been noted that the African leaders' decision to succumb to the agenda of the BWIs and remain noncommittal to the ECA's economic growth and developmental agenda might have been due to the economic strictures of debt or lack of foresight and confidence in alternative models.[51] Margaret Lee concluded that, after two decades of SAPs, there is a growing consensus that they have failed, leaving most African countries further marginalized within the world economy.[52] Without necessarily dabbling into the debate about the Berg Report and the LPA, this author shares in Kwame's view noting that:

> No matter the limitations of the LPA framework, and there were plenty of critics, it marked a serious attempt by the ECA to advance a normative policy agenda for Africa's development, unencumbered by the dictates of the Bretton Woods Institutions.[53]

Kwame therefore concluded on this point noting that, throughout the years since the international economic organizations got African states to adopt the neoliberal reformist policies, the ECA has been involved in half-hearted attempts to formulate 'alternative' development platforms for Africa including the APPER 1986–1990 (Africa's Priority Program for Economic Recovery) and NEPAD but with no sufficient or real intellectual leadership or challenge to the neoliberal agenda pushed by the BWI.[54]

Moving on after the LPA, on account of the likely failure to meet the objectives of the LPA and achieve the creation of the AEC by 2000, AU member states in 1991 reinforced their commitments and signed the Abuja Treaty, which creates the AEC and calls for the total integration of African economies by 2025. The commitment to the eventual merger of the RECs and the creation of the AEC earlier proposed by the LPA are enshrined in the 1991 Abuja Treaty, which lays down a 34-year timetable (1994–2028) in six different stages of different duration for the integration scheme. The Abuja Treaty of 1991 was largely influenced by Adedeji Adebayo, and the treaty eventually led to the 2012 ECA paper titled 'Boosting Intra-Africa Trade – Issues affecting Intra-Africa Trade, Proposed Action Plan for boosting Intra-Africa Trade and Framework for Fast Tracking of a Continental Free Trade Area',[55] which occasioned the launch of a Continental Free Trade Area discourse by the AU.[56] Ismail further noted that the 'Agenda 2063' adopted by African leaders at the AU Summit in 2015, calling for a prosperous Africa based on inclusive growth and sustainable

186 *CSR and regionalism in Africa*

development and expressing the vision that Africa shall be a continent where the free movement of people, capital, goods and services will result in significant increases in trade and investments amongst African countries. All these preceding efforts in light of the integration scheme culminated in the historic signing of an agreement creating the African Continental Free Trade Area Agreement (AfCFTA) on 21 March 2018 at the AU Summit in Kigali, Rwanda.[57]

6.4 CSR and sustainable development within the African Continental Free Trade Area (AfCFTA)

The African Continental Free Trade Area (AfCFTA)[58] covers the entire 55 member states of Africa with a market of 1.2 billion people and a gross domestic product of $2.5 trillion, and, as a result of the share number of participating countries, AfCFTA constitutes the world's largest free trade area since the formation of the World Trade Organization.[59] Article 3 of the main agreement of AfCFTA contains its general objectives, which include to:

(i) Create a single market for goods and services, facilitated by movement of persons in order to deepen the economic integration of the African continent and in accordance with the Pan African Vision of' An integrated, prosperous and peaceful Africa' enshrined in Agenda 2063;
(ii) Create a liberalized market for goods and services through successive rounds of negotiations;
(iii) Contribute to the movement of capital and natural persons and facilitate investments building on the initiatives and developments in the state parties and RECs;
(iv) Lay the foundation for the establishment of a Continental Customs Union at a later stage;
(v) Promote and attain sustainable and inclusive socio-economic development, gender equality and structural transformation of the state parties;
(vi) Enhance the competitiveness of the economies of state parties within the continent and the global market;
(vii) Promote industrial development through diversification and regional value chain development, agricultural development and food security;
(viii) Resolve the challenges of multiple and overlapping memberships and expedite the regional and continental integration processes.

Showing the connection between AfCFTA and sustainable development as a core CSR value as discussed in this book, the ECA confirms that:[60]

> The cumulative effect of AfCFTA is to contribute to the achievement of the United Nations 2030 Agenda, in particular, to the Sustainable Development Goals, from targets for decent work and economic growth (Goal 8) and the promotion of industry (Goal 9), to food security (Goal 2) and affordable access to health services (Goal 3).

On the question of what institutional arrangements are needed for the effective implementation of AfCFTA, it is noted that the responsibility for coordinating the implementation of the AfCFTA agreement will be within the AfCFTA secretariat,[61] which will form an autonomous institutional body within the African Union system and with an independent legal personality, akin to an agency of the African Union. It shall work closely with the African Union Commission and its departments, and the Commission shall provide the necessary transitional support until AfCFTA secretariat is fully operational. The funds of the secretariat shall be sourced from the overall budget of the African Union, and its headquarters, structure, roles and responsibilities shall be determined by the Council of Ministers responsible for trade.

The AfCFTA agreement is divided into seven parts, with thirty-one Articles in the main text of the agreement. The document has three protocols at the moment: one on trade in goods, the other on trade in services and the last on dispute settlement. AfCFTA is written in four original texts, which are in the Arabic, English, French and Portuguese languages, all of which are equally authentic.[62] While the AfCFTA agreement was adopted and opened for signature on 21 March 2018 in Kigali, it entered into force on 30 May 2019, 30 days after having received the twenty-second instrument of ratification on 29 April 2019. On 7 July 2019, its operational phase was launched at the 12th Extraordinary Session of the Assembly of African Union Heads of State and Government in Niamey, Niger. No doubt, the AfCFTA is truly emblematic of the flagship projects of Agenda 2063 of the African Union, with widespread reception across the continent. Both Nigeria and Benin having signed the AfCFTA agreement at the Niamey summit, and the AfCFTA having 28 ratifications, Eritrea remains the only African country not part of the trading bloc as of 5 November 2019.

Free trade is a means to the end of sustainable development, and it is one thing to pay lip service or at least casually mention CSR and sustainable development in the AfCFTA agreement, but mainstreaming the implementation of the core values of these CSR and sustainability constructs within the AfCFTA framework is another. It is remarkable that the drafters of the AfCFTA agreement have mentioned the phrase 'sustainable development goals' just once in the entire agreement, with no clear strategy or details about the methodology of attaining the SDGs. The word 'sustainable' features six times, while the phrase 'sustainable development' features four times in the entire document, and those mentions made are included in a protocol to the agreement. Beyond this, while AfCFTA recognizes the right of state parties to, for instance, regulate towards their overall sustainable development[63] and confirms its general objective to promote sustainable development in accordance with the sustainable development goals (SDGs),[64] apart from the previous passing mention and comments about SDGs and overall sustainable development, the AfCFTA agreement appears to discount the need for a properly defined framework through which the said objectives can be realized. Such mere mentioning appears to have no real value in practically promoting the ideas of CSR and

188   *CSR and regionalism in Africa*

sustainable development. In other words, it should not be simply a question of inserting the words 'sustainable development' or even CSR in the AfCFTA but rather seeking to mainstream throughout the document what is meant by such and how to be realized in more practical terms. For instance, there is the Southern African Development Community (SADC) Model Bilateral Investment Treaty Template and Commentary, which was completed in June 2012 by member states of SADC (the 'SADC Model Treaty').[65] Article 1 of this template treaty mentions that:

> The Main objective of this Agreement is to encourage and increase investments . . . that support the sustainable development of each Party, and in particular the Host State where an investment is to be located.

This stated objective by the drafters did not start and end with the previous quotation. Unlike with the AfCFTA, the drafters of the SADC Model Treaty ensured its stated objective was sustained throughout the agreement, making certain the treaty incorporated sustainable development thinking from the beginning to the end of the text. Practically speaking, the SADC Model Treaty had gone ahead to provide specific clauses that properly mainstream the intended development agenda into the treaty beyond mere mentioning.[66] It is important to also underscore that this mere mentioning of the subject as some 'grandiose western concept' in the AfCFTA is a repetition of previous mistakes that led to the failures of past integration efforts and suggestive of not having undertaken proper legal integration as required for the achievement of the AfCFTA objectives. There have been a few problems encountered in previous regional integration attempts in Africa including:[67]

(i) Divergent legal systems;
(ii) Non-ratification and non-implementation of key obligations;
(iii) Lack of fully developed legal principles within the municipal law;
(iv) Conflict of laws;
(v) Ambiguity of treaty language;
(vi) Lack of (financial) incentive to ensure compliance;
(vii) Inadequate (financial and human) resources and technical expertise for implementation;
(viii) Weak economic structure of African states;
(ix) Differing macro-economic policies;
(x) Unbridled attachment to national sovereignty, to political instability and conflicts.

Perhaps, the most crucial of the previously mentioned, which appears to remain elusive to date, is the absence of a proper legal harmonization through an effective legal integration exercise.[68] The fact is that the regional integration process is a creation of the law, and while the process usually germinates from the political interactions and negotiations between and/or among states, legal instruments, such as treaties and protocols, outline the road-map of such process.[69] The present AfCFTA framework appears to have ignored the importance of a properly defined, integrated and shared CSR and sustainable development policy and regulatory framework, having only paid such nominal significance to such shared CSR values within the integration scheme. This diminishes the seriousness of the African integration agenda in relation to CSR implementation and, to be clear, achieving the SDGs. Further, the previous status appears to run in the opposite direction of research showing that effective regional integration and mechanisms are no longer confined to trade and finance but have increasingly also been linked to regional social policies across a wide range of sectors. Upon reviewing the provisions of the AfCFTA including the statements contained in the ECA publication, the author reiterates the view that the drafters and negotiators of the AfCFTA agreement might have focused too much on regional integration in the area of trade liberalization in terms of goods, services and investment as an end in itself without paying adequate attention to important principles embedded in concepts such as developmental regionalism, transformative regionalism[70] and effective legal harmonization, especially in relation to CSR and sustainable development. It must be further reiterated that the incidence of free trade constitutes only a means towards achieving the end of sustainable development and not an end in itself. If Africa intends to achieve sustainable development, state parties must properly harmonize their legal systems and integrate the core values of CSR within their trade agreements. This will provide relevant framework with which the globalization-driving corporations may act socially responsibly and sustainably on the continent.

In conclusion, consequent upon the previous discussions, CSR can no longer be treated as something antithetical to trade liberalization or regional integration scheme in Africa. The AfCFTA framework appears inadequate and/or seems to have insufficiently provided the necessary and workable framework to meet the realities of modern times that have shown the transboundary nature of social, economic and environmental challenges arising from economic globalization and regional integration. This warrants more robust and deliberate regional social policy efforts. This is where the core values of CSR become imperative. It is important that the AfCFTA framework does not foster a situation of business as usual for multinational enterprises with double operations standards in their activities in developed economies (with relatively strong CSR policies) as opposed to their operations in developing markets (perceived with weak systems). The policy proposal towards mainstreaming effective CSR within the African regional integration scheme and ensuring businesses behave responsibly within the integration framework is underpinned by the RSM framework discussed in Chapter 7. Instead of policy makers paying half-hearted attention to the principles of CSR and sustainable development in the course of regional integration in Africa, especially within the AfCFTA regime, there is need to realize the potentials of using CSR for trade facilitation and at the same time ensuring that responsible corporate behaviours underpin such

190 *CSR and regionalism in Africa*

facilitated trade. This approach stands a better chance of ensuring that the vision of the founding fathers of regional integration in Africa towards a regionalism emphasizing the need for trade to serve as an instrument of accelerated industrialization and structural transformation in Africa is not only realized but also ensures that Africa is indeed not left behind in the attainment of the SDGs.

6.5 Chapter summary

This chapter examined the role played (and capable of being played) by CSR and sustainable development in tempering the adverse effects of globalization and unfettered corporate-driven (and driving) trade liberalization. It underscored the point that, although there have been some legislative advancements in the CSR domain in the two case study jurisdictions of Nigeria and South Africa, the practice of CSR across Africa appears still underpinned and dominated by the atavistic conceptualization of corporate philanthropy as many businesses in Africa only pay lip service to a robust CSR practice. Incidences of empty and mindless compliance with the otherwise impressive provisions in corporate governance codes hold sway. After a brief background to the establishment of the World Trade Organisation as peace dividend of the Second World War, the chapter demonstrated that any antipathies towards a robust CSR regime within Africa are not justifiable as the principles and values of CSR are not against the trade liberalization agenda of Africa and that CSR practices are indeed justifiable within the WTO framework. In other words, the chapter confirmed that there is nothing intrinsically incompatible between CSR values and sustainable development on the one hand and the WTO laws and free trade principles on the other. The chapter appraised the latest regional integration arrangement within the continent, the Africa Continental Free Trade Area (AfCFTA) and decried the seeming focus on trade liberalization and economic industrialization at all costs, having paid little attention to integration of the core values of CSR and sustainable development into the AfCFTA framework. Although the chapter sets the agenda for mainstreaming CSR in the world's largest regional integration initiative, it did not make the exact proposal through which CSR may be mainstreamed into the AfCFTA; in aligning flow of information and maintaining the structure of the book, this is reserved for Chapter 7, to be discussed alongside a CSR implementation proposal for Africa within the theoretical and regulatory ambits of the responsible stakeholder model (RSM).

Notes

1 Joseph Stiglitz, *Globalisation and Its Discontents* (London: Penguin 2002) 9.
2 Kato Kimbugwe, Nicholas Perdikis, May T. Yeung and William A. Kerr, *Economic Development through Regional Trade: A Role for the New East African Community?* (United Kingdom: Palgrave Macmillan 2012) chapter 1.
3 Faizel Ismail, *Transformative Industrialization and Trade in the Context of the CFTA: Opportunities and Challenges* (Addis Ababa: United Nations Economic Commission for Africa, UNECA 2017) 36. A succinct description of the hierarchy involved in regional trade

Roadmap to embedding CSR in Africa 191

arrangements was provided by Brendan Vickers in *A Handbook on Regional Integration in Africa: Towards Agenda 2063* (London: The Commonwealth Secretariat 2017) 9.

4 This proved to be successful until recently re-negotiated with the emergence of the latest President of the United States of America, Donald J. Trump as 'United States–Mexico–Canada Agreement' (USMCA).

5 Peter van den Bossche and Werner Zdouc, *The Law and Policy of the World Trade Organization: Text Cases and Materials* (4th edn, Cambridge: Cambridge University Press 2017) 673, 674.

6 Just like the EU, in several other cases – most notably China, India and some other Asian countries – integration appears to be paying off, and the promises of globalization are getting delivered; high-productivity employment opportunities have expanded, and structural change has contributed to overall growth.

7 Joseph Stiglitz, 'We Have Become Rich Countries of Poor People' *Financial Times* (7 September 2006).

8 Research has shown that, among developing countries, consequences of globalization depend on the manner in which countries integrate into the global economy. In other cases in Latin America and sub-Saharan Africa, integration and globalization appear not to have really fostered the desirable results. See Margaret McMillan and Dani Rodrik, 'Globalization, Structural Change and Productivity Growth' in M. Bacchetta and M. Jansen (eds.), *Making Globalization Socially Sustainable International Labour Organization and World Trade Organization* (Geneva: WTO Secretariat 2011) 50. Research also confirms that large industrialized societies and their MNEs take advantage of policy incoherencies and weak regulatory framework in the smaller and less developed economies by sometimes irresponsibly exporting potentially liability-attractive activities from their societies to the less developed systems (such as in Africa), which are considered safe havens for double standard irresponsible corporate behaviour. Janet Dine, 'Jurisdictional Arbitrage by Multinational Companies: A National Law Solution?' (2012) 3 *Journal of Human Rights and the Environment* 44, 49; Tom Hadden, *Company Law and Capitalism* (2nd edn, London: Weidenfeld and Nicolson 1972) 486–487, 506.

9 The forced business shut down by Shell Petroleum Development Company of Nigeria over human rights abuses in the oil rich Niger-Delta region of Nigeria appears instructive. *Wiwa v. Royal Dutch Petroleum Company* 226 F.3d 88 (2d cir 2000), 532US 941(2001).

10 UN Press Release SG/SM/6881, *Secretary-General Proposes Global Compact on Human Rights, Labour, Environment in Address to World Economic Forum in Davos* (Text of Speech by Kofi Annan, 1 February 1999) 1, available at: www.un.org/press/en/1999/19990201.sgsm6881. html accessed 9 November 2019. See further discussions about this in Chapter 3.

11 Nicola Yeates, *Beyond the Nation State: How Can Regional Social Policy Contribute to Achieving the Sustainable Development Goals?* (Issue Brief 05, Geneva: UNRISD 2017) 1.

12 For detailed discussions about CSR implementation within the framework of the EU, see Section 3.5 of Chapter 3. There are other efforts towards CSR implementation and taming powerful businesses in other developed parts, such as in the United States. See *Doe v. Unocal*, 395 F.3d 932, 937–42 (9th Cir. 2005); and *Wiwa v. Royal Dutch Petroleum Co.*, 226 F.3d 88, 92–93 (2d Cir. 2000); *Esther Kiobel et al v. Royal Dutch Petroleum Company, Shell Transport and Trading Company US Court of Appeal* (2nd Circuit) 06–4800-cv, 06–4876-cv (September 17 2010).

13 See the 2018 Nigerian Code of Corporate Governance, issued by the Financial Reporting Council of Nigeria; see also Institute of Directors in Southern Africa, 'King IV Report on Governance for South Africa 2016'. Despite some identified shortcomings, both documents were respectively analysed and commended for their impressive CSR conception and regulatory provisions. See Section 4.4 in Chapter 4 and Section 5.4 in Chapter 5 for discussions on Nigeria and South Africa respectively.

14 K.A. Ollong, 'Corporate Social Responsibility and Community Development in Cameroon' Conference Paper (12th International Conference on Corporate Social Responsibility, ISSN 2048–0806, Niteroi and Rio de Janeiro, Brazil, June 2013).

192 CSR and regionalism in Africa

15 See, Abiola Odutola, 'GTBank, Zenith, Access, FBN, 10 Others Spend Over N8 Billion on CSR' *Nairametrics* (3 November 2019) available at: https://nairametrics.com/2019/11/03/gtbank-zenith-access-fbn-10-others-spend-over-n8-billion-on-csr/ accessed 3 November 2019; also see, 'Cosgrove Gets NITP, COREN Commendation for CSR' *Thisday* (2 April 2019); Raheem Akingbolu, 'CSR as a Launchpad for Development' *Thisday* (25 October 2018); further, the website of the CSR affiliate or subsidiary of Dangote group of companies notes that Aliko Dangote 'Foundation is the Corporate Social Responsibility arm of Dangote Group' (and) 'responsible for contributing over $100 million in charitable funds to several causes in Nigeria and Africa over the past four years'. See www.devex.com/organizations/dangote-foundation-8101 accessed 3 November 2019; see also, FSDH Merchant Bank Limited, 'Corporate Social Responsibility (CSR) Activities in 2015' *The Guardian* (19 January 2016); Kaine Agary, 'Is CSR Worth the Trouble for Companies? (1)' *Punch* (26 July 2015); Raheem Akingbolu, 'Building Equity through CSR: The Grand Oak Example' *Thisday* (22 March 2013) 36; Raheem Akingbolu, 'CSR: Groups Hail Nigerite's Efforts' *Thisday* (14 May 2010).
16 Wayne Visser, 'Research on Corporate Citizenship in Africa: A Ten Year Review (1995–2005)' in W. Visser, M. McIntosh and C. Middleton (eds.), *Corporate Citizenship in Africa: Lessons from the Past: Paths to the Future* (Sheffield: Greenleaf Publishing 2006) 18–28.
17 J.N. Muthuri, 'Corporate Social Responsibility in Africa: Definition, Issues and Process' in R.T. Lituchy, B.J. Punnett and B.B. Puplampu (eds.), *Management in Africa: Macro and Micro Perspective* (New York and London: Routledge 2013) 90–111.
18 V.A. Bagire, I. Tusiime, G. Nalweyiso and J.B. Kakooza, 'Contextual Environment and Stakeholder Perception of Corporate Social Responsibility Practices in Uganda' (2013) 18 *Corporate Social Responsibility and Environmental Management* 102–109.
19 Mumo Kivuitu, Kavwanga Yambayamba and Tom Fox, 'How Can Corporate Social Responsibility Deliver in Africa? Insights from Kenya and Zambia' (2005) *Perspectives on Corporate Responsibility for Environment and Development, International Institute for Environment and Development* available at: https://pubs.iied.org/pdfs/16006IIED.pdf accessed 9 November 2019.
20 Ibid. 2.
21 David Fig, 'Manufacturing Amnesia: Corporate Social Responsibility in South Africa' (2005) 81 *International Affairs* 599–617, 603.
22 The defects in the codes in both jurisdictions (as mismatched with the primary corporate legislations) seem accentuated by the position of law in both Nigeria and South Africa that subsidiary legislations provisions *in pari materia* with primary legislations provisions cannot amend the provisions in the primary enactments. Executive Council, *Western Cape v. Minister for Provincial Affairs and Constitutional Development and Another; Executive Council, KwaZulu-Natal v. President of the Republic of South Africa* 2000 1 SA 661 (CC); *Adene and Ors v. Dantubu* (1994) 2 NWLR (Part 382) 509; *Eko Hotels Limited v. Financial Reporting Council of Nigeria* (FHC/L/CS/1430/2012); *NNPC v. Famfa Oil Ltd* (2012) 17 NWLR (Pt. 1328) 148; *Bernard Amasike v. The Registrar General of the Corporate Affairs Commission* (2010) NWLR (Pt. 1211) 337; *Olanrewaju v. Oyeyemi & Ors* (2001) 2 NWLR (Pt. 697) 229; *Din v. A.G. Federation* (1998) 4 NWLR (Pt. 87) 147 at 154; *Gov. Oyo State v. Folayan* (1995) 8 NWLR (Pt.413) 292 at 327. *Attorney General of Lagos State v. Eko Hotels Limited and Oha Limited* (2006) NWLR (Pt. 1011) 3782; *Noble Drilling Nigeria Limited v. Nigerian Maritime Administration and Safety Agency*, (2013) LPELR-22029 (CA).
23 Corporate governance codes give effect to legislated primary law provisions, and, as noted in the 2015 G20/OECD Principles of Corporate Governance, corporate governance codes should be consistent with the rule of law and complement the primary corporate legislations. See, Organisation for Economic Cooperation and Development (OECD) *G20/OECD Principles of Corporate Governance* (OECD Publishing 2015) 13, 14 *et seq.*

Roadmap to embedding CSR in Africa 193

24 Craig VanGrasstek, *The History and Future of the World Trade Organization* (Geneva: WTO 2013) 8.

25 Effective 1 January 1995, the TRIPS Agreement is Annex 1C of the Marrakesh Agreement Establishing the World Trade Organization, signed in Marrakesh, Morocco on 15 April 1994. Among other things covered, TRIPS covers how nations should give adequate protection to intellectual property rights (IPRs), how countries should enforce those rights and how to settle disputes on IP between members of the WTO. TRIPS was amended through the Protocol of 6 December 2005 that entered into force on 23 January 2017.

26 Article III of the General Agreement on Tariffs and Trade (GATT), 30 October 1947, United Nations, Treaty Series, vol. 55.

27 Ibid. Article I.

28 Ibid. Article XI.

29 Article 2.4 and Article 2.5 of the Agreement on Technical Barriers to Trade (TBT). The TBT framework is said to constitute an avenue to achieving international harmonization of technical regulations including marking and labelling standards through the recognition of international standards. See also Article XX, GATT.

30 VanGrasstek (n 24) x.

31 Annex 1 1, Agreement on Technical Barriers to Trade (TBT).

32 Annex I 2, TBT.

33 In the sense of, particularly, Article XI GATT, which prohibits unnecessary restrictions to trade.

34 Carola Glinski, 'CSR and the Law of the WTO: The Impact of Tuna Dolphin II and EC–Seal Products' (2017) 1 *Nordic Journal of Commercial Law* 121, 125; see also, M. Joshi, 'Are Eco-Labels Consistent with World Trade Organization Agreements?' (2004) 38 *Journal of World Trade* 69, 72, who refers, among others, to a study of the WTO Committee on Trade and Environment on discriminatory effects of environmental labelling; also see C. Vidal-Léon, 'Corporate Social Responsibility, Human Rights and the World Trade Organisation' (2013) 16 *Journal of International Economic Law* 893, 899 *et seq.*, who refers to several studies on the effects of CSR codes of conduct on international trade.

35 Glinski (n 34) 126 citing R. Howse and D. Regan, 'The Product/Process Distinction: An Illusory Basis for Disciplining "Unilateralism" in Trade Policy' (2000) 11 *European Journal of International Law* 249, 269 *et seq.*; see also, S. Charnovitz, 'The Law of Environmental "PPMs" in the WTO: Debunking the Myth of Illegality' (2002) 27 *Yale Journal of International Law* 59.

36 John Ruggie, 'Taking Embedded Liberalism Global: The Corporate Connection' in D. Held and M. Koenig-Archiburgi (eds.), *Taming Globalization: Frontiers of Governance* (Cambridge: Cambridge University Press 2003) 93.

37 See also, for instance, the 2019 *Guide for General Counsel on Corporate Sustainability* Version 2.0 designed to help legal professionals drive change and become leaders in embedding sustainability into their companies' strategies and operations. The guidance issued by the UNGC basically helps general counsel to advance the CSR agenda and make their companies behave responsibly. This latest 2019 version replaces the 2015 version available at: www.unglobalcompact.org/library/1351 accessed 9 November 2019.

38 Steven Bernstein and Erin Hannah, 'Non-State Global Standard Setting and the WTO: Legitimacy and the Need for Regulatory Space' (2008) 11 *Journal of International Economic Law* 575.

39 Especially where not used as a disguised restriction on international trade in an arbitrary and unjustifiable discriminatory manner. See US-Shrimp-Turtle case (*United States-Import Prohibition of Certain Shrimp and Shrimp Products*, WT/DS58/AB/R 1998) at para. 185 and 186.

40 Glinski (n 34) footnotes 53–55 and accompanying text. See also US – Gasoline case (*United States – Standards for Reformulated and Conventional Gasoline*, WT/DS2 1996); US-Shrimp-Turtle (1998), earlier at note 39; the EC – Seal Products case (*EC – Seal*

194 *CSR and regionalism in Africa*

Products, WT/DS/400/AB/R, WT/DS 401/AB/R 2014); and EC-Sardines case (*European Communities – Trade Description of Sardines*, WT/DS231/AB/R 2002), amongst others.

41 US-Shrimp-Turtle (1998), previous note 39, paras. 129–131, 185 and 186; see also, Birgitte Egelund Olsen, 'Trade and the Environment' in Birgitte Egelund Olsen, Michael Steinicke and Karsten Engsig Sorensen (eds.), *WTO Law from a European Perspective* (Alphen aan den Rijn, The Netherlands: Wolters Kluwer 2012) 187, 188, *et seq.*

42 Susan Ariel Aaronson, 'A Match Made in the Corporate and Public Interest: Marrying Voluntary CSR Initiatives and the WTO' (2007) 41 (3) *Journal of World Trade* 22, 23.

43 Margaret Lee, 'Regionalism in Africa: A Part of Problem or A Part of Solution' (2002) 9 *Polis Revue Camerounaise de Science Politique* 1–24.

44 Ibid. 21.

45 H.K. Mutai, *Compliance with International Trade Obligations: The Common Market for Eastern and Southern Africa* (The Netherlands: Kluwer 2017) 31, 32; see also, F. Laursen, *Comparative Regional Integration: Europe and Beyond* (Aldershot: Ashgate Publishing Limited 2010) 3 and 4.

46 The RECs have been and remain central institutional actors in Africa's efforts to resolve its economic development dilemmas. They are the regional groupings of African states, and the AU recognizes eight of them viz: Arab Maghreb Union (UMA); Common Market for Eastern and Southern Africa (COMESA); Community of Sahel – Saharan States (CEN – SAD); East African Community (EAC); Economic Community of Central African States (ECCAS); Economic Community of West African States (ECOWAS); Intergovernmental Authority on Development (IGAD)2 and Southern African Development Community (SADC).

47 Kwame Akonor, *African Economic Institutions* (Abingdon, UK: Routledge 2010) 4.

48 United Nations Economic Commission for Africa (ECA), *Greening Africa's Industrialization* (Economic Report on Africa 2016); ECA, *Economic Report on Africa 2015: Industrializing through Trade* (Economic Report on Africa 2015) also available at: www.uneca.org/publications/economic-report-africa-2015 accessed 5 November 2019.

49 Africa turned out the worst performing region in a global audit conducted about the long-term development trends covering 1960 to 1975 by the Economic Commission for Africa at the urging of the United Nations General Assembly, and missed targets set by the UN's Second Development Decade. Akonor (n 47) 21.

50 See Adedeji Adebayo, 'From the Lagos Plan of Action to the New Partnership for the African Development and from the Final Act of Lagos to the Constitutive Act: Whither Africa?' A keynote Address to the African Forum for envisioning Africa, 26–29 April, 2002, Nairobi, Kenya, at para 12 available at: www.worldsummit2002.org/texts/adebayoadedeji2.pdf2002, cited in Akonor (n 47) note 32.

51 Akonor (n 47) 23.

52 Lee (n 43) 5.

53 Akonor (n 47) 23.

54 Ibid.

55 African Union/Economic Commission for Africa (AU/ECA), 'Boosting Intra-Africa Trade: Issues affecting Intra-Africa Trade, Proposed Action Plan for Boosting Intra-Africa Trade and Framework for Fast Tracking of a Continental Free Trade Area' (23–30 January 2012, Addis Ababa, Ethiopia).

56 Faizel Ismail, *Advancing the Continental Free Trade Area (CFTA) and Agenda 2063 in the Context of the Changing Architecture of Global Trade* (Trade & Industrial Policy Strategies, Working Paper 2016) 6.

57 AfCFTA was actually preceded by the 2015 Tri-Partite Free Trade Agreement (TFTA) signed among: SADC, the Southern African Development Community; COMESA, the Common Market for Eastern and Southern Africa and EAC, the East African Community.

58 See the Agreement Establishing the African Continental Free Trade Area and its Protocols, Annexes and Appendices at: https://au.int/en/treaties/agreement-establishing-african-continental-free-trade-area accessed 5 November 2019.

59 African Trade Policy Centre United Nations Economic Commission for Africa, 'African Continental Free Trade Area: Questions & Answers' available at: www.uneca.org/publications/african-continental-free-trade-area-questions-answers accessed 5 November 2019.

60 Ibid. 4.

61 Ibid. 9. A conference of state parties will meet to adopt the structure and organigram of AfCFTA secretariat, the staff rules and regulations, and the secretariat budget. AfCFTA secretariat is to be established in Ghana as decided and approved by the AU Assembly on 7 July 2019.

62 Article 31, Part VII, AfCFTA.

63 See the preamble and paragraph 2 (b) of Article 3 in the Protocol on Trade in Services.

64 See paragraph (e) of Article 3 of the main agreement.

65 www.iisd.org/itn/wp-content/uploads/2012/10/SADC-Model-BIT-Template-Final.pdf accessed 5 November 2019.

66 See, for instance, Part 3 of the SADC Model Treaty. Article 10 has practical provisions in terms of the compliance of the investment plan with relevant anti-bribery and corruption policies. Article 13 deals with compliance with environmental and social impact assessment screening. Article 15 provides for maintaining best labour standards and safeguarding human rights, and Article 16 speaks to compliance with applicable corporate governance codes and standards and, very importantly to discussions in this article, Article 20 underscores its earlier stated objective and gives practical provisions about the recognition of the legitimate responsibility of states, in line with customary international law, to regulate towards the attainment of sustainable development. For more discussions, see Howard Mann, 'The SADC MODEL BIT Template: Investment for Sustainable Development' (IISD Investment Treaty News 2019) available at: www.iisd.org/itn/2012/10/30/the-sadc-model-bit-template-investment-for-sustainable-development/ accessed 5 November 2019.

67 Babatunde Fagbayibo, 'Exploring Legal Imperatives of Regional Integration in Africa' (2012) 45 *Comparative and International Law Journal of Southern Africa* 64–76, 68.

68 Legal integration is indeed indispensable for trade facilitation and effective regional integration. Muna Ndulo, 'The Need for the Harmonisation of Trade Laws in the Southern African Development Community' in Abdulqawi A. Yusuf (ed.), *African Yearbook of International Law* (The Netherlands: Kluwer Law International 1996) 195–225, 196; Jean Alain Penda Matipe, 'Legal Integration in Colonial and Immediate Post-Colonial Sub-Saharan Africa' in Claire Moore Dickerson (ed.), *Unified Business Laws for Africa* (2nd edn, London: IEDP 2012) 7–27.

69 Fagbayibo (n 67) 65, citing Joseph Weiler, *The Constitution of Europe: Do the New Clothes Have an Emperor? And Other Essays on European Integration* (Cambridge: Cambridge University Press 1999) 221.

70 Patrick N. Osakwe, *Transformative Regionalism, Trade and the Challenge of Poverty Reduction in Africa* (ALDC/UNCTAD 2015) available at: https://unctad.org/en/Publications Library/webaldc2015d1_en.pdf accessed 5 November 2019.

7 Model CSR framework for Africa – the Responsible Stakeholder Model

7 Background

Although the two dominant models (of shareholder primacy and stakeholder theories) have their respective strong and weak assumptions, following the appraisal of CSR regulatory and implementation regime in both corporate Nigeria and South Africa, evidence abounds of the undue reliance and focus on shareholder-centric approach in the primary corporate legislations. While it is imperative to recognize and adopt some of the assumptions within these dominant models, some other arguments embedded in these theories appear simply unacceptable. In fact, Professor Andrew Keay, in establishing the need for a new corporate law model, had noted that many of the existing traditional and dominant corporate law theories were devised in old societal contexts and that new ones are required in response to the ever changing nature of the firm and commerce.[1] As shown in Chapter 2, while the shareholder primacy model appears both normatively indefensible and morally untenable (some CEOs openly describing it as a 'dumb idea')[2] the stakeholder-centric theories, on the other hand, in trying to provide solutions to the criticisms of the shareholder primacy model, present an unworkable and impractical framework for CSR implementation. Further, discussions in Chapters 4 and 5 identified the shareholder primacy model as a common ideological obstacle to CSR implementation in the two case study jurisdictions of Nigeria and South Africa. This is coupled with other obstacles such as the faulty legal transplantation of foreign laws and principles; policy incoherence in the primary and secondary legal instruments for CSR enforcement; the unwarranted CSR antipathies in Africa and an undue confinement of CSR practices to corporate philanthropy. The previous challenges appear to provide necessary justifications for some re-thinking in corporate law and CSR re-theorizing for alternative ideological and implementation strategies.

This author proposed a theory labelled the responsible stakeholder model (RSM), embodying two key notions:

(i) A default legal duty on companies to balance competing stakeholder interests;

Model CSR framework for Africa   197

(ii) A presumption of verifiable corporate irresponsibility whenever alleged by a qualified stakeholder.

RSM does not de-legitimize wealth enhancement or maximization for shareholders, simpliciter. However, it draws a distinction between arguing that companies *exist for* the sole purpose of shareholders on the one hand and that companies should be *managed for* the sole purpose of the shareholders on the other hand. The shareholders bring the entity into existence, gave it life (as the realist would argue) or, at least, provided the platform on which the state could grant concession to exist (as the state concession theorists would argue) they have therefore 'paid it forward', sown seeds and should legitimately reap therefrom by participating in dividends and in the final assets sharing (as residual claimants) in the final hours of the entity. Therefore, it seems not totally incorrect to maintain that the company exists *but for* their investments and conscious efforts and can (and should) be deployed by corporate executives to enhance shareholder value. While RSM adopts the assumption that there is the need to enhance shareholder value, conjunctively it also assumes the need for social efficiency, the employment of the principles of corporate law to advance the aggregate welfare of corporate stakeholders. This stakeholder group that the RSM envisages may indeed be without contracts with the company but will usually have stakes and interests that are relevant to the long-term survival of the company and that have been genuinely impacted by corporate decisions.

Further to the wide recognition and inevitable interactions with the state and society for smooth operations and long term survival of businesses, RSM proposes the assignment of an extra corporate governance presumptive duty on companies to self-develop an appropriate and suitable technique towards responsibly balancing competing stakeholder interests. RSM assumes that companies exist for shareholders' wealth maximization but to be fundamentally conditioned by another assumption that the legitimate stakes of other corporate constituents (even if not equated with the interests of the shareholders in priority) must be safeguarded in the course of the said wealth maximization for shareholders. Therefore, RSM treats shareholder wealth maximization as a conditional and rebuttable assumption which treatment underpins its proposal of a default obligation to ensure the safeguard of relevant stakes in the company.

As earlier mentioned, RSM does not de-legitimize shareholder value enhancement by corporate executives and supports keeping the commercial focus of the business, devoid of unnecessary detractions and distractions. Therefore, only qualified stakeholders with legitimate interests that are relevant to the long term survival of the firm/company will be safeguarded within the RSM framework. Therefore, once any qualified stakeholder with a legitimate interest (be it employee, creditor, financier, supplier, contractor, customer, host community et cetera) alleges corporate irresponsibility (directly occasioned by a corporate decision) that is established to affect its legitimate stake in the company, then, in addition to (or as an alternative to) any other remedy or respite afforded in other aspects of the law (human rights law, environmental law, contracts law, torts law, consumer protection law or labour law), recourse should be had to this corporate law remedy of a presumptive duty to balance interests that the company involved must discharge (on a scale of probability that it acted responsibly in due regard to the stakeholder and having effectively balanced all other relevant stakeholders' interests in the circumstance). Such allegations of injury or oppression may include instances of: disregard to employee rights, for instance, in takeover bids or in the process of dividend declaration; in the determination of directors' remuneration; in cases of environmental degradation of host and impacted community infrastructure in business operations or violations of executed agreements with host communities.

7.1 Responsible Stakeholder Model for corporate Africa

While the previous discussions expose the need to further re-think the ideological foundation of corporate objectives and by extension CSR practices, this section of the chapter focuses on the regulatory, implementation and enforcement consequences of the proposed model. In the CSR implementation discourse world over, little progress appears recorded, especially against opportunistic greenwashing companies who choose to fly under the radar of soft law and self-regulatory CSR implementation. No doubt, therefore, some regulatory adjustments are required to the otherwise focus on the business case[3] argument in CSR discourse; the continued dominance of the shareholder primacy model and the open markets system promoted by the Bretton Woods Institutions and integrated within corporate law systems around the world including Africa,[4] together with the attendant weak, soft law and self-regulatory CSR regime at the global and domestic level, need some adjustments. Also calling for more action towards regulation, Dine had noted:

> It needs to be recognised that all of us living in comfort in the rich nations of the world are benefiting from the deeds of corporations regularly vilified in the anti-globalisation press [and that] . . . moral indignation about the terrible behaviour of some corporations . . . must not be allowed to obscure the fact that companies are designed by societies and their profits underpin much of our wealth. So when they strike bargains with evil regimes, repatriate their profits and sell us goods produced at low prices because of sweated or slave labour, this is not because of the inherent evil of the people that work in corporations but as a direct result of the legal design of corporations and the operation of the international legal system which provides them with many opportunities yet fails to regulate.[5]

The need for such regulatory adjustments was also prompted in Drutman and Cray's conclusion that:

> the most effective way to control corporations will be to restore citizen democracy and to reclaim the once widely accepted principle that

corporations are but creatures of the state, chartered under the premise that they will serve the public good, and entitled to only those rights and privileges granted by citizen-controlled governments . . . just and sustainable economy . . . driven by the values of human life . . . instead of the current suicide economy driven only by the relentless pursuit of financial profit at any cost.[6]

In line with the corporate law perspective adopted in this book to CSR implementation and upon a critical review of the challenges bedevilling the CSR regulatory and enforcement framework, this author submits that effective solutions to corporate irresponsibility are not outside but within the corporate law field and in the respective corporate law systems of domestic jurisdictions in Africa and beyond. In this regard, Professor Kent Greenfield noted that:

> Corporate law is a big deal. . . . The largest corporations in the world have economic power of nations. By establishing the obligations and priorities of companies and their management, corporate law affects everything from employees' wages rates (whether in Silicon Valley or Bangladesh), to whether companies will try to skirt environmental laws, to whether they will tend to look the other way when doing business with governments that violate human rights.[7]

Greenfield continued that:

> Only after we recognise the place of corporate law as one small element of a larger political landscape can we then craft a bundle of legal rules and regulatory programs that are likely to move us toward our collective goals.

Social efficiency and the values and interests of a good society do and should underlie corporate law as much as they underlie other areas of the law; there is no longer any need to keep isolating corporate law from other benefits available in other aspects of the law. The author has no question in his mind therefore that, once the field of corporate law and practice is set on proper reformatory pattern towards getting companies to behave responsibly, the world (Africa included) will more likely witness better disciplined and responsible business communities. This author therefore recommends that further attention needs to be paid to the respective corporate law systems across Africa, and the assumptions of the RSM together with the regulatory consequences of the model should be implemented across the continent. Further to earlier recommendations in Chapters 4 and 5, adoption of the theoretical and regulatory ambits of the RSM will entail specific amendments to the primary corporate legislations of African countries. Even where necessary guidance emanates on CSR implementation from the African integration scheme towards a shared, harmonized and integrated CSR framework across Africa (as shall be demonstrated in Section 7.2 later), the RSM theoretical and regulatory proposals must however be

200   CSR and regionalism in Africa

domesticated (legally transposed) within the municipal corporate law system of respective states. This is because, apart from guaranteeing effectiveness, it remains the primary obligation of municipal jurisdictions to regulate, and it is only upon the notorious failure or inadequacies of national legal regimes to so do that recourse is had to international law.[8] Besides, as already demonstrated in Chapter 3, there are already various regulatory challenges[9] with the international regulatory initiatives on the CSR domain. Against the backdrop of the mentioned challenges, while some scholars had expressed hope that voluntary self-regulatory CSR regime at the international level can become hardened eventually,[10] many other prominent experts rather maintain that the solution to corporate abuses at the global level seems almost inconceivable[11] or, at least, remotely far and not possible in the near or foreseeable future.[12] Noting the assertion of John Ruggie that one size (or style or feature) of regulation may not fit all types of companies across jurisdictions, the author therefore advocates the need for individual African countries to undertake a comparative study of the peculiarities of their respective jurisdictions, their history, culture and socio-economic dimensions in fashioning an effective CSR implementation framework within the RSM regime.

The proposed CSR implementation framework embodies a default[13] (presumptive) rule, as opposed to a mandatory[14] or permissive rule, which automatically applies to companies regardless of the contents of their memorandum or articles of association and may only be avoided by discharging the duty to the reasonable satisfaction of adjudicatory bodies (regulators and domestic courts). Discharging the duty will entail demonstration of an internalized CSR implementation corporate policy framework (for instance, voluntarily incorporating binding CSR and sustainability commitments in the company's articles and memorandum of association) that complies with: international best standards and practices or guidelines within the framework of the UNGC, the UNGPs, the OECD Guidelines for Multinational Enterprises, or other similar soft law and self-regulatory initiatives and/or by membership of an international certification or global reporting scheme for responsible business conduct such as the GRI, ISO 26000 and others. Again, compliance with these international best practices, international certification or effective stakeholder engagement and management only constitutes a rebuttable presumption and prima facie evidence and is in no way conclusive proof that such a company has acted or behaved responsibly in any particular circumstance. The conclusiveness of such actions will have to be determined, on a scale of probabilities, by judicial authorities (probably regular courts) acting both judiciously and judicially on a case-by-case basis, depending on circumstances of time, facts or even industry peculiarities. If a company is found in contravention of this default rule, remediation orders including any one or combination of the following may be applied: published apology, restitution, rehabilitation, financial or non-financial compensation and punitive sanctions (whether criminal or administrative, such as fines), as well as the prevention of harm through, for example, injunctions or guarantees of non-repetition.

Very central to the regulatory features of the RSM is its attribute of being meta-regulatory;[15] it adopts more subtle, lighter principles, instead of purely mandatory mechanism, to require compliance. The proposed RSM-inspired CSR implementation framework is anticipated to be acceptable within business communities in Africa as companies are still enjoined to maintain their voluntary self-regulatory CSR model; only that corporate stakeholders are also afforded the opportunity to simply establish their legitimate interest in the long term survival of the company and allege violations of rights protected by CSR (like human rights, environmental or labour rights) and show a resultant injury. The onus of discharging the burden of proving there was no violation is on companies.

This proposal ensures that corporate greenwashing, free riding and opportunistic rogue companies (willing and ready to do business regardless of elements of unlawfulness and irregularities involved, exemplified in Groups C and D of Thomas McInerney's analysis[16]) will find it more difficult to reasonably discharge this onus. By this incidence, corporate greenwashing and empty or mindless compliance with corporate governance codes, identified as obstacles in corporate Nigeria and South Africa, may be curbed.

It is imperative to note that this proposal is, however, not suggesting that the interests of shareholders and of the other stakeholder are the same, nor is it a radical prescription demanding the organization of formalized stakeholder meetings in corporate governance discourse to rival shareholder meetings in corporate legislations. That, again, will essentially defeat the commercial focus of the company and may discourage investment in the jurisdiction adopting such a model. The proposal is to impose a duty on company itself to consider, manage and balance competing stakeholder interests, which will expand the traditional meaning of 'the best interest of the company' in primary corporate legislations. It will not distract companies from their pure commercial focus but only ensure credible protection is afforded qualified stakeholders with genuine, material and legitimate stakes in the company.

As a regulatory technique for business communities in Africa, it is important to reiterate that the adoption of the RSM proposals does not entail an imposition of corporate tax unlike as attempted by the aborted 2007 Nigerian CSR Bill, nor does it introduce some highly prescriptive external hard law initiatives, which may scare off investment opportunities and result in regulatory jurisdictional arbitrage such as the potentials of the mandatory community development agreement (CDA) under Section 116 of the Nigerian Minerals and Mining Act, 2007.

In consideration of the foregoing and further to earlier discussions in Chapters 4 and 5, what is missing (and should be incorporated in the ongoing primary corporate law amendments in Nigeria and South Africa) is a specific duty on the company itself (and not on corporate executives or directors as done in India[17]) to ensure qualified, material and legitimate stakeholder interests are properly considered, managed and balanced in determining the best interest of the company. This will give impetus to the environment, social and

202 *CSR and regionalism in Africa*

governance (ESG) reporting under Principle 28 of the Nigerian Code and the stakeholder-inclusive approach under King IV. This will correct the policy incoherence and mismatch between the primary and secondary legislations on CSR implementation within corporate Nigeria and South Africa. With this proposal, the activities of the social and ethics committee under Section 72(4) of the South African Companies Act No. 71 of 2008 (SACA) would have also been enhanced in providing real value to stakeholders and ensuring more mindful compliance with stakeholder protection requirements in the corporate governance codes. The previous RSM-proposed CSR amendment in the corporate legislations is justifiable as there is no unassailable reason why corporate law principles, theories and rules should only focus on creating a conducive environment for corporate executives to maximize profits for shareholders and not afford credible requirements for safeguarding all stakeholder rights. All aspects and areas of law, environmental law, contracts law, intellectual property law, torts law, human rights law, international law and corporate law among others should be instrumental towards moving our society closer to what we want it to be.[18]

The adoption of the RSM is also facilitated on the ground that, as discussed in Chapter 2, the revolution away from shareholder primacy-oriented provisions in corporate legislations (primacy and subsidiary) appears to have already begun. Sections 11(a) and 50 (f) of the Nigerian Financial Reporting Council of Nigeria and Sections 7(d) and (k) together with Section 72(4) of the SACA are promising provisions and could be built upon in adopting the amendments proposals in this chapter.

This author reiterates the view expressed in Chapter 5 that any expansive or creative interpretation afforded the provisions under Sections 279(3) and 283(1) of the Nigerian Companies and Allied Matters Act, 1990 as amended (CAMA) and under Sections 7(d) and (k), 72(4), 76(3) (b), 218(2) of SACA are not only stretching the limits of those provisions too far but also amount to precarious handling of such an important aspect of public welfare and the promotion of social efficiency through corporate law. The reality is that, while such expansive arguments will appear to safeguard stakeholder interests, they are actually without any real benefits to any victim stakeholder. A serious danger to CSR implementation from this will be that proliferation of this so-called creative and expansive thinking may crowd out other proposals such as the RSM proposal in this chapter for head-on, direct and clear changes to primary corporate legislations. The so-called expansive or creative thinking might end up being used to divert policy makers' attention at a domestic and international level from taking steps such as recommended in this book.

The RSM-imposed obligation on the company means that shareholders, as residual owners, will ensure wholehearted and mindful compliance with corporate sustainability and integrated reporting requirements since they know that violation of legitimate interest of a qualified stakeholder may be very costly to the company and affect available profits for sharing as dividends or other assets to share as residual claimants. Upon the adoption of the foregoing recommendations, the business judgment rule with which corporate law has imposed a duty on corporate executives to promote the financial interests and assets of companies will be further expanded to accommodate directors' wholehearted pursuit of an effective and robust CSR beyond philanthropy and compliance with stakeholder protection requirements in the best interest of the company. Further, in light of prevailing modern socio-economic, political and environmental realities, corporate law has come of age to justifiably impose a duty on companies allowing their directors, guided by the business judgment rule (which safeguards disinterested, informed, and good-faith decisions of directors), to act responsibly and exercise their discretions and balance competing interests of constituents without imposing any specific one-size-fits-all measures for companies to adopt. Within the framework of the advocated RSM, company activities and assets will now be managed for the ultimate benefit of the shareholders only in the sense that they constitute the residual risk-bearers or claimants. For such residual risk, shareholders will retain the privilege of appointing competent and responsible corporate executives and directors who shall ensure, while avoiding unnecessary risks to corporate assets, that the business of the business is responsible business. And if such corporate executives as appointed by shareholders fail in this legal obligation, qualified and material stakeholders with legitimate interests will have credible and enforceable legal rights to seek redress with the regulators or the courts as either jurisdiction may choose. The much-touted RSM as an alternative theoretical and regulatory approach to CSR implementation in corporate Africa is again illustrated in the following figure:

A set of model CSR implementation provisions underpinned by the RSM and with which Nigeria and South Africa may amend their respective primary corporate legislations is provided in the following list:

(i) Every company organised for profit shall manage the social, economic and environmental impacts of its operations on stakeholders; such a company shall be corporate socially responsible by effectively balancing its legal, economic, ethical and discretionary responsibilities;

(ii) The stakeholders of a company may include its shareholders, employees, creditors, customers, consumers, host communities or any other qualified constituent in the society who may not have a subsisting or enforceable contract with it but with a genuine and legitimate interest in the company's long term survival;

(iii) For the purposes of this section, upon the presentation of a petition for alleged violation of paragraph (i) any time before any winding up or liquidation proceeding involving the company, such company may be presumed to have acted irresponsibly but shall be afforded the opportunity and shall therefore establish its corporate social responsibility towards the aggrieved stakeholder on the scale of probability;

(iv) If a company is found in contravention of the duty imposed in paragraph (i), remediation orders to be applied may include any one or combination

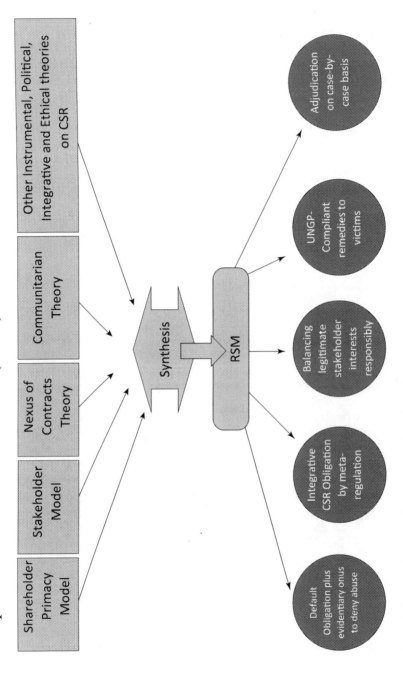

Figure 7.1 Illustrating RSM formulation and regulatory features

of: published apology, restitution, rehabilitation, financial or non-financial compensation and punitive sanctions (whether criminal or administrative, such as fines), as well as the prevention of harm through, for example, injunctions or guarantees of non-repetition;

(v) The obligation imposed on the company under this section shall be enforceable by petition filed at the High Court (in case of Nigeria, Federal High Court; for South Africa or other jurisdictions in Africa, any equivalent High Court of superior records handling company law matters) by any qualified stakeholder having established a verifiable injury to his or her legitimate interests in the long term survival of the company;

(vi) For the proper implementation and administration of the provisions in this section, the minister assigned with the responsibilities of trade, finance and investment matters shall have powers to publish supplementary rules, subsidiary regulations or guidelines in consonance with international or regional best practices, and such supplementary rules shall be published in the gazette.

The earlier RSM-inspired CSR implementation proposal is hereby subjected to some standards and tests. The Hague Institute for the Internationalisation of Law (HiiL)[19] provides some guidance. HiiL identified four pillars in assessing the appropriateness (success) or otherwise of regulatory regimes. These pillars include:

(i) Quality;
(ii) Enforcement;
(iii) Legitimacy;
(iv) Effectiveness.

The previous testing standards are interrelated, as one may be used to explain the other.[20] The 'quality' element of a framework relates to the question of how practicable and workable it is. 'Enforcement' relates to the question: are there legal or non-legal mechanisms to monitor or ensure compliance with the framework? 'Legitimacy' relates to whether the basic underlying goals or ideals for the introduction of the regulation are accepted by the addressees (business community) and others. And finally, 'effectiveness' is an empirical test monitoring the impact on compliance and the degree to which the framework has succeeded in regulating the intended conducts or misconducts. This author is of the view that the proposed model framework passes the first three pillars. In respect of the last pillar of effectiveness, while this is a regime not already tested, it is argued that it is likely to be successful as its contours are expected to be further developed over time by judicial authorities just as many procedural requirements of other traditional legal doctrines in the past have been developed by way of judicial precedents.

RSM is hinged on the principles of law and regulation, and as law and regulation have their limitations as possibly not constituting the best way to regulate

206 CSR and regionalism in Africa

behaviour,[21] RSM may not be without a few challenges. It may, for instance, be criticized (as other propositions have been in Australia[22]) to have the implication of undue expansion of directors' duties without necessarily guaranteeing stakeholder interests-protection. It may also be contended that, since it is the shareholders' investment that creates the company, the duties of corporate executives and the definition of the success of the company should be designed to protect that investment, without more.[23] While the previous statement may be true that without shareholders' investment there may not be companies in the first place, however, even if the shareholders have 'created' the company, risking their investment, does that investment exist or operate in isolation? Can it be concluded that only the shareholders contribute to the maintenance, maximization, safeguard or protection of that (capital) investment in view of the modern methods of doing business? This author submits that but for the concession of the state, coupled with wide recognition and inevitable interactions with the employees, creditors and the host communities amongst other stakeholders, such (capital) investment may not be very productive and would likely be nugatory in yielding expected returns for the shareholders.

The adoption of the previous proposal only at the domestic corporate law systems of states may not also be without its limitations in combating cross-border corporate abuses. Further, while an exterritorial application of the previous proposal by an African country will facilitate checks on the powers, influences and threats of the large corporations to constitute engines of further conflicts in conflict zones, such adoption runs the usual risk of inter-state friction on the continent. Further, jurisdictional arbitrage and forum shopping may likely become the order of the day whereby companies move around scouting for favourable jurisdictions and countries with weak CSR implementation framework to invest in. This appears to warrant the mainstreaming of CSR (using the assumptions such as proposed within the RSM framework) within the African integration discourse.

7.2 Mainstreaming CSR into AfCFTA

Discussions of the African integration scheme, together with appraising the African Continental Free Trade Area (AfCFTA) agreement in relation to its CSR provisions in Chapter 6 set the agenda for a regional strategy for CSR implementation towards attaining the objectives of trade liberalization and meeting the sustainable development goals (SDGs). This part of the book builds on relevant arguments in Sections 6.3 and 6.4 of Chapter 6 and will underscore the need for a CSR policy framework within Africa's free trade area.

Africa must realize that, as one of the realities of economic globalization, it is not too far from the truth that 'no one is in charge'.[24] It is unlikely that other continents will integrate to fix Africa's problems for Africa when they have their own challenges to deal with. Who, how and what will constitute the countervailing powers in Africa to the powerful corporations and businesses driving globalization – if not CSR – or using the instrumentality of CSR implementation within business communities in Africa? While drawing necessary lessons from other continents, especially leveraging the successes recorded at the European Union,[25] Africa must design a suitable CSR implementation framework to get businesses (multinationals included) to make profits responsibly and accountably. Sufficient arguments are already canvassed in this book showing that antipathies against CSR implementation or simply considering CSR and its core values as some grandiose Western ideas targeted at further impoverishing Africa are completely mistaken. Any economic pressures of trade liberalization in Africa must be properly managed as the usual fear of losing out on free trade and foreign investments for incorporating otherwise-thought alien ideas should be jettisoned.[26] It is very comforting that a few African countries have already incorporated CSR into their trade and investment agreements. While it is arguable that the inserted CSR clauses in these agreements may have more to do with, for instance, Brazil's impressive focus on investment cooperation and facilitation (as opposed to protection), the fact, however, that these African countries participated and signed such agreements appears sufficient prima facie evidence that African countries no longer treat CSR as necessarily a Western concept or necessarily anti-free trade. Instances of such incorporation of CSR and sustainability clauses in the trade and investment agreements can be found in Article 13 of the 2019 Cooperation and Investment Facilitation Agreement (CIFA) between Brazil and Morocco incorporating CSR and sustainability development provisions and Article 14 of the 2018 agreement between Brazil and Ethiopia.[27]

It is useful to clarify that, while the author is not suggesting that all of Africa's economic and development problems will be solved by mainstreaming some shared CSR implementation strategy in the AfCFTA framework, any CSR and sustainable development strategy of the African integration initiative should certainly not be counterproductive to achieving the SDGs in Africa. Therefore, towards ensuring AfCFTA is actually part of the solution and not contributing to Africa's economic woes, this author proposes the negotiation and signing of a Protocol on Rules and Procedures towards an Overall Sustainable Development Strategy as part of the AfCFTA framework. Within the ambits of Article 8 (3)[28] of the AfCFTA agreement, the author proposes the negotiation and signing of such protocol on the implementation of a harmonized CSR framework, not promoted as corporate philanthropy or ad hoc community development projects expected from the multinational enterprises operating in African states but as a robust and comprehensive corporate governance and business management concept to be embedded by member states within their respective business communities and with which businesses can be accountable and responsible for or better manage the risks associated with the economic, social and environmental impacts of their operations. With the protocol, discussions around, for instance, addressing CSR greenwash, double standards operations and maintaining value chain supply discipline for multinational enterprises operating in Africa, can be had drawing from practices within the most successful regional integration, the EU.[29] This CSR implementation

208 CSR and regionalism in Africa

proposal aligns with CSR conception within international regulatory initiatives and dialogues such as the UNGC, the UNGPs and the OECD Guidelines and will promote the attainment of the SDGs in Africa. The drafting of the protocol will entail the constitution of a drafting committee[30] by the AfCFTA secretariat who will undertake a proper legal harmonization of the corporate social responsibility and sustainability framework within the member states through effective legal integration exercise. Legal harmonization will address the different member states' current CSR regulatory strategies within their respective municipal laws – if any – or even as differently approached while negotiating investment treaties or finalizing private contracts with multinational enterprises operating in Africa.[31] Such diversity of laws or plurality in legal approaches must be embraced but, again, with proper integration exercise undertaken towards the harmonization as opposed to unification of the relevant respective laws. The proposed protocol (which this author suggests to be underpinned by the theoretical underpinnings of the RSM) would provide an implementation framework, which will serve as a template for member states, providing necessary guides and directives for CSR implementation within their domestic jurisdictions. It will therefore provide a platform for regular release of soft law[32] guiding directives for implementation to fit local legislations within respective member states. This will foster a comprehensive harmonized approach to be articulated at a regional level, which member states can also draw upon in whole or in part, even in negotiating investment treaties with other countries outside of Africa or in finalizing private contracts with multinational enterprises. By way of further clarifications on legal transposition at municipal levels of African states, target dates will be set at the regional level for member states to implement any CSR and sustainable development directives made pursuant to such agreed protocol to enable the incorporation of such CSR requirements within the domestic laws of member states, where they are not already there. Once incorporated within the municipal laws of member states, they may therefore be enforced through domestic courts. For the avoidance of doubt, the proposed protocol cannot be, nor does it have to be, one overarching document addressing all aspects of CSR or settling all matters bordering on sustainable development once and for all. CSR is constantly evolving, so there will be need for regular releases of directives made pursuant to the agreed protocol towards adjusting to changes. It is anticipated that issuing policy guidelines and directives in piecemeal will also ensure there is sufficient time and resources to obtain the buy-in of key stakeholders before thereafter moving towards more complex issues over time.

As distilled from the previous discussions, the following list highlights a few benefits of CSR implementation and mainstreaming within the regional integration scheme of Africa:

(i) Mainstreaming CSR and sustainable development into the African Continental Free Trade Area (AfCFTA) discourse will clarify and sustain a CSR policy direction within the AfCFTA agreement and ensure that the single market trade liberalization objective within Africa is appreciated not as an end in itself but as a means towards achieving overall social responsible economic growth and sustainable development across Africa;

(ii) Just like the impact of the CSR provisions in the EU free trade agreements, properly mainstreaming CSR into the AfCFTA agreement would be very useful in checking certain claims brought by investors against African states before an investment tribunal; in the circumstance, tribunals will consider the CSR obligations of such investors in the trade agreements as inspired by the shared CSR regulatory model made pursuant to the AfCFTA framework, and, where such investor has violated such CSR provisions, the investor would not enjoy the investment protection obligations on the African state or, at least, such investor's rights would be somewhat reduced (probably by reducing the damages available to it as a remedy);[33]

(iii) A regional CSR implementation framework will help to create greater awareness in the area (as AfCFTA covers the entirety of the 55 member states) about the values of CSR and economic globalization discourse. This book has shown that many developing countries, especially from Africa, still confine CSR as simply corporate philanthropy and undertaking community development projects. A harmonized CSR policy framework at the level of the AU as mainstreamed into the AfCFTA will definitely drive awareness of the core values of the concept within the region;

(iv) An AfCFTA framework without a robust CSR policy properly implemented across the African region will likely aggravate the challenges of jurisdictional arbitrage and forum shopping whereby companies will move around different countries in Africa scouting for favourable jurisdictions and states with weak CSR regulatory framework to invest. This will also likely diminish the effectiveness of the RSM-inspired CSR implementation framework recommended in Section 7.1 for domestic adoption within the African states. Those challenges that CSR and the values of sustainable development are supposed to address are usually cross-border in nature. In such instances, narrowly implemented and disjointed individual domestic approaches to them may not be very effective.

(v) Mainstreaming CSR discourse in the AfCFTA will definitely galvanize support for regionally defined CSR values and standards and therefore foster ownership of these standards by other actors in the region. The drafting committee to be constituted should be composed of Africans from Africa but with requisite comparative law skills towards a proper legal harmonization and integration. This will equally foster pooling of resources (regionally) and improve social protection policies across the region;

(vi) Adopting the previously proposed Protocol on Rules and Procedures towards an Overall Sustainable Development Strategy will ensure the AfCFTA goes beyond just mentioning the SDGs towards actually legislating policies towards CSR implementation;

210   *CSR and regionalism in Africa*

(vii) It is rather obvious that, because of the huge economic potentials in Africa and population size, AfCFTA, as the world's largest free trade area, will always attract further trade liberalization discussions and arrangements with the rest of the world. The question then is, will Africa join the global economy to develop internationally accepted CSR standards and thereby facilitate its own trade in goods and services from Africa, or would the antipathies to CSR, continent-wide largely corporate philanthropy practices or CSR treatment as undue or disguised protectionist practices of the developed economies linger? A CSR framework within the African regional integration scheme will equally have significant implications on market access argument for goods originating from Africa. The protocol together with any guiding directives released pursuant thereto will provide a common basis for African national legislations to prescribe internationally acceptable technical regulations and standards within the ambits of Article XX of the GATT and Articles 2.4 and 2.5 of the TBT.

7.3 Chapter summary

This chapter concludes the book and harmonizes earlier discussions in previous chapters about seeking to embed effective, robust and comprehensive CSR in corporate Africa. It galvanized earlier discussions about the theoretical ambits of the responsible stakeholder model (RSM) earlier synthesized in Chapter 2. RSM was described as an alternative ideological foundation on which the true nature, objective and purpose of corporate actions may be understood and upon which efficient CSR practices may be embedded in business communities. RSM perceives a company as a hub or web of investments (not a contractual web or hub) dependent on state concession and inevitable interaction and cooperation of different relevant stakes for its survival in the long run. The stakeholders are the corporate constituents and have been carefully qualified, limited to only accommodate legitimate interests in order to forestall meddlesome interlopers from interfering with smooth day-to-day operations of companies or distracting corporate executives with frivolous claims of corporate irresponsibility. Within the framework of RSM, the challenges encountered by many African host communities or any other constituent(s) of the company in safeguarding their stakes may become largely mitigated. A company found culpable under the default duty should be made, amongst any other necessary remedies, to restore the particular stakeholder to a position in which such stakeholder would have been had the company acted responsibly by seeking wealth maximization for its shareholders in a responsible manner. Although most of the international regulatory dialogues (including the most comprehensive corporate responsibility framework in the world, the UNGC, together with specific regulatory attempts such as the UNGPs and the OECD Guidelines) were found wanting in relation to effective CSR implementation, their significance within the RSM framework was discussed.

Building on earlier recommendations in Chapters 4 and 5 that the primary and secondary corporate law instruments in these countries should be harmonized, this chapter proposed a set of model CSR implementation provisions with which the Nigerian Companies and Allied Matters Act 1990 as amended, the South African Companies Act No. 71 of 2008 and other primary corporate legislations in Africa can be amended. Such a recommended model, inspired by the RSM, was touted to resolve the policy incoherence in the corporate law systems of the countries and ensure that their secondary law instruments become more effective, giving effect to and complementing the primary law instruments towards getting businesses to behave responsibly and accountably to stakeholders.

Although this chapter did not suggest that CSR has all the answers to all developmental challenges or solutions to all corporate-related human rights abuses in Africa, the author nonetheless has no doubt in his mind that the dream of the 'Africa we want' – where domestic businesses behave responsibly, where multinational enterprises find double standard operations in Africa no longer efficient and where the global competitiveness of businesses, goods and services from Africa is greatly enhanced – is achievable but is not going to happen by chance, magically or overnight. It will take relevant compromises on the principle of state sovereignty by African countries and, for the purpose of this book, deliberate efforts to properly harmonize and integrate CSR implementation beyond corporate philanthropy within Africa's trade liberalization discourse. Africa is lagging behind already; efforts at legal harmonization must be intensified now if someone (Africa) does not really want to be left behind (yet again) in the attainment of the universally accepted SDGs.

Notes

1 Andrew Keay, 'Ascertaining the Corporate Objective: An Entity Maximisation and Sustainability Model' (2008) 71 *Modern Law Review* 663, 666.

2 Francesco Guerrera, 'Welch Condemns Share Price Focus' *Financial Times* (12 March 2009), saying 'The idea that shareholder value is a strategy is insane. It is the product of your combined efforts-from the management to the employees'; see also, Paddy Ireland, 'Corporate Schizophrenia: The Institutional Origins of Corporate Social Irresponsibility' in Nina Boeger and Charlotte Villiers (eds.), *Shaping the Corporate Landscape: Towards Corporate Reform and Enterprise Diversity* (Oxford: Hart 2018); Duff McDonald, 'Harvard Business School and the Propagation of Immoral Profit Strategies' *Newsweek* (14 April 2017) 11–13.

3 A 'business case' argument for CSR enjoins corporate executives to consider stakeholder interests or report on non-financial matters of CSR like employee or environmental matters so long as it will make *business sense* (cost-benefit implications) to do so and such considerations promote the overall economic performance of the company without prejudice to enhancing shareholder value; see Charlotte Villiers, 'Corporate Law Corporate Power and Corporate Social Responsibility' in Nina Boeger, Rachel Murray, and Charlotte Villiers (eds.), *Perspectives on Corporate Social Responsibility* (Cheltenham: Edward Elgar 2008) 85, 97, 98 *et seq.*

212 CSR and regionalism in Africa

4 Liesbeth F.H. Enneking, *Foreign Direct Liability and Beyond Exploring the Role of Tort Law in Promoting Corporate Social Responsibility and Accountability* (The Hague: Eleven International Publishing 2012) 11.

5 Janet Dine, *Companies, International Trade and Human Rights* (Cambridge: Cambridge University Press 2005) 4, 44.

6 L. Drutman and C. Cray, *The Peoples Business: Controlling Corporations and Restoring Democracy* (Citizen Works Corporate Reform Commission, San Francisco: Berrett-Koehler Publishers 2004) 280.

7 Kent Greenfield, *The Failure of Corporate Law: Fundamental Flaws and Progressive Possibilities* (Chicago: University of Chicago Press 2006) 4–5.

8 Ole Kristian Fauchald and Jo Stigen, 'Corporate Responsibility before International Institutions' (2009) 40 *The George Washington International Law Review* 1025, 1027, 1028.

9 For instance, earlier CSR regulatory attempts by the United Nations with the aim of producing an international legally binding treaty through the instrumentality of the UN Draft Code and the UN Sub-Commission Norms both resulted in a failure to agree on a unified approach to CSR standards, and ultimately the two projects collapsed, although for different reasons. The Draft Code was said to have collapsed for political reasons as developing countries played the card of their fledging sovereignty while the UN Sub-Commission Norms were said to have proposed a regulatory regime contrary to international law. The regulatory challenges of the UNGC, the UNGPs and the OECD Guidelines in terms of CSR implementation have also been discussed in Chapter 3.

10 Around the year 2011, Professor Tineke Lambooy had predicted that in five years' time we will be getting such results. Tineke Lambooy, *Corporate Social Responsibility: Legal and Semi-Legal Frameworks Supporting CSR Developments 2000–2010 and Case Studies* (Dissertation and Commercial Edition in IVOR Series, Leiden: Kluwer 2010) 273.

11 John Ruggie, 'The Construction of the UN "Protect, Respect and Remedy" Framework for Business and Human Rights: The True Confessions of a Principled Pragmatist' (2011) *European Human Rights Law Review* 127, 128.

12 Bryan Horrigan, *Corporate Social Responsibility in the 21st Century: Debates, Models and Practices across Government, Law and Business* (Cheltenham, UK: Edward Elgar 2010) 344; see also Jennifer Zerk, *Corporate Abuse in 2007: A Discussion Paper on What Changes in the Law Need to Happen* (The Corporate Responsibility (CORE) Coalition 2007) 31.

13 For detailed discussions on the three forms of corporate rules, see, generally, Brian R. Cheffins, *Company Law: Theory, Structure and Operation* (Oxford: Clarendon Press 1996) 218, 219 *et seq.*

14 See, for instance, mandatory CSR regime in the Indonesian Investment Law No. 25 of 2007, and the Limited Liability Company Law No. 40 of 2007.

15 Olufemi Amao, 'Mandating Corporate Social Responsibility: Emerging Trends in Nigeria' (2008) 6 *Journal of Commonwealth Law and Legal Education* 75, 79.

16 See Section 3.1.6 of Chapter 3.

17 See Section 166(2) of the 2013 Indian Companies Act. In acting in the best interest of the company, directors are mandated to consider the employees, the shareholders, the community and the protection of environment. This is a clear legislative expansion of directors' duty beyond consideration of shareholders' interests and for the benefit of the mentioned stakeholders, employees, host community and environment. It is unlike Section 172 of the English Companies Act, which says directors should have 'regard' for stakeholders. The previous provision leaves no one in doubt that the Indian primary corporate legislation has moved (even if slightly) away from a shareholder primacy-oriented model.

18 Corroborative of the foregoing is the submission that corporate law isolation or the claim that corporate law should serve only the interests of the shareholder and managerial elite is highly suspect, especially if we believe that the purpose of corporations is to serve society as a whole rather than a small, wealthy minority. W.W. Bratton and

M.L. Wachter, 'Shareholder Primacy's Corporatist Origins: Adolf Berle and the Modern Corporation' (2008) 34 (1) *The Journal of Corporate Law* 99 at 151.

19 Tineke Lambooy and Marie-Eve Rancourt, *The Added Value of Private Regulation in an Internationalised World? Towards a Model of the Legitimacy, Effectiveness, Enforcement and Quality of Private Regulation* (HiiL's Concept Paper 2008) cited in Lambooy (n 10) 250 fn 91; largely similar test mechanisms such as legitimacy, accessibility, predictability, equity, rights-compatibility, and transparency were identified by Professor Ruggie in John Gerrard Ruggie, 'Protect, Respect, and Remedy: The UN Framework for Business and Human Rights' in Mashood A. Baderin and Manisuli Ssenyonjo (eds.), *International Human Rights Law: Six Decades after the UDHR and Beyond* (Surrey: Ashgate 2010) 535.

20 Ibid. 4–7.

21 Jan Eijsbouts, *Corporate Responsibility, Beyond Voluntarism: Regulatory Options to Reinforce the Licence to Operate* (Inaugural Lecture, Maastricht: Maastricht University 2011) 45.

22 Senate Standing Committee on Legal and Constitutional Affairs, *Company Directors' Duties: Report on the Social and Fiduciary Duties and Obligations of Company Directors* (Parliament of Australia 1989) 83.

23 Ibid. 98.

24 Thomas Friedman, The Lexus and the Olive Tree 112 (1999) cited by Larry C. Backer, 'Governing Corporations: Corporate Social Responsibility and the Obligations of States' (2008) 2 *Berkeley Journal of International Law* 503, 506.

25 In this regard, Morten Boas and others noted: 'One thing, which at least seems to be obvious, is that actors in the South should think very carefully about the fruitfulness of following the blueprint of the European Union or other regional schemes from the North. If regional organisation is to play a real role in the economies of the South it has to be embedded into the real life context of these economies'. Morten Boås, Marianne H. Marchand and Timothy M. Shaw, 'The Weave-World: Regionalism in the South in the New Millennium' (1999) 20 (5) *Third World Quarterly* 1061, 1025.

26 Henry Steiner, Phillip Alston and Ryan Goodman, *International Human Rights Law in Context: Law Politics Morals* (3rd edn, Oxford: Oxford University Press 2007) 1388.

27 See also similar provisions in the 2015 Brazil and Mozambique, Angola and Brazil, together with Brazil and Malawi agreements respectively. Others are available at <https://investmentpolicy.unctad.org/international-investment-agreements/countries/27/brazil> accessed 10 November 2019. CSR clauses are now specifically added to EU trade agreements such as in Article 13.6 of the EU-Korea Free Trade Agreement; see also Article 271 (3) of the EU Columbia/Peru Free Trade Agreement.

28 Article 8 (3) of AfCFTA opens the opportunity for a protocol on CSR implementation. Such protocol fits within and aligns with the stated (though in passing) objectives of the AfCTA for the overall sustainable development of the continent.

29 See discussions in Section 3.5 of Chapter 3.

30 The framework may proceed from the relatively simple matters such as proper CSR conception in Africa and showing its key values with which corporations driven by and driving regional trade and integration in Africa are expected to imbibe in their operations. It may thereafter move into more complex issues of addressing shared CSR regulatory and enforcement mechanisms through effective legal harmonization and integration. The protocol must, however, in the minimum, work on a development strategy which, though it incorporates relevant lessons from the global North, must adopt proper comparative analysis and legal transplantation, making such a development agenda not only fit for Africa but also aligned with international standards. Areas of member states' laws that constitute obstacles to economic integration will be thoroughly investigated and relevant proposals made for legal harmonisation. The need for harmonization of laws was long adumbrated in the study that led to the establishment of the United Nations Commission on International Trade Law (UNCITRAL), which referred to difficulties faced by parties engaging in international commercial transactions as a result of the multiplicity of and divergences in national laws. See Report of the UN

214 *CSR and regionalism in Africa*

Secretary General on International Trade Law, I UNCITRAL yearbook (1968–1970) 18, 19, *et seq.*; see also, the 'Progressive development of the law of international trade: Report of the Secretary-General' Official Records of the General Assembly, Twenty-first Session, Annexes, agenda item, docs.A/6396, Add.1.

31 Further to discussions in Chapters 4 and 5, the CSR legislative and regulatory framework in Nigeria, for instance, focuses on promoting transparency, environmental accountability, and host community development within the extractive industry and occasioned the passage of laws such as: the 2007 Nigerian Minerals and Mining Act; the 2007 Nigeria Extractive Industries Transparency Initiative (NEITI) Act and the proposed 2018 Petroleum Host and Impacted Communities Development Trust Bill. The corporate citizenship framework and strategy in South Africa is slightly differently focused. Whereas, as a result of the imbalances in the South African society occasioned by the apartheid policy of the government of the Republic of South Africa pre-1995, its CSR framework is geared towards social and economic transformation of the majority black population and occasioning enactments such as: the 1998 Employment Equity Act No. 55; the Skills Development Act No. 97 of 1998; the Promotion of Equality and Prevention of Unfair Discrimination Act, 2000 and the Broad-Based Black Economic Empowerment Act No. 53 of 2003 among others. See other implementation strategies as given with the example of the 2018 investment treaty between Ethiopia and Brazil with robust CSR implementation clauses.

32 In terms of policy making and regulation, there is very high potential for CSR principles expressed initially in terms of voluntary non-binding soft law to harden into hard law, to which mandatory enforcement may be warranted. For detailed description of soft laws, see Section 3.1.2 of Chapter 3.

33 Eva van der Zee, 'Incorporating the OECD Guidelines in International Investment Agreements: Turning a Soft Law Obligation into Hard Law?' (2013) 40 *Legal Issues of Economic Integration* 33, 59; Angelica Bonfanti, 'Applying Corporate Social Responsibility to Foreign Investments: Failures and Prospects' in T. Treves and others (eds.), *Foreign Investment, International Law and Common Concern* (Abingdon, UK: Routledge 2014) 246; Laurence Dubin, 'Corporate Social Responsibility Clauses in Investment Treaties' (IISD Investment Treaty News 2018) available at: www.iisd.org/itn/2018/12/21/corporate-social-responsibility-clauses-in-investment-treaties-laurence-dubin/ accessed 5 November 2019.

Bibliography

Books/chapters in books

Abugu, J.E.O., *Foundations of Corporate Law* (Lagos: University of Lagos Press 2011).

Abugu, J.E.O., *Principles of Corporate Law in Nigeria* (Lagos: MIJ Professional Publishers 2014).

Adeyeye, A.O., *Corporate Social Responsibility of Multinational Corporations in Developing Countries: Perspectives on Anti-Corruption* (Cambridge: Cambridge University Press 2012).

Ajogwu, F., *Corporate Governance in Nigeria: Law and Practice* (Lagos: CCLD 2007).

Akonor, K., *African Economic Institutions* (Abingdon, UK: Routledge 2010).

Amao, O., *Corporate Social Responsibility, Human Rights and the Law: Multinational Corporations in Developing Countries* (Abingdon, UK: Routledge 2011).

Armour, J., and others, 'The Essential Elements of Corporate Law: What Is Corporate Law?' in R. Kraakman, and others (eds.), *The Anatomy of Corporate Law: A Comparative and Functional Approach* (Oxford: Oxford University Press 2009).

Barnes, K.D., *Cases and Materials on Nigerian Company Law* (Ibadan: Samadex Printing Works 1992).

Berle, Jr., A.A., and Means, G.C., *The Modern Corporation and Private Property* (New York: The Macmillan Company 1932).

Black, J., 'Law and Regulation: The Case of Finance' in C. Parker, C. Scott, N. Lacey, and J. Braithwaite (eds.), *Regulating Law* (Oxford: Oxford University Press 2004).

Bonfanti, A., 'Applying Corporate Social Responsibility to Foreign Investments: Failures and Prospects' in T. Treves, and others (eds.), *Foreign Investment, International Law and Common Concern* (Abingdon, UK: Routledge 2014).

Bowen, H.R., *Social Responsibilities of the Businessman* (New York: Harper and Row 1953).

Campbell, D., 'Why Regulate the Modern Corporation? The Failure of "Market Failure"' in J. McCahery, S. Picciotto, and C. Scott (eds.), *Corporate Control and Accountability* (Oxford: Clarendon 1993).

Campbell, T., 'The Normative Grounding of Corporate Social Responsibility: A Human Rights Approach' in D. McBarnet, A. Voiculescu, and T. Campbell (eds.), *The New Corporate Accountability: Corporate Social Responsibility and the Law* (Cambridge: Cambridge University Press 2007).

Carroll, A.B., 'The Pyramid of Corporate Social Responsibility: Toward the Moral Management of Organizational Stakeholders' (1991) 34 *Business Horizons* 39 reprinted in A. Craine, D. Matten, and L.J. Spence (eds.), *Corporate Social Responsibility: Readings and Cases in a Global Context* (Abingdon, UK: Routledge 2008).

Cheffins, B.R., *Company Law: Theory, Structure and Operation* (Oxford: Clarendon Press 1997).

216　*Bibliography*

Cheruiyot, T.K., and Onsando, P., 'Corporate Social Responsibility in Africa: Context, Paradoxes, Stakeholder Orientations, Contestations and Reflections' in A. Stachowicz-Stanusch (ed.), *Corporate Social Performance in the Age of Irresponsibility: Cross National Perspective* (Charlotte: Information Age Publishing Inc. 2016).

Chianu, E., *Company Law* (Lagos: LawLords Publications 2012).

Davies, P.L., *Gower and Davies' Principles of Modern Company Law* (8th edn, London: Sweet & Maxwell 2008).

Davies, P.L., *Gower's Principle of Modern Company Law* (6th edn, London: Sweet and Maxwell 2003).

Davis, K., and others, *Business and Society: Concepts and Policy Issues* (4th edn, New York: McGraw-Hill 1980).

Dine, J., *Companies, International Trade and Human Rights* (Cambridge: Cambridge University Press 2005).

Dine, J., *The Governance of Corporate Groups* (Cambridge: Cambridge University Press 2006).

Du Plessis, J.J., and others, *Principles of Contemporary Corporate Governance* (2nd edn, Cambridge: Cambridge University Press 2011).

Easterbrook, F., and Fischel, D., *The Economic Structure of Corporate Law* (Cambridge: Harvard University Press 1991).

Eijsbouts, J., *Corporate Responsibility, Beyond Voluntarism: Regulatory Options to Reinforce the Licence to Operate* (Inaugural Lecture, Maastricht: Maastricht University 2011).

Enneking, L.F.H., *Foreign Direct Liability and Beyond Exploring the Role of Tort Law in Promoting Corporate Social Responsibility and Accountability* (The Hague: Eleven International Publishing 2012).

Epstein, G. (ed.), *Financialization and the World Economy* (Cheltenham: Edward Elgar 2005).

Faracik, B., *Implementation of the UN Guiding Principles on Business and Human Rights* (Policy Department, Directorate-General for External Policies, Belgium: European Union 2017).

Farouk, H.I.C., and others, *Contemporary Company Law* (Cape Town: JUTA 2011).

Farrar, J.H., *Corporate Governance: Theories, Principles and Practice* (3rd edn, Oxford: Oxford University Press 2008).

Farrar, J.H., and others, *Farrar's Company Law* (3rd edn, London: Butterworth 1991).

Freeman, E., *Strategic Management: A Stakeholder Approach* (Cambridge: Cambridge University Press 2010).

Freeman, E., and others, *Stakeholder Theory: The State of the Art* (Cambridge: Cambridge University Press 2010).

Friedman, M., *Capitalism and Freedom* (Chicago: University of Chicago Press 1962).

Friedman, M., 'The Social Responsibility of Business' in Kurt R. Leube (ed.), *The Essence of Friedman* (Stanford: The Hoover Institution Press 1987).

Gower, L.C.B., *Gower's Principles of Modern Company Law* (4th edn, London: Stevens & Sons 1979).

Greenfield, K., *The Failure of Corporate Law: Fundamental Flaws and Progressive Possibilities* (Chicago: University of Chicago Press 2006).

Guobadia, A., 'Protecting Minority and Public Interests in Nigeria Company Law: The Corporate Affairs Commission as an Ombudsman' in F. McMillan (ed.), *International Company Law* (Annual Vol. 1, Oxford: Hart Publishing 2000).

Hadden, T., *Company Law and Capitalism* (2nd edn, London: Weidenfeld and Nicolson 1972).

Hansmann, H., and Kraakman, R., 'The End of History for Corporate Law' in J. Gordon and M. Roe (eds.), *Convergence and Persistence in Corporate Governance* (Cambridge: Cambridge University Press 2004).

Hendrikse, J.W., and Hefer-Hendrikse, L., *Corporate Governance Handbook: Principles and Practice* (2nd edn, Cape Town: JUTA 2012).

Hobbes, T., *Leviathan* (Oxford: Blackwell 1960).

Horrigan, B., *Corporate Social Responsibility in the 21st Century: Debates, Models and Practices across Government, Law and Business* (Cheltenham: Edward Elgar 2010).

Ireland, P., 'Corporate Schizophrenia: The Institutional Origins of Corporate Social Irresponsibility' in N. Boeger and C. Villiers (eds.), *Shaping the Corporate Landscape: Towards Corporate Reform and Enterprise Diversity* (Oxford: Hart Publishing 2018).

Ireland, P., and Pillay, R.G., 'Corporate Social Responsibility in a Neoliberal Age' in P. Utting and J.C. Marques (eds.), *Corporate Social Responsibility and Regulatory Governance Towards Inclusive Development?* (Basingstoke: Palgrave Macmillan 2010).

Ismail, F., *Advancing the Continental Free Trade Area (CFTA) and Agenda 2063 in the Context of the Changing Architecture of Global Trade* (Pretoria: Trade & Industrial Policy Strategies 2016).

Ismail, F., *Transformative Industrialization and Trade in the Context of the CFTA: Opportunities and Challenges* (Addis Ababa: United Nations Economic Commission for Africa, UNECA 2017).

Jones, T.M., and others, 'Stakeholder Theory: The State of the Art' in N.E. Bowie (ed.), *The Blackwell Guide to Business Ethics* (Oxford: Wiley-Blackwell 2001).

Kimbugwe, K., and others, *Economic Development through Regional Trade: A Role for the New East African Community?* (United Kingdom: Palgrave Macmillan 2012).

Lambooy, T., *Corporate Social Responsibility: Legal and Semi-Legal Frameworks Supporting CSR Developments 2000–2010 and Case Studies* (Dissertation and Commercial Edition in IVOR Series, Leiden: Kluwer 2010).

Laursen, F., *Comparative Regional Integration: Europe and Beyond* (Aldershot: Ashgate Publishing Limited 2010).

Lynch-Fannon, I., *Working within Two Kind of Capitalism: Corporate Governance and Employee Stakeholding: US and EU Perspectives* (Oxford: Hart Publishing 2003).

MacLeod, S., 'The Role of International Regulatory Initiatives on Business and Human Rights for Holding Private Military and Security Companies to Account' in F. Francioni and N. Ronzitti (eds.), *War by Contract: Human Rights, Humanitarian Law and Private Contractors* (Oxford: Oxford University Press 2011).

Marx, K., *Early Writings*, translated and edited T. Bottomore (New York: McGraw-Hill 1963).

Matipe, J.A.P., 'Legal Integration in Colonial and Immediate Post-Colonial Sub-Saharan Africa' in C.M. Dickerson (ed.), *Unified Business Laws for Africa* (2nd edn, London: IEDP 2012).

McBarnet, D., 'Corporate Social Responsibility, Beyond Law, Through Law, For Law: The New Corporate Accountability' in D. McBarnet, A. Voiculescu, and T. Campbell (eds.), *The New Corporate Accountability: Corporate Social Responsibility and the Law* (Cambridge: Cambridge University Press 2007).

McDonald, D., *The Golden Passport: Harvard Business School, the Limits of Capitalism, and the Moral Failure of the MBA Elite* (New York: HarperCollins Publishers 2017).

McMillan, M., and Rodrik, D., 'Globalization, Structural Change and Productivity Growth' in M. Bacchetta and M. Jansen (eds.), *Making Globalization Socially Sustainable International Labour Organization and World Trade Organization* (Geneva: WTO Secretariat 2011).

Mitchell, L.E. (ed.), *Progressive Corporate Law* (Boulder, Colorado: Westview Press 1995).

Monks, R., and Minow, N., *Corporate Governance* (Massachusetts: Blackwell Publishers 1995).

218 *Bibliography*

Morgan, T., *Cases and Materials on Economic Regulation of Business* (Illinois: West Publishing Co 1976).

Muchlinski, P., 'Corporate Social Responsibility and International Law: The Case of Human Rights and Multinational Enterprises' in D. McBarnet, A. Voiculescu, and T. Campbell (eds.), *The New Corporate Accountability: Corporate Social Responsibility and the Law* (Cambridge: Cambridge University Press 2007).

Mutai, H.K., *Compliance with International Trade Obligations-the Common Market for Eastern and Southern Africa* (The Netherlands: Kluwer 2017).

Muthuri, J.N., 'Corporate Social Responsibility in Africa: Definition, Issues and Process' in R.T. Lituchy, B.J. Punnett, and B.B. Puplampu (eds.), *Management in Africa: Macro and Micro Perspective* (New York and London: Routledge 2013).

Ndulo, M., 'The Need for the Harmonisation of Trade Laws in the Southern African Development Community' in A.A. Yusuf (ed.), *African Yearbook of International Law* (The Netherlands: Kluwer Law International 1996).

Odeleye, I., 'Corporate Social Responsibility and the In-House Counsel' in R. Mullerat (ed.), *Corporate Social Responsibility* (The Netherlands: Wolters Kluwer 2011).

Okoye, A., *Legal Approaches and Corporate Social Responsibility: Towards a Llewellyn's Law-Jobs Approach* (Abingdon, UK: Routledge 2017).

Olsen, B.E., 'Trade and the Environment' in B.E. Olsen, M. Steinicke, and K.E. Sorensen (eds.), *WTO Law from a European Perspective* (Alphen aan den Rijn, The Netherlands: Wolters Kluwer 2012).

Orojo, J.O., *Company Law and Practice in Nigeria* (5th edn, Durban: LexisNexis 2008).

Orojo J.O., *Company Law in Nigeria* (3rd edn, Lagos: Mbeyi & Associates 1992).

Parkinson, J.E., 'Corporate Governance and the Regulation of Business Behaviour' in S. Macleod (ed.), *Global Governance and the Quest for Justice* Volume II, *Corporate Governance* (Oxford and Portland: Oregon 2006).

Parkinson, J.E., *Corporate Power and Responsibility* (Oxford: Clarendon Press 1993).

Pennington, R.R., *Company Law* (6th edn, London: Butterworths 1990).

Pennington, R.R., *Company Law* (8th edn, London: Butterworths 2001).

Preston, L.E., and Post, J.E., *Private Management and Public Policy: The Principle of Public Responsibility* (Englewood Cliffs, NJ: Prentice-Hall 1975).

Ruggie, J.G., 'Protect, Respect, and Remedy: The UN Framework for Business and Human Rights' in M.A. Baderin and M. Ssenyonjo (eds.), *International Human Rights Law: Six Decades after the UDHR and Beyond* (Surrey: Ashgate Publishing 2010).

Ruggie, J.G., 'Taking Embedded Liberalism Global: The Corporate Connection' in D. Held and M. Koenig-Archiburgi (eds.), *Taming Globalization: Frontiers of Governance* (Cambridge: Cambridge University Press 2003).

Schwartz, B., and Goodman, A.L., *Corporate Governance: Law and Practice* (Vol. 1, Newark: LexisNexis 2005).

Selznick, P., 'Self-Regulation and the Theory of Institutions' in G. Farmer and E. Murphy (eds.), *Environmental Law and Ecological Responsibility* (Chichester: Wiley 1994).

Shaw, M., *International Law* (5th edn, Cambridge: Cambridge University Press 2003).

Sheikh, S., *A Practical Approach to Corporate Governance* (West Sussex: Tottel Publishing 2006).

Smerdon, R., *A Practical Guide to Corporate Governance* (3rd edn, London: Sweet & Maxwell 2007).

Smith, A., 'An Inquiry into the Nature and Causes of the Wealth of Nations' in Robert L. Heilbroner (ed.), *The Essential Adam Smith* (New York: W.W. Norton & Company 1987).

Steiner, H., and others, *International Human Rights Law in Context: Law Politics Morals* (3rd ed., Oxford: Oxford University Press 2007).

Steiner, J.A., and Steiner, G.A., *Business Government and Society: A Managerial Perspective* (11th edn, New York: McGraw-Hill 2006).

Stiglitz, J., *Globalisation and Its Discontents* (London: Penguin 2002).

Sunstein, C., *Legal Reasoning and Political Conflict* (Oxford: Oxford University Press 1996).

Umozurike, U.O., *International Law and Colonialism in Africa* (Enugu: Nwamife Publishers 1979).

Van den Bossche, P., and Zdouc, W., *The Law and Policy of the World Trade Organization: Text Cases and Materials* (4th edn, Cambridge: Cambridge University Press 2017).

VanGrasstek, C., *The History and Future of the World Trade Organization* (Geneva: WTO 2013).

Vickers, B., *A Handbook on Regional Integration in Africa: Towards Agenda 2063* (London: The Commonwealth Secretariat 2017).

Villiers, C., 'Corporate Law, Corporate Power and Corporate Social Responsibility' in N. Boeger, R. Murray, and C. Villiers (eds.), *Perspectives on Corporate Social Responsibility* (Cheltenham: Edward Elgar 2008).

Visser, W., 'Corporate Social Responsibility in Developing Countries' in A. Crane, A. McWilliams, D. Matten, J. Moon, and D.S. Siegel (eds.), *The Oxford Handbook of Corporate Social Responsibility* (Oxford: Oxford University Press 2008).

Visser, W., 'Research on Corporate Citizenship in Africa: A Ten Year Review (1995–2005)' in W. Visser, M. McIntosh, and C. Middleton (eds.), *Corporate Citizenship in Africa: Lessons from the Past: Paths to the Future* (Sheffield: Greenleaf Publishing 2006).

Watson, A., *Legal Transplants: An Approach to Comparative Law* (2nd edn, Edinburgh: Scottish Academic Press 1993).

Whitehouse, L., 'Corporate Social Responsibility as Regulation: The Argument from Democracy' in J. O'Brien (ed.), *Governing the Corporation, Regulation and Corporate Governance in an Age of Scandal and Global Market* (West Sussex: John Wiley & Sons 2005).

Yeates, N., *Beyond the Nation State: How Can Regional Social Policy Contribute to Achieving the Sustainable Development Goals?* (Issue Brief 05, Geneva: UNRISD 2017).

Zadek, S., *The Civil Corporation: The New Economy of Corporate Citizenship* (London: Earthscan 2001).

Zerk, J., *Multinational and Corporate Social Responsibilities: Limitations and Opportunities in International Law* (Cambridge: Cambridge University Press 2006).

Journals/articles

Aaronson, S.A., 'Corporate Responsibility in the Global Village: The British Role Model and the American Laggard' (2003) 108 *Business and Society Review* 309.

Aaronson, S.A., 'A Match Made in the Corporate and Public Interest: Marrying Voluntary CSR Initiatives and the WTO' (2007) 41 (3) *Journal of World Trade* 22.

Aina, K., 'Board of Directors and Corporate Governance in Nigeria' (2013) 1 *International Journal of Business and Finance Management Research* 21.

Abugu, J., 'Issues and Problems in Corporate Governance in Nigeria' (2015) 6 (3) *The Gravitas Review of Business and Property Law* 1.

Abugu, J., 'Primacy of Shareholders' Interests and the Relevance of Stakeholder Economic Theories' (2013) 7 *Company Lawyer* 201.

Abugu, J., and Amodu, N., 'Regulating Corporate Reporting in Nigeria: The Uncharitable Perception of an Outsider (External) Regulator' (2016) 2 *The Commercial and Industrial Law Review* 64.

Aigbokhaevbo, V., 'Evaluation of Corporate Governance in Nigeria and Directors Liability' (1997) *Nigerian Contemporary Law Journal Uniben* 82.

220 Bibliography

Ako, R.T., and others, 'Forging Peaceful Relationships between Oil-Companies and Host-Communities in Nigeria's Delta Region: A Stakeholder's Perspective to Corporate Social Responsibility' (2009) 2 *Journal of Enterprising Communities* 205.

Amaeshi, K.M., and others, 'Corporate Social Responsibility in Nigeria: Western Mimicry or Indigenous Influences?' (2006) 24 *JCC* 83.

Amao, O., 'Corporate Social Responsibility, Multinational Corporations and the Law in Nigeria: Controlling Multinationals in Host States' (2008) 52 *Journal of African Law* 89.

Amao, O., 'Mandating Corporate Social Responsibility: Emerging Trends in Nigeria' (2008) 6 *Journal of Commonwealth Law and Legal Education* 75.

Amao, O., 'Reconstructing the Role of the Corporation: Multinational Corporations as Public Actors in Nigeria' (2007) 29 *Dublin University Law Journal* 312.

Amodu, N., 'Regulation and Enforcement of Corporate Social Responsibility in Corporate Nigeria' (2017) 61 *Journal of African Law* 105.

Amodu, N., 'The Responsible Stakeholder Model: An Alternative Theory of Corporate Law' (2018) 5 *Journal of Comparative Law in Africa* 1.

Arya, B., and Bassi, B., 'Corporate Social Responsibility and Broad-Based Black Economic Empowerment Legislation in South Africa: Codes of Good Practice' (2011) 50 (4) *Business & Society* 674–695.

Backer, L.C., 'Governing Corporations: Corporate Social Responsibility and the Obligations of States' (2008) 2 *Berkeley Journal of International Law* 503.

Bagire, V.A., and others, 'Contextual Environment and Stakeholder Perception of Corporate Social Responsibility Practices in Uganda' (2013) 18 *Corporate Social Responsibility and Environmental Management* 102–109.

Berle, A., 'Corporate Powers as Powers in Trust' (1931) 44 *Harvard Law Review* 1049.

Bernstein, S., and Hannah, E., 'Non-State Global Standard Setting and the WTO: Legitimacy and the Need for Regulatory Space' (2008) 11 *Journal of International Economic Law* 575.

Bhatta, G., 'Corporate Governance and Public Management in Post-Crisis Asia' (2001) 23 *Asian Journal of Public Administration* 1.

Blair, M., and Stout, L., 'Specific Investment: Explaining Anomalies in Corporate Law' (2006) 31 *Journal of Corporate Law* 719.

Blair, M., and Stout, L., 'A Team Production Theory of Corporate Law' (1999) 85 *Virginia Law Review* 247.

Blowfield, M., and Frynas, J.G., 'Setting New Agendas: Critical Perspective on Corporate Social Responsibility in the Developing World' (2005) 3 *International Affairs* 499.

Boås, M., and others, 'The Weave-World: Regionalism in the South in the New Millennium' (1999) 20 (5) *Third World Quarterly* 1061.

Bolodeoku, I.O., 'Economic Theories of the Corporation and Corporate Governance: A Critique' (2002) *JBL* 420.

Bolodeoku, I.O., 'Contractarianism and Corporate Law: Alternative Explanations to the Law's Mandatory and Enabling/Default Contents' (2005) 2 *Cardozo Journal of International and Comparative Law* 433.

Bolodeoku, I.O., 'Corporate Governance: The Law's Response to Agency Costs in Nigeria' (2007) 32 *Brooklyn Journal of International Law* 467.

Branson, D.M., 'Corporate Governance "Reform" and the New Corporate Social Responsibility' (2001) 62 *University of Pittsburgh Law Review* 605.

Bratton, Jr., W.W., 'The New Economic Theory of the Firm: Critical Perspectives from History' (1989) 41 *Stanford Law Review* 1471.

Bibliography 221

Bratton, Jr., W.W., 'The "Nexus of Contracts" Corporation: A Critical Appraisal' (1989) 74 *Cornel Law Review* 407.

Bratton, Jr., W.W., and Wachter, M.L., 'Shareholder Primacy's Corporatist Origins: Adolf Berle and the Modern Corporation' (2008) 1 *Journal of Corporate Law* 99.

Butler, H.N., and Ribstein, L.E., 'Opting Out of Fiduciary Duties: A Response to the Anti-Contractarians' (1990) 65 *Washington Law Review* 1.

Carroll, A.B., 'Corporate Social Responsibility: Evolution of a Definitional Construct' (1999) 38 *Business & Society* 268.

Carroll, A.B., 'A Three: Dimensional Conceptual Model of Corporate Performances' (1979) 4 *Academy of Management Review* 499.

Charnovitz, S., 'The Law of Environmental "PPMs" in the WTO: Debunking the Myth of Illegality' (2002) 27 *Yale Journal of International Law* 59.

Cherry, M., 'The Law and Economics of Corporate Social Responsibility and Greenwashing' (2014) 14 *University of California Davis Business Law Journal* 281.

Cherry, M., and Sneirson, J.F., 'Chevron, Greenwashing and the Myth of "Green Oil Companies"' (2012) 3 *Washington and Lee Journal of Energy, Climate and the Environment* 133.

Davis, K., 'The Case for and against the Assumption of Social Responsibilities' (1973) 2 *Academy of Management Journal* 312.

Dewey, J., 'The Historic Background of Corporate Legal Personality' (1926) 35 *Yale Law Journal* 655.

Dine, J., 'Jurisdictional Arbitrage by Multinational Companies: A National Law Solution?' (2012) 1 *Journal of Human Rights and the Environment* 44.

Dodd, M., 'For Whom Are Corporate Managers Trustees?' (1932) 45 *Harvard Law Review* 1145.

Donaldson, T., and Preston, L.E., 'The Stakeholder Theory of the Corporation: Concepts, Evidence and Implications' (1995) 20 *The Academy of Management Review* 65.

Easterbrook, F., and Fischel, D., 'The Corporate Contract' (1989) 89 *Columbia Law Review* 1416.

Ekhator, E.O., 'Corporate Social Responsibility and Chinese Oil Multinationals in the Oil and Gas Industry of Nigeria: An Appraisal' (2014) 28 *Cadernos de Estudos Africanos* 119.

Emeseh, E., and others, 'Corporations, CSR and Self-Regulation: What Lessons from the Global Financial Crisis?' (2010) 2 *German Law Journal* 230.

Engel, D., 'An Approach to Corporate Social Responsibility' (1979) 32 *Stanford Law Review* 1.

Enuoh, R., and Eneh, S., 'Corporate Social Responsibility in the Niger Delta Region of Nigeria: In Who's Interest' (2015) 5 *Journal of Management and Sustainability* 74.

Esser, I., 'Corporate Social Responsibility: A Company Law Perspective' (2011) 23 *South African Mercantile Law Journal* 317.

Esser, I., and Delport, P., 'The Protection of Stakeholders: The South African Social and Ethics Committee and the United Kingdom's Enlightened Shareholder Value Approach: Part 1' (2017) 50 *De Jure* 97.

Esser, I., and Delport, P., 'The South African King IV on Corporate Governance: Is the Crown Shiny Enough?' (2018) 11 *Company Lawyer* 378.

Fagbayibo, B., 'Exploring Legal Imperatives of Regional Integration in Africa' (2012) 45 *Comparative and International Law Journal of Southern Africa* 64–76.

Fairfax, L.M., 'Easier Said Than Done? A Corporate Law Theory for Actualizing Social Responsibility Rhetoric' (2007) 59 *Florida Law Review*. 771.

Fairfax, L.M., 'The Rhetoric of Corporate Law: The Impact of Stakeholder Rhetoric on Corporate Norms' (2006) 31 *Journal of Corporation Law* 675.

222 *Bibliography*

Fama, E., 'Agency Problems and the Theory of the Firm' (1980) 99 *Journal of Political Economy* 288.

Fig, D., 'Manufacturing Amnesia: Corporate Social Responsibility in South Africa' (2005) 81 *International Affairs* 599–617.

Fischel, D., 'The Corporate Governance Movement' (1982) 35 *Vanderbilt Law Review* 1259.

Foster, N.H.D., 'Company Law Theory in Comparative Perspective: England and France' (2000) 4 *American Journal of Comparative Law* 573.

Freeman, E., and others, 'Stakeholder Theory and "the Corporate Objective Revisited"' (2004) 15 *Organization Science* 364.

Garriga, E., and Mele, D., 'Corporate Social Responsibility Theories: Mapping the Territory' (2004) *Journal of Business Ethics* 53.

Geva, A., 'Three Models of Corporate Social Responsibility: Interrelationship between Theory, Research and Practice' (2008) *Business and Society Review* 5.

Glinski, C., 'CSR and the Law of the WTO: The Impact of Tuna Dolphin II and EC: Seal Products' (2017) 1 *Nordic Journal of Commercial Law* 121.

Greenfield, K., 'Reclaiming Corporate Law in a New Gilded Age' (2008) 2 *Harvard Law and Policy Review* 1.

Hamann, R., and Acutt, N., 'How Should Civil Society (and the Government) Respond to "Corporate Social Responsibility?" A Critique of Business Motivations and the Potential for Partnerships' (2003) 20 *Development Southern Africa* 255.

Hayden, G.M., and Bodie, M.T., 'The Uncorporation and the Unravelling of the "Nexus of Contracts"' Theory (2011) 109 *Michigan Law Review* 1127.

Ho, V.H., 'Beyond Regulation: A Comparative Look at State-Centric Corporate Social Responsibility and the Law in China' (2013) 46 *Vanderbilt Journal of Transnational Law* 375.

Howse, R., and Regan, D., 'The Product/Process Distinction: An Illusory Basis for Disciplining "Unilateralism" in Trade Policy' (2000) 11 *European Journal of International Law* 249.

Idemudia, U., 'Corporate Social Responsibility and Development in Africa: Issues and Possibilities' (2014) 8 (7) *Geography Compass* 421–435.

Idemudia, U., and Ite, U.E., 'Corporate-Community Relations in Nigeria's Oil Industry: Challenges and Imperatives' (2006) 13 *Corporate Social Responsibility and Environmental Management* 194.

Ihugba, B.U., 'Compulsory Regulation of CSR: A Case Study of Nigeria' (2012) 2 *Journal of Politics and Law* 68.

Ijaiya, H., 'Challenges of Corporate Social Responsibility in the Niger Delta Region of Nigeria' (2014) 1 *Journal of Sustainable Development Law and Policy* 60.

Ireland, P., 'Capitalism without the Capitalist: The Joint Stock Company Share and the Emergence of the Modern Doctrine of Separate Corporate Personality' (1996) 17 *Journal of Legal History* 40.

Ireland, P., 'Company Law and the Myth of Shareholder Ownership' (1999) 62 *Modern Law Review* 32.

Ireland, P., 'Making Sense of Contemporary Capitalism Using Company Law' (2018) 33 *Australian Journal of Corporate Law* 379–401.

Jagers, N., 'Access to Justice for Victims of Corporate-Related Human Rights Abuse: An Echternach-Procession' (2015) 33 *Netherlands Quarterly of Human Rights* 269–273.

Jensen, M.C., and Meckling, W.H., 'Theory of the Firm: Managerial Behaviour, Agency Costs and Ownership Structure' (1976) 3 *Journal of Financial Economics* 305.

Johnson, L., 'The Delaware Judiciary and the Meaning of Corporate Life and Corporate Law' (1990) 68 *Texas Law Review* 865.

Bibliography 223

Johnson, L., and Millon, D., 'Corporate Takeovers and Corporate Law: Who's in Control?' (1993) 61 *George Washington Law Review* 1177.

Joshi, M., 'Are Eco-Labels Consistent with World Trade Organization Agreements?' (2004) 38 *Journal of World Trade* 69.

Kabir, M.H., and others, 'Corporate Social Responsibility Evolution in South Africa' (2015) 13 *Problems and Perspectives in Management* 281–289.

Kaplow, L., 'Rules versus Standards: An Economic Analysis' (1992) 42 *Duke Law Review* 557.

Karmel, R.S., 'Implications of the Stakeholder Model' (1993) 61 *George Washington Law Review* 1156.

Keay, A., 'Ascertaining the Corporate Objective: An Entity Maximisation and Sustainability Model' (2008) 71 *Modern Law Review* 663.

Keay, A., 'Stakeholder Theory in Corporate Law: Has It Got What It Takes?' (2010) 3 (9) *Richmond Journal of Global Law and Business* 249.

Keay, A., 'Tackling the Issue of the Corporate Objective: An Analysis of the United Kingdom's Enlightened Shareholder Value Approach' (2007) 29 *Sydney Law Review* 577.

Keay, A., and Loughrey, J., McNulty, T., Okanigbuan, F., and Stewart, A., 'Business Judgment and Director Accountability: A Study of Case-Law Over Time' (2019) *Journal of Corporate Law Studies*, available at https://doi.org/10.1080/14735970.2019.1695516 accessed 2 February 2020.

Keay, A., and Iqbal, T., 'The Impact of Enlightened Shareholder Value' (2019) 4 *Journal of Business Law* 304.

Kloppers, H.J., 'Driving Corporate Social Responsibility (CSR) through the Companies Act: An Overview of the Role of the Social and Ethics Committee' (2013) 16 *Potchefstroom Electronic Law Journal* 165–199.

Lee, M., 'Regionalism in Africa: A Part of Problem or a Part of Solution' (2002) 9 *Polis Revue Camerounaise de Science* 1–24.

Lesser, B., 'When Government Fails, Will the Market Do Better? The Privatization/Market Liberalization Movement in Developing Countries' (1991) 12 *Canadian Journals of Development Studies* 276.

Letza, S., and others, 'Shareholding versus Stakeholding: A Critical Review of Corporate Governance' (2004) 12 *Corporate Governance: An International Review* 242.

MacLeod, S., '*Maria Aguinda* v. *Texaco Inc.*: Defining the Limits of Liability for Human Rights Violations Resulting from Environmental Degradation' (1999) 2 *Contemporary Issues in Law* 189.

Marks, C., and Miller, P.S., 'Plato, The Prince and Corporate Virtue: Philosophical Approaches to Corporate Social Responsibility' (2010) 1 *University of San Francisco Law Review* 1.

Marks, C., and Rapoport, N.B., 'The Corporate Lawyer's Role in a Contemporary Democracy' (2009) 77 *Fordham Law Review* 1269.

McDonald, D., 'Harvard Business School and the Propagation of Immoral Profit Strategies' *Newsweek* (14 April, 2017).

McInerney, T., 'Putting Regulation Before Responsibility: Towards Binding Norms of Corporate Social Responsibility' (2007) 40 *Cornell International Law Journal* 171.

Meehan, J., and others, 'Corporate Social Responsibility: The 3C-SR Model' (2006) 33 *International Journal of Social Economics* 386.

Miles, L., and Jones, M., 'The Prospects for Corporate Governance Operating as a Vehicle for Social Change in South Africa' (2009) 1 *Deakin Law Review* 71.

Miller, R.T., 'The Coasean Dissolution of Corporate Social Responsibility' (2014) 2 *Chapman Law Review* 1.

Mitkidis, K.P., 'Sustainability Clauses in International Supply Chain Contracts: Regulation, Enforceability and Effects of Ethical Requirement' (2014) *Nordic Journal of Commercial Law* 1.

224   *Bibliography*

Muchlinski, P., 'The Changing Face of Transnational Business Governance: Private Corporate Law Liability and Accountability of Transnational Groups in a Post-Financial Crisis World' (2011) 18 *Indiana Journal of Global Legal Studies* 665.

Muswaka, L., 'Shareholder Value versus Stakeholders' Interests: A Critical Analysis of Corporate Governance from a South African Perspective' (2015) *Journal of Social Sciences* 217–225.

Nelson, II, W.A., 'Post-Citizens United: Using Shareholder Derivative Claims of Corporate Waste to Challenge Corporate Independent Political Expenditures' (2012) 13 *Nevada Law Journal* 134.

Nwangwu, G., 'The Influence of Companies on the Legal, Political and Economic History of Nigeria' (2018) 12 *Journal of Economics and Sustainable Development* 115.

Nwete, B., 'Corporate Social Responsibility and Transparency in the Development of Energy and Mining Projects in Emerging Markets: Is Soft Law the Answer?' (2007) 4 *German Law Journal* 311.

Ofoegbu, G.N., and others, 'Corporate Board Characteristics and Environmental Disclosure Quantity: Evidence from South Africa (Integrated Reporting) and Nigeria (Traditional Reporting)' (2018) 5 *Cogent Business & Management* 1–27.

Okon, E., 'Corporate Social Responsibility by Companies: The Liberal Perspective' (1997) *Nigerian Current Law Review* 193.

Osemeke, L., and Adegbite, E., 'Regulatory Multiplicity and Conflict: Towards a Combined Code on Corporate Governance in Nigeria' (2016) 133 *Journal of Business Ethics* 431–451.

Parkinson, J.E., 'Models of the Company and the Employment Relationship' (2003) 3 *British Journal of Industrial Relations* 481.

Pennington, R.R., 'Terminal Compensation for Employees of Companies in Liquidation' (1962) 25 *Modern Law Review* 715.

Post, J.E., and others, 'Managing the Extended Enterprise: The New Stakeholder View' (2002) 1 *California Management Review* 6.

Raimi, L., and others, 'How Adequate and Efficient Are Regulations on Corporate Social Responsibility and Social Reporting? Evidence from the Nigeria Telecommunication Industry' (2014) 6 *Asian Journal of Empirical Research* 315.

Ratner, D., 'The Government of Business Corporations: Critical Reflections on the Rule of "One Share, One Vote"' (1970) 56 *Cornell Law Review* I.

Ribstein, L., 'Accountability and Responsibility in Corporate Governance' (2006) 81 *Notre Dame Law Review* 1431.

Rieth, L.Z., and others, 'Is Corporate Citizenship Making a Difference?' (2001) 28 *The Journal of Corporate Citizenship* 99–112.

Rock, E.B., and Wachter, M.L., 'Islands of Conscious Power: Law, Norms, and Self-Governing Corporation' (2001) 149 *University of Pennsylvania Law Review* 1619.

Roe, M.J., 'The Shareholder Wealth Maximization Norm and Industrial Organisation' (2001) 149 *University of Pennsylvania Law Review* 2063.

Rott, P., 'Directors' Duties and Corporate Social Responsibility under German Law: Is Tort Law Litigation Changing the Picture?' (2017) 1 *NJCL* 9–27, 18.

Ruggie, J., 'Reconstituting the Global Public Domain: Issues, Actors, and Practices' (2004) 4 *European Journal of International Relations* 499.

Sacco, R., 'Legal Formants: A Dynamic Approach to Comparative Law' (1991) 39 *American Journal of Comparative Law* 10.

Schwartz, H., 'Governmentally Appointed Directors in a Private Corporation: The Communications Satellite Act of 1962' (1965) 79 *Harvard Law Review* 350.

Schwartz, H., and Carroll, A.B., 'Corporate Social Responsibility: A Three: Domain Approach' (2003) 13 *Business Ethics Quarterly* 503.

Smith, I.O., 'Corporate Social Responsibility towards a Healthier Environment' (2000) 4 *MPJFIL* 22.

Sneirson, J.F., 'Shareholder Primacy and Corporate Compliance' (2015) 26 *Fordham Environmental Law Journal* 1.

Spamann, H., 'Contemporary Legal Transplants: Legal Families and the Diffusion of (Corporate) Law' (2010) 6 *Brigham Young University Law Review* 1813.

Stevelman, F., 'Global Finance, Multinationals and Human Rights: With Commentary on Backer's Critique of the 2008 Report by John Ruggie' (2011) 9 *Santa Clara Journal of International Law* 101.

Thomsen, S., 'The Convergence of Corporate Governance Systems and European and Anglo-American Standards' (2003) 4 *European Business Organization Law Review* 31.

Van der Zee, E., 'Incorporating the OECD Guidelines in International Investment Agreements: Turning a Soft Law Obligation into Hard Law?' (2013) 40 *Legal Issues of Economic Integration* 33.

Van Zyl, A.S., 'Sustainability and Integrated Reporting in the South African Corporate Sector' (2013) 12 *International Business & Economics Research Journal* 903.

Vidal-Léon, C., 'Corporate Social Responsibility, Human Rights and the World Trade Organisation' (2013) 16 *Journal of International Economic Law* 893.

Williams, O.F., 'The UN Global Compact: The Challenge and the Promise' (2004) 14 *Business Ethics Quarterly* 755.

Yu, X., 'Impacts of Corporate Code of Conduct on Labor Standards: A Case Study of Reebok's Athletic Footwear Supplier Factory in China' (2008) 81 *Journal of Business Ethics* 513.

Internet sources

African Trade Policy Centre United Nations Economic Commission for Africa, 'African Continental Free Trade Area: Questions & Answers' available at www.uneca.org/publications/african-continental-free-trade-area-questions-answers accessed 5 November 2019.

Armour, J., and others, 'Shareholder Primacy and the Trajectory of UK Corporate Governance' (University of Cambridge Research Paper 266/ 2003) available at www.cbr.cam.ac.uk/fileadmin/user_upload/centre-for-business-research/downloads/working-papers/wp266.pdf accessed 5 November 2019.

MacLeod, S., 'Towards Normative Transformation: Re-Conceptualising Business and Human Rights' (Unpublished) PhD Thesis submitted to the School of Law, University of Glasgow, 2012 available at http://theses.gla.ac.uk/3714/1/2012macleodphd.pdf accessed 5 November 2019.

Mann, H., 'The SADC Model Bit Template: Investment for Sustainable Development' (IISD Investment Treaty News 2019) available at www.iisd.org/itn/2012/10/30/the-sadc-model-bit-template-investment-for-sustainable-development/ accessed 5 November 2019.

Mumo, K., and others, 'How Can Corporate Social Responsibility Deliver in Africa? Insights from Kenya and Zambia' (2005) *Perspectives on Corporate Responsibility for Environment and Development, International Institute for Environment and Development* available at https://pubs.iied.org/pdfs/16006IIED.pdf accessed 5 November 2019.

226   *Bibliography*

Osakwe, P.N., *Transformative Regionalism, Trade and the Challenge of Poverty Reduction in Africa* (ALDC/UNCTAD, 2015) available at https://unctad.org/en/PublicationsLibrary/webaldc2015d1_en.pdf accessed 5 November 2019.

Official documents

AU, Agreement Establishing the African Continental Free Trade Area and its Protocols, Annexes and Appendices available at https://au.int/en/treaties/agreement-establishing-african-continental-free-trade-area accessed 5 November 2019.

EU, Communication from the Commission to the European Parliament, the Council, the European Economic and Social Committee and the Committee of the Region: A Renewed European Union Strategy 2011–14 for Corporate Social Responsibility, COM (2011) 681 Final 6.

EU, Council Directive, 2003/51/EC, 18th June, 2003 Amending Directives 78/660/EEC, 83/635/EEC and 91/674/EEC on the Annual and Consolidated Accounts of Certain Types of Companies, Banks and Other Financial Institutions and Insurance Undertakings, OJ L178/16, 2003.

EU, Disclosure of Non-Financial and Diversity Information by Certain Large Undertakings and Groups, Directive 2014/95/EU.

ILO, Tripartite Declaration of Principles Concerning Multinational Enterprises and Social Policy, Adopted by the Governing Body of the International Labour Office at Its 204th Session, Geneva, November 1977/,/Text/, /Tripartite/Code of Conduct/, /Multinational Enterprise/, /Social Policy/. 03.04.2 ISBN 92-2-111631-X.

OECD, Declaration on International Investment and Multinational Enterprises (1979), Cmnd. 6525.

UN, Commentary on the Norms on the Responsibilities of Transnational Corporations and Other Business Enterprises with Regard to Human Rights', UN Doc. E/CN.4/Sub.2/2003/ 38/Rev.2 (2003); Sub-Commission Res. 2003/16, UN Doc. E/CN.4/Sub.2/2003/L.11, 52, 2003.

UN, Declaration on Principles of International Law Concerning Friendly Relations and Cooperation among States in Accordance with the Charter of the United Nations, UNGA/Res/2625/(XXV).

UN, Norms on the Responsibilities of Transnational Corporations and Other Business Enterprises with Regard to Human Rights, (2003) UN Doc. E/CN.4/Sub.2/2003/12 Rev.

UN, Secretary-General Proposes Global Compact on Human Rights, Labour, Environment in Address to World Economic Forum in Davos, Text of Speech by Kofi Annan, 1 February 1999, UN Press Release SG/SM/6881.

UN, World Commission on Environment and Development, Our Common Future, Report of the World Commission on Environment and Development, 1987, Annexed to United Nations General Assembly, Document A/42/427.

Appendix

Tables of cases and statutes

Table of cases

A

Abubakari v. Smith (1973) 6 S.C. 24

Adene and Ors v. Dantubu (1994) 2 NWLR (Pt. 382) 509

Alex Oladele Elufioye & Ors v. Ibrahim Halilu & Ors (1990) LPELR-20126(CA)

Amalgamated Society of Woodworkers of South Africa v. Die 1963 AmbagsaaWerenig-ing (1967) 1 SA 586 (T)

Attorney General of Lagos State v. Eko Hotels Limited and Oha Limited (2006) NWLR (Pt. 1011) 3782

B

Bernard Amasike v. The Registrar General of the Corporate Affairs Commission (2010) NWLR (Pt. 1211) 337

BCE Inc. v. 1976 Debentureholder (2008) 3. S. C. R.560

Bligh v. Brent (1837) 2 Y & C Ex. 268

Bowoto v. Chevron F. Supp. 2d 1229 (N.D. Cal. 2004)

Burwell v. Hobby Lobby Stores, Inc. 134 S. Ct. 2751, 2781 (2014)

C

CDBI v. COBEC (Nigeria) Ltd (2004) 13 NWLR (Pt. 948) 376

Christopher Okeke v. Securities and Exchange Commission & 2 Ors (2013) All FWLR (Pt. 687) 731

Christopher N. Okeke v. Cadbury Nigeria Plc (2015) 5 CLRN 22

Cobden Investments Ltd v. RWM Langport Ltd (2008) EWHC 2810 (Ch)

Compania del Desarrollode Santa Elena, S.A. v. Republic of Costa Rica ICSID case No. ARB/96/1, 15 ICSID Review (2000)

D

De Villiers v. BOE Bank Ltd [2004] (2) All SA 457 (SCA)

Dodge v. Ford Motor Co. (1919) 204 Mich. 459

228   *Appendix*

Doe v. Unocal 963 F. Supp. 880 (C.D. Cal. 1997) 110 F. Supp. 2d 1294
Din v. A.G. Federation (1998) 4 NWLR (Pt. 87) 147

E

Ebrahimi v. Westbourne Galleries (1973) AC 360
EC Sardines case (European Communities – Trade Description of Sardines, WT/ DS231/AB/R, 2002)
Edwards v. Halliwell (1950) 2 All E.R. 1064
Eko Hotels Limited v. Financial Reporting Council of Nigeria (FHC/L/CS/1430/ 2012)
Esther Kiobel et al v. Royal Dutch Petroleum Company (2013) 133 S.Ct. 1659
Evans v. Brunner, Mond & Co. (1921) 1 Ch. 359
Executive Council, Western Cape v. Minister for Provincial Affairs and Constitutional Development and Another; Executive Council, KwaZulu-Natal v. President of the Republic of South Africa 2000 1 SA 661

F

Foss v. Harbottle (1943) 2 Hare 461
Fulham Football Club Ltd v. Cabra Estates Plc (1994) 1 B. C. L. C. 363

G

Gottlieb v. Heyden Chemical Corp., 90 A. 2d 660 (Del. 1952)
Gov. Oyo State v. Folayan (1995) 8 NWLR (Pt.413) 292
Greenhalgh v. Arderne Cinemas Ltd (1951) Ch. 286, 291

H

Habib Nigeria Bank Limited v. Ochete (2001) FWLR (Pt. 54) 384
Hampson v. Price's Patent Candle Co (1876) 45 LJ Ch. 437
Harlowe's Nominees Pty Ltd v. Woodside Lakes Entrance Oil NL (1968) 121 CLR 48
Haston (Nig.) Ltd v. A.C.B. Plc (2002) 12 NWLR (Pt.7820)
Hutton v. West Cork Railway Co. (1883) 23 Ch D. 654

J

John Doe et al. v. Unocal Corp et al. 963 F. Supp. 880 (March 25 1997)

K

Kasky v. Nike Inc. 45 P. 3d 243 (Cal. 2002)
Katz v. Oak Industries, Inc. 508 A-2d 873, 878 (Del. Ch. 1986)

Appendix 229

L

Lonrho Ltd v. Shell Petroleum Co. Ltd (1980) 1 WLR 627 (HL)

M

Madoff Securities International Ltd (in liq) v. Raven (2013) EWHC 3147 (Comm)
Marina Nominees Ltd. v. Federal Board of Inland Revenue (1986) 2 NWLR (Pt. 20) 61
Mezu v. Co-operative Commerce Bank & Anor (2013) 12 W.R.N. 1
McQuillen v. National Cash Register Co., 27 F. Supp. 639 (D. Md. 1939)
Michelson v. Duncan 407 A. 2d 211 (Del 1979)
Miles v. Sydney Meat Preserving Co Ltd (1912) HCA 87
Minister of Water Affairs and Forestry v. Stilfontein Gold Mining Co. Ltd 2006 5 SA 333 (W)
Morrison v. National Australia Bank 547 F 3d 167 (2d Cir.2008)
Mthimunye-Bakoro v. Petroleum Oil and Gas Corporation of South Africa (SOC) Limited [2015] JOL 33744

N

Nike Inc. v. Marc Kasky 539 US 654 (2003)
NNPC v. Famfa Oil Ltd (2012) 17 NWLR (Pt. 1328) 148
Noble Drilling Nigeria Limited v. Nigerian Maritime Administration and Safety Agency (2013) LPELR-22029 (CA)

O

Olanrewaju v. Oyeyemi & Ors (2001) 2 NWLR (Pt. 697) 229
O'Neill & Anor v. Phillips & Anor (1999) 2 B.C.L.C. 1 HL

P

Parke v. Daily News Ltd (1962) 3 WLR 566
People's Department Stores Inc. v. Wise (2004) 3 S. C. R. 68
Percival v. Wright (1902) 2 Ch 421
Provident Int'l Corporation v. Int'l Leasing Corp Limited (1969) 1 NSWR 424

R

Re HLC Environmental Projects Ltd (2013) EWHC 2876 (Ch)
Re Lee, Behrens & Co Ltd (1932) Ch 46
Re Saul D Harrison & Sons Plc (1995) 1 B.C.L.C 14
Re West Coast Capital (LIOS) Ltd (2008) CSOH 72
Rogers v. Hill 289 U.S. 582 (1933)

230   *Appendix*

S

Salomon v. Salomon (1896) UKHL 1
Shlensky v. Wrigley (237 N.E 2d 776 ILL. App 1968)
Short v. Treasury Commissioners (1948) 1 KB 116
Smith Manufacturing Co. v. Barlow (1953) 346 U.S. 861

T

Teck Corporation Ltd v. Millar (1973) 33 DLR (3d) 288 (BCSC)
Tecnicas Medioambientales Tecmed S.A. v. United Mexican States, ICSID case No.
   ARB (AF)/00/2(2003)

U

Unocal Corporation v. Mesa Petro Co. (1985) Del. Supr. 493 A.2d 946
US–Shrimp–Turtle case (*United States-Import Prohibition of Certain Shrimp and
   Shrimp Products*, WT/DS58/AB/R, 1998)
US–Gasoline case (*United States – Standards for Reformulated and Conventional
   Gasoline*, WT/DS2, 1996)

V

Vedanta Resources Plc v. Lungowe [2019] UKSC 20
Velasquez Rodriguez v. Honduras (1988) Inter-Am Court HR (Ser. C) No. 4

W

Wiwa v. Royal Dutch Petroleum Company 226 F.3d 88 (2d cir 2000), 532US
   941(2001)

Table of statutes

Alien Torts Claims Act 1789 (USA)
Annual Reports Act 1995 (Sweden)
Constitution of the Republic of South Africa 1996
**Broad-Based Black Economic Empowerment Act No. 53 of 2003
   (South Africa)**
Companies Act 2006 (UK)
Companies Act 2013 (India)
Companies Act No. 71 of 2008 (South Africa)
Companies and Allied Matters Act, 1999 as amended (Nigeria)
Constitution of the Federal Republic of Nigeria 1990, as amended
Corporate Responsibility Bill 2002 (UK)
Corporate Social Responsibility Bill 2007 (Nigeria)

Corporations Act 2001 (Australia)

Dodd – Frank Wall Street Reform and Consumer Protection Act 2010 (USA)

Employment Equity Act No. 55 of 1998 (South Africa)

Financial Reporting Council of Nigeria Act 2011

Financial Statements Act 2008 (Denmark)

Foreign Corrupt Practices Act 1977 (USA)

Investment Law No. 25 of 2007 (Indonesia)

Investments and Securities Act 2007 (Nigeria)

Joint Stock Companies Act 1844 (UK)

Labour Relations Act No. 66 of 1995 (South Africa)

Limited Liability Act 1855 (UK)

Limited Liability Company Law No. 40 of 2007 (Indonesia)

Mine Health and Safety Act No. 29 of 1996 (South Africa)

Mineral and Petroleum Resources Development Act No. 28 of 2002 (South Africa)

National Environmental Management Act No. 107 of 1998 (South Africa)

Nigerian Extractive Industry Transparency Initiative Act 2007

Nigerian Minerals and Mining Act 2007

Nouvelles Regulations Economiques 2001 (France)

Occupational Health and Safety Act No. 85 of 1993 (South Africa)

Petroleum Host and Impacted Communities Development Trust Bill 2018

Petroleum Industry Bill 2012 (Nigeria)

Promotion of Access to Information Act No. 2 of 2000 (South Africa)

Promotion of Equality and Prevention of Unfair Discrimination Act 2000 (South Africa)

Sarbanes-Oxley Act 2002 (USA)

Skills Development Act No. 97 of 1998 (South Africa)

Index

3TG 90, 107, 108

Abugu, Joseph 129, 130, 147
Adebayo, Adedeji 184, 185
AfCFTA 30, 177, 186–190, 210; Agreement 31, 186–190, 206–209; Framework 188–190, 206–209; Secretariat 208
Africa 3, 4, 16, 17, 22, 27, 129–196
Africa Continental Free Trade Area *see* AfCFTA
African Economic Community 183, 184
African Union 187
agency cost problem 24, 25, 27, 42, 54, 70, 75
aggregate social welfare 53, 65, 66, 77, 85, 197
Ajogwu, Fabian 130
Alien Torts Claims Act *see* ATCA
Amnesty International 102, 115
annual reports 9, 10, 90, 108, 111, 112, 121, 124, 125, 149, 155
apartheid 158, 159, 162, 179, 214
ATCA 111, 125

balancing interests 20, 46, 65, 66, 68, 69, 70, 72, 83, 144, 158, 197, 203, 204
BBBEE 159, 162, 163, 214
Berle, Adolf 5, 11, 12, 24, 37, 40, 48, 74
bluewashing 98, 115
Bolodeoku, Ige Omotayo 25
Bowen, Howard 6
Branson, Douglas 5, 8, 24
Broad-Based Black Economic Empowerment Act *see* BBBEE
Burma/Myanmar 102
business case 46, 76, 91, 92, 109, 113, 124, 198, 211
business ethics 26, 132
business judgment rule 71, 75, 79, 203
business of business 7, 71, 85

Cadbury Committee report 9
cakes and ale 46, 137
CAMA 67, 88, 91, 133–140, 146, 149, 162, 165, 169, 179, 202, 211
capitalism 4, 7, 31
Carroll, Archie 14–16
CBN Code of Corporate Governance 135, 145
climate change 49, 51, 130
communitarianism 8, 40, 46, 52, 55–64, 72, 73, 80, 204
community development 17, 20, 29, 35, 113, 114, 129–135, 142, 143, 147, 149, 157, 177, 179, 207, 209, 214
community development agreement 143, 201
Companies Act 2006 (UK) 51, 67, 110, 136, 140
Companies Act 2008 (South Africa) 43, 51, 88, 89, 91, 158, 162, 168, 178, 202, 211
Companies Act 2013 (India) 17, 19, 35, 51, 89, 112, 114, 136
Companies and Allied Matters Act 1990 (Nigeria) *see* CAMA
competing interests 43, 67, 68, 69, 71, 203
Confederation of British Industry 9
Conflict Minerals Regulation 2017/821 (EU) 90, 107, 112
Constitution of the Federal Republic of Nigeria 78
Constitution of the Republic of South Africa 159, 162
contractarianism 8, 40, 52–63, 68, 73, 165
corporate accountability 23, 38, 46, 55, 61, 65, 71, 85, 87, 88, 97, 100, 103, 106, 111, 129, 131, 132, 138, 140, 146, 148, 157, 162, 165, 177, 179
corporate charity 10, 12, 16, 17, 21, 28, 29, 46, 91, 113, 129, 130, 131, 132, 135, 136, 137, 147, 157, 158, 177, 178, 181

Index   233

corporate citizenship 3, 46, 57, 58, 63, 97, 145, 157, 158, 163, 166
corporate culture 42, 111, 132, 140, 145
corporate governance and business management model 3, 10, 19, 23, 30, 31, 38, 48, 131, 157, 158, 178
corporate governance codes *see* King Reports on Corporate Governance; Nigerian Code of Corporate Governance
corporate governance, interconnectedness with CSR 23–27
corporate law: end of history for 42, 44; isolation and insulation of 85, 86, 100
corporate objective 28, 31, 40, 61, 73, 134, 198
Corporate Responsibility Bill (UK) 109, 110, 135
corporate scandal 36, 87, 114, 121, 171
corporate social and environmental responsibility and accountability 87, 97, 129, 131, 132, 146, 162, 165, 177
corporate social responsibility *see* CSR
Corporate Social Responsibility Bill (Nigeria) 135, 152
corporate sustainability 4, 17, 22, 23, 27, 31, 35, 96–100, 107–111, 129, 133, 145, 169, 179, 187, 200, 202, 207, 208
countervailing power *see* CSR
CSR: business case for (*see* business case); conception in developing and less industrialised economies 16, 22, 148, 181, 209, 112–114, 129–172; conceptual framework 10–27; core values 20, 25, 30, 50, 108, 132, 140, 176–179, 187–190, 207–209; as corporate governance and business model (*see* corporate governance and business management model); as countervailing power 6–9, 206; definition of 3, 10, 12, 17–20; detraction from serious business 12, 21, 66, 137, 138, 197; emergence and history of 3–10; implementation in Africa 129–172; implementation in industrialized economies 85–112; as neutral concept 19, 31; as philanthropy and charitable donations 10, 12, 16, 17, 21, 46, 91, 113, 129–137, 147, 157–159, 177, 178, 181; reception in business community 20–23; theoretical underpinnings of 38–84

Dine, Janet 52, 62, 71, 198
Directors, board of 23, 24, 44, 46, 51, 66, 69, 70, 89, 109, 113, 133, 136, 137, 145, 160, 161, 163, 164, 170

disclosure *see* annual reports
Dodd-Frank Wall Street Reform and Consumer Protection Act 111, 140
double standards 176, 179, 207, 211

economic integration 175–177, 184–186, 213
embedding CSR 27, 50, 61, 87, 89, 177
Employment Equity Act (South Africa) 159, 162, 163
EMS 70
enlightened shareholder value 43, 45, 51, 110
Enron 36, 75, 87, 114, 118
entity maximization and sustainability model *see* EMS
European Union 12, 19, 29, 106–115, 175, 176, 207
externalizing 57, 68, 93, 176
extraterritoriality 90, 91

Financial Reporting Council (UK) 9, 140
Financial Reporting Council of Nigeria 86, 91, 145, 202
Foreign Corrupt Practices Act (USA) 140
Freeman, Edward 48–50
free riders 21, 201
Friedman, Milton 7, 8, 11, 12, 41, 56, 75

Galbraith, John Kenneth 6
GATT 180, 182, 210
Global Compact 86, 90, 91, 94–98, 104, 106, 109, 179, 182, 200, 208, 210
globalization 22, 85, 97, 98, 175–183, 189, 190, 206, 209
global warming 49, 133
Greenfield, Kent 57, 199
greenwashing 21, 30, 31, 87, 92, 115, 178, 198, 201, 207

Hampel report 9, 10
Hansmann, Henry 42, 44
hard law 19, 31, 86–92, 109–115, 135, 136, 140, 146, 179, 201
harmonization 149, 179, 188, 189, 208, 209, 211
Higgs review 9
Horrigan, Bryan 10, 13, 22, 86, 93
human rights 11, 20, 25–28, 31, 47, 60, 85, 87, 90, 94–107, 111, 129–133, 148, 157, 179, 197, 199, 201, 202, 211

ICSID 148
indirect CSR implementation 112, 114, 115, 162, 165

234 *Index*

integrated reporting 134, 138, 149, 152, 166, 167, 169, 178, 202
international regulatory dialogues 85, 86, 91, 115, 210
Investments and Securities Act (Nigeria) 135, 138, 149
invisible hand of market forces 4–8, 61, 62
Ireland, Paddy 43, 47, 51, 59, 161

Jensen, Michael 53–55

Kaldor-Hicks efficiency 53–55
King Reports on Corporate Governance 162–165
Kraakman, Reinier 42, 44

Labour Relations Act (South Africa) 159, 162
Lagos Plan of Action and the Final Act of Lagos 184
Lambooy, Tineke 25, 26
Limited Liability Act (UK) 61
lip service *see* free riding; greenwashing
long term 22, 23, 43, 45, 55, 64–67, 70, 145, 178, 197, 201, 203, 205

MacLeod, Sorcha 102
mandatory or voluntary CSR 19, 31, 91–93, 108, 131
maximization of profits 12, 13, 21, 26, 38, 42, 44, 45, 56–70, 97, 103, 132, 197, 206, 210
Means, Gardiner 5, 24, 48
Meckling, William 53–55
Mine Health and Safety Act (South Africa) 162
Mineral and Petroleum Resources Development Act (South Africa) 162
model CSR implementation framework *see* RSM
morality 27, 58, 59, 65, 129
most favoured nation treatment 180
Muchlinski, Peter 43, 104

NAICOM Code of Corporate Governance for Insurance Companies (Nigeria) 135, 145
naming and shaming 106
National Action Plan 101, 102
National Code of Corporate Governance (Nigeria) 35, 86, 135, 145
National Contact Point 105
National Environmental Management Act (South Africa) 162

national treatment 180
NCC Code of Corporate Governance for the Telecommunications Industry 135, 145
NEITI 135–140, 149, 179
nexus-of-contracts theory
    see contractarianism
Nigerian Code of Corporate Governance 86, 91, 135, 145, 166, 178, 179
Nigerian Extractive Industry Transparency Initiative Act *see* NEITI
Nigerian Minerals and Mining Act 142–144
Nkrumah, Kwame 184
non-financial matters reporting 90, 110, 112, 134, 136, 138, 140, 149, 166, 178, 179

Occupational Health and Safety Act (South Africa) 162
OECD Guidelines for Multinationals 28, 86, 88, 91, 103–108, 179, 200, 208, 210
Ogoni nine 131
Orojo, Olakunle 130

pan African Vision 30, 184, 186
Parkinson, John Edward 47, 65
PENCOM Code of Corporate Governance for Licensed Pension Operators 135, 145
perfect market 44
Petroleum Host and Impacted Communities Development Trust Bill (Nigeria) 89, 131, 135, 141, 142
Petroleum Industry Bill (Nigeria) *see* PIB
PIB 131, 135, 141, 142
Promotion of Access to Information Act (South Africa) 162
Promotion of Equality and Prevention of Unfair Discrimination Act (South Africa) 162

regionalism *see* economic integration
regulation: definition of 87; formal versus informal regulations 88; internal versus external regulations 93; international versus domestic regulations 90; meta regulation 71, 72, 93, 94, 112, 201, 204; methods of regulation 87–94; principle-based versus rule-based regulations 91; private versus public regulations 89; self-regulation 12, 19–21, 29–31, 66, 86–89, 92, 97, 98, 103, 106, 115, 136, 149, 169, 198, 200, 201; soft law versus hard law regulations 88; voluntary versus mandatory regulations 91
regulatory chill 147–149
responsible stakeholder model *see* RSM

RSM 64–73, 144, 165, 169, 189, 190, 196–211
Ruggie, John Gerrard 98, 99, 101, 200

SADC Model Treaty 188
Sarbanes-Oxley Act (USA) 88, 91, 103, 111, 112, 140
Saro-Wiwa, Ken 48
SDGs 30, 31, 107, 186–190, 206–211
SEC Code of Corporate Governance for Public Companies (Nigeria) 135, 145
sectoral codes of corporate governance 145, 146, 149, 183
shareholder primacy model 41–48
shareholder wealth maximization *see* maximization of profits
Skills Development Act (South Africa) 162
Smith, Adam 7
social efficiency 47, 60, 61, 66, 77, 197, 199, 202
social license to operate 10
soft law 19, 30, 31, 66, 88–103, 106, 110–115, 135, 140, 146, 149, 167–169, 198, 200, 208
Specific Instance Procedure 105, 106
stakeholders, genuine and legitimate 83
stakeholder theories 48–51
state concession theory 56

Strategic Reports 110, 136
sustainability impact assessment 108
sustainable development 3, 7, 25, 31, 50, 51, 55, 58, 59, 114, 131, 141, 166, 178, 180, 182, 186–190, 207–209
sustainable development goals *see* SDGs

takeover 63, 66, 198
tax 135–138, 201
theoretical underpinnings of CSR *see* CSR
tokenism 21, 131, 178
trade liberalization 22, 30, 180–190, 206–211
triple bottom line 13, 87, 166, 178
TRIPS 180
two-tier board structure 109

UNGPs 28, 86, 98–103, 106–109, 115, 179, 182, 200, 208, 210
unification 208
United Kingdom's Combined Codes of Best Practice 9
United Nations Guiding Principles on Business and Human Rights *see* UNGPs

Visser, Wayne 158

WTO 179–183, 190

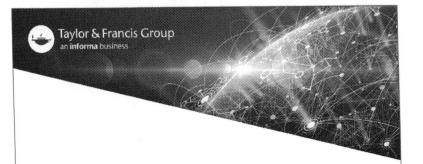

Taylor & Francis eBooks

www.taylorfrancis.com

A single destination for eBooks from Taylor & Francis with increased functionality and an improved user experience to meet the needs of our customers.

90,000+ eBooks of award-winning academic content in Humanities, Social Science, Science, Technology, Engineering, and Medical written by a global network of editors and authors.

TAYLOR & FRANCIS EBOOKS OFFERS:

A streamlined experience for our library customers

A single point of discovery for all of our eBook content

Improved search and discovery of content at both book and chapter level

REQUEST A FREE TRIAL
support@taylorfrancis.com

Printed in the United States
by Baker & Taylor Publisher Services